Writing Arguments

A Rhetoric with Readings
Concise Edition

Third Edition

John D. Ramage
Arizona State University

John C. Bean
Seattle University

June Johnson
Seattle University

PEARSON
Longman

New York   San Francisco   Boston
London   Toronto   Sydney   Tokyo   Singapore   Madrid
Mexico City   Munich   Paris   Cape Town   Hong Kong   Montreal

Senior Vice President and Publisher: Joseph Opiela
Vice President and Publisher: Eben W. Ludlow
Development Manager: Janet Lanphier
Development Editor: Marion B. Castellucci
Executive Marketing Manager: Ann Stypuloski
Senior Supplements Editor: Donna Campion
Media Supplements Editor: Nancy Garcia
Production Manager: Donna DeBenedictis
Project Coordination, Text Design, and Electronic Page Makeup:
    Elm Street Publishing Services, Inc.
Cover Design/Manager: Wendy Ann Fredericks
Cover Art: Inez Milholland Boissevain poster—Courtesy of the Historic National Woman's Party,
    Sewall-Belmont House and Museum, Washington, D.C.
Photo Researcher: Photosearch, Inc.
Manufacturing Buyer: Alfred C. Dorsey
Printer and Binder: RR Donnelley & Sons Company, Harrisonburg
Cover Printer: Phoenix Color Corporation

Library of Congress Cataloging-in-Publication Data
Ramage, John D.
        Writing arguments: A rhetoric with readings/John D. Ramage, John C. Bean, June
        Johnson—3rd ed.
                p.   cm.
        Includes bibliographical references and index.
        ISBN 0-321-16338-9 (alk. paper)
        1. English language—Rhetoric. 2. Persuasion (Rhetoric) 3. College readers. 4. Report writing.
        I. Bean, John C. II. Johnson, June. III. Title.

PE1431.R33 2004
808'.0427—dc21   2003044740

ISBN 0-321-16337-0 (Complete Edition)
ISBN 0-321-16341-9 (Brief Edition)
ISBN 0-321-16338-9 (Concise Edition)

1 2 3 4 5 6 7 8 9 10—DOH—06 05 04 03

Brief Contents

Appendixes   272

Detailed Contents

3   Writing Arguments   43

Part Two   Principles of Argument   63

4   The Core of an Argument: A Claim with Reasons   65

5   The Logical Structure of Arguments   76

Part Three   Claim Types in Argument   163

10   An Introduction to the Types of Claims   165

11   Categorical and Definitional Arguments: X Is (Is Not) a Y   174

12 Causal Arguments: X Causes (Does Not Cause) Y   194

15   Proposal Arguments: We Should (Should Not) Do X   249

Color Plates
(Insert following page 152)

A. Sustain, "What If Everything Was Labeled like Genetically Engineered Foods?" (advocacy advertisement)

B. Council for Biotechnology Information, "Would You Be Surprised to Know That Growing Soybeans Can Help the Environment?" (advocacy advertisement)

C. Tom Reese/The *Seattle Times*, Mosh Pit Crowd Surfer (news photo)

D. Alex Quesada/Matrix, Woman Crossing Bridge in Haitian Slum (news photo)

E. Save the Children, "She's the Best Qualified Teacher for Her Children" (advocacy advertisement)

F. Earth Justice, "It's Just Not the Same Without Bears" (advocacy advertisement)

G. General Motors, "Creatures of the Evergreen Forest" (product advertisement)

H. Center for Consumer Freedom, "PETA: Not as Warm and Cuddly as You Thought" (advocacy advertisement)

I. U.S. Network for Global Economic Justice, "Welcome to 50 Years Is Enough" (Web site)

Preface

Through six editions, *Writing Arguments* has established itself as the leading college textbook in argumentation. Available in three versions—a regular edition, which includes an anthology of readings; a brief edition, which offers the complete rhetoric without the anthology; or a concise edition with fewer readings and examples—*Writing Arguments* has been used successfully at every level, from first-year composition to advanced argumentation courses. In this third Concise Edition of *Writing Arguments*, we have tried to create the most up-to-date, accessible, and teachable short rhetoric of argument on the market. Based on the sixth edition of *Writing Arguments*, the third Concise Edition is a redaction of the complete rhetoric, covering the essentials of argument without sacrificing coverage, clarity, or flexibility. It can be used successfully as a stand-alone rhetoric text or as a compact companion to an anthology of readings.

As in the Regular and Brief Editions of *Writing Arguments*, our aim in this Concise Edition is to treat argument as a means of discovery as well as persuasion, introducing students to the role of argument in professional and civic life. The text shows students how argument entails productive dialogue in search of the best solutions to problems rather than pro–con debate with winners and losers. Users and reviewers have consistently praised the book for its teaching of the critical thinking that helps students *write* arguments: how to analyze the occasion for an argument; how to ground an argument in the values and beliefs of the targeted audience; how to develop and support an argument; and how to respond sensitively to objections and alternative views.

In this third Concise Edition, we have maintained the signature strengths of *Writing Arguments* while making important changes that reflect our own evolving understanding of the theory and practice of argumentation. As in previous editions, our aim is to integrate a comprehensive study of argument with an effective pedagogy that engages students' interest, builds their confidence as writers and critical thinkers, and gives them tools for effective problem solving and advocacy in academic, professional, and civic life. In both its treatment of argumentation and its approach to teaching writing, the text is rooted in current research and theory. Our emphasis throughout is on providing a student-friendly text that really works in the classroom.

What's New in the Third Concise Edition?

The third Concise Edition retains all the features that have made earlier concise editions successful. In addition, the third Concise Edition has been improved in the following ways:

- An attractive new design, including eight pages of color plates, enhances the book's visual appeal and supports an increased emphasis on visual rhetoric throughout the text. The color plates, along with other images and graphics interspersed throughout the text, highlight the function of political cartoons, advocacy ads, photographs, fliers, posters, Web sites, and quantitative graphics as important genres of argument in contemporary culture.

- A new Chapter 9, "Conducting Visual Arguments," provides an overview of visual arguments to help students create and incorporate effective images and graphics into their own arguments. It teaches students how to analyze visual arguments and how to use type, layout, color, and images to construct their own advocacy advertisements, posters, or fliers. The chapter also helps writers interpret tables and select and display numbers in rhetorically effective bar graphs, line graphs, or pie charts.

- A substantial revision of Chapter 2, "Reading Arguments," includes new material on the multiple genres of contemporary argument aimed at helping students understand how arguments are positioned in a rhetorical context and shaped by the constraints and purposes of a genre. The chapter teaches strategies for summarizing and interrogating texts, showing students how to analyze disagreements, cope with ambiguity, and produce questions for further research. In this edition, the controversy over genetic engineering of food replaces the articles on gender pay equity in the second Concise Edition; this issue, which holds high interest for today's students, integrates questions from science, agriculture, world trade, and the ethics of food production.

- Chapter 5, "The Logical Structure of Arguments," has been reorganized to integrate the treatment of audience-based reasons (formerly in Chapter 7) with the discussion of the enthymeme and the Toulmin system. Foregrounding audience-based reasons in Chapter 5 helps students understand Toulmin's concepts not as inert terms but as generative tools for creating successful arguments for particular audiences in particular contexts.

- A substantially revised Chapter 6 ("Using Evidence Effectively") presents helpful charts to explain the kinds of evidence available for arguments and to help students evaluate each kind's potential strengths and limitations for a given audience, purpose, or genre. This chapter also explains strategies for finding, evaluating, and selecting evidence and for framing it to anticipate an audience's queries and increase its rhetorical effectiveness.

- An extensively revised and expanded Appendix Two ("A Concise Guide to Finding, Evaluating, and Documenting Sources") uses an improved pedagogy for teaching research writing derived from our classroom research on students' difficulties in negotiating print and cyberspace sources. Appendix Two now emphasizes strategies for reading and evaluating sources rhetorically with special attention on the rhetoric of Web sites. It also provides updated models for the most frequently used types of citations in both MLA and APA styles. The appendix concludes with an engaging new student APA-style research paper by Megan Matthews on the danger to whales posed by the Navy's use of sonar. Student Mark Bonicillo's new MLA-style researched policy argument on medical insurance for the uninsured appears in Chapter 15.

- Throughout the text, shorter revisions improve the clarity, interest level, and effectiveness of instruction. For example, the revised section on Socrates and the Sophists in Chapter 1 explains more clearly philosophic disagreements about the meaning of "truth." In Chapter 3, new examples on hate speech show how the structure of classical argument can be used as a heuristic to help students generate ideas. Throughout the claim-type chapters (Chapters 11–15), updated examples explore recent controversies in a range of areas from national and international affairs to popular culture. In Chapter 14, the treatment of ethical arguments is now integrated with evaluation arguments to provide a more economical introduction to ethical arguing and to show how ethical claims are a subtype of evaluation claims.

- Seven new student essays or visual arguments have been selected for the quality of their arguments and the appeal of their subject matter. Drawn from popular culture issues and other contemporary concerns, these arguments connect effectively to the interests of today's students. For example, Tiffany Anderson's "A Woman's View of Hip-Hop" (Chapter 14) updates the previous edition's evaluation of the Spice Girls, and Leah Johnson's poster "Drink and Then Drive? Jeopardize My Future?" (Chapter 9) illustrates a visual genre of argument.

- The text includes six new professional essays chosen for the appeal of their subject matter and for the range of genres they represent. These new readings address such issues as the harms or benefits of genetically engineered food (Chapter 2); the admission of Taiwan to the United Nations (Chapter 11); and the ethics of reproductive technology (Chapter 14). In addition to new professional essays, the rhetoric portion also includes many new examples of visual arguments including advocacy advertisements promoting biotech food and addressing the problem of teenage pregnancy, a political cartoon about downloading music from the Internet, news photographs of President George W. Bush, and a Web site describing the effect of Navy sonar on whales.

What Hasn't Changed?
The Distinguishing Features of *Writing Arguments*

Building on earlier success, we have preserved the signature features of earlier editions praised by students, instructors, and reviewers:

- *Focus throughout on writing arguments.* Grounded in composition theory, this text combines explanations of argument with class-tested discussion tasks, exploratory writing tasks, and sequenced writing assignments aimed at developing skills of writing and critical thinking. This text builds students' confidence in their ability to enter the argumentative conversations of our culture, understand diverse points of view, synthesize ideas, and create their own persuasive texts.

- *Equal focus on the rhetoric of argument, particularly on analyzing audience, on understanding the real-world occasions for argument, and on appreciating the rhetorical context and genre of arguments.* Throughout the text, we have infused a philosophical view of argument with pedagogical concern for helping students think reflectively and critically at every stage of the construction of an argument.

- *Focus on both the reading and the writing of arguments with emphasis on argument as inquiry and discovery as well as persuasion.* The text emphasizes the critical thinking that underlies effective arguments, particularly the skills of critical reading, of believing and doubting, of empathic listening, of active questioning, and of negotiating ambiguity and seeking synthesis.

- *Integration of four different approaches to argument.* The text highlights the Toulmin system as a means of invention and analysis of arguments; the enthymeme as a logical structure rooted in the beliefs and values of the audience; the classical concepts of *logos, pathos,* and *ethos* as persuasive appeals; and stasis theory (called claim types) as an aid to inventing and structuring arguments through understanding of generic argumentative moves associated with different categories of claims.

- *Concise treatment of finding, evaluating, and documenting sources.* Quick Reference Guides provide models of common types of citations in MLA and APA style, and student examples of documented research papers—one using the MLA system and one using the APA system—are provided as models.

- *Numerous "For Class Discussion" exercises and sequenced Writing Assignments and Microthemes designed to teach critical thinking and build argumentative skills.* All "For Class Discussion" exercises can be used either for whole class discussions or for collaborative group tasks.

- *Effective student and professional arguments used to illustrate argumentative strategies and stimulate discussion, analysis, and debate.* The text includes seven essays and five visual arguments drawn from the public arena and nine essays and two visual arguments done by students.

Our Approaches to Argumentation

Our interest in argumentation grows out of our interest in the relationship between writing and thinking. When writing arguments, writers are forced to lay bare their thinking processes in an unparalleled way, grappling with the complex interplay between inquiry and persuasion, between issue and audience. In an effort to engage students in the kinds of critical thinking that argument demands, we draw on four major approaches to argumentation:

- *The enthymeme as a rhetorical and logical structure.* This concept, especially useful for beginning writers, helps students "nutshell" an argument as a claim with one or more supporting *because* clauses. It also helps them see how real-world arguments are rooted in assumptions granted by the audience rather than in universal and unchanging principles.

- *The three classical types of appeal*—logos, ethos, *and* pathos. These concepts help students place their arguments in a rhetorical context focusing on audience-based appeals; they also help students create an effective voice and style.

- *Toulmin's system of analyzing arguments.* Toulmin's system helps students see the complete, implicit structure that underlies an enthymeme and develop appropriate grounds and backing to support an argument's reasons and warrants. It also highlights the rhetorical, social, and dialectical nature of argument.

- *Stasis theory concerning types of claims.* This approach stresses the heuristic value of learning different patterns of support for different types of claims and often leads students to make surprisingly rich and full arguments.

Throughout the text these approaches are integrated and synthesized into generative tools for both producing and analyzing arguments.

Structure of the Text

The text has three main parts and two appendixes. Part One gives an overview of argumentation. These first three chapters present our philosophy of argument, showing how argument helps writers clarify their own thinking and connect with the values and beliefs of a questioning audience. Throughout we link the process of arguing—articulating issue questions, formulating propositions, examining alternative points of view, and creating structures of supporting reasons and evidence—with the processes of reading and writing.

Part Two examines the principles of argument. Chapters 4 through 6 show that the core of an effective argument is a claim with reasons. These reasons are often stated as enthymemes, the unstated premise of which must sometimes be brought to the surface and supported. In effective arguments, the reasons are audience-based so that the argument proceeds from underlying beliefs, values, or assumptions held by the intended audience. Discussion of Toulmin logic shows students how to discover both the stated and unstated premises of their arguments and how to provide audience-based structures of reasons and evidence to support them. Chapter 7 focuses on *ethos* and *pathos* as means of persuasion, while Chapter 8 focuses on strategies for accommodating arguments to different kinds of audiences from sympathetic to neutral to hostile. Finally, Chapter 9 focuses on the theory and practice of visual arguments—both images and quantitative graphics—giving students the tools for analyzing visual arguments and for creating their own.

Part Three discusses six different types of argument: simple categorical arguments, definitional arguments, causal arguments, resemblance arguments, evaluation arguments including ethics, and proposal arguments. These chapters introduce students to two recurring strategies of argument that cut across the different category types: Criteria-match arguing in which the writer establishes criteria for making a judgment and argues whether a specific case does or does not meet those criteria, and causal arguing in which the writer shows that one event or phenomenon can be linked to others in a causal chain.

The appendixes provide important supplemental information useful for courses in argument. Appendix One gives an overview of informal fallacies while Appendix Two presents a concise guide to finding, evaluating, and documenting research sources.

Writing Assignments

The text provides a variety of sequenced writing assignments. Parts One and Two include exploratory tasks for discovering and generating arguments, "microthemes" for practicing basic argumentative moves (for example, supporting a reason with evidence), and numerous other assignments calling for complete arguments. Thus, the text provides instructors with a wealth of options for writing assignments on which to build a coherent course.

The Instructor's Manual

The Instructor's Manual has been revised to make it more useful for teachers and writing program administrators. Written by co-author June Johnson, the revised Instructor's Manual has the following features:

■ Discussion of planning decisions an instructor must make in designing an argument course: for example, how to use readings, how much to emphasize Toulmin or claim-type theory; how much time to build into the course for invention, peer review of drafts, and other writing instruction; and how to select and sequence assignments.

■ Three detailed syllabi showing how *Writing Arguments* can support a variety of course structures and emphases:

Syllabus #1: This course emphasizes argumentative skills and strategies, uses readings for rhetorical analysis, and asks students to write on issues drawn from their own interests and experience.

Syllabus #2: This more rigorous course works intensely with the logical structure of argument, the classical appeals, the Toulmin schema, and claim-type theory. It uses readings for rhetorical analysis and for an introduction to the argumentative controversies that students will address in their papers.

Syllabus #3: This course asks students to experiment with genres of argument (for example, op-ed pieces, visual arguments, white papers, and researched freelance or scholarly arguments) and focuses on students' choice of issues and claim-types.

- For instructors who include Toulmin, an independent, highly teachable introductory lesson on the Toulmin schema, and an additional exercise giving students practice using Toulmin to generate argument frames.

- For new instructors, a helpful discussion of how to sequence writing assignments and how to use a variety of collaborative tasks in the classroom to promote active learning and critical thinking.

- Chapter-by-chapter responses to the For Class Discussion exercises.

- Numerous teaching tips and suggestions placed strategically throughout the chapter material, including several sample quizzes asking students to explain and apply argumentative concepts.

- For instructors who teach visual arguments, suggestions for encouraging students to explore how visual arguments have molded public thinking in historical controversies, as in the poster argument on the cover of this text.

- For instructors who like to use student essays in class exercises and discussions, a number of new student essays showing how students responded to assignments in the text. Several of these student pieces exemplify stages of revision.

- Helpful suggestions for using the exercises on critiquing readings in Part Three, "Claim Types in Argument." By focusing on rhetorical context as well as the strengths and weaknesses of these arguments, our suggestions will help students connect their reading of arguments to their writing of arguments.

Companion Website

The Companion Website to accompany the *Writing Arguments* series (http://www.ablongman.com/ramage), written by Laurie Cubbison of Radford University and Jonathan Sabol of Fordham University, offers a wealth of resources for both students and instructors. Students will have access to reviews of the concepts in each chapter of their book, exploratory writing exercises, online activities, and Web resources to help them develop their skills of argumentation. In addition, instructors will find Web resources and the Instructor's Manual available for download.

Acknowledgments

We are happy for this opportunity to give public thanks to the scholars, teachers, and students who have influenced our approach to composition and argument. We would like to thank our student researchers who helped us explore current civic controversies: LeaEllen Ren, for her excellent library skills; Chris Ronk, for his witty, novel views of contemporary culture; and Megan Matthews, for the complexity and keenness of her assessment of environmental issues. We would especially like to thank Megan, as well as Tiffany Anderson and Mark Bonicillo, for contributing their writing to this text and for their enthusiasm and professionalism. We are also grateful to all our students whom we have been privileged to teach in our writing classes; a number of their arguments from these classes appear in this text. They have inspired us and have profoundly affected how we understand and teach argumentation. We thank too the many users of our texts who have given us encouragement about our successes and offered helpful suggestions for improvements. Particularly we thank the following scholars and teachers who reviewed the new edition of *Writing Arguments* in its various stages: Janet Eldred, Univeristy of Kentucky; Judy Gardner, University of Texas at San Antonio; Gregory R. Glau, Arizona State University; Tammy D. Harvey, State University of West Georgia; Heidi A. Huse, The University of Tennessee at Martin; Karen Kornweibel, Stephen F. Austin State University; Dixie Lee Larson, North Carolina State University; Mary Massier, Baylor University; Linda Moore, University of West Florida; Gary L. Myers, Mississippi State University; Roy Stamper, North Carolina State University; Abby Wallace, Owensboro Community College; and Rebecca M. Whitten, Mississippi State University.

Our deep thanks also to our editor, Eben Ludlow, whose unflagging good humor and faith in our approach to both composition and argument have kept us writing and revising for the better part of eighteen years. We especially want to express our gratitude to Marion Castellucci, our development editor, for her indispensable teamwork, for the brilliance and organizational wizardry with which she has managed both the big picture and the myriad of details of this project, and for her expert and candid advice. She has been a model of patience, professionalism, and good humor.

Finally, we would like to thank our families. John Bean thanks his wife, Kit, also a professional composition teacher and director of a writing center, and his children, Matthew, Andrew, Stephen, and Sarah, who have grown to adulthood since he first began writing textbooks. June Johnson thanks her husband, Kenneth Bube, a mathematics professor and researcher, who has been an invaluable supporter of this intellectual endeavor, offering astute insights into civic arguments, knowledge of teaching and scientific writing, and Internet expertise. She also thanks her daughter, Jane Ellen, who knows well how much time and work textbook writing takes and who has contributed her own wisdom and delightful humor.

John D. Ramage
John C. Bean
June Johnson

Part One

Overview of Argument

This political cartoon presents one of the major perspectives in the public controversy over genetically modified foods, an issue discussed in Chapter 2.

Source: Steve Breen and Copley News Service.

1 Argument

An Introduction

One ought to begin a book on argument by telling the reader straight out what argument is. But we can't. Philosophers and rhetoricians have disagreed for centuries about the meaning of the term and about the goals that arguers should set for themselves. So in place of a simple definition, we'll show you several different ways of thinking about argument as a way of helping you become a more powerful arguer yourself.

After explaining how arguments make claims and provide justifications for those claims, we will consider argument from two different perspectives—as product and process. We'll also explain how arguments combine two distinct and sometimes conflicting purposes—truth seeking and persuasion. Because of the importance of this last distinction, we'll explore extensively the debate over truth versus victory as the goal of argument.

What Do We Mean by Argument?

Let's begin by rejecting two popular synonyms for "argument": *fight* and *debate*.

Argument Is Not a Fight or a Quarrel

The word *argument* often connotes anger, as when we say, "I just got in a huge argument with my roommate!" We may picture heated disagreements, rising pulse rates, and slamming doors. We may conjure up images of shouting talk-show guests or fist-banging speakers.

But to our way of thinking, argument doesn't necessarily imply anger. In fact, arguing can be pleasurable. It can be a creative and productive activity that engages our minds and our hearts in conversations with people we respect about ideas that we cherish. For your primary image of argument, we invite you to think not of a fist-banging speaker but of a small group of reasonable persons seeking the best solution to a problem. We will return to this image throughout the chapter.

Argument Is Not Pro-Con Debate

Another popular conception of argument is debate—a presidential debate, perhaps, or a high school or college debate tournament, in which, according to one popular dictionary, "opposing speakers defend and attack a given proposition." While formal debates can develop our critical thinking powers, they stress winning and losing, often to the detriment of cooperative inquiry.

To illustrate the limitations of debate, consider one of our former students, a champion high school debater who spent his senior year debating prison reform. Throughout the year he argued for and against such propositions as "The United States should build more prisons" and "We must find innovative alternatives to prison." One day we asked him, "What do you personally think is the best way to reform prisons?" "I don't know," he replied. "I've never thought about it that way."

Nothing in the atmosphere of pro-con debate had engaged this bright, articulate student in the important process of clarifying his own values and taking a personal stand. As we explain throughout this text, argument entails a desire for truth seeking, not necessarily Truth with a capital T but truth as a desire to find the best solutions to complex problems. Of course, arguers often passionately support their own points of view and expose weaknesses in other views. However, arguers' passionate defenses and relentless probings are not moves in a win-lose game but rather moves toward discovering and promoting the best belief or best course of action.

Arguments Can Be Explicit or Implicit

Before proceeding to some defining features of argument, we should note also that arguments can be either explicit or implicit. An *explicit* argument states directly a controversial claim and supports it with reasons and evidence. An *implicit* argument, in contrast, doesn't look like an argument. It may be a poem or short story, a photograph or cartoon, a personal essay, or an autobiographical narrative. But like an explicit argument, it persuades an audience toward a certain point of view. For example, a famous World War I poem (Wilfred Owen's "*Dulce et Decorum Est*") challenges the patriotic notion that it is "sweet and fitting" to die for one's country. Instead of using the ordered thesis, reasons, and evidence found in explicit arguments, this poem employs a horrible image—a soldier drowning in his own fluids from a mustard gas attack—to impel readers to see the gruesome senselessness of war.

Visual images can also make implicit arguments, often by evoking powerful emotions in audiences. The perspective that photos take, the stories they tell, or the vivid details of place and time they display compel viewers literally to see the issue from a particular angle. Take, for instance, Figure 1.1, a photo of homeless Albanian refugees during the Kosovo War. By foregrounding the old woman, probably a grandmother, perched precariously atop a heavily loaded wheelbarrow, her canes or crutches sticking out from the pile, and the six persons in the scene hastening down a stark road against an ominous gray background, the photographer conveys the nightmare of this war. Here *showing* the urgency of the Albanians' flight for their

FIGURE 1.1   *Albanian refugees during the Kosovo War*

lives and the helplessness of the two who can't walk is an effective strategy to arouse sympathy for the Albanians. Photographs of this kind regularly appeared in American newspapers during the war, serving to heighten U.S. support of NATO's bombing. Meanwhile, Serbs complained that no American newspapers showed photographs of KLA (Kosovo Liberation Army) atrocities against Serbs.

For Class Discussion

Working individually or in small groups, describe a photograph that would create an implicit argument persuading (1) teenagers to avoid smoking, (2) teenagers to avoid becoming sexually active, (3) the general public to ban handguns, or (4) the general public to save endangered species.

EXAMPLE: To create an implicit argument against legalizing hard drugs, you might photograph a blank-eyed, cadaverous teenager plunging a needle into her arm.

We'll return to implicit arguments later, especially in Chapter 7, where we describe the persuasive power of stories, narratives, and visual images. For now, however, and in most of this text, our predominant focus is on explicit argument.

Argument Requires Justification of Its Claims

To begin defining argument, let's turn to a humble but universal site of disagreement: the conflict between a parent and a teenager over rules. In what way and in what circumstances do these conflicts constitute arguments?

Consider the following dialogue:

YOUNG PERSON (*racing for the front door while putting coat on*):   Bye. See you later.

PARENT: Whoa! What time are you planning on coming home?

YOUNG PERSON (*coolly, hand still on doorknob*):   I'm sure we discussed this earlier. I'll be home around two A.M. (*the second sentence, spoken very rapidly, is barely audible.*)

PARENT (*mouth tightening*):   We did *not* discuss this earlier, and you're *not* staying out till two in the morning. You'll be home at twelve.

At this point in the exchange, we have a quarrel, not an argument. Quarrelers exchange antagonistic assertions without any attempt to support them rationally. If the dialogue never gets past the "Yes-you-will/No-I-won't" stage, it either remains a quarrel or degenerates into a fight.

Let us say, however, that the dialogue takes the following turn:

YOUNG PERSON (*tragically*):   But I'm *sixteen years old!*

Now we're moving toward argument. Not, to be sure, a particularly well-developed or cogent one, but an argument all the same. It's now an argument because one of the quarrelers has offered a reason for her assertion. Her choice of curfew is satisfactory, she says, *because* she is sixteen years old.

The parent can now respond in one of several ways that will either advance the argument or turn it back into a quarrel. The parent can simply invoke parental authority ("I don't care—you're still coming home at twelve"), in which case argument ceases. Or the parent can provide a reason for his or her view ("You will be home at twelve because your dad and I pay the bills around here!"), in which case the argument takes a new turn.

So far we've established two necessary conditions that must be met before we're willing to call something an argument: (1) a set of two or more conflicting assertions and (2) the attempt to resolve the conflict through an appeal to reason. But good argument demands more than meeting these two formal requirements. For an argument to be effective, the arguer must clarify and support the reasons presented.

For example, "But I'm sixteen years old!" is not yet a clear support for the assertion "I should be allowed to set my own curfew." On the surface, Young Person's argument seems absurd. Her parent, of all people, knows precisely how old she is. What makes it an argument is that behind her claim lies an unstated assumption—all sixteen-year-olds are old enough to set their own curfews. What Young Person needs to do now is to support that assumption.* In doing so, she must anticipate the sorts of questions the assumption will raise in the minds of her parent: What is the legal status of sixteen-year-olds? How psychologically mature, as opposed to chronologically mature, is Young Person? What is the actual track record of Young Person in being responsible? Each of these questions will force Young Person to reexamine and clarify her assumptions about the proper degree of autonomy for sixteen-year-olds. And her response to those questions should in turn force the parents to reexamine their assumptions about the dependence of sixteen-year-olds on parental guidance and wisdom. (Likewise, the parents will need to show why "paying the bills around here" automatically gives them the right to set Young Person's curfew.)

As the argument continues, Young Person and Parent may shift to a different line of reasoning. For example, Young Person might say: "I should be allowed to stay out until two A.M. because all my friends get to stay out that late." (Here the unstated assumption is that the rules in this family ought to be based on the rules in other families.) The parent might in turn respond, "But I certainly never stayed out that late when I was your age"—an argument assuming that the rules in this family should follow the rules of an earlier generation.

As Young Person and Parent listen to each other's points of view (trying to figure out why their initial arguments are unpersuasive), both parties find themselves in the uncomfortable position of having to examine their own beliefs and to justify assumptions that they have taken for granted. Here we encounter one of the earliest senses of the term *to argue,* which is "to clarify." In response to her audience's failure to understand or assent to her view, the arguer must reshape her argument to help her audience "see" her position. In the process she may, perhaps for the first time, come to understand that position herself. Thus Young Person might recast her argument so that it relates more directly to her parent's values:

> I should be allowed to stay out until two A.M. on a trial basis because I need enough space to demonstrate my maturity and show you I won't get into trouble.

The assumption underlying this argument is that it is good to give teenagers freedom to demonstrate their maturity. Because this reason is likely to appeal to her parent's values (the parent wants the daughter to mature) and because it is tempered by the qualifier "on a trial basis" (which reduces some of the threat of Young Person's initial demands), it may prompt productive discussion.

---

*In Chapter 5 we will call the assumption underlying a line of reasoning its *warrant.*

Whether or not Young Person and Parent can work out the best solution, the preceding scenario illustrates how argument leads persons to clarify their reasons and provide justifications that can be examined rationally. The scenario also illustrates two specific aspects of argument that we will explore in detail in the next sections: (1) Argument is both a process and a product. (2) Argument combines truth seeking and persuasion.

Argument Is Both a Process and a Product

In the preceding scenario, argument functioned as a *process* whereby two or more parties sought the best solution to a question or problem. But if we stopped the process at a given moment and looked at each person's contribution to the conversation, these contributions would be *products*. In an informal discussion, these products are usually brief, comprising a few sentences. In a more formal setting, such as an open-mike discussion of a campus issue or a PowerPoint presentation at a business meeting, the oral argument might be considerably longer.

Written versions of informal conversations occur online among members of chat groups or listservs. These e-mail messages are usually short and informal, albeit more carefully crafted than real-time oral rejoinders. And as these discussions (or *threads*) play out over several days, you may well see participants' ideas shift and evolve as they negotiate some sort of collectively agreeable view, or perhaps a simple truce.

Written versions of formal speeches may take the form of an academic argument for a college course; a grant proposal; a guest op-ed* piece; a legal brief; a letter to a member of Congress; or an article for an organizational newsletter, popular magazine, or professional journal. In such instances, the written argument (a product) enters a conversation (a process)—in this case, a conversation of readers, many of whom will carry on the conversation by writing their own responses or by discussing the writer's views with others.

Argument Combines Truth Seeking and Persuasion

In producing her argument, the writer will find herself continually moving back and forth between truth seeking and persuasion—that is, between questions about the subject matter (What is the best solution to this problem?) and about audience (What reasons and evidence best speak to my audience's values?). Back and forth she'll weave, alternately absorbed in the subject matter of her argument and in the persuasiveness of her argument to her audience.

---

*Op-ed stands for "opposite-editorial." It is the generic name in journalism for signed arguments that voice the writer's opinion on an issue, as opposed to news stories, which are supposed to report events objectively.

Rarely is either focus ever completely ignored, but their relative importance shifts during different phases of the argument's development. We could thus place "concern for truthfulness" at one end of a continuum and "concern for persuasiveness" at the other, and fit any argument somewhere along that continuum. At the far truth-seeking end might be an exploratory piece that lays out several alternative approaches to a problem and weighs the strengths and weaknesses of each. At the other end of the continuum would be outright propaganda, such as a political campaign advertisement that reduces a complex issue to sound bites. (At its most blatant, propaganda obliterates truth seeking; it will do anything, including distorting or inventing evidence, to win over an audience.) In the middle ranges of the continuum, writers shift their focuses back and forth between truth seeking and persuasion but with varying degrees of emphasis.

To illustrate the need for a shifting focus, consider the case of Kathleen, who in her college argument course addressed the definitional question "Should American Sign Language meet the university's foreign language requirement?" Kathleen had taken two years of ASL at a community college. When she transferred to a four-year college, her ASL proficiency was dismissed by the foreign language department chair. "ASL isn't a 'language,' " he said summarily. "It's not equivalent to learning French, German, or Japanese."

Kathleen disagreed and immersed herself in her argument. In her initial research she focused almost entirely on subject matter, searching for what linguists, neurologists, cognitive psychologists, and sociologists had said about ASL. She was only tacitly concerned with her audience, whom she mostly envisioned as her classmates and those sympathetic to her view. She wrote a well-documented paper, citing several scholarly articles, that made a good case to her classmates (and her professor) that ASL was indeed a distinct language.

Proud of the big red A the professor had placed on her paper and more secure in her position, Kathleen resubmitted her request (this time buttressed with a copy of her paper) to count ASL for her language requirement. The chair of the foreign language department read her paper, congratulated her on her good writing, but said her argument was not persuasive. He disagreed with the definition of *language* she used in the paper, and he took issue with several of the linguists she cited. He again turned down her request.

Stung by what she considered a facile rejection of her argument, Kathleen embarked on a second ASL paper for her argument class—this time aimed directly at the foreign language chair. She researched the history of her college's foreign language requirement and discovered that after being dropped in the 1970s, the requirement was revived in the 1990s, partly (her math professor confided) to revive flagging enrollments in foreign languages. She also interviewed foreign language teachers to uncover their assumptions about ASL. She discovered that many of them thought ASL was "easy to learn" and that given the option, many students would take ASL to avoid the rigors of "real" language classes. Additionally, she learned that foreign language teachers valued immersing students in a foreign culture; in fact, the foreign language requirement was seen as a key component in the college's attempt to improve multicultural education.

With her newly acquired understanding of her target audience, Kathleen reconceptualized her argument. She emphasized how difficult ASL was to learn (to counter her audience's belief that learning ASL was easy), how the deaf community formed a distinct culture with its own customs and literature (to show how ASL met the goals of multiculturalism), and how few students would transfer in with ASL credits (to allay fears that accepting ASL would threaten language enrollments). She concluded by citing her college's mission statement, which called for eradicating social injustice and for reaching out to the oppressed. Surely, she argued, encouraging hearing people to learn ASL would help integrate the deaf community more fully into the larger campus community. In sum, all her revisions—the reasons selected, the evidence used, the arrangement and tone—were guided by her desire to persuade.

Our point, then, is that all along the continuum writers are concerned both to seek truth and to persuade, but not necessarily with equal balance. Kathleen could not have written her second paper, aimed specifically at persuading the chair of foreign languages, if she hadn't first immersed herself in truth-seeking research that convinced her that ASL was indeed a distinct language. Nor are we saying that her second argument was better than her first. Both fulfilled their purposes and met the needs of their intended audiences. Both involved truth seeking and persuasion, but the first focused primarily on subject matter whereas the second focused primarily on audience.

Argument and the Problem of Truth

The tension that we have just examined between truth seeking and persuasion raises an ancient issue in the field of argument: Is the arguer's first obligation to truth or to winning the argument? And just what is the nature of the truth to which arguers are supposed to be obligated?

In Plato's famous dialogues from ancient Greek philosophy, these questions were at the heart of Socrates' disagreement with the Sophists. The Sophists were professional rhetoricians who specialized in training orators to win arguments. Socrates, who valued truth seeking over persuasion and believed that truth could be discovered through philosophic inquiry, opposed the Sophists. For Socrates, Truth resided in the ideal world of forms, and through philosophic rigor humans could transcend the changing, shadowlike world of everyday reality to perceive the world of universals where Truth, Beauty, and Goodness resided. Through his method of questioning his interlocutors, Socrates would gradually peel away layer after layer of false views until Truth was revealed. The good person's duty, Socrates believed, was not to win an argument but to pursue this higher Truth. Socrates distrusted rhetoricians because they were interested only in the temporal power and wealth that came from persuading audiences to the orator's views.

Let's apply Socrates' disagreement with the Sophists to a modern instance. Suppose your community is divided over the issue of raising environmental standards versus keeping open a job-producing factory that doesn't meet new guidelines for waste discharge. The Sophists would train you to argue any side of this issue on behalf of any lobbying group willing to pay for your services. If, however, you followed the spirit of Socrates, you would be inspired to listen to all sides of the dispute, peel away false arguments, discover the Truth through reasonable inquiry, and commit yourself to a Right Course of Action.

But what is the nature of Truth or Right Action in a dispute between jobs and the environment? The Sophists believed that truth was determined by those in power; thus they could enter an argument unconstrained by any transcendent beliefs or assumptions. When Socrates talked about justice and virtue, they could reply contemptuously that these were fictitious concepts invented by the weak to protect themselves from the strong. Over the years, the Sophists' relativist beliefs were so repugnant to people that the term *sophistry* became synonymous with trickery in argument.

However, in recent years the Sophists' critique of a transcendent Universal Truth has been taken seriously by many philosophers, sociologists, and other thinkers who doubt Socrates' confident belief that arguments, properly conducted, necessarily arrive at a single Truth. For these thinkers, as for the Sophists, there are often different degrees of truth and different kinds of truths for different situations or cultures. From this perspective, when we consider questions of interpretation or value, we can never demonstrate that a belief or assumption is true—not through scientific observation, not through reason, and not through religious revelation. We get our beliefs, according to these contemporary thinkers, from the shared assumptions of our particular cultures. We are condemned (or liberated) to live in a pluralistic, multicultural world with competing visions of truth.

If we accept this pluralistic view of the world, do we then endorse the Sophists' radical relativism, freeing us to argue any side of any issue? Or do we doggedly pursue some modern equivalent of Socrates' truth?

Our own sympathies are with Socrates, but we admit to a view of truth that is more tentative, cautious, and conflicted than his. For us, truth seeking does not mean finding the "Right Answer" to a disputed question, but neither does it mean a valueless relativism in which all answers are equally good. For us, truth seeking means taking responsibility for determining the "best answer" or "best solution" to the question for the good of the whole community when taking into consideration the interests of all stakeholders. It means making hard decisions in the face of uncertainty. This more tentative view of truth means that you cannot use argument to "prove" your claim, but only to make a reasonable case for your claim. One contemporary philosopher says that argument can hope only to "increase adherence" to ideas, not absolutely convince an audience of the necessary truth of ideas. Even though you can't be certain, in a Socratic sense, that your solution to the problem is the best one available, you must ethically take responsibility for the consequences of your claim and you must seek justice for stakeholders beyond yourself. You must, in other words, forge a personal stance based on your examination of all the evidence and your articulation of values that you can make public and defend.

To seek truth, then, means to seek the best or most just solution to a problem while observing all available evidence, listening with an open mind to the views of all stakeholders, clarifying and attempting to justify your own values and assumptions, and taking responsibility for your argument. It follows that truth seeking often means delaying closure on an issue, acknowledging the pressure of alternative views, and being willing to change one's mind. Seen in this way, learning to argue effectively has the deepest sort of social value: It helps communities settle conflicts in a rational and humane way by finding, through the dialectic exchange of ideas, the best solutions to problems without resorting to violence or to other assertions of raw power.

For Class Discussion

On any given day, newspapers provide evidence of the complexity of living in a pluralistic culture. Issues that could be readily decided in a completely homogeneous culture raise many questions for us in a society that has few shared assumptions. Use the following story as the subject for a "simulation game" in which class members represent the points of view of the persons involved in the mosh pit controversy.

MOSH PITS: IT'S NOT ALL FUN AND MUSIC

This article begins with the case of a fourteen-year-old boy who suffered brain damage when he was dropped while crowd surfing at a Rage Against the Machine concert in Seattle. The article then discusses the controversy over crowd safety at grunge concerts:

> Most concerts do not result in injuries and deaths. But the increasing frequency of serious injuries—including broken bones, brain damage and paralysis—is shining a spotlight on what some critics see as fun and freedom pushed to irresponsible limits.
>
> The injuries have prompted a handful of U.S. cities and some bands to ban crowd surfing and stage diving, but there are no national standards for concert safety, and no one has exact numbers on how many people are injured in mosh pits every year. One survey cites at least 10 deaths and more than 1,000 injuries resulting from just 15 U.S. concerts last year.

Your task: Imagine a public hearing in which city officials are trying to develop a city policy on mosh pits at concerts. Should they be banned altogether? If not, how might they be regulated and who is responsible for injuries? Hold a mock hearing in which classmates present the views of the following: (a) a rock band that values crowd surfing and stage diving; (b) several concert fans who love mosh pits; (c) parents of a teenager seriously injured in a mosh pit accident; (d) a woman who was groped while crowd surfing; (e) local police; (f) concert promoters; (g) a venue owner fearing a liability lawsuit; (h) a city attorney fearing a liability lawsuit.

A Successful Process of Argumentation:
The Well-Functioning Committee

We have said that neither the fist-banging speaker nor the college debate team represents our ideal image of argument. The best image for us, as we have implied, is a well-functioning small group seeking a solution to a problem. In professional life such small groups usually take the form of committees.

We use the word *committee* in its broadest sense to indicate all sorts of important work that grows out of group conversation and debate. The Declaration of Independence is essentially a committee document with Thomas Jefferson as the chair. Similarly, the U.S. Supreme Court is in effect a committee of nine judges who rely heavily, as numerous books and articles have demonstrated, on small-group decision-making processes to reach their judgments and formulate their legal briefs.

To illustrate our committee or small-group model for argument, let's briefly consider the workings of a university committee on which coauthor John Ramage once served, the University Standards Committee. The Arizona State University (ASU) Standards Committee plays a role in university life analogous to that of the Supreme Court in civic life. It's the final court of appeal for ASU students seeking exceptions to various rules that govern their academic lives (such as registering under a different catalog, waiving a required course, or being allowed to retake a course for a third time).

The Standards Committee is a large committee, comprising nearly two dozen members who represent the whole spectrum of departments and offices across campus. Every two weeks, the committee meets for two or more hours to consider between twenty and forty appeals. The issues that regularly come before the committee draw forth all the argumentative strategies discussed in detail throughout this text. For example, all of the types of claims discussed in Part Three regularly surface during committee deliberations. The committee deals with definition issues ("Is math anxiety a 'learning disability' for purposes of exempting a student from a math requirement? If so, what criteria can we establish for math anxiety?"); cause/consequence issues ("What were the causes of this student's sudden poor performance during spring semester?" "What will be the consequences of approving or denying her appeal?"); resemblance issues ("How is this case similar to an earlier case that we considered?"); evaluation issues ("Which criteria should take precedence in assessing this sort of appeal?"); and proposal issues ("Should we make it a policy to allow course X to substitute for course Y in the General Studies requirements?").

On any given day, the committee's deliberations showed how dialogue can lead to clarification of thinking. On many occasions, committee members' initial views shifted as they listened to opposing arguments. Unlike some committees, this committee made many decisions, the consequences of which were not trivial for the people involved. Because of the significance of these outcomes, committee members were more willing than they otherwise might have been to concede a point to another member in the name of reaching a better decision and to view their deliberations as an ongoing process of negotiation rather than a series of win-lose debates.

To give you firsthand experience at using argument as a process of clarification, we conclude this chapter with an actual case that came before the University Standards Committee. We invite you to read the following letter, pretending that you are a member of the University Standards Committee, and then proceed to the exercises that follow.

Petition to Waive the University Mathematics Requirement

Standards Committee Members,

1   I am a 43-year-old member of the Pawnee Tribe of Oklahoma and a very nontraditional student currently pursuing Justice Studies at the Arizona State University (ASU) College of Public Programs. I entered college as the first step toward completion of my goal—becoming legal counsel for my tribe, and statesman.

2   I come before this committee in good faith to request that ASU suspend, in my special case, its mathematics requirement for undergraduate degree completion so I may enter the ASU College of Law during Fall 1993. The point I wish to make to this committee is this: I do not need algebraic skills; I will never use algebra in my intended profession; and, if forced to comply with ASU's algebra requirement, I will be needlessly prevented from graduating in time to enter law school next fall and face an idle academic year before my next opportunity in 1994. I will address each of these points in turn, but a few words concerning my academic credentials are in order first.

3   Two years ago, I made a vow of moral commitment to seek out and confront injustice. In September of 1990, I enrolled in college. Although I had only the benefit of a ninth grade education, I took the General Equivalency Diploma (GED) examination and placed in the top ten percent of those, nationwide, who took the test. On the basis of this score I was accepted into Scottsdale Community College (SCC). This step made me the first in my entire family, and practically in my tribe, to enter college. During my first year at SCC I maintained a 4.0 GPA, I was placed on the President's list twice, was active in the Honors Program, received the Honors Award of Merit in English Humanities, and was conferred an Honors Scholarship (see attached) for the Academic year of 1991–1992 which I declined, opting to enroll in ASU instead.

4   At the beginning of the 1991 summer semester, I transferred to ASU. I chose to graduate from ASU because of the courses offered in American Indian studies, an important field ignored by most other Universities but necessary to my commitment. At ASU I currently maintain a 3.6 GPA, although my cumulative GPA is closer to 3.9. I am a member of the Honors and Justice Colleges, was appointed to the Dean's List,

and awarded ASU's prestigious Maroon and Gold Scholarship twice. My academic standing is impeccable. I will enter the ASU College of Law to study Indian and criminal law during the Fall of 1993—if this petition is approved. Upon successful completion of my juris doctorate I will return to Oklahoma to become active in the administration of Pawnee tribal affairs as tribal attorney and advisor, and vigorously prosecute our right to sovereignty before the Congress of the United States.

When I began my "college experience," I set a rigid time schedule for the completion of my goal. By the terms of that self-imposed schedule, founded in my belief that I have already wasted many productive years, I allowed myself thirty-five months in which to achieve my Bachelor of Science degree in Justice Studies, for indeed justice is my concern, and another thirty-six months in which to earn my juris doctorate—summa cum laude. Consistent with my approach to all endeavors, I fell upon this task with zeal. I have willingly assumed the burden of carrying substantial academic loads during fall, spring and summer semesters. My problem now lies in the fact that in order to satisfy the University's math requirement to graduate I must still take MAT-106 and MAT-117. I submit that these mathematics courses are irrelevant to my goals, and present a barrier to my fall matriculation into law school.

Upon consideration of my dilemma, the questions emerged: Why do I need college algebra (MAT-117)? Is college algebra necessary for studying American Indian law? Will I use college algebra in my chosen field? What will the University gain or lose, from my taking college algebra—or not? I decided I should resolve these questions.

I began my inquiry with the question: "Why do I need college algebra (MAT-117)?" I consulted Mr. Jim _____ of the Justice College and presented this question to him. He referred to the current ASU catalog and delineated the following answer: I need college algebra (1) for a minimum level of math competency in my chosen field, and (2) to satisfy the university math requirement in order to graduate. My reply to the first answer is this: I already possess ample math skills, both practical and academic; and, I have no need for algebra in my chosen field. How do I know this? During the spring 1992 semester at ASU I successfully completed introductory algebra (MAT-077), scoring the highest class grade on one test (see attached transcript and test). More noteworthy is the fact that I was a machine and welding contractor for fifteen years. I used geometry and algebra commonly in the design of many welded structures. I am proficient in the use of Computer Assisted Design (CAD) programs, designing and drawing all my own blueprints for jobs. My blueprints and designs are always approved by city planning departments. For example, my most recent job consisted of the manufacture, transportation and installation of one linear mile of anodized, aluminum handrailing at a luxury resort condo on Maui, Hawaii. I applied extensive use of math to calculate the amount of raw materials to order, the logistics of mass production and transportation for both men and materials from Mesa to Maui, the job site installation itself, and cash flow. I have successfully completed many jobs of this nature—all without a mathematical hitch. As to the application of math competency in my chosen field, I can guarantee this committee that there will not be a time in my practice of Indian law that I will need algebra. If an occasion ever occurs that I need algebra, I will hire a mathematician, just as I would an engineer if I need engineering, or a surgeon if I need an operation.

8   I then contacted Dr. _____ of the ASU Mathematics Department and presented him with the same question: "Why do I need college algebra?" He replied: (1) for a well-rounded education; (2) to develop creative thinking; and (3) to satisfy the university math requirement in order to graduate. Responding to the first answer, I have a "well-rounded education." My need is for a specific education in justice and American Indian law. In fact, I do not really need the degree to practice Indian law as representative of my tribe, just the knowledge. Regarding the second, I do not need to develop my creative thinking. It has been honed to a keen edge for many years. For example, as a steel contractor, I commonly create huge, beautiful and intricate structures from raw materials. Contracting is not my only experience in creative thinking. For twenty-five years I have also enjoyed the status of being one of this country's foremost designers and builders of racebikes. Machines I have designed and brought into existence from my imagination have topped some of Japan and Europe's best engineering efforts. To illustrate this point, in 1984 I rode a bike of my own design to an international victory over Honda, Suzuki, Laverda, BMW and Yamaha. I have excelled at creative thinking my entire life—I called it survival.

9   Expanding on the question of why I need college algebra, I contacted a few friends who are practicing attorneys. All responded to my question in similar manner. One, Mr. Billy _____, Esq., whose law firm is in Tempe, answered my two questions as follows: "When you attended law school, were there any courses you took which required algebra?" His response was "no." "Have you ever needed algebra during the many years of your practice?" Again, his response was "no." All agreed there was not a single occasion when they had need for algebra in their professional careers.

10   Just to make sure of my position, I contacted the ASU College of Law, and among others, spoke to Ms. Sierra _____. I submitted the question "What law school courses will I encounter in which I will need algebra?" The unanimous reply was, they knew of none.

11   I am not proposing that the number of credit hours I need for graduation be lowered. In fact, I am more than willing to substitute another course or two in its place. I am not trying to get out of anything hard or distasteful, for that is certainly not my style. I am seeking only to dispose of an unnecessary item in my studies, one which will prevent me from entering law school this fall—breaking my stride. So little holds up so much.

12   I agree that a young adult directly out of high school may not know that he needs algebraic skills. Understandably, he does not know what his future holds—but I am not that young adult. I claim the advantage. I know precisely what my future holds and that future holds no possibility of my needing college algebra.

13   Physically confronting injustice is my end. On reservations where government apathy allows rapacious pedophiles to pose as teachers; in a country where a million and a half American Indians are held hostage as second-rate human beings whose despair results in a suicide, alcohol and drug abuse rate second to no other people; in prisons where helpless inmates are beaten like dogs by sadistic guards who should be the inmates—this is the realm of my chosen field—the disenfranchised. In this netherworld, algebra and justice exist independently of one another.

In summary, I am convinced that I do not need college algebra for a minimum   14
level of math competency in my chosen field. I do not need college algebra for a well
rounded education, nor to develop my creative thinking. I do not need algebra to
take the LSAT. I do not need algebra for any courses in law school, nor will I for any
purpose in the practice of American Indian law. It remains only that I need college
algebra in order to graduate.

I promise this committee that ASU's integrity will not be compromised in any   15
way by approving this waiver. Moreover, I assure this committee that despite not
having a formal accreditation in algebra, I will prove to be nothing less than an
asset to this University and its Indian community, both to which I belong, and I will
continue to set a standard for integrity, excellence and perseverance for all who
follow. Therefore, I ask this committee, for all the reasons described above, to approve and initiate the waiver of my University mathematics requirement.

[Signed: Gordon Adams]

For Class Discussion

1. Before class discussion, decide how you would vote on this issue. How
   persuasive is Gordon Adams's letter? Should Adams be exempted from
   the math requirement?

2. Working in small groups or as a whole class, pretend that you are the
   University Standards Committee and arrive at a group decision on
   whether to exempt this student from the math requirement.

3. After the discussion, write for several minutes in a journal or notebook describing how your thinking evolved during the discussion. Did any of
   your classmates' views cause you to rethink your own? Class members
   should share with each other their descriptions of how the process of argument led to the clarification of their own thinking.

Conclusion

In this chapter we have explored some of the complexities of argument, showing
you why we believe that argument is a matter not of fist banging or of win-lose
debate but of finding, through a process of rational inquiry, the best solution to a
problem. What is our advice for you at the close of this introductory chapter?
Briefly, it is to accept both responsibilities of argument: truth seeking and persuasion. To argue responsibly, you should seek out a wide range of views, especially
ones different from your own, and treat those views as rationally defensible, paying special attention to the reasons and evidence on which they rest.

Our goal in this text is to help you learn skills of argument. If you choose, you
can use these skills cynically to argue any side of any issue. But we hope you

choose to use these skills in the service of your deepest beliefs—beliefs that you discover or clarify through open-minded inquiry. Thus we hope that on some occasions you will modify your position on an issue while writing a rough draft (a sure sign that the process of arguing has complicated your views). If our culture sets you adrift in pluralism, argument can help you take a stand, to say, "These things I believe." In this text we will not pretend to tell you what position to take on any given issue. But if this text helps you define and defend your beliefs—to say, "Here are the reasons that I consider choice A better than choice B, and why you ought to share my view"—then we'll consider it a success.

2 Reading Arguments

Why Reading Arguments Is Important for Writers

In the previous chapter we explained how argument is a social phenomenon in which communities search for the best answers to disputed questions. As you'll see in this chapter, we live in an environment saturated with oral, visual, print, and hypertext arguments. When we enter an argumentative conversation, we need to position ourselves as inquirers as well as persuaders, listening attentively to alternative points of view and reexamining our values, assumptions, and behaviors. In this chapter, we present five strategies that will help you listen to the arguments you encounter, resist simplistic answers, delve into multiple views, and emerge from your intellectual wrestling with informed, deepened, and supportable solutions to problems.

Because argument begins in disagreements within a social community, you should examine any argument as if it were only one voice in a larger conversation. We therefore recommend the following sequence of strategies:

1. Read as a believer.
2. Read as a doubter.
3. Explore how the rhetorical context and genre are shaping the argument.
4. Seek alternative views and analyze sources of disagreement.
5. Use disagreement productively to prompt further investigation.

Let's now examine each of these strategies in turn.

Strategy 1: Reading as a Believer

When you read an argument as a believer, you practice what psychologist Carl Rogers calls *empathic listening*. Empathic listening requires that you see the world through the author's eyes, adopt temporarily the author's beliefs and values, and suspend your skepticism and biases long enough to hear what the author is saying.

Because empathic listening is such a vital skill, we soon will invite you to practice it on a brief argument opposing the genetic engineering of food. Before we ask you to read the argument, however, we want to introduce you to this issue. Since 1994, when genetically modified foods first appeared in supermarkets, they have become increasingly more prevalent, but not without resistance from some consumers. Antibiotechnology groups have labeled genetically modified foods "Frankenfoods" after the power-seeking scientist who created the monster in Mary Shelley's novel *Frankenstein*. This catchy and shrewd word "Frankenfoods" connotes God-playing scientists whose work backfires into an uncontrollable destructive force. The proponents of biotechnology, in contrast, see genetic engineering as beneficial and progressive, offering ways to create disease-resistant plants, more environmentally friendly agricultural methods, and more promising ways to feed the world. With this background, you are now ready to examine for yourself some of the controversies surrounding genetic engineering of food.

For Class Discussion

1. Suppose you are thumbing through a magazine and come across the advocacy advertisement shown in Color Plate A. The ad is sponsored by three groups called "Citizens for Health," the "Center for Food Safety," and "Sustain." Working as a whole class or in small groups, respond to the following questions:

   a. What is the claim of this ad? Whom or what is it arguing against?

   b. Does this ad make you nervous about eating genetically modified foods? What aspects of the ad are most effective in influencing your response? (Consider both the text of the ad and its visual elements.)

2. Now suppose you saw in the op-ed section of your local newspaper the political cartoon shown at the beginning of Part One of this text (p. 1).

   a. What is the claim of this cartoon? Whom or what is it arguing against?

   b. How does this cartoon speak back to the "Keep Nature Natural" ad in Color Plate A?

3. What is your current view of genetically modified foods? (If you buy your food from supermarkets, you are probably eating some genetically modified ingredients. According to some sources, 33 percent of corn, 50 percent of soy, and 50 percent of cotton crops are genetically modified.)

4. Based on the "Keep Nature Natural" ad and the political cartoon, what do you think are the major arguments for and against genetically modified foods?

Now that you have done some thinking about genetic modification of food, read carefully the following article, which appeared in a health food magazine called *Better Nutrition* in June 2000.

Playing with Our Food
Genetic Engineering and Irradiation
Lisa Turner

It used to be that getting clean food wasn't so hard. A trip to the local health food store and a quick scan of food labels, and you could fill your 'fridge with whole, healthy foods. Now, even tofu is likely to be tainted with genetically modified organisms, and your favorite natural tabouli mix may contain irradiated herbs and spices. Is nothing sacred? Not in the brave new world of "biotech" foods. 1

GENETIC ENGINEERING WEIRD SCIENCE

Flounder genes in your pasta sauce? Insect genes in your mashed potatoes? Welcome to the high-tech process of artificially shuffling genes from one organism to another. Proponents of *genetic engineering* say it's a sure way to boost food supply, reduce pesticide use and possibly breed super-foods with extraordinary nutritional profiles. The problem is, no one really knows the long-term effects of such complex *genetic*manipulation—and the potential *dangers* to humans and the environment are substantial. 2

Don't think that *genetic engineering* is merely a stepped-up version of traditional cross-breeding techniques. It's a new, weird science that allows the insertion of genes from any plant or animal into any other organism. One example: an "anti-freeze" gene that allows flounder to survive in very cold water is inserted into tomatoes to boost their tolerance to frost. Or insect-killing genes from bacteria may be inserted into corn or potatoes to up their defenses against pests. 3

Shuffling genes between species raises plenty of scary possibilities. The technology is new enough to be frighteningly imprecise, with generally uncertain outcomes. And because no long-term safety tests have been conducted, no one really knows the full scope of potential health risks. According to an editorial in a 1996 issue of the *New England Journal of Medicine.* "Questions of safety vex federal regulators and industry as well as the public. The transfer of genes from microbes, plants or animals into foods raises issues about the unintended consequences of such manipulations." 4

Some of these consequences include the production of new allergens in foods and unexpected mutations in an organism, which can create new and higher levels of toxins. One example: in 1993, 37 people died and more than 1,500 people suffered partial paralysis from a disease called eosinophilia-myalgia, which was eventually linked to a tryptophan supplement made with genetically engineered bacteria. 5

6   Another worrisome possibility is that insects, birds and the wind can carry genetically altered seeds into neighboring fields and beyond, where they can cross-pollinate, threatening the future of wild crops, genetically natural crops and organic foods.

7   And once genetically modified organisms are introduced into the food supply, they can't be recalled. "Unlike pesticide use, *genetic engineering* introduces living organisms that will be replicated in other living organisms," says Susan Haeger, president/CEO of Citizens for Health, a non-profit consumer advocacy group based in Boulder, Colorado. "Once they're in the environment, there's no way to bring them back."

IRRADIATION: ZAPPING OUR FOOD

8   What happens when you cross a potato with 10,000 rads of ionizing radiation—more than 2,500,000 times the dose of a chest X-ray? Better find out before you eat your next order of french fries. Irradiation, used to extend shelf life and kill microorganisms in food, can also lower nutritional value, create environmental hazards, promote the growth of toxins and produce compounds called unique radiolytic products, which have been associated with a variety of biological abnormalities.

9   Food irradiation was proposed by the Atomic Energy Commission in the early 1950s as a way of dealing with a formidable nuclear waste problem from the manufacture of nuclear weapons, according to Michael Colby, editor of the *Food & Water Journal.* In the mid-1980s, the FDA began to approve a huge range of foodstuffs for irradiation, including meat, poultry, produce, herbs and spices. Since then, permissible levels of radiation have been dramatically increased, and the amount now allowed is substantial.

10   Proponents say irradiation destroys harmful microorganisms and may reduce outbreaks of salmonella and trichinosis from meat. It is also said that irradiation increases shelf life of various foods and can reduce the use of toxic chemicals as post-harvest fumigants. Absurd, say irradiation opponents. "Irradiation is destroying our food supply," says Gary Gibbs, D.O., author of *The Food That Would Last Forever.* "It is nothing more than a toxic band-aid approach to the problems."

11   Adequate cooking, sanitary handling and preparation and hygienic processing methods are better ways to reduce illness from microorganisms in meat. Shelf life is an unfounded concern in the United States, and the cost of irradiation in less-developed countries would usually offset savings from extended shelf life. As for the argument that irradiation would reduce the need for post-harvest chemical fumigants, some say that irradiated foods are more prone to infection by certain fungi.

12   The FDA and irradiation proponents claim the process is safe, but compelling evidence to the contrary says otherwise. Meanwhile, considerable controversy exists regarding safety studies. Although 441 studies have been conducted on food irradiation, the FDA based their toxicity evaluation on only five animal studies, according to Gibbs. Of these five studies, two were found to be methodologically flawed, one suggested that irradiated food could have adverse effects on older animals and two investigated foods irradiated at doses well below FDA-approved levels.

Few human trials exist, because of obvious ethical considerations, but some small studies have raised concerns, suggesting that food irradiation can cause chromosomal abnormalities. [13]

Irradiation of food can lead to cardiac disease, cancer, kidney disease, fetal malformations and a dramatic shortening of the life span, according to Gibbs. "A lot of studies have shown problems with the heart, specifically that irradiation causes bleeding in the heart," he says. "Also, when food is irradiated, it creates benzene and formaldehyde, which are known mutagens and suspected carcinogens." [14]

Irradiation also appears to cause significant nutrient loss in foods, especially of vitamins A, B, C and E. Generally, the higher the amount of radiation, the greater the nutrient loss. Add to that environmental concerns, including hazards in transporting and handling radioactive isotopes, danger of exposure to workers and possible security problems at irradiation facilities. Right now, there are about 50 irradiation facilities in the United States, says Colby, but a huge increase is expected if irradiation is embraced in the marketplace. The result: a substantial increase in potential environmental disasters. [15]

WHAT TO DO

Because biotech foods are still new, the core issues are safety testing and consumer awareness. "It may be that there are some positive aspects to biotech food," says Haeger. "We don't know. Our concern is that the commercialization of biotech foods and their integration in the food system is outpacing the science and is being promoted without the awareness of the public." [16]

More stringent safety testing is critical, as are more comprehensive labeling requirements. Under current laws, irradiated foods must be labeled as such, with a written notice and a "radura"—the international irradiation symbol—but processed foods and foods prepared for restaurants, hospitals or school cafeterias are exempt from such labeling. Additionally, no labeling requirements exist for genetically engineered foods. [17]

Some say *genetic engineering* and food irradiation should be banned. "This is beyond labeling considerations," says Gibbs. "It should be completely outlawed. We shouldn't even have to have conversations about labeling." In the meantime, the primary thrust is toward public awareness. [18]

"Our main concern is for consumers to be aware of food manipulation," says Haeger. "We want to ensure that they are informed and have adequate information on what they're purchasing, so they can make their own choices." [19]

References

Belongia, F.A., et al. "The eosinophilia-myalgia syndrome and tryptophan," *Annu Rev Nutr* 12: 235–56, 1992.

Bhaskaram, C., Sadasivan, G. "Effects of feeding irradiated wheat to malnourished children," *American Journal of Clinical Nutrition* 28(2): 130–35, 1975.

Hickman, J.R., McLean, L.A., Ley, F.J. "Rat feeding studies on wheat treated with gamma radiation," *Food and Cosmetic Toxicology* 2(2): 175–180, 1964.

Khattak, A.B., Klopfenstein, C.F. "Effects of gamma irradiation on the nutritional quality of grains and legumes," *Cereal Chemistry* 66(3): 171–72, 1989.

McGivney, W.T. "Preservation of food products by irradiation," *Seminars in Nuclear Medicine* 18: 36, 1998.

Nyhan, W.L., et al. "New approaches to understanding Lesch-Nyhan disease," *New England Journal of Medicine* 334(24): 1602–4, 1996.

Piccioni, R. "Food irradiation: Contaminating our food," *The Ecologist* 18(2): 48, 1988.

Radomski, J.L., et al. "Chronic toxicity studies in irradiated beef stew and evaporated milk," *Toxicology and Applied Pharmacology* 7(1): 113–21, 1965.

Raica, N., Scott, J., Nielson, N. "Nutritional quality of irradiated foods," *Radiation Research Review* 3(4): 447–57, 1972.

Shanghai Institute of Radiation Medicine and Shanghai Institute of Nuclear Research. "Safety evaluation of 35 kinds of irradiated human foods," *Chinese Medical Journal* 100(9): 715–18, 1987.

Summary Writing as a Way of Reading to Believe

Now that you have finished the article, ask yourself how well you "listened" to it. If you listened well, you should be able to write a summary of Turner's argument in your own words. A *summary* (also called an *abstract*, a *précis*, or a *synopsis*) presents only a text's major points and eliminates supporting details. Writers often incorporate summaries of other writers' views into their own arguments, either to support their own claims or to represent opposing arguments that they intend to refute. Summaries can be any length, depending on the writer's purposes, but they usually range from several sentences to one or two paragraphs.

Practicing the following steps should help you be a better summary writer.

Step 1: Read the argument first for general meaning. Don't judge it; just follow the writer's meaning, trying to see the issue from the writer's perspective. Try to adopt the writer's values and belief system.

Step 2: Read the argument slowly a second and a third time, writing in the margins brief *does* and *says* statements for each paragraph (or group of closely connected paragraphs). A *does* statement identifies a paragraph's function, such as "summarizes an opposing view," "introduces a supporting reason," or "gives an example." A *says* statement summarizes a paragraph's main point. What follows are our *does* and *says* statements for the first five paragraphs of Turner's article.

DOES/SAYS ANALYSIS OF TURNER'S ARTICLE

Paragraph 1: *Does*: Introduces the problem of "the brave new world of 'biotech' foods." *Says*: It is becoming difficult today to find foods that have not been irradiated or genetically modified.

Paragraph 2: *Does*: Briefly sketches the benefits of genetic engineering and shifts to the potential dangers. *Says*: Advocates claim that biotechnology can increase the food supply, reduce the use of pesticides, and increase the nutritional value of foods, but no one knows the long-term effects of genetic engineering on humans or the environment.

Paragraph 3: *Does:* Elaborates on how genetic engineering works with some specific examples. *Says:* Genetic engineering alters plants and animals far beyond crossbreeding.

Paragraph 4: *Does:* Elaborates on the potential dangers of genetic engineering. *Says*: Imprecision and unpredictable long-term consequences make this biotechnology frightening.

Paragraph 5: *Does*: Offers examples of some of the dangerous consequences so far. *Says*: Genetic engineering created toxins that caused deaths and partial paralysis in 1993.

For Class Discussion

Working individually or in groups, write *does* and *says* statements for the remaining paragraphs of Turner's article.

Step 3: Examine your *does* and *says* statements to determine the major sections of the argument, and create a list of major points and subpoints. If you are visually oriented, you may prefer to make a flowchart or diagram of the article.

Step 4: Turn your list, flowchart, or diagram into a prose summary. Typically, writers do this in one of two ways. Some start by joining all their *says* statements into a lengthy paragraph-by-paragraph summary and then prune it. Others start with a one-sentence summary of the argument's thesis and major supporting reasons and then gradually flesh it out with more supporting ideas. Your goal is to be neutral, objective, and accurate in presenting the writer's main points and emphasis on those points.

Step 5: Revise your summary until it is the desired length and is sufficiently clear, concise, and complete. When you incorporate a summary of someone else's argument into your own essay, you must distinguish that author's words and ideas from your own by using *attributive tags* (expressions like "Turner says," "according to Turner," or "Turner further explains"), by putting any directly borrowed language in quotation marks, and by citing the original author using appropriate conventions for documenting sources.[*]

As illustration, we will show our summaries of Turner's article—a one-paragraph version and a single-sentence version. In the one-paragraph version, we illustrate the MLA documentation system in which page numbers for direct

---

[*]The most frequently used documentation systems in academic writing are those of the Modern Language Association (MLA) and the American Psychological Association (APA). Both are explained in Appendix Two, "A Concise Guide to Finding, Evaluating, and Documenting Sources."

quotations are placed in parentheses after the quotation and complete bibliographic information is placed in a Works Cited list at the end of the paper. See Appendix Two for a brief explanation of the MLA and APA documentation systems.

ONE-PARAGRAPH SUMMARY OF TURNER'S ARGUMENT

Identification of author and source

Insertion of short quotation; MLA documentation shows page numbers in parentheses

Attributive tags

Continued use of attributive tags

In an article entitled "Playing with Our Food" from the magazine Better Nutrition, health food advocate Lisa Turner warns readers that much of our food today is genetically modified or irradiated. She describes genetic engineering as "artificially shuffling genes," which differs completely from "traditional cross-breeding" (21). She argues that the potential, unforeseen, harmful consequences of this "new, weird science" (21) offset the possible benefits of increasing the food supply, reducing the use of pesticides, and boosting the nutritional value of foods. Turner asserts that genetic engineering is imprecise, untested, unpredictable, irreversible, and also uncontrollable due to animals, insects, and winds. She also objects to the use of irradiation to enable foods to stay fresh longer and to kill harmful microorganisms. Claiming that the FDA has not tested irradiation at the levels that it allows, she suggests that irradiation has many harmful effects: depleting vitamins in foods, causing cancer and cardiac problems, and increasing amounts of radioactive material in the environment. Turner concludes by saying that the marketing of these products has proceeded much more quickly than scientific knowledge about them warrants. If we don't ban genetic engineering and irradiation completely (a course that some people propose), Turner argues that at the very least more safety testing and labeling are needed. We consumers must know how our food has been manipulated. (220 words)

Works Cited

Correct citation of article in MLA format. (In a formal paper the "Works Cited" list begins a new page.)

Turner, Lisa. "Playing with Our Food." Better Nutrition June 2002: 56-59. Rpt. in Writing Arguments: A Rhetoric with Readings. John D. Ramage, John C. Bean, and June Johnson. 3rd Concise ed. New York: Longman, 2004. 21–24.

ONE-SENTENCE SUMMARY OF TURNER'S ARGUMENT

In her article in Better Nutrition, health food writer Lisa Turner warns readers of the prevalence, risk, and potential health and environmental dangers of genetic modification and irradiation of food, arguing that these products should undergo more stringent testing for safety and should be labeled for consumer protection.

Whether you write a very short summary or a more detailed one, your goal should be to come as close as possible to a fair, accurate, and balanced condensation of the author's argument and to represent the relationships among the parts fairly and accurately. We don't want to pretend that summary writing is easy; often it's not, especially if the argument is complex and if the author doesn't explicitly highlight his or her thesis and main supporting reasons. Nonetheless, being able to summarize the arguments of others in your own words is an important skill for arguers.

Suspending Doubt: Willing Your Own Belief in the Writer's Views

Summarizing an argument is only the first step in your effort to believe it. You must also suspend doubt and will yourself to adopt the writer's view. Suspending doubt is easy if you already agree with the author. But if an author's views affront your own values, then "believing" can be a hard but valuable exercise. By struggling to believe strange, threatening, or unfamiliar views, we can grow as learners and thinkers.

To believe an author, search your mind for personal experiences, values, and beliefs that affirm his or her argument. Here is how one student wrote a journal entry trying to believe Turner's argument.

> JOURNAL ENTRY SHOWING STUDENT'S ATTEMPT TO BELIEVE TURNER
>
> Although I had heard of genetic modification of plants, I never thought about how I might be affected. Turner's article made me worry about how many of the things I eat have been produced by artificial genetic processes. How much do scientists actually know about long-term effects of growing and eating biotech food? I know of lots of cases where scientists have tried to fix environmental problems, and ended up causing new problems. My biology teacher told us about a failed scientific intervention involving cane toads brought into Australia to eat the beetles and grubs plaguing the sugar cane. The natural cycles of the grubs, beetles and toads didn't match. Now these poisonous cane toads have proliferated out of control because they have no native predators. What will we say about genetic engineering in ten years? Turner's article has also made me want to know how the government is regulating what biotech foods are sold. Maybe I should spend more time reading the labels on all the food I buy. How much more will I have to pay to avoid foods that have been genetically modified?

Strategy 2: Reading as a Doubter

Reading as a believer is only half of being a powerful reader. You must also read as a doubter by raising objections, asking questions, expressing skepticism, and withholding assent. In the margins of the text, as a doubter, you add a new layer of notes demanding more proof, doubting evidence, challenging the author's assumptions and values, asking what is left out, and speaking back to the author.

For Class Discussion

Return to Turner's article, reading it skeptically. Raise questions, offer objections, express doubts. Then, working as a class or in small groups, list all your doubts about Turner's argument.

Now that you have doubted Turner's article, compare your doubts to some raised by our students.

- In the third sentence of her article, Turner says that tofu is "likely to be tainted with genetically modified organisms." Her word "taint" suggests a strong bias against technology right from the start.

- She mentions the possible advantages of genetic engineering in only one sentence—boosting food supply, reducing needs for pesticides, and so forth. These seem like major advantages that should be investigated. How successful has biotechnology been at achieving its stated goals? What scientific breakthroughs has genetic engineering made? What good has it done so far?

- She gives no sources for her claim that an anti-freeze gene from flounders is inserted into tomatoes. We would like to learn if this claim is true and see how scientists describe the purpose and results. There may be another side to this story.

- Turner doesn't claim that biotech foods are not safe. She just claims that they haven't been tested enough. The only negative evidence she provides is the thirty-seven persons killed by a disease that was "linked" to genetically engineered bacteria. Why the weak word "linked"? Did scientists prove that the disease was caused by genetic engineering? Is this case exceptional?

- The case against irradiation is not supported by evidence but by testimony from Gary Gibbs and Susan Haeger, whose scientific credentials aren't clearly stated. Turner does not provide or document the "compelling evidence" she claims exists for her numerous frightening statements about irradiation.

These are only some of the objections that might be raised against Turner's argument. Perhaps you and your classmates have other objections that are equally important. Our point is that you should practice "doubting" an argument as well as "believing" it. Both skills are essential. *Believing* helps you expand your view of the world or modify your arguments and beliefs in response to others. *Doubting* helps protect you from becoming overpowered by others' arguments and teaches you to stand back, consider, and weigh points carefully.

Strategy 3: Exploring How Rhetorical Context and Genre Shape the Argument

The strategies of believing and doubting an argument urge you toward further exploration and inquiry. In the next stage of analysis, you should consider the rhetorical context of the argument as well as its genre. In this section we'll explain these concepts and show you why they are important.

Understanding the Genres of Argument

Knowing the genre of an argument helps you understand how the writer's purpose, intended audience, and angle of vision or bias have shaped the argument. A "genre" is a recurring type or pattern of argument such as a letter to the editor, a scholarly journal article, or the home page of an advocacy Web site. Genres are often categorized by format, purpose, or type of publication; as we'll see, they place on writers certain demands (such as the need for a particular tone or kind of evidence) and constraints (such as limits on length).

When you read arguments anthologized in a textbook, you lose clues about the argument's original genre. (You should therefore note the information about genre provided in our introductions to readings.) You can also lose clues about genre when you download articles from the Internet or from licensed databases such as LexisNexis or ProQuest. (See Appendix Two for explanations of these research tools.) When you do your own research, you therefore need to be aware of the original genre of what you are reading: Is this piece a newspaper editorial, an article from a magazine, an organizational white paper, an academic argument in a peer-reviewed journal, a student paper posted to a Web site, or something else?

In the following list, we identify most of the genres of argument through which readers and writers carry on the conversations of a democracy.

- *Personal correspondence.* This category includes letters or e-mail messages to specific decision makers to achieve the writer's purpose (complaint letter, request for a certain action). The style can range from a formal business letter to an informal note. The tone depends on purpose and audience.

- *Letters to the editor.* Published in newspapers and some public affairs magazines, letters to the editor are aimed at the readers of the publication and enable ordinary citizens to speak out and influence opinion on public issues from a variety of perspectives. They are very short (fewer than three hundred words) and time sensitive.

- *Newspaper editorials and op-ed columns.* Often written in response to a recent occurrence, political event, or social problem in the news, editorials and op-ed pieces are widely read, influential types of arguments. Editorials, which appear on the editorial page of a newspaper and promote the views of the editors, are short (usually fewer than five hundred words), and are written in a journalistic style, often without detailed evidence. They can range from conservative to liberal depending on the political bias of the editors. Op-ed columns appear "opposite the editorial page" (hence the abbreviation "op-ed") and are usually written by syndicated columnists who are professional writers. Op-ed columns typically average 500–1,000 words and can vary from explicit thesis-driven arguments to implicit arguments with stylistic flair.

■ *Public affairs or niche magazine articles.* Public affairs magazines such as *National Review*, *New Republic*, *Atlantic Monthly*, or *The Progressive* are outlets for in-depth studies of current issues. Written by staff writers or freelancers, articles in public affairs magazines usually reflect the political bias of the magazine. The articles are often well researched, have a journalistic style with informal documentation, and frequently include narrative elements rather than explicit thesis-and-reasons organization. In contrast to public affairs magazines, niche magazines advocate for the interests of a particular profession or target audience. Niche magazines include trade publications such as *Automotive Week* or *Construction Marketing Today*, arts and entertainment magazines such as *Rolling Stone* or *Cinema*, and culture and society magazines aimed at particular audiences, such as *The Advocate* (gay and lesbian issues) or *Minority Business Entrepreneur*.

■ *Scholarly journals.* Scholarly journals are nonprofit magazines subsidized by universities or scholarly societies. They publish academic articles that have been reviewed by scholars in the field. Although scholars try scrupulously to collect evidence in an unbiased way and analyze it objectively, their work necessarily reflects the biases, methods, and strategies associated with a specific school of thought or theory within a discipline. Scholarly articles usually employ a formal academic style and include academic documentation and bibliographies. Sometimes scholars seek to influence public opinion, use a more popular style, and write for public affairs magazines or academic Web sites. (Student papers in an argument class often fit this genre—academic argument aimed at a popular audience on a public issue.)

■ *Organizational white papers.* White papers, a common genre of argument in organizational and professional settings, are written as in-house documents by individuals or committees to influence organizational decisions or policies or give informed advice to clients. Sometimes they are written for external audiences to influence public opinion favorable to the organization, in which case they reflect the organization's bias and perspective (external white papers are often posted on Web sites or sent to legislators). Usually desktop published and written in a utilitarian style with thesis-and-reasons organization and formal documentation, they often include graphics and other visuals.

■ *Proposals.* Typed or desktop published, proposals identify a problem, propose a specific solution, and support the solution with a justifying argument. Proposals focus on the needs of the targeted audience, using the audience's values and desires to justify the writer's proposed solution. They are often used to seek grant funding or secure contracts with clients.

■ *Legal briefs and court decisions.* Legal briefs are written by attorneys to support the position of one of the parties in a trial or judicial review. "Friends of the court" briefs are serious reasons-and-evidence position papers, written by stakeholders in a case to influence appeals courts such as the U.S. Supreme Court. Briefs are usually written in legalese, but use a logical, well-organized reasons-and-evidence structure. Once a judge or court makes a decision, the "court decision" is often published to explain the judge's reasoning and minority arguments if the decision was not unanimous.

- *Public affairs advocacy advertisements.* Published as posters, fliers, Web pages, or paid advertisements in newspapers and magazines, these condensed arguments seek to influence public opinion on civic issues. Using a succinct "sound bite" style, these ads often employ document design, bulleted lists, and visual elements such as graphics, photographs, or drawings for rhetorical effect. They have an explicit bias and often ignore the complexities of an issue by focusing strongly on one view.

- *Advocacy Web sites.* Often identified by the extension ".org" in the Web site address, advocacy Web sites support the views of the site owner on civic issues. Web sites by well-financed advocacy groups such as the NRA (National Rifle Association) or PETA (People for the Ethical Treatment of Animals) are professionally designed with extensive links to other sites supporting the same views. Well-designed sites use visuals and hyperlinked texts aimed at creating an immediate visceral response favorable to the site owner's views. Ethically responsible sites explicitly announce their bias and purpose in an "About us" link on the home page. (For further discussion of reading and evaluating Web sites, see Appendix Two, pp. 284–288.)

- *Postings to chat rooms, MOOs, electronic bulletin boards.* These postings are written in truncated, informal style often using the jargon and code words of a particular audience. They are posted by individuals to influence opinions of other participants in an online discussion. They usually reflect a wide range of perspectives and are excellent places to try out ideas-in-progress.

- *Visual arguments.* Although seldom appearing without some accompanying text, photographs, drawings, political cartoons, and graphics can have an intense rhetorical impact (see Chapter 9). Visuals make strong emotional appeals, often reducing complex issues to one powerful perspective.

- *Speeches.* Many of the important arguments in our culture, including those in print, begin initially as speeches—either formal speeches such as a presidential address or a keynote speech at a professional meeting, or more informal speeches such as presentations at hearings or interviews on talk shows. Often transcriptions of speeches are printed in newspapers or made available on the Web.

Now that you have a brief overview of the genres of argument, we can apply this knowledge to the issue we have been examining—the genetic engineering of food. As we did our own research on this issue, we found that the public debate about genetic engineering of foods is being carried on across the total spectrum of argument genres, from letters to the editor, to op-ed pieces, to scholarly academic articles, to political speeches and advocacy ads.

Analyzing Rhetorical Context and Genre

Besides understanding an argument's genre, you need to reconstruct its rhetorical context—that is, learn more about the conversation the writer is joining and about the writer's credentials, purpose, audience, and motivation. Awareness of genre and rhetorical context can help you determine how much influence an argument should have on your own thinking about an issue. To explore the rhetorical context of an argument, you can use the following guide questions:

Questions about Rhetorical Context and Genre

1. Who is the author? What are the author's credentials and what is his/her investment in the issue?
2. What audience is he or she writing for?
3. What motivating occasion prompted this writing? What is the author's purpose?
4. What genre of argument is this? How do the conventions of that genre help determine the depth, complexity, and even appearance of the argument?
5. What information about the publication or source (magazine, newspaper, advocacy Web site) helps explain the angle of vision that shapes the argument?

Consider how we applied these questions to Lisa Turner's article "Playing with Our Food." We began by investigating the identity of the author and the kind of publication. Checking on Lisa Turner's background (by entering her name into a Web search engine), we discovered that she specializes in alternative health therapies and has training in Chinese herbal medicine, yoga, and meditation techniques. She has written five books on nutrition and health published by presses associated with alternative medicine, regularly appears on talk shows to promote natural health, teaches cooking classes at Whole Foods Market (one of the biggest organic food chains), and owns a catering company called "The Healthy Gourmet." We learned that *Better Nutrition* is a popular magazine about consumer health and alternative therapies distributed primarily at health food stores. It is indexed in CINAHL, the main nursing index, but not in MEDLINE, one of the main medical indexes, suggesting that it is not regarded as rigorous scientific scholarship.

When we returned to the article "Playing with Our Food" and analyzed it rhetorically, we saw more clearly how Turner's background, the type of magazine, and her sense of audience shaped her argument. She is strongly biased toward organic foods and alternative approaches to medicine and health. Because *Better Nutrition* is a natural health magazine, Turner assumes that her audience will share her opposition to scientific intervention in farming and food processing and will be moved by her alarmist tone, vehement language, and general statements. Although this article does include references, they are not the most current or the most exact. The two sources that she quotes directly—the CEO of the advocacy group Citizens for Health and the author of the book *The Food That Would Last Forever*—do not appear in her list of references. We decided that this article represents a "health foods" point of view in the biotech foods controversy but provides only a starting point for inquiry into this complex issue.

Strategy 4: Seeking Alternative Views and Analyzing Sources of Disagreement

If you were an arbitrator, you wouldn't think of settling a dispute between A and B on the basis of A's testimony alone. You would insist on hearing B's side of the story, and perhaps also C's and D's if they are stakeholders in the dispute. By the same token, you can't fairly evaluate an argument detached from the controversy out of which it arose or isolated from the alternative views to which it speaks. You must seek out those views.

When analyzing disagreements among various points of view, you'll find they typically fall into two categories: (1) disagreements about the facts or their relevance and (2) disagreements about underlying beliefs, values, or assumptions. Let's consider each in turn.

Disagreement About Facts or Their Relevance

Often disputants in an argument disagree about facts in a case or about the relevance of certain facts. Consider the controversies over global warming. Although the majority of scientists believe that the earth is getting hotter and that at least some portion of this increase is caused by the emission of greenhouse gases, scientists have factual disputes about the rate of global warming, about its causes (How much is natural? How much is human-caused?), and about its environmental effects. Additionally, disputants can disagree on the significance or relevance of a fact. For example, global warming activists often cite the dramatic shrinking of the glacial ice cap on Africa's Mount Kilimanjaro as evidence of human-caused global warming. But some climatologists, who agree that Kilimanjaro's ice cap is shrinking, argue that nonhuman causes such as natural climate variability may be the primary factors. In this case, a fact that urges one person to propose political action to combat global warming leaves another person unmoved. Other disagreements about facts or their relevance include the following:

- In arguing whether silver-mercury amalgam tooth fillings should be banned, dental researchers disagree on the amount of mercury vapor released by older fillings. They also disagree how much mercury vapor has to be present before it is harmful.

- In arguing about the legalization of drugs, writers disagree about the degree to which Prohibition reduced alcohol consumption; they also disagree whether crack cocaine is "crimogenic" (has chemical properties that induce violent behavior).

Disagreements About Values, Beliefs, or Assumptions

A second source of disagreement concerns differences in values, beliefs, or assumptions.

- Persons A and B may agree that a huge tax on gasoline would cut down on the consumption of petroleum. They may agree further that the world's supply of petroleum will eventually run out. Thus A and B agree at the level of facts. But they may disagree about whether the United States should enact a huge gas tax. Person A may support a tax increase to conserve oil, whereas person B may oppose it, perhaps because B believes that scientists will find alternative energy sources before the petroleum runs out or because B believes that the short-term harm of such a tax outweighs distant benefits.

Sometimes disagreements about assumptions present themselves as disagreements about definitions or analogies.

- Social theorist A and social theorist B might disagree about whether the covers of some women's magazines, such as *Cosmopolitan,* are pornographic. This disagreement turns on the definition of *pornography,* with different definitions reflecting different underlying values and beliefs.
- Person A and Person B might disagree on whether it is ethically acceptable for Down's syndrome children to undergo plastic surgery to correct some of the facial abnormalities associated with this genetic condition. Person A supports the surgery, arguing it is analogous to any other cosmetic surgeries done to improve appearance. Person B argues against such surgery, saying that the motivation for the surgery is analogous to the racial self-hatred of some minority persons who have tried to change their ethnic appearance. (The latter analogy argues that Down's syndrome is nothing to be ashamed of and that persons should take pride in their difference.)

We now invite you to consider a different view of biotechnology. Examine Color Plate B, which is an advocacy advertisement sponsored by the Council for Biotechnology Information. This ad, promoting biotech soybeans, appeared in a July 2002 issue of *Time* magazine. Then read this same organization's argument opposing consumer labels for genetically engineered foods. (We found the argument on the Council's Web site.) These pro-biotech arguments—in conversation with Turner's article and the "Keep Nature Natural" ad (Color Plate A)—vividly exemplify the differing values and beliefs that compete for our allegiance in a pluralistic world.

Why Biotech Labeling Can Confuse Consumers
Council for Biotechnology Information

Consumers want food product labels with clear, meaningful information.   1

A grocery shopper, for example, finds a wealth of factual information on labels,   2
whether it's about nutrient and caloric content or specific health aspects of a food
product.

Should that same shopper also be able to read on the label whether those corn   3
chips or that bottle of cooking oil contains biotech ingredients? Some say yes. Given
the concerns raised by a few about biotech safety, there's an important "right to
know," they contend.

Others say there's no need to label foods with biotech ingredients that are the   4
same as foods with ingredients from conventional crops. Requiring a label for
biotech ingredients, they say, would confuse consumers, not inform them.

The U.S. Food and Drug Administration (FDA), which oversees food safety issues   5
in the United States, takes the second view. The agency performs exhaustive safety
tests on every biotech food entering the marketplace, and requires special labeling only
when the new food product is significantly different from its conventional counterpart.

TESTED FOR SAFETY

Before they reach a farmer's field, biotech corn, soybeans and other genetically   6
enhanced foods undergo years of review by researchers, university scientists,
farmers and other government agencies in addition to the FDA.

The results are unambiguous. Biotech crops are safe to eat. No studies or test   7
results have said otherwise. There hasn't been a single documented case of an illness caused by biotech foods.[1] A report issued in 2000 by the National Academy
of Sciences, an independent group of scientists and scholars, confirmed that all
approved biotech products are as safe as their conventional counterparts.[2]

So safety is not at issue in labeling biotech food. Instead, the FDA considers   8
whether a biotech orange, for example, is "substantially equivalent" to a traditional
orange. Does it produce the same nutrients? If it does, there's no need for a label. If
it doesn't—if the orange has a higher or lower level of vitamin C—then the FDA requires a label.

Under this line of thinking, labeling *all* biotech foods would make a distinction   9
without a difference. Rather than communicating relevant health or safety information, it would merely explain the *process* by which the food was developed. And in so
doing it could sow confusion among consumers. Ninety-two percent of food industry
leaders, for example, believe that mandatory biotech food labeling—which proponents often position simply as an informational tool—will instead be perceived as a
"warning" by at least some consumers.[3]

The American Medical Association (AMA) has stated that "there is no scientific   10
justification for special labeling of genetically modified foods, as a class."[4]

11   Statistics show that the current FDA policy—labeling biotech foods when there's a meaningful reason to do so—is what consumers want. When surveyed for their opinions, two-thirds to three-quarters consistently approve of the existing system once it's explained that biotech foods have been reviewed and found safe by experts, and would be specially labeled if the nutritional content has been significantly changed.[5]

12   When asked in an open-ended way what information they'd like more of on product labels, only 1 percent of consumers mentioned biotechnology. Three percent said ingredients, four percent nutrition and 75 percent said they wanted no additional information.[6]

COSTLY AND CONFUSING

13   Countries and trading blocs that want to require labels have had to develop a long list of exemptions and loopholes.[7] That's the case in Europe, which enacted labeling requirements and other restrictions. An article in the *Wall Street Journal* pointed out that the European system has "confused consumers" and "spawned a bewildering array of marketing claims, counterclaims and outright contradictions that only a food scientist possibly could unravel."[8]

14   Labeling requirements also increase costs. Keeping biotech commodity crops separate from traditional ones requires new expenses in the agricultural supply chain—in added handling measures, testing requirements, and so on—that inevitably will be passed on to consumers.

15   A Canadian study estimated that mandatory labeling would cost that country's consumers $700 million to $950 million annually[9]—arguably, a food tax on the majority to pay for the labeling demands of a few.[10]

16   An alternative is the voluntary labeling guidelines for biotech and nonbiotech products currently being developed by the FDA. Under this system, manufacturers can let consumers know if a food was developed using biotechnology to have a beneficial trait such as reduced saturated fat—or, conversely, if biotech ingredients were not used in making a food.[11]

17   Professor Thomas Hoban, director of the Center for Biotechnology in Global Society at North Carolina State University, points out that voluntary labeling can provide choice "without imposing costs on . . . the majority of consumers who support or have no objection to biotechnology."[12]

FOCUSING DEBATE

18   Biotechnology is a fast-changing science that's raising environmental, economic and ethical issues. Given the importance of food in a fast-growing world where about 840 million people go hungry, those issues deserve to be considered on their merits.

19   By raising questionable concerns in the minds of consumers, and introducing unnecessary costs, mandatory labeling requirements may only distract from what's truly important: a rational, fact-informed debate about the risks of biotechnology, balanced against the benefits it offers.

Notes

[1] Aaron, David L., U.S. Undersecretary of Commerce for Trade, Reuters, September 16, 1999; also, "In Support of Biotechnology (Expert Views)" The Alliance for Better Foods, <www.betterfoods.org/Expert/Expert.htm>.

[2] Woo, Robin Y., "No Room for Politics on Food Labels," *Des Moines Register,* May 11, 2000, reprinted at <index.asp?id=1226&redirect=con508mid17%2Ehtml>.

[3] Hoban, Thomas J., "Market Acceptance of Agricultural Biotechnology," North Carolina State University, electronic multimedia presentation.

[4] "Genetically Modified Crops and Foods," American Medical Association (AMA), <www.ama-assn.org/ama/pub/article/2036-3604.html>.

[5] Hoban, Thomas J., "Biotechnology," *Forum,* Fourth Quarter 2000, p. 102.

[6] Hoban, Thomas, J., "Biotechnology," *Forum,* Fourth Quarter 2000, p. 95.

[7] Chin, Mary Lee, "Confusing Customers," *Denver Post,* June 17, 2001.

[8] Stecklow, Steve, "Genetically Modified Label Confuses U.K. Shoppers," *The Wall Street Journal,* October 27, 1999.

[9] "Economic Impact Study: Potential Costs of Mandatory Labeling of Food Products Derived from Biotechnology in Canada," KPMG Consulting, December 1, 2000.

[10] "Labeling Biotechnology Foods and the Organic Lobby," Economic & Agricultural Trade 2000, <www.eat2k.org/issues/laveling_backgrounder.html>.

[11] "Guidance for Industry: Voluntary Labeling Indicating Whether Foods Have or Have Not Been Developed Using Bioengineering," U.S. Food and Drug Administration, January 2001, <www.cfsan.fda.gov/dms/biolabgu.html>.

[12] Hoban, Thomas, J., "Biotechnology," *Forum,* Fourth Quarter 2000, p. 103.

For Class Discussion

Working as a whole class or in small groups, respond to the following questions about the readings and visual arguments you have just considered.

1. What claims about biotech foods does the soybean ad (Color Plate B) make?

2. Consider this ad in dialogue with Turner and the "Keep Nature Natural" ad (Color Plate A). How does this ad try to allay the fears and answer the objections of the opponents of genetically engineered foods?

3. The genre of the advocacy ad requires brevity and strong, clear, audience-based appeals to a target audience. Why did the Council for Biotechnology Information choose to publish its ads in *Time* and other magazines like *Atlantic Monthly*? What audiences is it trying to reach?

4. What does this advocacy ad do to establish its authority and credibility?

5. Now consider the Council's policy argument on biotech labeling. To what extent do Lisa Turner and the Council disagree about the basic facts concerning genetically engineered foods?

6. To what extent do Turner and the Council disagree about values, beliefs, and underlying assumptions?

Writing an Analysis of a Disagreement

A common writing assignment in argument courses asks students to analyze the sources of disagreement between two or more writers who take different positions on an issue. In writing such an analysis, you need to determine whether the writers disagree primarily about facts/relevance, about values, or about both. To illustrate an analysis of a disagreement, we've constructed the following model: our own brief analysis of the sources of disagreement between Turner and the Council for Biotechnology Information. We've written it as a short, formal paper following the MLA documentation style.

An Analysis of the Sources of Disagreement Between Lisa Turner and the Council for Biotechnology Information

1   Lisa Turner and the Council for Biotechnology Information clash about facts and values in their arguments over the genetic engineering of food. Turner stresses the dangers of biotechnology while the Council stresses the value of scientific advancement.

2   At the heart of their controversy is disagreement about facts. Have genetically engineered foods been appropriately tested for safety? "No," says Turner; "yes," says the Council. These antithetical views determine the stand each source takes on the need for biotech labeling. Turner argues that biotech foods are risky. Her strategy is to raise doubts about the safety of genetically engineered food, mainly by suggesting frightening hypothetical scenarios. She emphasizes the experimental quality of these modifications, arguing that they are imprecise, uncontrollable, and irreversible because they alter living things that pass on genetic modifications when they propagate and they affect natural cycles that involve other plants and animals. She mentions the creation of new allergens that could provoke dangerous allergic reactions. She cites one example of deaths and paralysis in 1993, but she does not explain what food product caused this response. (The Council states that no death or disease has ever resulted from biotech foods.) Her main point is that scientists, farmers, and marketers are foisting these entirely experimental foods on an uninformed public.

3   In contrast, the Council for Biotechnology Information assumes the safety of genetically engineered foods. It has confidence in the U.S. Food and Drug Administration's declaration that biotech foods are safe and agrees with the FDA rule that labels are needed only when a biotech food substantially differs from its natural counterpart. The Council asserts that these biotech foods have undergone rigorous tests "by researchers, university scientists, farmers and other government

agencies in addition to the FDA" (paragraph 6). However, in the conclusion of the article, the Council does mention that "[b]iotechnology is a fast-changing science" (paragraph 18) and there is a need for "a rational, fact-informed debate about the risks of biotechnology" (paragraph 19).

The "facts" in these two arguments derive from the authors' dramatically different   4
values and assumptions. Turner's article appeared in a health food magazine, and she writes to an audience who shares her distrust of technology. Turner reveals her angle of vision as a health and natural foods practitioner in her strong alarmist tone and her antagonism to genetic engineering, which come through her choice of language. Words such as "tainted," "nothing sacred," "brave new world of 'biotech foods,'" "artificially shuffling genes," and "new, weird science" express her antitechnology bias (paragraphs 1-3). Clearly, she believes that plants, animals, and foods in their natural state are superior to anything that is artificially created.

In contrast, the Council for Biotechnology Information makes an effort to sound   5
balanced, rational, and knowledgeable, but this article also reveals its underlying values. The Council, which is an advocacy organization for the biotechnology industry, believes that biotechnology is a beneficent force that uses human ingenuity to improve nature. Its slogan "Good ideas are growing" (found on its Web site home page) encodes the idea that progress results when humans can manipulate natural processes. This article enhances its credibility by citing the American Medical Association's endorsement of the safety of genetically engineered foods and documenting its reputable sources. However, under the guise of concern for cost to consumers, the Council hides its pro-big business and pro-government bias. The hidden reality here is that the creation and marketing of genetically modified foods are highly profitable enterprises. It also assumes that the FDA and other government regulatory agencies are completely neutral and have consumers' well-being foremost in mind. Thus while Turner sees the labeling of biotech ingredients as a needed warning to consumers, the Council sees its costs as a tax on food brought about by a small minority.

These arguments sketch out in bold strokes two alternative views of geneti-   6
cally engineered foods, demonstrating how different values cause persons to perceive different realities and construct different facts.

Works Cited

"Biotech Labeling." <u>Council for Biotechnology Information.</u> 2002: 2 pp. 11 July 2002 <http://whybiotech.com/index.asp?id+1812>. Rpt. in <u>Writing Arguments: A Rhetoric with Readings</u>. John D. Ramage, John C. Bean, and June Johnson. 3rd Concise ed. New York: Longman, 2004. 35–37.

Turner, Lisa. "Playing with Our Food." <u>Better Nutrition</u> June 2002: 56-59. Rpt. in <u>Writing Arguments: A Rhetoric with Readings</u>. John D. Ramage, John C. Bean, and June Johnson. 3rd Concise ed. New York: Longman, 2004. 21–24.

Strategy 5: Using Disagreement Productively to Prompt Further Investigation

Our fifth strategy—using disagreement productively to prompt further investigation—is both a powerful strategy for reading arguments and a bridge toward constructing your own arguments. Our goal is to suggest ways to help you proceed when the experts disagree.

Accepting Ambiguity and Uncertainty

When confronted with conflicting positions, you must learn to cope with ambiguity. If there were no disagreements, of course, there would be no need for argument. It is important to realize that experts can look at the same data, can analyze the same arguments, can listen to the same authorities, and still can reach different conclusions. Seldom will one expert's argument triumph over another's in a field of dissenting claims. Accepting ambiguity enables you to delve deeply into an issue and to resist easy answers.

As you sort through conflicting viewpoints, your goal is not to identify one of them as "correct" but to ask what is the best solution to the problem being debated here. You may eventually decide that one of the current viewpoints is indeed the best solution. Or you may develop a synthesis that combines strengths from several divergent viewpoints. In either case, you will emerge from the process with an enlarged, informed understanding. You will have developed the ability to remain intellectually flexible while listening to alternative viewpoints. Responding productively to disagreement thus becomes part of your preparation for writing ethically responsible arguments.

To illustrate the process of responding to disagreements, we now show you how we responded to the disagreement between Turner and the Council for Biotechnology Information over genetically engineered food.

Seeking Sources of Facts and More Complete Versions of Alternative Views

After analyzing the sources of disagreement between Turner and the Council for Biotechnology Information (see our sample essay on pp. 35–37), we pondered how we would continue our search for personal clarity on the issue. We decided to seek alternative views through vigorous library and online research. (see Appendix Two for instruction on research strategies), particularly exploring these questions:

- Are genetically engineered foods safe? What kinds of tests are currently used to verify short-term and long-term safety? How rigorous are they? How accurate are Turner's claims that these foods are potentially dangerous?
- What are the current regulations on the sale and labeling of genetically engineered crops and food? What legislation is being proposed?

- Among disinterested scientists who don't have contracts with the biotech industry, what is the view of the potential benefits and dangers of genetically modified foods? What is the view of the dangers and benefits to the environment?
- What is the feasibility and practicality of labeling foods with biotech ingredients?
- What are alternatives to using biotechnology?

When we began our research, we found major disagreement among scientists. For example, the Union of Concerned Scientists (http://www.ucsusa.org) gives a detailed list of the specific crops that have been modified, the corporations or companies that control the modification, and the traits that genetic engineers are trying to create. This organization raises questions about the safety of these food products, proposing a slower investigative process—basically calling for more science and less business in the whole biotech movement. On the other hand, the American Council on Science and Health (www.asch.org), consisting of physicians, scientists, and policy advisers, actively campaigns for further implementation of what it considers to be highly advantageous and beneficial scientific processes. We discovered that other scientific groups such as the American Medical Association (www.ama-assn.org) take a middle position, praising current advances in genetic engineering of foods but recommending closer monitoring of these crops and more scientifically sound criteria for testing them.

The range of views on testing and labeling of genetically modified foods revealed to us the complexity of this issue. The arguments we found most useful acknowledged the potential value of genetic engineering of foods while realistically confronting the risks and calling for more pre-market testing. We were also drawn to arguments that exposed the profit-making motives driving much of the experimentation with biotech foods. Finally, we welcomed discussions of the real challenges of accurately and helpfully labeling these food products.

Determining What Values Are at Stake for You and Articulating Your Own Values

In responding to disagreement, you need to articulate your own values and to try to justify them by explaining the reasons you hold them. The authors of this text, for instance, support the pursuit of scientific knowledge but often question the motives and actions of big business. We believe in the value of strong oversight of scientific experimentation—both from peer review by disinterested scientists and from government regulatory agencies that represent the common good. We like the idea of health food stores, of organic farming, of small family farms, and of less commercialism, but we also appreciate inexpensive food and the convenience of supermarkets. Additionally, we are drawn to technologies that might help feed the world's poor. Therefore, we are trying to stake out our own positions within the complex middle ground on genetic engineering.

Considering Ways to Synthesize Alternative Views

As a final step in your evaluation of conflicting sources, you should consider what you have gained from the different perspectives. How do alternative views modify each other or otherwise "speak to each other"? How might we synthesize the apparently polarized views on genetic engineering of food?

Environmentalists and organic food supporters like Lisa Turner teach us the need for long-range thinking. They prompt us to be more active in exploring alternative solutions to agricultural problems. They advise society to weigh human health and well-being against profits, and they exhort us to be responsible, pro-active citizens and knowledgeable, assertive consumers. At the same time, the Council for Biotechnology Information shows us that the "science as bad guy" view is much too simplistic and that science and technology may help us solve otherwise intractable problems. In trying to synthesize these divergent perspectives, we would look for ways to combine sensible caution and rigorous science.

When you try to synthesize points from conflicting views, as we begin to do here, you tap into the dialectical nature of argument, questioning and modifying ideas and your position in response to new perspectives. Your ultimate goal is to find a position that is reasonable and responsible in light of the available facts and your own values.

Conclusion

This chapter has explained why reading arguments is crucially important to writers of arguments and has offered five main strategies for deep reading: (1) Read as a believer. (2) Read as a doubter. (3) Explore how rhetorical context and genre shape an argument. (4) Seek alternative views and analyze sources of disagreement. (5) Use disagreement productively to prompt further investigation. This chapter has also shown you how to summarize an article and incorporate summaries into your own writing through the use of attributive tags. It has explained who writes arguments and how writer, purpose, audience, and the genre of the argument are closely connected and must be considered in any thoughtful response to an argument.

In the next chapter we turn from the reading of arguments to the writing of arguments, suggesting ways that you can generate ideas for arguments, structure your arguments, and improve your own writing processes.

3 Writing Arguments

As the opening chapters suggest, when you write an argument, you try to achieve two goals: (1) to see the issue complexly enough so that your stance reflects an ethical consideration of conflicting views and (2) to persuade your audience toward your stance on an issue. Because managing these tasks takes time, the quality of any argument depends on the quality of the thinking and writing processes that produced it. In this chapter, we suggest ways that you can improve these processes. We begin by looking at the social contexts that produce arguments, asking who writes arguments and why. We then present some writing tips based on the composing practices of experienced writers. Finally we describe nuts-and-bolts strategies for generating ideas and organizing an argument for an intended audience, concluding with two sets of exploratory exercises that can be adapted to any kind of argumentative task.

Who Writes Arguments and Why?

To help you see how writers operate in a social context—how they are spurred to write by a motivating occasion and by a desire to change the views of particular audiences—we begin by asking you to consider more fully who writes arguments.

In the classical period of ancient Greece and Rome, when the discipline of rhetoric was born, arguers usually made speeches before deliberative bodies. Arguers today, however, can present their views in a wide range of media and genres: speeches at public hearings, at committee meetings, or on talk radio; letters to legislators, bosses, or newspaper editors; professional proposals, marketing plans, or workplace memos; white papers advising lawmakers on issues; posters and pamphlets advocating a cause; e-mail letters or posts to chat rooms or personal Web sites; paid advertisements—even T-shirts and bumper stickers. Experienced writers and media specialists have even more options: freelance articles, books, syndicated columns, and TV documentaries. If we asked who in our culture actually writes arguments—let's say, for example, arguments on biotechnology and food—a partial list would include lobbyists and advocacy groups, legislators, people in businesses and corporations, lawyers and judges, media commentators, professional freelance or staff writers, scholars and academics, and average citizens.

As a student, you are already a member of two of these groups—"scholars and academics" and "average citizens." Moreover, as a professional-in-training, you have the opportunity to practice the kinds of arguments written by other groups on our list, whether advocacy arguments or inquiry-based research pieces. You might publish your writing as letters to the editor or as guest editorials, present your arguments at undergraduate research conferences, write persuasive letters to legislators, submit proposals to decision makers in the workplace, or post your arguments on Web sites.

What all these writers have in common is a deep engagement with their issues. They share a strong belief that an issue matters, that decisions have consequences, and that the stakes are often high. You can engage an issue either by having a position to advocate or by seeking to clarify your stand. What is important to note is how fluid a writer's position can be along this continuum ranging from "advocate" to "inquirer." An advocate, while writing an argument, might discover an issue's complexity and be drawn into inquiry. Likewise, an inquirer, in the course of studying an issue, might clarify her thinking, establish a strong claim, and become an advocate. It is also possible to write arguments from any position on the continuum: You can be a tentative advocate as well as an avidly committed one, or you can be a cautious skeptic. You can even remain an inquirer by arguing that no proposed solution to a problem is yet adequate.

So how do you become engaged? We suggest that you immerse yourself in the arguments of the communities to which you belong—your classroom community, your dorm or apartment community, your work community, your civic communities—and look for points of entry into these conversations: either places where you can take a stand or places where you are puzzled and uncertain. By opening yourself to the conversations of your culture, and by initiating these conversations when you encounter situations you would like to change, you will be ready to write arguments.

Tips for Improving Your Writing Process

Once you are motivated to write, you can improve your arguing ability if you know something about the writing processes of experienced writers. Too often inexperienced writers cut this process short, producing undeveloped arguments that don't speak effectively to the needs of the intended audience. Although no two writers follow the same process, we can describe the evolution of an argument in a loose way and offer tips for making your writing processes more effective. You should regard the writing process we are about to describe as recursive, meaning that writers often loop back to earlier phases by changing their minds on an issue, by throwing out a draft and starting over, or by going back to do more research late in the process.

Starting Point

Most writers of arguments start with a problem they want to solve or a claim they want to assert. At the outset, they may pose questions such as these: Who are the interested parties in this conversation? What are the causes of disagreement? What is the best way to solve the problem being debated? Who is the audience that must be persuaded? What is the best means of persuading that audience? Often a specific occasion spurs them to write. They feel hooked.

Tips for Starting the Process

- In many cases arguers are motivated to write because they find situations in their lives that they want to change. You can often focus an argument by asking yourself who has the power to make the changes you desire. How can you craft an argument that connects your desired changes to this audience's beliefs and values? What obstacles in your audience's environment might constrain that audience from action? How can these obstacles be overcome? This rhetorical focus—identifying the decision makers who have the power to change a situation and looking at the constraints that keep them from action—can give you a concrete sense of audience and clarify how your argument might proceed.

- In a college context you may sometimes have only a secondary occasion for writing—an assignment due date rather than an issue that hooks you. In such cases you can use the exploratory exercises described later in this chapter. These exercises help you inventory issues within the communities to which you belong, find points of engagement, and articulate the values and consequences that are at stake for you. Knowing why an issue matters to you can help you make it matter to others.

- Discuss issues with friends and classmates. Talking about ideas in small groups may help you discover claims that you want to make or issues that you find significant yet perplexing. By questioning claims and presenting multiple points of view, groups can help you understand points of disagreement on an issue.

Exploring, Researching, and Rehearsing

To discover, refine, and support their claims, writers typically research their issues carefully, trying to understand arguments on all sides, to resolve disagreements about facts or reality, to clarify their own values, and to identify the beliefs and values of their audience. While researching their issues, writers often discover that their own views evolve. During research, writers often do exploratory writing in online chat rooms, e-mail exchanges, or a writer's journal, sometimes drafting whole pieces of an argument.

Tips for Exploring, Researching, and Rehearsing

- When you research an issue, focus on your rhetorical context. You need to research the issue itself, but also the values and beliefs of your targeted audience, and the obstacles in your audience's social environment that might prevent audience members from acting on your claim or adopting your beliefs.

■ As you explore divergent views on your issue through library or Internet research or through interviews and field research, pay particular attention to why your views may be threatening to others. Later chapters in this text explain strategies for overcoming audience resistance.

■ Stay in conversation with others. Active discussion of your issue—especially with persons who don't agree with you—is a powerful way to explore an argument and find the best means of persuasion. As you talk through your argument, note where listeners look confused or skeptical and where they question your points. Skeptics may find holes in your reasoning, argue from different values, surprise you by conceding points you thought had to be developed at length, and challenge you by demanding more justification of your claim.

Writing a First Draft

At some point in the process, a writer's attention shifts temporarily away from gathering data and probing an issue to composing a first draft. The act of writing a draft forces deep and focused thinking, which may then send the writer back to do more research and exploration. Effective first drafts are likely to be jumbled, messy, and full of gaps. Ideas appear at the point the writer thought of them rather than where readers need them. The writer's tone and style may be inappropriate, needed evidence may be entirely missing, the audience's beliefs and values may not be adequately addressed, and the whole draft may be confusing to an outside reader. Moreover, writers may discover that their own views are still shifting and unstable. Nevertheless, such drafts are a crucial first step. They get your ideas onto paper and give you material to work with.

Tips for Writing a First Draft

■ Try lowering your expectations. If you get blocked, keep writing. Don't worry about grammar, correctness, or polish. Just get ideas on paper.

■ Rehearse your ideas orally. Working in pairs with another student, talk through your argument orally before you write it down. Make a scratch outline first to prompt you as you talk. Then let your partner question you to help you flesh out your argument with more details.

■ For a first draft, try following the template for a "classical argument" described on pages 55–57. This strategy will help you consider and respond to opposing views as well as clarify the reasons and evidence that support your own claim.

■ Do the exploration tasks entitled "Set 2: Exploration and Rehearsal" (pp. 59–60) prior to writing a first draft. These exercises will help you brainstorm most of the ideas you'll need for an initial draft.

Revising Through Multiple Drafts

After completing a first draft, you now have materials out on the table to work with. Most writers need multiple drafts to convert an early draft into a persuasive finished product. They also often need to return to the earlier stage of exploration and research now that writing a draft has revealed gaps in their arguments or provided a clearer understanding of their audience.

Tips for Revising

- Don't manicure your drafts; rebuild them. Cross out whole paragraphs and rewrite them from scratch. Move blocks of text to new locations. Make a mess. Inexperienced writers often think of revision as polishing and correcting rather than as making substantial changes (what writing teachers call "global revision"). Revising means to rethink your whole argument. Some writers even throw away the first draft and start fresh.

- Improve your mechanical procedures. We recommend that you revise off double-spaced hard copy rather than off the computer screen. Leave lots of space between lines and in margins on your drafts so that you have room to draw arrows and make pencil or pen deletions and inserts. When your draft becomes too messy, keyboard your changes back into the computer. If you manage all your drafts on computer, you may find that copying to a new file for each new draft gives you more freedom to experiment with changes (since you can always recover an earlier draft).

- As you revise, think of your audience. Many first drafts show why the writer believes his or her claim but not why the intended audience should believe it or act on it. How can you hook into your audience's beliefs and values using audience-based rather than writer-based reasons? Look also at the obstacles or constraints that keep your audience from adopting your beliefs or acting on your claim. How can you address those constraints in your revision?

- As you revise, also consider the image of yourself conveyed in your tone and style. Do you want to come across as angry? As sarcastic? As conciliatory and sympathetic? Also, to what extent do you want to appeal to audience members' emotions and imagination as well as to their logical intellects? These concerns are discussed in Chapter 7 under the headings *ethos* and *pathos*.

- Exchange drafts with classmates. Ask classmates where your argument is not persuasive, where your tone is offensive, where they have doubts, where your writing is unclear or undeveloped. Ask your classmates to role-play members of your intended audience. Explain the values and beliefs of this audience and the constraints members face. Let your classmates give you their reactions and advice. Classmates also can help you meet your readers' needs for effective organization, development, and style.

- Loop back to do more exploration and research. Revising your first draft may involve considerably more research and exploration.

Editing for Style, Impact, and Correctness

Writers now polish their drafts, rephrasing sentences, finding the precise word, and establishing links between sentences. At this point, you should turn to surface features such as spelling, punctuation, and grammar as well as to the appearance and form of the final manuscript.

Tips for Editing

- Read your draft out loud. Your ear can often pick up problems that your eye missed.
- Use your computer's spell check program. Remember, however, that spell checkers won't pick up mistakes with homonyms like *to/two/too, here/hear,* or *affect/effect.* Be skeptical of computerized grammar checkers, which cannot "read" with human intelligence but can only mechanically count, sort, and match. Your instructor can guide you on what grammar checkers can and cannot do.
- Use a good handbook for up-to-date advice on usage, punctuation, style, and manuscript form.
- Ask a classmate or friend to proofread your paper.
- Be prepared to loop back again to earlier stages. Sometimes thinking of a better way to word a sentence uncovers larger problems of clarity and meaning requiring you to rewrite a whole section of your argument.

Using Exploratory Writing to Discover Ideas and Deepen Thinking

What follows is a compendium of strategies to help you discover and explore ideas. None of these strategies works for every writer. But all of them are worth trying. Each requires practice, so don't give up on the strategy if it doesn't work at first. We recommend that you keep your exploratory writing in a journal or in easily identified files in your word processor so you can review it later and test the "staying power" of ideas produced by the different strategies.

Freewriting or Blind Writing

Freewriting is useful at any stage of the writing process. When you freewrite, you put pen to paper and write rapidly *nonstop,* usually ten to fifteen minutes at a stretch. The object is to think of as many ideas as possible without stopping to edit your work. On a computer, freewriters often turn off the monitor so that they can't see the text being produced. Such "blind writing" frees the writer from the urge to edit or correct the text and simply lets ideas roll forth. Some freewriters or blind writers achieve a stream-of-consciousness style, recording their ideas at the very moment they bubble into consciousness, stutters and stammers and all. Others produce more focused chunks, though without clear connections among them. You will probably find your initial reservoir of ideas running out in three to five minutes. If so, force yourself to keep writing or typing. If you can't think of anything to say, write "relax" or "I'm stuck" over and over until new ideas emerge.

Here is an example of a freewrite from a student named Jean, exploring her thoughts about hate speech following a class discussion of the "Machado Case" in which a Los Angeles man, Richard Machado, was convicted in 1998 for sending e-mail death threats to fifty-nine Asian students at the University of California, Irvine. He sent the e-mails from a campus computer and signed them "Asian hater."

> I was really disturbed in class today when we talked about the Machado case of the man who made e-mail death threats to Asians saying that he would hunt them down and kill them if they did not leave the campus—I think it was in California somewhere—anyway I just shivered and shuddered to think about this creepy guy. I haven't heard anything like this on our campus but after 9/11 a lot of discussions have gotten really heated with people saying hateful things about Arabs and also about Jews. The whole Israeli/Palestinian conflict divides people and creates stereotypes that get really close to hate speech. Do I think hate speech ought to be banned? I don't know it is such a hard question because I can see both sides of this issue. I don't think people should be allowed to use hateful words for races or sexes in class discussions but just banning the words doesn't mean that people still don't feel the same hate. I wish people could just be nicer to each other, but that's relax relax relax what do I think about hate speech? A lot of hate speech can lead to violence it has the effect of making people want to fight and shout rather than conduct real conversations. Hate speech is like the Jerry Springer show instead of an intelligent discussion. But does that mean it should be banned? I don't know. I hope we get to discuss this more in class.

For Class Discussion

Individual task: Choose one of the following controversial claims (or another chosen by your instructor) and freewrite your response to it for five or ten minutes. **Group task:** Working in pairs, in small groups, or as a whole class, share your freewrite with classmates. Don't feel embarrassed if your freewrite is fragmentary or disjointed. Freewrites are not supposed to be finished products; their sole purpose is to generate a flow of thought. The more you practice the technique, the better you will become.

1. A student should report a fellow student who is cheating on an exam or plagiarizing an essay.
2. States should legalize marriages between homosexuals.

3. Companies should not be allowed to enforce English-only policies in the workplace.
4. It is permissible to use racial profiling for airport screening.
5. Violent video games such as Soldier of Fortune should be made illegal.

Idea Mapping

Another good technique for exploring ideas is *idea mapping.* When you make an idea map, draw a circle in the center of the page and write some trigger idea (a broad topic, a question, or working thesis statement) in the center of the circle. Then record your ideas on branches and subbranches extending from the center circle. As long as you pursue one train of thought, keep recording your ideas on the branch. But when that line of thinking gives out, start a new branch. Often your thoughts jump back and forth between branches. That's a major advantage of "picturing" your thoughts; you can see them as part of an emerging design rather than as strings of unrelated ideas.

Idea maps usually generate more ideas, though less well-developed ones, than freewrites. Writers who practice both techniques report that each strategy causes them to think about their ideas very differently. When Jean, the student who produced the freewrite on hate speech, decided to explore this issue further, she created the idea map shown in Figure 3.1.

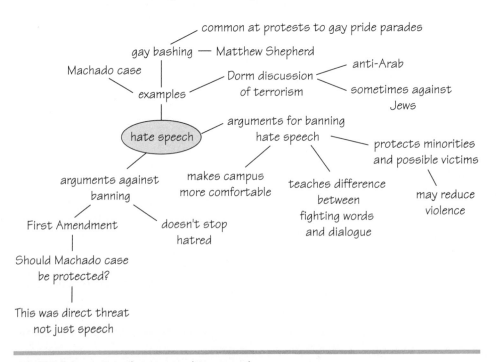

FIGURE 3.1   *Jean's idea map on hate speech*

For Class Discussion

Choose a controversial issue—national, local, or campus—that's interesting to the class. The instructor will lead a class discussion on the issue, recording ideas on an idea map as they emerge. Your goal is to appreciate the fluidity of idea maps as a visual form of idea generation halfway between an outline and a list.

Playing the Believing and Doubting Game

The believing/doubting game* is an excellent way to imagine views different from your own and to anticipate responses to those views. As a believer, your role is to be wholly sympathetic to an idea, to listen carefully to it, and to suspend all disbelief. You must identify all the ways in which the idea might appeal to different audiences and all the reasons for believing the idea. The believing game is easy so long as you already accept an idea. But when dealing with ideas that strike you as shaky, false, or threatening, you will find that the believing game can be difficult, even frightening.

The doubting game is the opposite of the believing game. As a doubter, your role is to be judgmental and critical, to find faults with an idea. You do your best to find counterexamples and inconsistencies that undermine the idea. It is easy to play the doubting game with ideas you reject. Doubting ideas you've invested in can be threatening.

When you play the believing and doubting game with an assertion, simply write two different chunks, one chunk arguing for the assertion (the believing game) and one chunk opposing it (the doubting game). Freewrite both chunks, letting your ideas flow without censoring. Or, alternatively, make an idea map with believing and doubting branches.

Here is how one student played the believing and doubting game as part of a class discussion about the following classified ad seeking young college women to be egg donors for an infertile couple:

> Infertile professional couple seeks egg-donor for artificial insemination. Donor should be slim, athletic, blue-eyed with 1400 SATs or better. $50,000 and all medical expenses. Must be discrete and willing to sign documents giving up all legal rights to a baby that might be produced.

The student responded to the assertion "Recent advances in reproductive technology, including the use of egg donors, are good for society."

BELIEVING EXAMPLE

The latest advances in reproductive technology are good for society. Up until now, infertile couples had only adoption to turn to if they wanted a child. Using egg donation enables the parents to feel like real parents because the mother does carry the child.

---

*A term coined by Peter Elbow, *Writing without Teachers* (New York: Oxford UP, 1973), 147–90.

The parents can be a bit more selective about the child they get because egg donors are carefully screened. I think egg donors are more stable and safe than women who carelessly or accidentally get pregnant and give up their babies for adoption. Egg donors can be smart, healthy young women, such as college students. These young women also get an opportunity to make some money. Another point is that women can preserve some of their own eggs from their youth and actually have a child much later in life when they are ready for such a commitment. I can see how egg donation can help infertile couples, young women, and older women.

DOUBTING EXAMPLE

While egg donation sounds promising, I think the supporters of it often leave out the dark side and the moral implications. The process is changing having babies from a natural experience to a completely commercial one. Eggs are bought and judged like any other product. The high prices reaching even tens of thousands of dollars mean that only rich couples will be able to afford the process. The fact that the preferred egg donors have common traits (are Ivy League students, are tall, blonde, and blue eyed) only serves to increase a certain elitism. The donor part has pitfalls too. I can understand the attraction of the large sums of money, but the medical process is not easy. The young women must take fertility drugs and injections to boost their egg production. These drugs may have side effects and long-term complications. I wouldn't want my girlfriend to undergo this process.

Although this writer condemns these medical advances in reproductive technology, he does a good job of trying to sympathize with women who are involved in them. Playing the believing and doubting game has helped him see the issue more complexly.

For Class Discussion

Return to the five controversial claims in the For Class Discussion exercise on pages 49–50. **Individual task:** Choose one of the claims and play the believing and doubting game with it by freewriting for five minutes trying to believe the claim and then for five minutes trying to doubt the claim. Or, if you prefer, make an idea map by creating a believing spoke and a doubting spoke off the main hub. Instead of freewriting, enter ideas onto your idea map, moving back and forth between believing and doubting. **Group task:** Share what you produced with members of your group or with the class as a whole.

Repeat the exercise with another claim.

Brainstorming for Pro and Con *Because* Clauses

This activity is similar to the believing and doubting game in that it asks you to brainstorm ideas for and against a controversial assertion. In the believing and doubting game, however, you simply freewrite or make an idea map on both sides of the issue. In this activity, you try to state your reasons for and against the proposition as *because* clauses. The value of doing so is discussed in depth in Chapter 4, which shows how a claim with *because* clauses can form the core of an argument.

Here is an example of how you might create *because* clauses for and against the claim "Recent advances in reproductive technology, including the use of egg donors, are good for society."

PRO

Recent advances in reproductive technology, including the use of egg donors, are good for society

- because children born using this technology are really wanted and will be given loving homes
- because this technology overcomes infertility, a medical disorder that can destroy marriages
- because curing this disorder will support marriages and create loving families
- because this technology restores to parents some measure of control over their reproductive capabilities

CON

Recent advances in reproductive technology, including the use of egg donors, are dangerous to society

- because this technology could lead to situations in which persons have no idea to whom they are genetically related
- because the technology might harm persons such as the egg donors who do not know what the long-term consequences of tampering with their reproductive systems through the use of fertility drugs might be
- because using donor eggs is equivalent to "special ordering" children who may not live up to the parents' expectations (to be smart, tall)
- because the expense of reproductive technology (especially when it results in multiple births) is too large for individuals, insurance companies, or the state to bear

For Class Discussion

Generating *because* clauses like these is an especially productive discussion activity for groups. Once again return to the five controversial claims in the For Class Discussion exercise on pages 49–50. Select one or more of these claims (or others provided by your instructor) and, working in small groups, generate pro and con *because* clauses supporting and attacking the claim. Share your group's *because* clauses with those of other groups.

Brainstorming a Network of Related Issues

The previous exercise helps you see how certain issues can provoke strong pro-con stances. Occasionally in civic life, an issue is presented to the public in just such a pro-con form, as when voters are asked to approve or disapprove a referendum or when a jury must decide the guilt or innocence of a defendant. But in most contexts, the argumentative situation is more open-ended and fluid.

You can easily oversimplify an issue by reducing it to two opposing sides. Most issues are embedded in a network of subissues, side issues, and larger issues, and seeing an issue in pro-con terms can often blind you to other ways to join a conversation. For example, a writer might propose the middle ground between adversarial positions, examine a subissue in more depth, connect an issue to a related side issue, or redefine an issue to place it in a new context.

Consider, for example, the assertion about reproductive technology. Rather than arguing for or against this claim, a writer might focus on reproductive technology in a variety of other ways:

- Who should determine the ethics of reproductive technology? Families? Doctors? Government?
- How can risky physical outcomes such as multiple births (mothers carrying seven and eight babies) be avoided?
- What effect will the new reproductive technologies have on concepts of motherhood and family?
- In case of divorce, who has legal rights to frozen embryos and other genetic material?
- Will reproductive technology lead to control over the sex and genetic makeup of children? Should it?
- What is the difference between paying someone to donate a kidney (which is illegal) and paying a woman to donate her eggs (which is currently legal)?
- Many adopted children want to seek out their birth mothers. Would children born from donated eggs want to seek out their genetic mothers?
- Who should pay for reproductive technology?

For Class Discussion

Working as a whole class or in small groups, choose one or more of the controversial assertions on pages 49–50. Instead of arguing for or against them, brainstorm a number of related issues (subissues, side issues, or larger issues) on the same general subject.

Shaping Your Argument: Using Classical Structure as an Initial Guide

We turn now from discovery strategies to organizing strategies. As you begin drafting, you need some sort of plan. How elaborate that plan is varies considerably from writer to writer. Some writers plan extensively before writing; others write extensively before planning. But somewhere along the way all writers must develop a structure.

In making an initial plan, writers often rely on knowledge of typical argument structures to guide their thinking. One of the oldest models is the *classical argument*—so called because it follows a pattern recommended by ancient rhetoricians. In traditional Latin terminology, classical argument has the following parts: the *exordium* (which gets the audience's attention); the *narratio* (which provides needed background); the *propositio* (which introduces the speaker's proposition or thesis); the *partitio* (which forecasts the main parts of the speech); the *confirmatio* (which presents arguments supporting the proposition); the *confutatio* (which refutes opposing views); and the *peroratio* (which sums up the argument, calls for action, and leaves a strong last impression). Classical arguments are often best suited for undecided or neutral audiences (See Chapter 8).

In slightly homelier terms (see Figure 3.2), writers of classical argument typically begin with a dramatic story or a startling statistic that commands attention. Then they focus the issue, often by stating it directly as a question and perhaps by briefly summarizing opposing views. Next, they contextualize the issue by providing needed background, explaining the immediate context, or defining key terms. They conclude the introduction by presenting the thesis and forecasting the argument's structure.

The body of a classical argument has two major sections—one presenting the writer's own position and the other summarizing and critiquing alternative views. Figure 3.2 shows that the writer's own position comes first. But writers can reverse that order. If you have a resistant audience initially hostile to your views, it is advantageous to summarize and respond to opposing views before you present your own argument. Doing so reassures skeptics that you have considered alternative positions, thus reducing their initial hostility to your own argument. In contrast, if you have an undecided audience, it is probably better to present your argument before you summarize and respond to alternative views. In Chapter 8, we explain these considerations in more detail and give you additional options for addressing resistant audiences.

Whether you place your own argument before or after your summary and critique of opposing views, this section is usually the longest part of a classical argument. Here writers present the reasons and evidence supporting their claims, typically choosing reasons that tie into their audience's values, beliefs, and assumptions (see Chapter 5, pp. 86–91). Usually each reason is developed in its own paragraph or sequence of paragraphs.

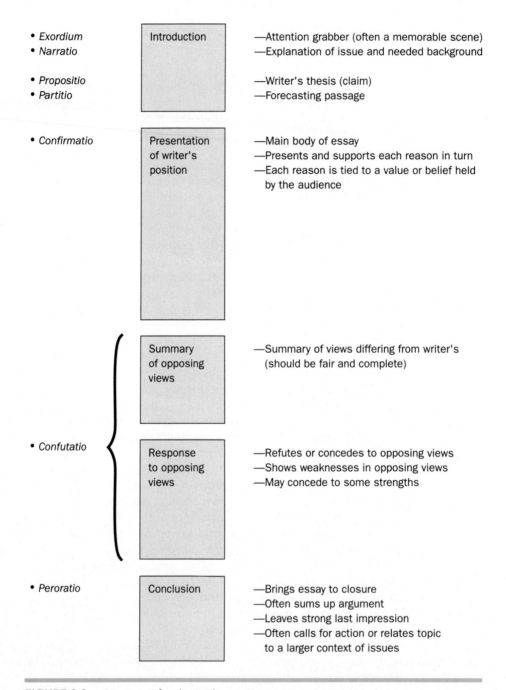

- *Exordium*
- *Narratio*

- *Propositio*
- *Partitio*

Introduction

—Attention grabber (often a memorable scene)
—Explanation of issue and needed background

—Writer's thesis (claim)
—Forecasting passage

- *Confirmatio*

Presentation of writer's position

—Main body of essay
—Presents and supports each reason in turn
—Each reason is tied to a value or belief held by the audience

- *Confutatio*

Summary of opposing views

—Summary of views differing from writer's (should be fair and complete)

Response to opposing views

—Refutes or concedes to opposing views
—Shows weaknesses in opposing views
—May concede to some strengths

- *Peroratio*

Conclusion

—Brings essay to closure
—Often sums up argument
—Leaves strong last impression
—Often calls for action or relates topic to a larger context of issues

FIGURE 3.2   *Diagram of a classical argument*

When summarizing and responding to opposing views, writers have several options. If there are several opposing arguments, writers may summarize all of them together and then compose a single response, or they may summarize and respond to each argument in turn.

Finally, in their conclusion, writers sum up their argument, often calling for some kind of action, thereby creating a sense of closure and leaving a strong final impression.

For all its strengths, the classical argument may not always be your best model. In some cases, for example, delaying your thesis or ignoring alternative views may be justified (see Chapter 8). Even in these cases, however, the classical argument is a useful planning tool. Its call for a thesis statement and a forecasting statement in the introduction helps you see the whole of your argument in miniature. And by requiring you to summarize and consider opposing views, classical argument alerts you to the limits of your position and to the need for further reasons and evidence. Moreover, the classical argument is a particularly persuasive mode of argument when you address a neutral or undecided audience.

Using Exploratory Writing to Discover Ideas and Deepen Thinking: Two Sets of Exploratory Tasks

The following tasks use exploratory writing to help you generate ideas. The first set of tasks helps you gather ideas early in a writing project either by helping you think of issues to write about or by deepening and complicating your response to readings. The second set of tasks helps you think about your ideas systematically before you compose a first draft.

Set 1: Starting Points

Task 1: Make an Inventory of the Communities to Which You Belong and the Issues that Arise in Those Communities   All of us belong to a variety of communities. For example, you have a classroom community for each course you are taking. Each club or organization has its own community, as does the community where you live (dorm, apartment, your family). Beyond these small communities, you have your campus community and beyond that your city, state, region, nation, and world communities. You may also belong to a work or job community, to a church/mosque/synagogue community, or to communities related to your hobbies or avocations.

The occasion for argument grows out of your life in these communities—your desire to make a difference on some issue that divides or troubles the community. As an arguer, you might tackle a big issue in your world community (What is the best way to prevent destruction of rain forests?) or a small issue in your dorm (Should quiet hours be enforced?). In your classroom community, you might tackle a practical problem (What should the instructor do about persons coming in late?) or intellectual issues in the discipline itself (Was Hamlet really mad? Is Freud's view of dreams defensible?).

For this task, make a list of the communities to which you belong. Then brainstorm controversies in these communities—issues that are being debated or that you would like to see debated. You might find one or more of the following "trigger questions" helpful:

- Persons in my dorm (at work, in the state legislature, at the United Nations) disagree about . . . .
- Our campus (this dorm, my hometown, our state, our country) would be a better place if . . . .
- Something that really makes me mad about this campus (my apartment life, city government, our society) is . . . .
- In the career I hope to pursue, X is a serious problem that needs to be addressed.
- Person X believes . . . ; however, I believe . . . .

Task 2: Make an Inventory of Issues That Interest You   The previous task can overwhelm students with the sheer number of issues that surround them. Once you broaden out to the large communities of city, state, nation, and world, the number of issues multiply rapidly. Moreover, each large issue has numerous subissues. For this task make an inventory of ten to fifteen possible issues that you would like to explore more deeply and possibly write about. Share your list with classmates, adding their ideas to yours.

Task 3: Choose Several Areas of Controversy for Exploration   For this task, choose two or three possible controversies from the Task 2 list and explore them through freewriting or idea mapping. Try responding to the following questions: (a) What is my position on this issue and why? (b) What are opposing or alternative positions on this issue? (c) Why do people disagree about this issue? (Do they disagree about the facts of the case? About underlying values, assumptions, and beliefs?) (d) To argue a position on this issue, what evidence do I need to find, and what further research will be required?

Task 4: Choose a Local Issue and Explore Its Rhetorical Context   For this task choose a local issue (some situation that you would like to see changed on your campus, in your place of work, or in your town or city) and explore its rhetorical context. (a) What is the situation you would like to change? (b) Who has the power to change that situation? (c) What are the values and beliefs of these decision makers? (d) What obstacles or constraints may prevent these decision makers from acting on your desires? (e) What reasons and evidence would exert the most pressure on these decision makers? (How can you make acting on your proposal a good thing for them?)

Task 5: Identify and Explore Issues That Are Problematic for You   A major assignment often given in argument courses is to write a research-based argument on an issue or problem initially puzzling to you. Perhaps you don't know enough about the issue (for example, establishing international controls on pesticides), or perhaps the issue draws you into an uncomfortable conflict of values (for example, assisted suicide, legalization of drugs, noncriminal incarceration of sexual predators). Your goal for this task is to identify several issues about which you are undecided, to choose one, and to explore your current uncertainty. Why can't you make up your mind on this issue?

Task 6: Deepen Your Response to Readings   This task requires you to read a collection of arguments on an issue and to explore them thoughtfully. As you read the arguments assigned by your instructor, annotate the margins with believing and doubting notes as explained in Chapter 2. Then respond to one or more of the following prompts, using freewriting or idea mapping:

- Why do the writers disagree? Are there disagreements about facts? About underlying values, beliefs, and assumptions?
- Identify "hot spots" in the readings—passages that evoke strong agreement or disagreement, anger, confusion, or any other memorable response—and explore your reaction to these passages.
- Explore the evolution of your thinking as you read and later review the essays. What new questions have they raised? How did your thinking change? Where do you stand now and why?
- If you were to meet one of the authors on a plane or at a ball game, what would you say to him or her?

Set 2: Exploration and Rehearsal

The following tasks are designed to help you once you have chosen a topic and begun to clarify your thesis. While these tasks may take two or more hours to complete, the effort pays off by helping you produce a full set of ideas for your rough draft. We recommend using these tasks each time you write a paper for this course.

Task 1   What issue do you plan to address in this argument? Try wording the issue as a one-sentence question. Reword your question in several different ways because each version will frame the issue somewhat differently. Then put a box around your best version of the question.

Task 2   Now write out your tentative answer to the question. This will be your beginning thesis statement or claim. Put a box around this answer. Next write out one or more different answers to your question. These will be alternative claims that a neutral audience might consider.

Task 3 Why is this a controversial issue? Is there insufficient evidence to resolve the issue, or is the evidence ambiguous or contradictory? Are definitions in dispute? Do the parties disagree about basic values, assumptions, or beliefs?

Task 4 What personal interest do you have in this issue? What are the consequences for you if your argument succeeds or doesn't succeed? How does the issue affect you? Why do you care about it? (Knowing why you care about it might help you get your audience to care about it.)

Task 5 Who is the audience that you need to persuade? If your argument calls for an action, who has the power to act on your claim? Can you address these persons of power directly? Or do you need to sway others (such as voters) to exert pressure on persons in power? With regard to your issue, what are the values and beliefs of the audience you are trying to sway?

Task 6 What obstacles or constraints in the social or physical environment prevent your audience from acting on your claim or accepting your beliefs? What are some ways these obstacles can be overcome? If these obstacles cannot be overcome, should you change your claim?

Task 7 In this task you will rehearse the main body of your paper. Using freewriting or idea mapping, think of the main reasons and evidence you could use to sway your intended audience. Brainstorm everything that comes to mind that might help you support your case. Because this section will eventually provide the bulk of your argument, proceed rapidly without worrying whether your argument makes sense. Just get ideas on paper. As you generate reasons and evidence, you are likely to discover gaps in your knowledge. Where could your argument be bolstered by additional data such as statistics, examples, and expert testimony? Where and how will you do the research to fill these gaps?

Task 8 Now reread what you wrote for Tasks 5 and 6, in which you examined your audience's perspective. Role playing that audience, imagine all the counterarguments audience members might make. Where does your claim threaten them or oppose their values? What are the obstacles or constraints in their environment that they are likely to point to. ("I'd love to act on your claim, but we just don't have the money" or "If we grant your request, it will set a bad precedent.") Brainstorm all the objections your audience might raise to your argument.

Task 9 How can you respond to those objections? Take them one by one and brainstorm possible responses.

Task 10 Explore again why this issue is important. What are its broader implications and consequences? What other issues does it relate to? Thinking of possible answers to these questions may prove useful when you write your introduction or conclusion.

WRITING ASSIGNMENTS
FOR CHAPTERS 1–3

Option 1: *An Argument Summary*   Write a 250-word summary of an argument selected by your instructor. Then write a one-sentence summary of the same argument. Use as models the summaries of Lisa Turner's argument on biotech foods in Chapter 2 (p. 26).

Option 2: *An Analysis of Sources of Disagreement in a Controversy*   Using as a model the analysis of the controversy between Turner and the Council for Biotechnology Information in Chapter 2 (pp. 38–40), write an analysis of the sources of disagreement in any two arguments that take differing views on the same issue.

Option 3: *Propose a Problem for a Major Course Project*   An excellent major project for an argument course is to research an issue about which you are initially undecided. Your final essay for the course could be an argument in which you take a stand on this issue. Choose one of the issues you listed in Task 5 on page 59 (issues that are problematic for you), and make this issue a major research project for the course. During the term keep a log of your research activities and be ready, in class discussion or in writing, to explain what kinds of arguments or evidence turned out to be most persuasive in helping you take a stand.

For this assignment, write a short letter to your instructor identifying the issue you have chosen and explain why you are interested in it and why you can't make up your mind at this time.

Principles of Argument

This poster voices a protest against the pollution and stress of our car-based lifestyle and proposes an alternative.

Source: Courtesy of Doug Minkler, San Francisco Bay area poster maker.

4 The Core of an Argument

A Claim with Reasons

The Rhetorical Triangle

Before we examine the structure of arguments, we should explain briefly their social context, which can be visualized as a triangle with interrelated points labeled *message, writer/speaker,* and *audience.* Effective arguments consider all three points on this *rhetorical triangle.* As we will see in later chapters, when you alter one point of the triangle (for example, when you change the audience for whom you are writing), you often need to alter the other points (by restructuring the message itself and perhaps by changing the tone or image you project as writer/speaker). We have created a series of questions based on the "rhetorical triangle" to help you plan, draft, and revise your argument (see Figure 4.1).

Each point on the triangle in turn corresponds to one of the three kinds of persuasive appeals that ancient rhetoricians named *logos, ethos,* and *pathos.*

Logos (Greek for "word") refers primarily to the internal consistency and clarity of the message and to the logic of its reasons and support. The impact of *logos* on an audience is referred to as its *logical appeal.*

Ethos (Greek for "character") refers to the credibility of the writer/speaker. *Ethos* is often conveyed through the tone and style of the message, through the care with which the writer considers alternative views, and through the writer's investment in his or her claim. In some cases, it's also a function of the writer's reputation for honesty and expertise independent of the message. The impact of *ethos* on an audience is referred to as its *ethical appeal* or *appeal from credibility.*

Our third term, *pathos* (Greek for "suffering" or "experience") is often associated with emotional appeal. But *pathos* appeals more specifically to our audience's imaginative sympathies—their capacity to feel and see what the writer feels and sees. Thus, when we turn the abstractions of logical discourse into a palpable and immediate story, we are making a pathetic appeal. Appeals to *logos* and *ethos* can further intellectual assent to our claim, but appeals to *pathos* engage imagination and feelings, moving the audience to deeper appreciation of the argument's significance.

Message
(LOGOS: *How can I make the argument
internally consistent and logical?
How can I find the best reasons and
support them with the best evidence?*)

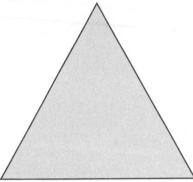

Audience
(PATHOS: *How can I make the reader
open to my message? How can I best
appeal to my reader's values and
interests? How can I engage my
reader emotionally and imaginatively?*)

Writer or Speaker
(ETHOS: *How can I present myself
effectively? How can I enhance my
credibility and trustworthiness?*)

FIGURE 4.1   *The rhetorical triangle*

In Part Two, we treat all three elements of the rhetorical triangle in detail. Although all three terms overlap, Chapters 4, 5, and 6 focus primarily on *logos*, and Chapters 7 and 8 focus primarily on *ethos* and *pathos*.

Given this background on the rhetorical triangle, let's turn now to *logos*—the logic and structure of arguments.

Issue Questions as the Origins of Argument

At the heart of any argument is a controversial question, or issue question, that gives rise to alternative answers. Any topic area, such as "the labeling of genetically engineered foods" or "racial profiling," has embedded within it a number of issue questions. Thus the topic area "abortion" gives rise to issue questions such as "Should abortion be legal?", "Should the federal government underwrite the cost of abortion?", and "When does a fetus become a human being?" Each of these issue questions opens up one strand of the complex debate on abortion.

Difference between an Issue Question and an Information Question

Of course, not all questions are issue questions. Some may simply call for more information, not argument. Keeping this distinction in mind, consider the following two questions:

> How does the teenage pregnancy rate in the United States compare with the rate in Sweden? If the rates are different, why?

Although both questions seem to call for information rather than for argument, we believe that the second one would be an issue question if reasonable people disagreed on the answer. Thus, different writers might agree that the teenage pregnancy rate in the United States is four times higher than the rate in Sweden. But they might disagree about why. One writer might emphasize Sweden's practical, secularized sex education courses in the schools, leading to more consistent use of contraceptives among Swedish teenagers. Another writer might point to the higher use of oral contraceptives among teenage girls in Sweden (partly a result of Sweden's generous national health program) and to less reliance on condoms for preventing pregnancy. Another might argue that moral decay in the United States is at fault. Still another might argue that the American welfare system helps promote teenage pregnancy (a popular conservative argument in the late 1990s). Thus, underneath the surface of what looks like a simple explication of the "truth" is really a controversy.

To determine if a given question is an issue question or an information question, examine the role it calls you to play in relation to your audience. If the question asks you to be a teacher providing new information or knowledge, then it is probably an information question. But if the question asks you to be an advocate, persuading your audience toward your point of view in a controversy, then it is probably an issue question. Sometimes context will determine if a given question is an issue question or an information question. Consider the following examples:

- How does a diesel engine work? (Almost surely an information question, posed by an audience of learners who regard you as a teacher.)
- What is the most cost-effective way to produce diesel fuel from crude oil? (This would be an information question if experts agreed on the answer and you were teaching this knowledge to new learners. But if experts disagreed—imagine a roomful of petroleum engineers seeking ways to reduce the production costs of diesel fuel—it would be an issue question.)
- Should the tax on diesel fuel be reduced? (A slam-dunk issue question sure to provoke controversy in almost any context.)

For Class Discussion

Working as a class or in small groups, decide whether the following questions are information questions or issue questions. Some questions could be either, depending on the context. For such questions, create a hypothetical context that justifies your choice.

1. What is the percentage of U.S. public schools that are failing?
2. What causes U.S. public schools to fail?
3. Are chiropractors legitimate health professionals?
4. How does chiropractic treatment of illness differ from a medical doctor's treatment?
5. What is the effect of violent TV shows on children?

Difference Between a Genuine Argument and a Pseudo-Argument

While every argument features an issue question with alternative answers, not every dispute over answers is a rational argument. Rational arguments require two additional factors: (1) reasonable participants who operate within the conventions of reasonable behavior and (2) potentially shareable assumptions that can serve as a starting place or foundation for the argument. Lacking one or both of these conditions, disagreements remain stalled at the level of pseudo-arguments.

Pseudo-Arguments: Fanatical Believers and Fanatical Skeptics

A reasonable argument assumes the possibility of growth and change; disputants may modify their views as they acknowledge strengths in an alternative view or weaknesses in their own. Such growth becomes impossible—and argument degenerates to pseudo-argument—when disputants are fanatically committed to their positions. Consider the case of the fanatical believer or the fanatical skeptic.

Fanatical believers believe their claims are true because they say so, period. They may cite some authoritative text—the Bible, the *Communist Manifesto*, or *The Road Less Traveled*—but in the end it's their narrow and quirky reading of the text or their faith in the author (which others might not share) that underlies their argument. Disagreeing with a fanatical believer is like ordering the surf to quiet down. The only response is another crashing wave.

The fanatical skeptic, in contrast, dismisses the possibility of proving anything. So what if the sun has risen every day of recorded history? That's no proof that it will rise tomorrow. Short of absolute proof, which never exists, fanatical skeptics accept nothing. In a world where the most we can hope for is increased audience adherence to our ideas, the fanatical skeptic demands an ironclad logical demonstration of our claim's rightness. In the presence of fanatical believers or skeptics, then, genuine argument is impossible.

Another Source of Pseudo-Arguments: Lack of Shared Assumptions

A reasonable argument is difficult to conduct unless the participants share common assumptions on which the argument can be grounded. Like axioms in geometry, these shared assumptions serve as the starting point for the argument. Consider the following conversation, in which Randall refuses to accept Rhonda's assumptions.

RHONDA: Smoking should be banned because it causes cancer.

RANDALL: So it causes cancer. What's so bad about that?

RHONDA: Don't be perverse, Randy. Cancer causes suffering and death.

RANDALL: Rhonda, my dear girl, don't be such a twinkie. Suffering and death are just part of the human condition.

RHONDA: But that doesn't make them desirable, especially when they can be avoided.

RANDALL: Perhaps in particular cases they're avoidable for a while, but in the long run, we all suffer and we all die, so who cares if smoking causes what's inevitable anyway?

This, we would suggest, is a doomed argument. Without any shared assumptions (for example, that cancer is bad, that suffering should be minimized and death delayed), there's no "bottom" to this argument, just an endless regress of reasons based on more reasons. While calling assumptions into question is a legitimate way to deepen and complicate our understanding of an issue, the unwillingness to accept any assumption makes argument impossible.

While our smoking example may be a bit heavy-handed, less obvious variants of this debate happen all the time. Whenever we argue about purely personal opinions—opera is boring, soccer is better than baseball, pizza is tastier than nachos—we're condemned to a bottomless dispute. Because there are no common criteria for "boring" or "better" or "tastier," we can't put our claims to any common test. We can only reassert them.

Of course, reasonable arguments about these disputes become possible once common assumptions are established. For example, a nutritionist could argue that pizza is better than nachos because it provides a better balance of nutrients per calorie. Such an argument can succeed if the disputants accept the nutritionist's assumption that "a better balance of nutrients per calorie" is a criterion for "better." But if one of the disputants responds, "Nah, nachos are better than pizza because nachos taste better," then he makes a different assumption—"My sense of taste is better than your sense of taste." This is a wholly personal standard, an assumption that others are unable to share.

For Class Discussion

The following questions can all be answered in alternative ways. However, not all of them will lead to reasonable arguments. Try to decide which questions will lead to reasonable arguments and which will lead only to pseudo-arguments.

1. Is Spike Lee a good film director?
2. Is postmodern architecture beautiful?
3. Should cities subsidize professional sports venues?
4. Is this abstract oil painting by a monkey smearing paint on a canvas a true work of art?
5. Are nose rings and tongue studs attractive?

Frame of an Argument: A Claim Supported by Reasons

In writing an argument, you take a position on an issue and support it with reasons and evidence. You state your position in the form of a claim, which functions as the thesis statement of your argument. A claim should provide a one-sentence answer to the issue question. Your task, then, is to make a claim and support it with reasons and evidence, which together comprise your argument's framework.

What Is a Reason?

A reason is a claim used to support another claim. Reasons are usually linked to their claims with words like *because, thus, since, consequently,* and *therefore* to underscore their logical connection.

Let's take an example. In one of our classes, a female naval ROTC student ignited a heated discussion by suggesting that women should not be allowed to serve on submarines. The ensuing discussion expanded into a more general debate about women's fitness to serve in combat units. Here are frameworks the class developed for two alternative positions on this issue.

One View

CLAIM: Women should be barred from military combat units.

REASON 1:   Most women lack the strength and endurance needed for combat.

REASON 2:   Serving in combat isn't necessary for female soldiers' career advancement.

REASON 3:   Female soldiers would hurt morale by introducing sexual jealousy into combat units.

REASON 4:   Pregnancy or need to care for infants would render women unreliable soldiers.

REASON 5:   Women haven't been socialized into warrior roles and thus would be more reluctant than males to kill the enemy.

Alternative View

CLAIM: Women should be allowed to serve as combat soldiers.

REASON 1:   Millions of women do have the strength and endurance to serve in combat roles.

REASON 2:   Female combat soldiers would offer a positive role model to young women and help society overcome harmful gender stereotyping.

REASON 3:   Serving in combat would open up new career advancement opportunities for female soldiers.

REASON 4:   Simple justice demands that women be allowed to serve in combat units.

Formulating a list of reasons in this way breaks your persuasive task into a series of more manageable subtasks. Thus, in the first view given, five possible lines of support are laid out. A writer might use all five or select only two or three, depending on which would most persuade the intended audience. Each line of reasoning would compose a distinct section of the argument.

For example, one section of an argument opposing women in combat might open with the following sentence: "Women should be excluded from combat units because they lack strength or endurance necessary for combat roles." The writer thereby assumes the burden of showing that women can't meet the prescribed physical requirements for combat duty. Further, the writer may also need to support the unstated assumption underlying this reason—namely, that meeting these physical requirements is a necessary condition for combat effectiveness.

The writer could develop each section of the argument in the same way. After a clear statement of the reason to be developed, the writer would offer evidence or chains of reasons in support. Depending on the intended audience, the writer might also articulate and support assumptions underlying the reason.

We can summarize the gist of this section as follows: The frame of an argument consists of a claim (the thesis statement of the essay), which is supported by one or more reasons, which are in turn supported by evidence or sequences of further reasons.

Advantages of Expressing Reasons in *Because* Clauses

Chances are that when you were a child the word *because* contained magical explanatory powers:

DOROTHY: I want to go home now.

TOMMY: Why?

DOROTHY: Because.

TOMMY: Because why?

DOROTHY: Just because.

Somehow *because* seemed decisive. It persuaded people to accept your view of the world; it changed people's minds. Later, you discovered that *because* only introduced your arguments and that it was the reasons following *because* that made the difference. But for most of us the word retains some residual magic and is persuasive in and of itself.

Of course, there are many other ways to express the logical connection between a reason and a claim. Our language is rich in ways of stating *because* relationships:

- Women shouldn't be allowed to join combat units because they don't have the strength or endurance for combat roles.
- Women don't have the strength or endurance for combat roles. Therefore women should not be allowed to join combat units.
- Women don't have the strength or endurance for combat roles, so they should not be allowed to join combat units.
- One reason why women should not be allowed to join combat units is that they don't have the strength or endurance for combat roles.

But even though logical relationships can be stated in various ways, writing out one or more *because* clauses remains the most succinct way to clarify an argument for oneself. We therefore suggest that sometime in the writing process you create a *working thesis statement* that summarizes your main reasons as *because* clauses attached to your claim.* Some writers compose their working thesis statement

---

*A working thesis statement for an argument opposing women in combat units might look like this: *Women should not be allowed to join combat units because they lack the strength, endurance, and "fighting spirit" needed in combat; because being pregnant or having small children would make them unreliable for combat at a moment's notice; and because women's presence would hurt morale of tight-knit combat units.* (A working thesis statement for an argument supporting women in combat is found on p. 74.)

You might choose not to put a bulky thesis statement like this into your essay itself. A working thesis statement offers a behind-the-scenes way of summarizing your argument for yourself, so that you can see it whole and clear.

before they write their rough draft. Others discover their thesis as they write. Still others compose their working thesis statement in mid-draft in order to rein in an argument headed off in too many directions. Some wait until the very end, using their thesis statement to check the unity of the final product.

No matter when you write your working thesis statement, you will find doing so both thought provoking and frustrating. On the plus side, composing *because* clauses can be a powerful discovery tool, causing you to think of many different kinds of arguments to support your claim. But often it is difficult to wrestle your ideas into because clauses, which sometimes seem to be overly tidy for the complex network of ideas you are trying to work with. In the end, though, constructing a scale-model version of your argument in your working thesis statement is immensely helpful and worth the effort.

For Class Discussion

Try the following group exercise to help you see how writing *because* clauses can be a discovery procedure.

Divide into small groups. Each group member should contribute an issue that he or she might like to explore. Discussing one person's issue at a time, help each member develop a claim supported by several reasons. Express each reason as a *because* clause. Then write out the working thesis statement for each person's argument by attaching the *because* clauses to the claim. Finally, try to create *because* clauses in support of an alternative claim for each issue. Recorders should select two or three working thesis statements from the group to present to the class as a whole.

Applying This Chapter's Principles to Your Own Writing

In Chapter 2, we discussed the difficulties of summarizing various types of arguments. Generally, an argument is easiest to summarize when the writer places the thesis in the introduction and uses explicit transitions to highlight the argument's reasons and structural frame. Such arguments are said to have a *self-announcing structure* because they announce their thesis (and sometimes supporting reasons) and forecast their shape at the outset. Self-announcing arguments typically follow the conventional format of classical argument discussed in Chapter 3. The invention strategies set forth in this chapter—generating parallel *because* clauses and nutshelling them in a working thesis statement—lead naturally to a classical argument with a self-announcing structure. Each *because* clause, together with its supporting evidence, becomes a separate section of the argument.

An argument with an *unfolding structure,* in contrast, is considerably harder to summarize. In an unfolding structure, the thesis is delayed until the end or is unstated and left to be inferred by the reader from a narrative that may be both complex and subtle. As we explain in Chapter 8, unfolding structures can be especially effective when dealing with hostile audiences or with troubling or tangled issues. In contrast, classical arguments are often more effective for neutral or un-decided audiences weighing alternative views on a clear-cut issue.[*]

In our own classes, we ask students initially to write arguments with self-announcing structures, thereby forcing them to articulate their arguments clearly to themselves and helping them to master the art of organizing complex ideas. Later in the course, we invite them to experiment with structures that unfold their meanings in subtler, more flexible ways.

In writing classical arguments, students often ask how much of the argument to summarize in the introduction. Consider the following options. You might an-nounce only your claim:

> Women should be allowed to join combat units.

Or you could also predict a series of parallel reasons:

> Women should be allowed to join combat units for several reasons.

Or you could forecast the actual number of reasons:

> Women should be allowed to join combat units for four reasons.

Or you could forecast the whole argument:

> Women should be allowed to join combat units because they are physically capable of doing the job; because the presence of women in combat units would weaken gender stereotypes; because opening combat units to women would expand their military ca-reer opportunities; and because doing so would advance the cause of civil rights.

These are not, of course, your only options. If you choose to delay your thesis until the end (a typical kind of unfolding argument), you might place the issue question in the introduction without giving away your own position:

> Is the nation well served by allowing women to join combat units?

No formula can tell you how much of your argument to forecast in the intro-duction. In Chapters 7 and 8 we discuss how forecasting or withholding your thesis affects your *ethos*. We also show how a delayed-thesis argument may be a better option for hostile audiences. It is clear at this point, though, that the more

---

[*]Instead of the terms self-announcing and unfolding, rhetoricians sometimes use *closed form* and *open form*. A *closed-form structure* tells the reader in advance where the argument is headed. Choosing a closed form, which forecasts the structure in the introduction, obligates the writer to follow through with that structure in a straightforward, undeviating way. In contrast, an *open-form structure* is like a story or nar-rative, keeping the reader in suspense about the argument's final destination.

you forecast, the clearer your argument is to your reader, whereas the less you forecast, the more surprising your argument will be. The only general rule is this: Readers sometimes feel insulted by too much forecasting. In writing a self-announcing argument, forecast only what is needed for clarity. In short arguments readers often need only your claim. In longer arguments or in especially complex ones, readers appreciate your forecasting the complete structure of the argument (claim with reasons).

Applying This Chapter's Principles to Reading Arguments

When you read a complex argument that lacks explicit forecasting, it is often hard to discern its structural core, to identify its claim, and to sort out its reasons and evidence. The more "unfolding" its structure, the harder it is to see exactly how the writer makes his or her case. Moreover, extended arguments often contain digressions and subarguments. Thus there may be dozens of small interlinked arguments going on inside a slowly unfolding main argument.

When you feel yourself getting lost in an unfolding structure, try converting it to a self-announcing structure. (It might help to imagine that the argument's author must state the argument as a claim with *because* clauses. What working thesis statement might the writer construct?) Begin by identifying the writer's claim. Then ask yourself: What are the one, two, three, or four main lines of argument this writer puts forward to support that claim? State those arguments as *because* clauses attached to the claim. Then compare your *because* clauses with your classmates'. You can expect disagreement—indeed, that disagreement can enrich your understanding of a text—because the writer has left it to you to infer her intent. You should, however, find considerable overlap in your responses. Once you have converted the support for the claim to *because* clauses and reached consensus on them, you will find it much easier to analyze the writer's reasoning, underlying assumptions, and use of evidence.

Conclusion

This chapter has introduced you to the rhetorical triangle and its key concepts: *logos, ethos,* and *pathos.* It has also shown how arguments originate in issue questions, how issue questions differ from information questions, and how arguments differ from pseudo-arguments. At the heart of this chapter we explained that the frame of an argument is a claim supported by reasons. As you generate reasons to support your own arguments, it is often helpful to articulate them as *because* clauses attached to the claim. Finally, we explained how you can apply the principles of this chapter to your own writing and reading of arguments.

In the next chapter we will see how to support a reason by examining its logical structure, uncovering its unstated assumptions, and planning a strategy of development.

5 The Logical Structure of Arguments

In Chapter 4 you learned that the core of an argument is a claim supported by reasons and that these reasons can often be stated as *because* clauses attached to a claim. In the present chapter we examine the logical structure of arguments in more depth.

An Overview of *Logos:* What Do We Mean by the "Logical Structure" of an Argument?

As you will recall from our discussion of the rhetorical triangle, *logos* refers to the strength of an argument's support and its internal consistency. *Logos* is the argument's logical structure. But what do we mean by "logical structure"?

First of all, what we *don't* mean by logical structure is the kind of precise certainty you get in a philosophy class in formal logic. Logic classes deal with symbolic assertions that are universal and unchanging, such as "If all ps are qs and if r is a p, then r is a q." This statement is logically certain so long as p, q, and r are pure abstractions. But in the real world, p, q, and r turn into actual things, and the relationships among them suddenly become fuzzy.

For example, p might be a class of actions called "sexual harassment," and q could be the class "actions that justify dismissal from a job." If r is the class "telling off-color stories," then the logic of our p–q–r statement suggests that telling off-color stories (r) is an instance of sexual harassment (p), which in turn is an action justifying dismissal from one's job (q). Now, most of us would agree that sexual harassment is a serious offense that might well justify dismissal from a job. In turn, we might agree that telling off-color stories, if the jokes are sufficiently raunchy and are inflicted on an unwilling audience, constitutes sexual harassment. But few of us would want to say categorically that all people who tell off-color stories are harassing their listeners and ought to be fired. Most of us would want to know the particulars of the case before making a final judgment.

A key difference, then, between formal logic and real-world argument is that real-world arguments are not grounded in abstract, universal statements. Rather, as we shall see, they must be grounded in beliefs, assumptions, or values granted by the audience. A second important difference is that in real-world arguments these beliefs, assumptions, or values are often unstated. So long as writer and audience share the same assumptions, then it's fine to leave them unstated. But if these underlying assumptions aren't shared, the writer has a problem. To illustrate the nature of this problem, consider one of the arguments we introduced in the last chapter.

> Women should be allowed to join combat units because the image of women in combat would help eliminate gender stereotypes.

On the face of it, this is a plausible argument. But the argument is persuasive only if the audience agrees with the writer's assumption that it is a good thing to eliminate gender stereotyping.

The writer assumes that gender stereotyping (for example, seeing men as the fighters who are protecting the women and children back home) is harmful and that society would be better off without such fixed gender roles. But what if you believed that some gender roles are biologically based, divinely intended, or otherwise culturally essential and that society should strive to maintain these gender roles rather than dismiss them as "stereotypes"? If such were the case, you might believe as a consequence that our culture should socialize women to be nurturers, not fighters, and that some essential trait of "womanhood" would be at risk if women served in combat. If these were your beliefs, the argument wouldn't work for you because you would reject its underlying assumption. To persuade you with this line of reasoning, the writer would have to show not only how women in combat would help eliminate gender stereotypes but also why these stereotypes are harmful and why society would be better off without them.

The previous core argument ("Women should be allowed to join combat units because the image of women in combat would help eliminate gender stereotypes") is an incomplete logical structure called an *enthymeme*. Its persuasiveness depends on an unstated assumption or belief that the audience must accept. To complete the enthymeme and make it effective, the audience must willingly supply a missing premise—in this case, that gender stereotypes are harmful and should be eliminated. The Greek philosopher Aristotle showed how successful enthymemes, which he considered the main underlying structure of argument, root the speaker's argument in assumptions, beliefs, or values held by the audience. If the audience is unwilling to supply the missing premise, then the argument fails. Our point is that successful arguments depend both on what the arguer says and on what the audience already has in mind.

To clarify the concept of the enthymeme, let's go over this same territory again more slowly, examining what we mean by "incomplete logical structure." The original claim with *because* clause is an enthymeme. It combines a claim ("Women should be allowed to join combat units") with a reason expressed as a *because* clause ("because the image of women in combat would help eliminate gender stereotypes"). To render this enthymeme logically complete, you must supply an unstated assumption—that gender stereotypes are harmful and should be eliminated. If your audience accepts this assumption, then you have a starting place on which to build an effective argument. If your audience doesn't accept this assumption, then you must supply another argument to support it, and so on until you find common ground with your audience. To sum up:

1. Claims are supported with reasons. You can usually state a reason as a *because* clause attached to a claim (see Chapter 4).

2. A *because* clause attached to a claim is an incomplete logical structure called an enthymeme. To create a complete logical structure from an enthymeme, the unstated assumption (or assumptions) must be articulated.

3. To serve as an effective starting point for the argument, this unstated assumption should be a belief, value, or principle that the audience grants.

Let's illustrate this structure by putting the previous example—plus a new one—into schematic form.

INITIAL ENTHYMEME: Women should be allowed to join combat units because the image of women in combat would help eliminate gender stereotypes.*

CLAIM: Women should be allowed to join combat units.

STATED REASON: because the image of women in combat would help eliminate gender stereotypes

UNSTATED ASSUMPTION: Gender stereotypes are harmful and should be eliminated.

INITIAL ENTHYMEME: Cocaine and heroin should be legalized because legalization would eliminate the black market in drugs.

CLAIM: Cocaine and heroin should be legalized.

STATED REASON: because legalization would eliminate the black market in drugs

UNSTATED ASSUMPTION: An action that eliminates the black market in drugs is good.

---

*Most arguments have more than one *because* clause or reason in support of the claim. Each enthymeme thus develops only one line of reasoning, one piece of your whole argument.

For Class Discussion

Working individually or in small groups, identify the claim, stated reason, and unstated assumption that complete each of the following enthymemic arguments.

EXAMPLE:

Rabbits make good pets because they are gentle.

CLAIM: Rabbits make good pets.

STATED REASON: Because they are gentle

UNSTATED ASSUMPTION: Gentle animals make good pets.

1. We should not choose Joe as committee chairperson because he is too bossy.
2. Buy this stereo system because it has a powerful amplifier.
3. Drugs should not be legalized because legalization would greatly increase the number of drug addicts.
4. Practicing the piano is good for kids because it teaches discipline.
5. Airport screeners should use racial profiling because doing so will increase the odds of stopping terrorists.
6. Racial profiling should not be used by airport screeners because it violates a person's civil rights.
7. We should strengthen the Endangered Species Act because doing so will preserve genetic diversity on the planet.
8. The Endangered Species Act is too stringent because it severely damages the economy.
9. The doctor should not perform an abortion in this case because the mother's life is not in danger.
10. Abortion should be legal because a woman has the right to control her own body. (This enthymeme has several unstated assumptions behind it. See if you can re-create all the missing premises.)

Adopting a Language for Describing Arguments: The Toulmin System

Understanding a new field usually requires us to learn a new vocabulary. For example, if you were taking biology for the first time, you'd spend days memorizing dozens of new terms. Luckily, the field of argument requires us to learn a mere handful of new terms. A particularly useful set of argument terms, one we'll be using throughout the rest of this text, comes from philosopher Stephen Toulmin. In the 1950s, Toulmin rejected the prevailing models of argument based on formal logic in favor of a very audience-based courtroom model.

Toulmin's courtroom model differs from formal logic in assuming that (1) all assertions and assumptions are contestable by "opposing counsel" and (2) all final "verdicts" about the persuasiveness of alternative arguments will be rendered by a neutral third party, a judge or jury. Keeping in mind the "opposing counsel" forces us to anticipate counterarguments and to question our assumptions. Keeping in mind the judge and jury reminds us to answer opposing arguments fully, without rancor, and to present positive reasons for supporting our case as well as negative reasons for disbelieving the alternative views. Above all else, Toulmin's model reminds us not to construct an argument that appeals only to those who already agree with us, and it helps arguers tailor arguments to their audiences.

The system we use for analyzing arguments combines Toulmin's system with Aristotle's concept of the enthymeme. It builds on the system you have already been practicing. We simply need to add a few more key terms from Toulmin. The first term is Toulmin's *warrant*, the name we will now use for the unstated assumption that turns an enthymeme into a complete logical structure. For example:

INITIAL ENTHYMEME: Women should be allowed to join combat units because the image of women in combat would help eliminate gender stereotypes.

CLAIM: Women should be allowed to join combat units.

STATED REASON: because the image of women in combat would help eliminate gender stereotypes

WARRANT: Gender stereotypes are harmful and should be eliminated.

INITIAL ENTHYMEME: Cocaine and heroin should be legalized because legalization would eliminate the black market in drugs.

CLAIM: Cocaine and heroin should be legalized.

STATED REASON: because legalization would eliminate the black market in drugs

WARRANT: An action that eliminates the black market in drugs is good.

Toulmin derives his term *warrant* from the concept of a warranty or guarantee. The warrant is the value, belief, or principle that the audience has to hold if the soundness of the argument is to be guaranteed or warranted. We sometimes make similar use of this word in ordinary language when we say "That is an unwarranted conclusion."

But arguments need more than claims, reasons, and warrants. These are simply one-sentence statements—the frame of an argument, not a developed argument. To flesh out our arguments and make them convincing, we need what Toulmin calls *grounds* and *backing*. Grounds are the evidence you use to support your *because* clause (your stated reason). Toulmin suggests that grounds are "what you have to go on" in an argument—the facts, data, statistics, testimony, or examples you use to support your reason. It sometimes helps to think of grounds as the answer to a "How do you know that . . . ?" question prefixed to your stated reason. (How do you know that letting women into combat units would help eliminate gender stereotypes? How do you know that legalizing drugs will end the black market?) Here is how grounds fit into our emerging argument schema:

CLAIM: Women should be allowed to join combat units.

STATED REASON: because the image of women in combat would help eliminate gender stereotypes

GROUNDS: data and evidence showing that a chief stereotype of women is that they are soft and nurturing whereas men are stereotyped as tough and aggressive; images of women in combat gear packing rifles, driving tanks, firing machine guns from a foxhole, or radioing for artillery support would shock people into seeing women not as "soft and nurturing" but as equal to men.

CLAIM: Cocaine and heroin should be legalized.

STATED REASON: because legalization would eliminate the black market in drugs

GROUNDS: data and evidence showing how legalizing cocaine and heroin would eliminate the black market (statistics, data, and examples showing the size of the current black market and explaining why legalization would eliminate it)

In many cases, successful arguments require just these three components: a claim, a reason, and grounds. If the audience already accepts the unstated assumption behind the reason (the warrant), then the warrant can safely remain in the background unstated and unexamined. But if there is a chance that the audience will question or doubt the warrant, then the writer needs to back it up by providing an argument in its support. *Backing* is the argument that supports the warrant. Backing answers the question "How do you know that . . . ?" or "Why do you believe that . . . ?" prefixed to the warrant. (Why do you believe that gender stereotyping is harmful? Why do you believe that ending the black market is good?) Here is how *backing* is added to our schema:

WARRANT: Gender stereotypes are harmful and should be eliminated.

BACKING: arguments showing how the existing stereotype of soft and nurturing women and tough and aggressive men is harmful to both men and women (examples of how the stereotype keeps men from developing their nurturing sides and women from developing autonomy and power; examples of other benefits that come from eliminating gender stereotypes including a more egalitarian society, no limits on what persons can pursue, deeper respect for both sexes)

WARRANT: An action that eliminates the black market in drugs is good.

BACKING: an argument supporting the warrant by showing why the benefits of eliminating the black market outweigh the social cost of legalizing drugs (statistics and examples about the ill effects of the black market, data on crime and profiteering, evidence that huge profits make drug dealing more attractive than ordinary jobs, the high cost of crime created by the black market, the cost to taxpayers of waging the war against drugs, the high cost of prisons to house incarcerated drug dealers, etc.)

Next Toulmin's system asks us to imagine how a resistant audience would try to refute our argument. Specifically, this adversarial audience might challenge our reason and grounds, our warrant and backing, or both. In the case of the argument supporting women in combat, an adversary might offer one or more of the following rebuttals:

CONDITIONS OF REBUTTAL

Rebutting the reasons and grounds: evidence that letting women join combat units wouldn't overcome gender stereotyping (very few women would want to join combat units; those who did would be considered freaks; most girls would still identify with Barbie doll models, not with female infantry)

Rebutting the warrant and backing: arguments showing it is important to maintain gender role differences because they are biologically based, divinely inspired, or otherwise important culturally; women should be nurturers and mothers, not fighters; essential nature of "womanhood" sullied by putting women in combat

Likewise, a skeptical audience might rebut the legalization of drugs argument in one or more of the following ways:

CONDITIONS OF REBUTTAL

Rebutting the reasons and grounds: evidence that legalizing drugs might not end the black market (perhaps taxes would keep prices high or perhaps new designer drugs would be developed and sold on the black market)

Rebutting the warrant and backing: arguments showing that the costs of eliminating the black market by legalizing drugs outweigh the benefits (an unacceptably high number of new drug users and addicts; a catastrophic increase in health care costs because of increased drug use; harm to the social structure from increased acceptance of drugs; high social costs to families and communities associated with addiction or erratic behavior during drug-induced "highs")

Toulmin's final term, used to limit the force of a claim and indicate the degree of its probable truth, is *qualifier.* The qualifier reminds us that real-world arguments almost never prove a claim. We may add words like *very likely, probably,* or *maybe* to indicate the strength of the claim we are willing to draw from our grounds and warrant. Thus if your grounds or warrant can be rebutted, you will have to qualify your claim. For example, you might say, "Except in rare cases, women should not be allowed in combat units," or "With full awareness of the potential dangers, I suggest that legalizing drugs may be the best way to eliminate the social costs of the black market."

For Class Discussion

Working individually or in small groups, imagine that you have to write arguments developing the ten enthymemes listed in the For Class Discussion exercise on page 79. Use the Toulmin schema to help you determine what you need to consider when developing each enthymeme. As an example, we have applied the Toulmin schema to the first enthymeme.

ORIGINAL ENTHYMEME: We should not choose Joe as committee chairperson because he is too bossy.

CLAIM: We should not choose Joe as committee chair.

STATED REASON: because he is too bossy

GROUNDS: various examples of Joe's bossiness; testimony about his bossi-

CONDITIONS OF REBUTTAL: *Rebuttal of reason and grounds:* Perhaps Joe isn't really bossy (counterevidence of Joe's cooperativeness and kindness, testimony that Joe is easy to work with, etc.).

Rebuttal of the warrant and backing: Perhaps bossy people sometimes make good chairpersons (arguments showing that at times a group needs a bossy person who can make decisions

ness from people who have worked
with him

WARRANT: Bossy people make bad
committee chairs.

BACKING: arguments showing that
other things being equal, bossy people
tend to bring out the worst rather than
the best in those around them; bossy
people tend not to ask advice, make
bad decisions, etc.

and get things done). Perhaps Joe has
other traits of good leadership that
outweigh his bossiness (evidence that,
despite his bossiness, Joe has many
other good leadership traits such as
high energy, intelligence, and
charisma).

QUALIFIER: In most circumstances,
bossy people make bad committee
chairs.

Using Toulmin's Schema to Determine a Strategy of Support

Having introduced you to Toulmin's terminology for describing the logical structure of arguments, we can turn directly to a discussion of how to use these
concepts for developing your own arguments. As we have seen, the claim, supporting reasons, and warrant form the frame for a line of reasoning. The majority
of words in an argument, however, are devoted to grounds and backing—the supporting sections that develop the argument frame.

For an illustration of how a writer can use the Toulmin schema to generate
ideas for an argument, consider the following hypothetical case. A student,
Ramona, wants to write a complaint letter to the head of the philosophy department about a philosophy professor, Dr. Choplogic, whom Ramona considers
incompetent. Ramona plans to develop two different lines of reasoning: first, that
Choplogic's courses are disorganized and, second, that Choplogic is unconcerned
about students. Let's look briefly at how she can develop her first main line of
reasoning, which is based on the following enthymeme:

> Dr. Choplogic is an ineffective teacher because his courses are disorganized.

The grounds for this argument will be evidence that Choplogic's courses are
disorganized. Using the Toulmin schema, Ramona lists under "grounds" all the
evidence she can muster that Choplogic's courses are disorganized. Here is how
this argument might look when placed into written form:

A LINE OF ARGUMENT DEVELOPED WITH EVIDENCE

Claim and reason   One reason why Dr. Choplogic is ineffective is that his courses are
poorly organized. I have had him for two courses—Introduction
to Philosophy and Ethics—and both were disorganized. He never

Grounds (evidence in support of reason)	gave us a syllabus or explained his grading system. At the beginning of the course he wouldn't tell us how many papers he would require, and he never seemed to know how much of the textbook material he planned to cover. For Intro he told us to read the whole text, but he covered only half of it in class. A week before the final I asked him how much of the text would be on the exam and he said he hadn't decided. The Ethics class was even more disorganized. Dr. Choplogic told us to read the text, which provided one set of terms for ethical arguments, and then he told us he didn't like the text and presented us in lecture with a wholly different set of terms. The result was a whole class of confused, angry students.

As you can see, Ramona has plenty of evidence to support her contention that Choplogic is disorganized. But how effective is this argument as it stands? Is this all she needs? The Toulmin schema also encourages Ramona to examine the warrant, backing, and conditions of rebuttal for this argument. She believes that no one can challenge her reason and grounds—Choplogic is indeed a disorganized teacher. But she recognizes that some people might challenge her warrant ("Disorganized teachers are ineffective"). A supporter of Dr. Choplogic might say that some teachers, even though they are hopelessly disorganized, might nevertheless do an excellent job of stimulating thought and discussion. Moreover, such teachers might possess other valuable traits that outweigh their disorganization. Ramona therefore decides to address these concerns by adding another section to this portion of her argument.

CONTINUATION OF RAMONA'S ARGUMENT

Backing for warrant (shows why disorganization is bad)	Dr. Choplogic's lack of organization makes it difficult for students to take notes, to know what to study, or to relate one part of the course to another. Moreover, students lose confidence in the teacher because he doesn't seem to care enough to prepare for class.
Response to conditions of rebuttal	In Dr. Choplogic's defense, it might be thought that his primary concern is involving students in class discussions or other activities to teach us thinking skills or get us involved in philosophical discussions. But this isn't the case. Students rarely get a chance to speak in class. We just sit there listening to rambling, disorganized lectures.

This section of her argument backs the warrant that disorganized teachers are ineffective and anticipates some of the conditions for rebuttal that an audience might raise to defend Dr. Choplogic. Throughout her draft, Ramona has supported her argument with evidence. Although Ramona takes her evidence from personal experience, in other cases evidence might come primarily from interviews, surveys, reading, and research. Chapter 6 is devoted to a more detailed discussion of evidence in arguments.

1. Working individually or in small groups, consider ways you could use evidence to support the stated reason in each of these following partial arguments.

   a. Another reason to oppose a state sales tax is that it is so annoying.

   b. Rap music has a bad influence on teenagers because it promotes disrespect for women.

   c. Professor X is an outstanding teacher because he (she) generously spends so much time outside of class counseling students with personal problems.

2. Now create arguments to support the warrants in each of the partial arguments in exercise 1. The warrants for each of the arguments are stated below.

   a. Support this warrant: We should oppose taxes that are annoying.

   b. Support this warrant: It is bad to promote disrespect for women.

   c. Support this warrant: Time spent counseling students with personal problems is an important criterion for identifying outstanding teachers.

3. Using Toulmin's conditions of rebuttal, work out a strategy for refuting either the stated reasons or the warrants or both in each of the arguments above.

The Power of Audience-Based Reasons

As we have seen, both Aristotle's concept of the enthymeme and Toulmin's concept of the warrant focus on the arguer's need to create what we will now call "audience-based reasons." Whenever you ask whether a given piece of writing is persuasive, the immediate rejoinder should always be "Persuasive to whom?" What seems like a good reason to you may not be a good reason to others. Finding audience-based reasons means finding arguments whose warrants the audience will accept—that is, arguments effectively rooted in your audience's beliefs and values.

Difference Between Writer-Based and Audience-Based Reasons

To illustrate the difference between writer-based and audience-based reasons, consider the following hypothetical case. Suppose you believed that the government should build a dam on the nearby Rapid River—a project bitterly opposed by several environmental groups. Which of the following two arguments might you use to address environmentalists?

1. The government should build a dam on the Rapid River because the only alternative power sources are coal-fired or nuclear plants, both of which pose greater risk to the environment than a hydroelectric dam.

2. The government should build a hydroelectric dam on the Rapid River because this area needs cheap power to attract heavy industry.

Clearly, the warrant of Argument 1 ("Choose the source of power that poses least risk to the environment") is rooted in the values and beliefs of environmentalists, whereas the warrant of Argument 2 ("Growth of industry is good") is likely to make them wince. To environmentalists, new industry means more congestion, more smokestacks, and more pollution. However, Argument 2 may appeal to out-of-work laborers or to the business community, to whom new industry means more jobs and a booming economy.

From the perspective of logic alone, Arguments 1 and 2 are both sound. They are internally consistent and proceed from reasonable premises. But they will affect different audiences very differently. Neither argument proves that the government should build the dam; both are open to objection. Passionate environmentalists, for example, might counter Argument 1 by asking why the government needs to build any power plant at all. They could argue that energy conservation would obviate the need for a new power plant. Or they might argue that building a dam hurts the environment in ways unforeseen by dam supporters. Our point, then, isn't that Argument 1 will persuade environmentalists. Rather, our point is that Argument 1 will be more persuasive than Argument 2 because it is rooted in beliefs and values the intended audience shares.

Let's consider a second example by returning to student Gordon Adams's petition to waive the university math requirement (Chapter 1, pp. 14–17). Gordon's central argument, as you will recall, had the following core:

> I should be exempted from the algebra requirement because in my chosen field of law I will have no need for algebra.

The warrant for Gordon's argument is that general education requirements should be based on career utility (that is, if a course isn't needed for a particular student's career, it shouldn't be required).

In our discussions of this case with students and faculty, students generally vote to support Gordon's request, whereas faculty members generally vote against it. And in fact, the University Standards Committee rejected Gordon's petition, thus delaying his entry into law school.

Why do faculty members and students differ on this issue? Mainly they differ because faculty members reject Gordon's warrant that general education requirements should serve students' individual career interests. Most faculty members believe that general education courses, including math, provide a base of common learning that links us to the past and teaches us modes of understanding that remain useful throughout life. Gordon's argument thus challenges one of college professors' most cherished beliefs—that the liberal arts are innately valuable. Further, it threatens his immediate audience, the committee, with a possible flood of student requests to waive other general education requirements on the grounds of their irrelevance to a particular career choice.

How might Gordon have created a more persuasive argument? In our view, Gordon might have prevailed had he accepted the faculty's belief in the value of the math requirement and argued that he had fulfilled the "spirit" of that requirement through alternative means. He could have based his argument on an enthymeme like this:

> I should be exempted from the algebra requirement because my experience as a contractor and inventor has already provided me with equivalent mathematical knowledge.

Following this audience-based approach, Gordon would drop all references to algebra's uselessness for lawyers and expand his discussion of the mathematical savvy he acquired on the job. This argument would honor faculty values and reduce faculty members' fears of setting a bad precedent. Few students are likely to have Gordon's background, and those who did could apply for a similar exemption without threatening the system. Again, this argument may not have won, but it would have gotten a more sympathetic hearing.

For Class Discussion

Working in groups, decide which of the two reasons offered in each instance would be more persuasive to the specified audience. Be prepared to explain your reasoning to the class. Write out the implied warrant for each *because* clause, and decide whether the specific audience would likely grant it.

1. Audience: a beleaguered parent
   a. I should be allowed to stay out until 2 A.M. because all my friends do.
   b. I should be allowed to stay out until 2 A.M. because only if I'm free to make my own decisions will I mature.
2. Audience: people who oppose the present grading system on the grounds that it is too competitive
   a. We should keep the present grading system because it prepares people for the dog-eat-dog pressures of the business world.
   b. We should keep the present grading system because it tells students that certain standards of excellence must be met if individuals are to reach their full potential.
3. Audience: conservative proponents of "family values"
   a. Same-sex marriages should be legalized because doing so will promote public acceptance of homosexuality.
   b. Same-sex marriages should be legalized because doing so will make it easier for gay people to establish and sustain long-term stable relationships.

Finding Audience-Based Reasons:
Asking Questions About Your Audience

As the preceding exercise makes clear, reasons are most persuasive when linked to your audience's values. This principle seems simple enough, yet it is easy to forget. For example, employers frequently complain about job interviewees whose first concern is what the company will do for them, not what they might do for the company. Conversely, job search experts agree that most successful job candidates do extensive background research on a prospective company so that in an interview they can relate their own skills to the company's problems and needs. Successful arguments typically grow out of similar attention to audience needs.

To find out all you can about an audience, we recommend that you explore the following questions:

1. *Who is your audience?* Your audience might be a single, identifiable person. For example, you might write a letter to your student body president arguing for a change in intramural policies, or your audience might be a decision-making body such as an influential committee. At other times your audience might be the general readership of a newspaper, church bulletin, magazine, or journal, or you might produce a flier to be handed out on street corners.

2. *How much does your audience know or care about your issue?* Are audience members currently part of the conversation on this issue, or do they need considerable background information? If you are writing to specific decision makers (for example, the administration at your college about restructuring the student orientation program), are they currently aware of the problem or issue you are addressing, and do they care about it? If not, how can you get their attention? Your answers to these questions will especially affect your introduction and conclusion.

3. *What is your audience's current attitude toward your issue?* Are members supportive of your position on the issue? Neutral or undecided? Skeptical? Strongly opposed? What other points of view besides your own will your audience be weighing? In Chapter 8 we will explain how your answers to these questions can help you decide the structure, content, and tone of your argument.

4. *What will be your audience's likely objections to your argument?* What weaknesses will members find? What aspects of your position will be most threatening to them and why? How are your basic assumptions, values, or beliefs different from your audience's? Your answers here will help determine the content of your argument and will alert you to extra research you may need to do to bolster your response to audience objections.

5. *What values, beliefs, or assumptions about the world do you and your audience share?* Despite differences of view on this issue, where can you find common links with your audience? How might you use these links to build bridges to your audience?

Suppose, for example, that you support racial profiling (rather than random selection) for determining who receives intensive screening at airports. It's important from the start that you understand and acknowledge the interests of those opposed to your position. Middle-Eastern men, the most likely candidates for racial profiling, will object to your racial stereotyping, which lumps all persons of Arabic or Semitic appearance into the category "potential terrorists." African Americans and Hispanics, frequent victims of racial profiling by police in U.S. cities, may object to further extension of this hated practice. Also, most political liberals, as well as many moderates and conservatives, may object to the racism inherent in selecting persons for airport screening on the basis of ethnicity.

What shared values might you use to build bridges to those opposed to racial profiling at airports? Suppose that you are writing a guest op-ed piece for a liberal campus newspaper and imagine readers repulsed by the notion of racial profiling. (Indeed you too feel repulsed by racial profiling.) You need to develop a strategy to reduce your audience's fears and to link your reasons to their values. Your thinking might go something like this:

Problem: How can I create an argument rooted in shared values? How can I reduce fear that racial profiling in this situation endorses racism or will lead to further erosion of civil liberties?

Bridge-building goals: I must try to show that my argument's goal is to increase airline safety by preventing terrorist acts like those of 9/11/01. My argument must show my respect for Islam and for Arabic and Semitic peoples. I must also show my rejection of racial profiling as normal police practice.

Possible strategies: ■ Stress the shared value of protecting innocent people from terrorism.

■ Show how racial profiling significantly increases the efficiency of secondary searches. (If searches are performed at random, then we waste time and resources searching the elderly, women, children, and others who are statistically unlikely to be terrorists.)

■ Argue that airport screeners must also use indicators other than race to select persons for searches (for example, traits that might indicate a domestic terrorist like Timothy McVeigh).

■ Show my respect for Islam.

■ Show sympathy for persons selected for searching via racial profiling and acknowledge that this practice would normally be despicable except for the extreme importance of airline security, which over-rides personal liberties in this case.

- Show my rejection of racial profiling in situations other than airport screening—for example, stopping African Americans for traffic violations more often than whites and then searching their cars for drugs or stolen goods.

The preceding example shows how a writer's focus on audience can shape the actual invention of the argument.

For Class Discussion

Working individually or in small groups, plan an audience-based argumentative strategy for one or more of the following cases. Follow the thinking process used by the writer of the racial profiling argument: (1) State several problems that the writer must solve to reach the audience. (2) Develop possible solutions to those problems.

1. An argument for the right of software companies to continue making and selling violent video games: Aim the argument at parents who oppose their children's playing these games.

2. An argument to reverse grade inflation by limiting the number of A's and B's a professor can give in a course: Aim the argument at students who fear the results of getting lower grades.

3. An argument supporting a $1-per-gallon increase in gasoline taxes as an energy conservation measure: Aim your argument at business leaders who oppose the tax for fear it will raise the cost of consumer goods.

4. An argument supporting the legalization of cocaine: Aim your argument at readers of *Reader's Digest*, a conservative magazine that supports the current war on drugs.

Conclusion

Chapters 4 and 5 have provided an anatomy of argument. They have shown that the core of an argument is a claim with reasons that usually can be summarized in one or more *because* clauses attached to the claim. Often, it is as important to support the unstated assumptions in your argument as it is to support the stated reasons because a successful argument must eventually be rooted in beliefs and values held by your audience. In order to plan an audience-based argument strategy, arguers can use the Toulmin schema, which helps writers discover grounds, warrants, and backing for their arguments and test them through conditions of rebuttal. Finally, a search for audience-based reasons helps you keep your audience in mind from the start whenever you plan an argument.

6 Using Evidence Effectively

In Chapters 4 and 5 we introduced you to the concept of *logos*—the logical structure of reasons and evidence in an argument. In this chapter we explain in more detail how to use evidence. By "evidence," we mean all the verifiable information a writer might use as support for an argument, such as facts, observations, examples, cases, testimony, experimental findings, survey data, statistics, and so forth. In Toulmin's terms, evidence is part of the "grounds" or "backing" of an argument in support of reasons or warrants.

We begin by explaining some general principles for the persuasive use of evidence. Next we describe and illustrate various kinds of evidence and then present a rhetorical way to think about evidence, particularly the way writers select and frame evidence to support the writer's reasons while simultaneously guiding and limiting what the reader sees. We conclude the chapter by suggesting strategies to help you gather evidence for your arguments, including advice on conducting interviews and using questionnaires.

General Principles for the Persuasive Use of Data

Consider a target audience of educated, reasonable, and careful readers who approach an issue with healthy skepticism, open-minded but cautious. What demands would such readers make upon a writer's use of evidence? To begin to answer that question, let's look at some general principles for using evidence persuasively.

Apply the STAR Criteria to Data

Our open-minded but skeptical audience would first of all expect your evidence to meet what rhetorician Richard Fulkerson calls the STAR criteria:*

---

*Richard Fulkerson, *Teaching the Argument in Writing* (Urbana: National Council of Teachers of English, 1996), 44–53. In this section we are indebted to Fulkerson's discussion.

Sufficiency: Is there enough evidence?

Typicality: Are the chosen data representative and typical?

Accuracy: Are the data accurate and up-to-date?

Relevance: Are the data relevant to the claim?

Let's examine each in turn.

Sufficiency of Evidence   How much evidence you need is a function of your rhetorical context. In a court trial, opposing attorneys often agree to waive evidence for points that aren't in doubt in order to concentrate on contested points. The more a claim is contested or the more your audience is skeptical, the more evidence you may need to present. If you provide too little evidence, you may be accused of *hasty generalization* (see Appendix One), a reasoning fallacy in which a person makes a sweeping conclusion based on only one or two instances. On the other hand, if you provide too much evidence your argument may become overly long and tedious. You can guard against having too little or too much evidence by appropriately qualifying the claim your evidence supports.

> **Strong claim:** Working full time seriously harms a student's grade point average. [much data needed—probably a combination of examples and statistical studies]
>
> **Qualified claim:** Working full time often harms a student's grade point average. [a few representative examples may be enough]

Typicality of Evidence   Whenever you select data, readers need to believe the data are typical and representative rather than extreme instances. Suppose that you want to argue that students can combine full-time work with full-time college and cite the case of your friend Pam who pulled a straight-A grade average while working forty hours per week as a night receptionist in a small hotel. Your audience might doubt the typicality of Pam's case since a night receptionist can often use work hours for studying. What about more typical jobs, they'll ask, where you can't study while you work?

Accuracy of Evidence   Data can't be used ethically unless they are accurate and up-to-date, and they can't be persuasive unless the audience believes in the writer's credibility. As a writer, you must be scrupulous in using the most recent and accurate data you can find. We have already encountered a case of doubtful data in the two articles on biotech food in Chapter 2. Lisa Turner cites a 1993 case in which thirty-seven people died from a rare disease allegedly linked to bioengineered food (see Chapter 2, p. 21), yet the Council for Biotechnology Information states, "There hasn't been a single documented case of an illness caused by biotech foods" (p. 35). One of these writers must be using inaccurate data—a problem the reader can unravel only through additional research. Faith in the accuracy of a writer's data is one function of *ethos*—the audience's confidence in the writer's credibility and trustworthiness (see Chapter 7, p. 112).

Relevance of Evidence   Finally, data will be persuasive only if the reader considers them relevant to the contested issue. Consider the following student argument: "I deserve an A in this course because I worked exceptionally hard." The student then cites substantial evidence of how hard he worked—a log of study hours, copies of multiple drafts of papers, testimony from friends, and so forth. Such evidence is ample support for the claim "I worked very hard" but is irrelevant to the claim that "I deserve an A." Although some instructors may give partial credit for effort, the criteria for grades usually focus on the quality of the student's performance, not on the student's time spent studying.

Use Sources That Your Reader Trusts

Another way to enhance the persuasiveness of your evidence is to choose data, whenever possible, from sources you think your readers will trust. Because questions of fact are often at issue in arguments, readers may be skeptical of certain sources. When you research an issue, you soon get a sense of who the participants in the conversation are and what their reputations tend to be. Knowing the political biases of sources and the extent to which a source has financial or personal investment in the outcome of a controversy will also help you locate data sources that both you and your readers can trust. Citing a peer-reviewed scholarly journal is often more persuasive than citing an advocacy Web site. Similarly, citing a conservative magazine such as the *National Review* may be unpersuasive to liberal audiences, just as citing a Sierra Club publication may be unpersuasive to conservatives. (See Appendix Two for further discussion of how to evaluate research sources.)

Rhetorical Understanding of Evidence

In the previous section we presented some general principles for the effective use of evidence. We now want to deepen your understanding of how evidence persuades by asking you to consider more closely the rhetorical context in which evidence operates. We'll look first at the kinds of evidence used in arguments and then show you how writers select and frame evidence for persuasive effect.

Kinds of Evidence

Writers have numerous options for the kinds of evidence they can use in an argument, ranging from personal experience data to research findings to hypothetical examples. To explain these options, we present a series of charts that categorize different kinds of evidence, illustrate how each kind might be worked into an argument, and add comments about the strengths and limitations of each.

Data from Personal Experience   One powerful kind of evidence comes from personal experience:

CATEGORY	EXAMPLE	STRENGTHS AND LIMITATIONS
Examples from personal experience or knowledge	Despite recent criticism that Ritalin is overprescribed for hyperactivity and attention deficit disorder, it can often seem like a miracle drug. My little brother is a perfect example. Before he was given Ritalin he was a terror in school. . . . [Tell the "before" and "after" story of your little brother.]	■ Personal experience examples help readers identify with writer; they show writer's personal connection to issue. ■ Vivid stories capture imagination. ■ Skeptics may sometimes argue that personal experience examples are insufficient (writer is guilty of hasty generalization), not typical, or not adequately scientific or verifiable.
Personal observation or field research	The intersection at fifth and Montgomery is particularly dangerous because pedestrians almost never find a comfortable break in the heavy flow of cars. On April 29, I watched fifty-seven pedestrians cross the street. Not once did cars stop in both directions before the pedestrian stepped off the sidewalk onto the street. [Continue with observed data about danger.]	■ Field research gives feeling of scientific credibility. ■ It increases typicality by expanding data base beyond example of one person. ■ It enhances *ethos* of writer as personally invested and reasonable. ■ Skeptics may point to flaws in how observations were conducted, showing how data are insufficient, inaccurate, or nontypical.

Data from Interviews, Questionnaires, Surveys   You can also gather data by interviewing stakeholders in a controversy, creating questionnaires, or doing surveys. (See pp. 104–106 for advice on how to conduct this kind of field research.)

EXAMPLE	STRENGTHS AND LIMITATIONS
In the first two months after the terrorist attacks on September 11, 2001, Muslim students on our campus suffered from anxiety at an especially severe rate. In a survey I conducted	■ Interviews, questionnaires, and surveys enhance sufficiency and typicality of evidence by expanding data base beyond experiences of one person.

EXAMPLE	STRENGTHS AND LIMITATIONS
through the Student Affairs Office, 87 percent of Muslim students reported . . . . [Give details of survey.] Additionally, in my interviews with three Muslim students—two international students from Saudi Arabia and one American student born and raised in Chicago—I discovered that . . . . [Report interview data.]	■ Quantitative data from questionnaires and surveys often increase scientific feel of argument. ■ Surveys and questionnaires often uncover local or recent data not available in published research. ■ Interviews can provide engaging personal stories enhancing *pathos*. ■ Skeptics can raise doubts about research methodology, questionnaire design, or typicality of interview subjects.

Data from Reading and Research   For many arguments, evidence is derived from reading, particularly through library or Internet research. Appendix Two of this text offers detailed advice on conducting research.

CATEGORY	EXAMPLE	STRENGTHS AND LIMITATIONS
Facts, examples, illustrative cases drawn from reading	Although reproductive technology cannot solve all infertility problems, breakthroughs continue. In addition to fertilizing eggs in petri dishes, reproductive technology can detect abnormalities in embryos before they are implanted. To combat male infertility, which makes up nearly half the infertility problems, reproductive technology can concentrate sperm for artificial insemination and inject a sperm directly into an egg. Since 1970, the number of women in their thirties and forties having their first child has quadrupled, partly as a result of these scientific advances (Kalb 40–43).*	■ Researched evidence is often powerful, especially when sources are respected. ■ Skeptics might doubt accuracy of facts or credentials of source. ■ Skeptics might raise doubts about sufficiency, typicality, or relevance of data.
Findings from experimental reports; summaries of research studies	The belief that a high-carbohydrate–low-fat diet is the best way to lose weight has been challenged by research conducted by Walter Willett and his colleagues in the department of nutrition in the Harvard	■ Reports and studies are an excellent source of persuasive data, especially if studies are peer reviewed in respected journals. ■ These enhance writer's *ethos* if writer composes

*Examples of parenthetical citations in this section follow the MLA documentation system. See Appendix Two for a discussion of how to cite and document sources.

CATEGORY	EXAMPLE	STRENGTHS AND LIMITATIONS
	School of Public Health. Willett's research suggests that complex carbohydrates such as pasta and potatoes spike glucose levels, increasing the risk of diabetes. Additionally, some fats may be good for you—especially monounsaturated and polyunsaturated fats found in nuts, fish, and most vegetable oils, which help lower "bad" cholesterol levels (45).	clear summaries in writer's own voice without insider jargon. ■ Skeptics might doubt the research design of the study or cite other studies with different results.
Testimony	Although the Swedish economist Bjorn Lomborg claims that acid rain is not a significant problem, many environmentalists disagree. According to David Bellamany, president of the Conservation Foundation, "Acid rain does kill forests and people around the world, and it's still doing so in the most polluted places, such as Russia" (qtd. in BBC News).	■ Testimony is frequently used when data are too technical or complex for lay audience to understand; it can also supplement use of actual data. ■ By itself, it is generally less persuasive than direct data. ■ Persuasiveness can be increased if source has impressive credentials, which writer must state. ■ Skeptics might undermine testimonial evidence by questioning credentials of source, showing source's bias, or quoting a counter-source.

Statistical Data Many contemporary arguments rely heavily on statistical data, often supplemented by visual graphics such as tables, pie charts, and graphs. (See Chapter 9 for a discussion of the use of visual graphics in argument.)

EXAMPLE	STRENGTHS AND LIMITATIONS
Americans are delaying marriage at a surprising rate. In 1970, 85 percent of Americans between the ages of 15 and 29 were married. In 2000, however, only 54 percent were married (U.S. Census Bureau).	■ Statistics can give powerful snapshots of aggregate data from a wide data base. ■ They are often used in conjunction with visual graphics (see pp. 154–160). ■ They can be calculated and displayed in different ways to achieve different rhetorical effects, so reader must be wary (see pp. 157–159). ■ Skeptics might question statistical methods, research design, and interpretation of data.

Hypothetical Examples, Cases, and Scenarios   Arguments occasionally use hypothetical examples, cases, or scenarios, particularly to illustrate conjectured consequences of an event or to test philosophical hypotheses.

EXAMPLE	STRENGTHS AND LIMITATIONS
Consider what might happen if we continue to use biotech soybeans that are resistant to herbicides. The resistant gene, through cross-pollination, might be transferred to an ordinary weed, creating an out-of-control superweed that herbicides couldn't kill. Such a superweed could be an ecological disaster.	■ Scenarios have strong imaginative appeal. ■ They are persuasive only if they seem plausible. ■ A scenario narrative often conveys a sense of "inevitability," even if the actual scenario is unlikely; hence rhetorical effect may be illogical. ■ Skeptics might show implausibility of scenario or offer an alternative scenario.

Reasoned Sequence of Ideas   Sometimes arguments are supported with a reasoned sequence of ideas rather than with concrete facts or other forms of empirical evidence. The writer's concern is to support a point through a logical progression of ideas. Such arguments are conceptual, supported by linked ideas, rather than evidential. This kind of support occurs frequently in arguments and is often intermingled with evidentiary support.

EXAMPLE	STRENGTHS AND LIMITATIONS
Embryonic stem cell research, despite its promise in fighting diseases, may have negative social consequences. This research encourages us to place embryos in the category of mere cellular matter that can be manipulated at will. Currently we place animals in this category when we genetically alter them for human purposes such as engineering pigs to grow more human-like heart valves for use in transplants. Placing human embryos in the same category by treating them as material that can be altered and destroyed at will may benefit society materially, but this quest for greater knowledge and control involves a reclassifying of embryos that could potentially lead to a devaluing of human life.	■ These sequences are often used in causal arguments to show how causes are linked to effects or in definitional or values arguments to show links among ideas. ■ They have great power to clarify values and show the belief structure upon which a claim is founded. ■ They can sketch out ideas and connections that would otherwise remain latent. ■ Their effectiveness depends on audience's acceptance of each link in the sequence of ideas. ■ Skeptics might raise objections at any link in the sequence, often by pointing to different values or outlining different consequences.

Angle of Vision and the Selection and Framing of Evidence

You can increase your ability to use evidence effectively—and to analyze how other arguers use evidence—by becoming more aware of a writer's rhetorical choices when using evidence to support a claim. When writers select evidence for an argument, they are guided by an "angle of vision" determined by their underlying beliefs, values, or purposes. (Instead of "angle of vision," we could also use other words or metaphors such as *perspective, bias, lens,* or *filter*—all terms that suggest that our way of seeing the world is shaped by our values and beliefs.) A writer's angle of vision, like a lens or filter, helps determine what stands out for that writer in a field of data—that is, what data are important or trivial, significant or irrelevant, worth focusing on or worth ignoring.

To illustrate this concept of selective seeing, we ask you to consider the selection of evidence regarding homeless persons in two arguments presented to a city council at a planning conference. The first speaker, arguing that the city should provide more services to the homeless, wishes to select and frame evidence to create positive feelings for homeless people. (The word "frame" derives metaphorically from a window frame or the frame of a camera's viewfinder. When you look through a frame, some part of your field of vision is blocked off, thus emphasizing the material within the frame. Through framing, a writer maximizes the reader's focus on some data, minimizes the reader's focus on other data, and otherwise guides the reader's vision and response.) She begins by telling the story of a homeless man's struggle to find shelter and then provides data on the number of homeless persons in the downtown area and on the inadequacy of current shelters and food bank programs. In contrast, the second speaker has a different agenda. Promoting downtown development, he focuses on the decline of shoppers in downtown stores. His argument also includes data about the homeless (citing some of the same statistics used by the first speaker), but he frames the homeless as "panhandlers" who need to be removed from picturesque downtown tourist areas. As arguers, both speakers want their audience to see the homeless from their own angles of vision. Consequently, lost shopping revenues don't show up at all in the first speaker's argument while the story of a homeless man's night in the cold doesn't show up in the second speaker's argument. As this example shows, writers select and frame evidence to bring the reader's view of the subject into alignment with the writer's angle of vision. The writer selects and frames evidence to limit and control what the reader sees.

To help you better understand the concept of angle of vision, we offer the following class discussion exercise. As you do this exercise, we invite you to observe your own processes for selecting and framing evidence according to an angle of vision.

For Class Discussion

Suppose that your city has scheduled a public hearing on a proposed city ordinance to ban mosh pits at rock concerts. (See p. 12, where we introduced this issue.) Among the factual data available to various speakers for evidence are the following:

Possible Data for Mosh Pit Argument

- Some bands, like Nine Inch Nails, specify festival seating that allows a mosh pit area.

- A female mosher writing on the Internet says: "I experience a shared energy that is like no other when I am in the pit with the crowd. It is like we are all a bunch of atoms bouncing off of each other. It's great. Hey, some people get that feeling from basketball games. I get mine from the mosh pit."

- A student conducted a survey of fifty students on her campus who had attended rock concerts in the last six months. Of the respondents, 80 percent thought that mosh pits should be allowed at concerts.

- Narrative comments on these questionnaires included the following:

  - Mosh pits are a passion for me. I get an amazing rush when crowd surfing.

  - I don't like to be in a mosh pit or do crowd surfing. But I love festival seating and like to watch the mosh pits. For me, mosh pits are part of the ambience of a concert.

  - I know a girl who was groped in a mosh pit, and she'll never do one again. But I have never had any problems.

  - Mosh pits are dangerous and stupid. I think they should be outlawed.

  - If you are afraid of mosh pits just stay away. Nobody forces you to go into a mosh pit! It is ridiculous to ban them because they are totally voluntary. They should just post big signs saying, "City assumes no responsibility for accidents occurring in mosh pit area."

- A fourteen-year-old boy suffered permanent brain damage from a mosh pit accident when he went to hear Rage Against the Machine in Seattle in 1996.

- A teenage girl suffered brain damage and memory loss at a 1998 Pearl Jam concert in Rapid City, South Dakota. According to her attorney, she hadn't intended to bodysurf or enter the mosh pit but "got sucked in while she was standing at its fringe."

- There were twenty-four concert deaths recorded in 2001, most of them in the area closest to the stage where people are packed in.

- A twenty-one-year-old man suffered cardiac arrest at a Metallica concert in Indiana and is now in a permanent vegetative state. Because he was jammed into the mosh pit area, nobody noticed he was in distress.

Tasks: Working individually or in small groups, complete the following tasks:

1. Compose two short speeches from different angles of vision—one supporting the proposed city ordinance to ban mosh pits and one opposing it. How you use these data is up to you, but be able to explain your reasoning in the way you select and frame them. Share your speeches with classmates.

2. After you have shared examples of different speeches, explain the approaches that different classmates employed. What principle of selection

was used? If arguers included evidence contrary to their positions, how did they handle it, respond to it, minimize its importance, or otherwise channel its rhetorical effect?

Rhetorical Strategies for Framing Evidence

What we hope you learned from the preceding exercise is that an arguer's angle of vision causes the arguer to select evidence from a wide field of data and then frame these data through rhetorical strategies that emphasize some data, minimize others, and guide the reader's response. Now that you have a basic idea of what we mean by framing evidence, here are some strategies writers can use to guide what the reader sees and feels.

Strategies for Framing Evidence

- *Controlling the space given to supporting versus contrary evidence*: Depending on their audience and purpose, writers can devote most of their space to supporting evidence and minimal space to contrary evidence (or omit it entirely). Thus persons arguing in favor of mosh pits may have used lots of evidence supporting mosh pits, including enthusiastic quotations from concertgoers, while omitting (or summarizing very rapidly) the data about the dangers of mosh pits.

- *Emphasizing a detailed story versus presenting lots of facts and statistics:* Often, writers can choose to support a point with a memorable individual case or with aggregate data such as statistics or lists of facts. A memorable story can have a strongly persuasive effect. For example, to create a negative view of mosh pits, a writer might tell the heartrending story of a teenager suffering permanent brain damage from being dropped on a mosh pit floor. In contrast, a supporter of mosh pits might tell the story of a happy music lover turned on to the concert scene by the rush of crowd surfing. A different strategy is to use facts and statistics rather than case narratives—for example, data about the frequency of mosh pit accidents, financial consequences of lawsuits, and so forth. The single narrative case often has a more powerful rhetorical effect, but it is always open to the charge that it is an insufficient or nonrepresentative example. Vivid anecdotes make for interesting reading, but by themselves they may not be compelling logically. In contrast, aggregate data, often used in scholarly studies, can provide more compelling logical evidence but sometimes make the prose wonkish and dense.

- *Providing contextual and interpretive comments when presenting data*: When citing data, writers can add brief contextual or interpretive comments that act like lenses over the readers' eyes to help them see the data from the writer's perspective. Suppose you want to support mosh pits, but want to admit that mosh pits are dangerous. You could make that danger seem irrelevant or inconsequential by saying: "It is true that occasional mosh pit accidents happen, just as accidents happen in any kind of recreational activity from swimming to weekend softball games." The concluding phrase frames the danger of mosh pits by comparing them to other recreational accidents that don't require special laws or regulations. The implied argument is this: banning mosh pits because of an occasional accident would be as silly as banning recreational swimming because of occasional accidents.

- *Putting contrary evidence in subordinate positions:* Just as a photographer can place a flower at the center of a photograph or in the background, a writer can place a piece of data in a subordinate clause or main clause of a sentence. Note how the structure of the following sentence minimizes the fact that mosh pit accidents are rare: "Although mosh pit accidents are rare, the danger to the city of multimillion-dollar liability lawsuits means that the city should nevertheless ban them for reasons of fiscal prudence." The factual datum that mosh pit accidents are rare is summarized briefly and tucked away in a subordinate *"although* clause," while the writer's own position is elaborated in the main clause where it receives grammatical emphasis. A writer with a different angle of vision might say, "Although some cities may occasionally be threatened with a lawsuit, serious accidents resulting from mosh pits are so rare that cities shouldn't interfere with the desires of music fans to conduct concerts as they please."

- *Choosing labels and names that guide the reader's response to data:* One of the most subtle ways to control your reader's response to data is to choose labels and names that prompt them to see the issue as you do. If you like mosh pits, you might refer to the seating arrangements in a concert venue as "festival seating, where concertgoers have the opportunity to create a free-flowing mosh pit." If you don't like mosh pits, you might refer to the seating arrangements as "an accident-inviting use of empty space where rowdies can crowd together, slam into each other, and occasionally punch and kick." The labels you choose, along with the connotations of the words you select, urge your reader to share your angle of vision.

- *Using images (photographs, drawings) to guide the reader's response to data:* Another strategy for moving your audience toward your angle of vision is to include a photograph or drawing that portrays a contested issue from your perspective. (See Chapter 9 for a complete discussion of the use of visuals in argument.) Consider the photograph of crowd surfing shown in Color Plate C. This photograph supports a positive view of mosh pits. The crowd looks happy (rather than rowdy or out of control) and the young woman lifted above the crowd smiles broadly, her body relaxed, her arms extended.

- *Revealing the value system that determines the writer's selection and framing of data:* Ultimately, how a writer selects and frames evidence is linked to the system of values that organize his or her argument. If you favor mosh pits, you probably favor maximizing the pleasure of concertgoers, promoting individual choice, and letting moshers assume the risk of their own behavior. If you want to forbid mosh pits, you probably favor minimizing risks, protecting the city from lawsuits, and protecting individuals from the danger of their own out-of-control actions. Sometimes you can foster connections with your audience by openly addressing your underlying values that you hope your audience shares with you. You can often frame your selected data by stating explicitly the values that guide your argument.

Special Strategies for Framing Statistical Evidence

Numbers and statistical data can be framed in so many ways that this category of evidence deserves its own separate treatment. By recognizing how writers frame numbers to support the story they want to tell, you will always be aware that other stories are also possible. Ethical use of numbers means that you use reputable sources for your basic data, that you don't invent or intentionally distort numbers for your own purposes, and that you don't ignore alternative points of view. Here are some of the choices writers make when framing statistical data:

■ *Raw numbers versus percentages.* You can alter the rhetorical effect of a statistic by choosing between raw number or percentages. In summer 2002, many American parents panicked over what seemed like an epidemic of child abductions. If you cited the raw number of these abductions reported in the national news, this number, although small, could seem scary. But if you computed the actual percentage of American children who were abducted, that percentage was so infinitesimally small as to seem insignificant. You can apply this framing option directly to the mosh pit case. To emphasize the danger of mosh pits, you can say that twenty deaths occurred at rock concerts in the year 2001. To minimize this statistic, you could compute the percentage of deaths by dividing this number by the total number of persons who attended rock concerts during the year, certainly a number in the several millions. From the perspective of percentages, the death rate at concerts is extremely low.

■ *Median versus mean.* Another way to alter the rhetorical effect of numbers is to choose between the median and the mean. The mean is the average of all numbers on a list. The median is the middle number when all the numbers are arranged sequentially from high to low. In 1998 the mean annual income for retired families in the United States was $32,600—not a wealthy amount but enough to live on comfortably if you owned your own home. However, the median income was only $19,300, a figure that gives you a much more striking picture of income distribution among older Americans. This median figure means that half of all retired families in the United States had annual incomes of $19,300 or less. The much higher mean income indicates that many retired Americans are extremely wealthy. This wealth raises the average of all incomes (the mean) but doesn't effect the median.

■ *Unadjusted versus adjusted numbers.* Suppose your boss told you that you were getting a 5 percent raise. You might be happy—unless inflation rates were running at 6 percent. Economic data can be hard to interpret across time unless the dollar amounts are adjusted for inflation. This same problem occurs in other areas. For example, comparing grade point averages of college graduates in 1970 versus 2002 means little unless one can somehow compensate for grade inflation.

■ *Base point for statistical comparisons.* In the summer of 2002, the stock market was in precipitous decline if one compared 2002 prices with 2000 prices. However, the market still seemed vigorous and healthy if one compared 2002 against 1990. One's choice of the base point for a comparison often makes a significant rhetorical difference.

For Class Discussion

A proposal to build a new ballpark in Seattle, Washington, yielded a wide range of statistical arguments. All of the following statements are reasonably faithful to the same facts:

■ The ballpark would be paid for by raising the sales tax from 8.2 percent to 8.3 percent over a twenty-year period.

■ The sales tax increase is one-tenth of 1 percent.

■ This increase represents $750 per five-person family over the twenty-year period of the tax.

■ For a family building a new home in the Seattle area, this tax will increase building costs by $200.

■ This is a $250 million tax increase for the residents of the Seattle area.

How would you describe the costs of the proposed ballpark if you opposed the proposal? How would you describe the costs if you supported the proposal?

Gathering Evidence

We conclude this chapter with some brief advice on ways to gather evidence for your arguments. We begin with a list of brainstorming questions that may help you think of possible sources for evidence. We then provide suggestions for conducting interviews and creating surveys and questionnaires, since these powerful sources are often overlooked by students.

Creating a Plan for Gathering Evidence

As you begin contemplating an argument, you can use the following checklist to help you think of possible sources for evidence.

A Checklist for Brainstorming Sources of Evidence

- What personal experiences have you had with this issue? What details from your life or the lives of your friends, acquaintances, or relatives might serve as examples or other kinds of evidence?
- What observational studies would be relevant to this issue? How could you gather data by observing people, events, or other phenomena or by doing field or laboratory research?
- What persons could you interview to provide insights or expert knowledge on this issue?
- What questions about your issue could be addressed in a survey or questionnaire?
- What evidence could you gather by doing library research, including a licensed database search for print articles in magazines, newspapers, and scholarly journals? (See Appendix Two.)
- What evidence could you find by doing a rhetorically savvy search of Internet and Web sources? (See Appendix Two.)

Gathering Data from Interviews

Conducting interviews is a useful way not only to gather expert testimony and important data but also to learn about alternative views. To make interviews as productive as possible, determine your purpose in advance. Prepare by doing background reading so that you will be informed on the issue, establish your credibility, and build a bridge between you and your source. It is also a good idea to formulate questions in advance, but be ready to move in unexpected directions if the interview opens up new territory. As part of your professional demeanor, be sure to have with you all the necessary supplies (notepaper, pens, pencils, perhaps a tape recorder, if your interviewee is willing). Take brief but clear notes, recording the main ideas and being accurate with quotations. Ask for clarification of any points you don't understand. Immediately after the interview, while your memory is still fresh, rewrite your notes more fully and completely.

When you use interview data in your writing, put quotation marks around any direct quotations. In most cases, you will also want to identify your source by name and indicate his or her title or credentials—whatever will convince the reader that this person's remarks are to be taken seriously.

Gathering Data from Surveys or Questionnaires

A well-constructed survey or questionnaire can provide lively, current data for your argument. To give you useful information and avoid charges of bias, you will want to include a range of questions, including both closed-response questions and open-response questions. Closed-response questions, asking

participants to check a box or number on a scale, yield quantitative data that
you can report statistically, perhaps in tables or graphs. Open-response questions elicit varied responses and often short narratives that allow participants to
offer their own input. These may contribute new insights to your perspective on
the issue. Make your questionnaire clear and easy to complete and explain your
purpose at the outset. Respondents are usually more willing to participate if
they know how the knowledge gained from the questionnaire or survey will
benefit others. Also seek a random sample of respondents. For example, if a
questionnaire about the university library went only to dorm residents, then
you wouldn't learn how commuting students felt. When you have collected the
questionnaires or finished the survey interviews, tally the usable data and summarize responses.

Conclusion

Effective use of evidence is an essential skill for arguers. In this chapter we introduced you to the STAR criteria evaluating data. We then illustrated various kinds
of evidence, examined how a writer's angle of vision influences the selection and
framing of evidence, and described framing strategies for emphasizing evidence,
de-emphasizing it, and guiding your reader's response to it. We concluded with
advice on how to gather evidence, including the use of interviews, surveys, and
questionnaires.

WRITING ASSIGNMENTS
FOR CHAPTERS 4–6

OPTION 1: A Microtheme   Write a one- or two-paragraph argument in which
you support one of the following enthymemes, using evidence from personal
experience, field observation, interviews, or data from a brief questionnaire or
survey. Most of your microtheme should support the stated reason with evidence.
However, also include a brief passage supporting the implied warrant. The opening sentence of your microtheme should be the enthymeme itself, which serves as
the thesis statement for your argument. (Note: If you disagree with the enthymeme's argument, recast the claim or the reason to assert what you want to
argue.)

1. Reading fashion magazines can be detrimental to teenage girls because
   such magazines can produce an unhealthy focus on beauty.
2. Learning to surf the Web might harm your studying because it causes you
   to waste time.

3. Service-learning courses are valuable because they allow you to test course concepts against real-world situations.

4. Summer internships in your field of interest, even without pay, are the best use of your summer time because they speed up your education and training for a career.

5. Any enthymeme (a claim with a *because* clause) of your choice that can be supported without library or Internet research. (The goal of this microtheme is to practice using data from personal experience or from brief field research.) You may want to have your instructor approve your enthymeme in advance.

OPTION 2: A Classical Argument Write a classical argument that uses at least two reasons to support your claim (classical argument is explained in detail in Chapter 3, pp. 55–57). As we explain further in Chapter 8, classical argument is particularly effective when you are addressing neutral or undecided audiences. It has a self-announcing or closed-form structure in which you state your claim at the end of the introduction, begin body paragraphs with clearly stated reasons, and use effective transitions throughout to keep your reader on track. In developing your argument, place your most important reason last, where it will have the greatest impact on your readers. Typically, a classical argument also summarizes anticipated objections to the writer's argument and responds to them appropriately. You can place this section either before or after you develop your main argument. (Chapter 8, pp. 122–127, gives a detailed explanation of how to respond to objections and alternative views.)

The following student essay illustrates a classical argument. This essay grew out of a class discussion about alternative sports, conflicts between traditional sports and newer sports (downhill skiing and snowboarding), and middle-aged prejudices against groups of young people.

"Half-Criminals" or Urban Athletes?
A Plea for Fair Treatment of Skateboarders
David Langley (student)

For skateboarders, the campus of the University of California at San Diego is a wide-open, huge, geometric, obstacle-filled, stair-scattered cement paradise. The signs posted all over campus read "No skateboarding, biking, or rollerblading on campus except on Saturday, Sunday, and Holidays." I have always respected these signs at my local skateboarding spot. On the first day of 1999, I was skateboarding here with my hometown skate buddies and had just landed a trick when a police officer rushed out from behind a pillar, grabbed me, and yanked me off my board. Because I didn't have my I. D. (I had emptied my pockets so I wouldn't bruise my legs if I fell—a little trick of the trade), the officer started treating me like a criminal. She told me to spread my legs and put my hands on my head. She frisked me and then called in my name to police headquarters.

2   "What's the deal?" I asked. "The sign said skateboarding was legal on holidays."

3   "The sign means that you can only *roll* on campus," she said.

4   But that's *not* what the sign said. The police officer gave one friend and me a warning. Our third friend received a fifty-dollar ticket because it was his second citation in the last twelve months. Like other skateboarders throughout cities, we have been bombarded with unfair treatment. We have been forced out of known skate spots in the city by storeowners and police, kicked out of every parking garage in downtown, compelled to skate at strange times of day and night, and herded into crowded skateboard parks. However, after I was searched by the police and detained for over twenty minutes in my own skating sanctuary, the unreasonableness of the treatment of skateboarders struck me. Where are skateboarders supposed to go? Cities need to change their unfair treatment of skateboarders because skateboarders are not antisocial misfits as popularly believed, because the laws regulating skateboarding are ambiguous, and because skateboarders are not given enough legitimate space to practice their sport.

5   Possibly because to the average eye most skateboarders look like misfits or delinquents, adults think of us as criminal types and associate our skateboards with antisocial behavior. But this view is unfair. City dwellers should recognize that skateboards are a natural reaction to the urban environment. If people are surrounded by cement, they are going to figure out a way to ride it. People's different environments have always produced transportation and sports to suit the conditions: bikes, cars, skis, ice skates, boats, canoes, surfboards. If we live on snow, we are going to develop skis or snowshoes to move around. If we live in an environment that has flat panels of cement for ground and lots of curbs and stairs, we are going to invent an ingeniously designed flat board with wheels. Skateboards are as natural to cement as surfboards are to water or skis to snow. Moreover, the resulting sport is as healthful, graceful, and athletic. A fair assessment of skateboarders should respect our elegant, nonpolluting means of transportation and sport, and not consider us hoodlums.

6   A second way that skateboarders are treated unfairly is that the laws that regulate skateboarding in public places are highly restrictive, ambiguous, and open to abusive application by police officers. My being frisked on the UCSD campus is just one example. When I moved to Seattle to go to college, I found the laws in Washington to be equally unclear. When a sign says "No Skateboarding," that generally means you will get ticketed if you are caught skateboarding in the area. But most areas aren't posted. The general rule then is that you can skateboard so long as you do so safely without being reckless. But the definition of "reckless" is up to the whim of the police officer. I visited the front desk of the Seattle East Precinct and asked them exactly what the laws against reckless skateboarding meant. They said that skaters are allowed on the sidewalk as long as they travel at reasonable speed and the sidewalks aren't crowded. One of the officers explained that if he saw

a skater sliding down a handrail with people all around, he would definitely arrest the skater. What if there were no people around, I asked? The officer admitted that he might arrest the lone skater anyway and not be questioned by his superiors. No wonder skateboarders feel unfairly treated.

One way that cities have tried to treat skateboarders fairly is to build skate- 7 board parks. Unfortunately, for the most part these parks are no solution at all. Most parks were designed by nonskaters who don't understand the momentum or gravity pull associated with the movement of skateboards. For example, City Skate, a park below the Space Needle in Seattle, is very appealing to the eye, but once you start to ride it you realize that the transitions and the verticals are all off, making it unpleasant and even dangerous to skate there. The Skate Park in Issaquah, Washington, hosts about thirty to fifty skaters at a time. Collisions are frequent and close calls, many. There are simply too many people in a small area. The people who built the park in Redmond, Washington, decided to make a huge wall in it for graffiti artists to "tag" on legally. They apparently thought they ought to throw all us teenage "half criminals" in together. At this park, young teens are nervous to skate near a gangster "throwing up his piece," and skaters become dizzy as they take deep breaths from their workouts right next to four or five cans of spray paint expelling toxins in the air.

Of course, many adults probably don't think skateboarders deserve to be 8 treated fairly. I have heard the arguments against skateboarders for years from parents, storeowners, friends, police officers, and security guards. For one thing, skateboarding tears up public and private property, people say. I can't deny that skating leaves marks on handrails and benches, and it does chip cement and granite. But in general skateboarders help the environment more than they hurt it. Skateboarding places are not littered or tagged up by skaters. Because skaters need smooth surfaces and because any small object of litter can lead to painful accidents, skaters actually keep the environment cleaner than the average citizen does. As for the population as a whole, skateboarders are keeping the air a lot cleaner than many other commuters and athletes such as boat drivers, car drivers, and skiers on ski lifts. In the bigger picture, infrequent repair of curbs and benches is cheaper than attempts to heal the ozone.

We skateboarders aren't going away so cities are going to have to make room 9 for us somewhere. Here is how cities can treat us fairly. We should be allowed to skate when others are present as long as we skate safely on the sidewalks. The rules and laws should be clearer so that skaters don't get put into vulnerable positions that make them easy targets for tickets. I do support the opening of skate parks, but cities need to build more of them, need to situate them closer to where skateboarders live, and need to make them relatively wholesome environments. They should also be designed by skateboarders so that they are skater-friendly and safe to ride. Instead of being treated as "half criminals," skaters should be accepted as urban citizens and admired as athletes; we are a clean population, and we are executing a challenging and graceful sport. As human beings grow, we go from crawling to walking; some of us grow from strollers to skateboards.

7 Moving Your Audience:
Ethos and *Pathos*

In Chapters 4, 5, and 6 we focused primarily on *logos*—the logical structure of reasons and evidence in an argument. In this chapter, we turn our attention to the other two points on the rhetorical triangle introduced in Chapter 4 (p. 66)—*ethos* and *pathos*—through which the writer hopes to win the reader's trust and engage the reader's sympathies, emotions, and imagination. We hope to show you how knowledge of all three classical appeals can increase the persuasiveness of your arguments.

Ethos and *Pathos* as Persuasive Appeals: An Overview

To see how *logos, ethos,* and *pathos* work together to create an impact on the reader, consider the different impacts of the following arguments:

1. People should adopt a vegetarian diet because only through vegetarianism can we prevent the cruelty to animals that results from factory farming.

2. I hope you enjoyed your fried chicken this evening. You know, of course, how much that chicken suffered just so you could have a tender and juicy meal. Commercial growers cram the chickens so tightly together into cages that their beaks must be cut off to keep them from pecking each other's eyes out. The only way to end the torture is to adopt a vegetarian diet.

3. People who eat meat are no better than sadists who torture other sentient creatures to enhance their own pleasure. Unless you enjoy sadistic tyranny over others, you have only one choice: Become a vegetarian.

4. People committed to justice might consider the extent to which our love of eating meat requires the agony of animals. A visit to a modern chicken factory—where chickens live their entire lives in tiny darkened coops without room to spread their wings—might raise doubts about our right to inflict such suffering

on sentient creatures. Indeed, such a visit might persuade us that vegetarianism is a more just alternative.

Each argument has roughly the same logical core:

CLAIM: People should adopt a vegetarian diet.

STATED REASON: because only vegetarianism will end the suffering of animals subjected to factory farming

GROUNDS: the evidence of suffering in commercial chicken farms, where chickens are crammed together and lash out at each other; evidence that only widespread adoption of vegetarianism will end factory farming

WARRANT: If we have an alternative to making animals suffer, we should adopt it.

But the impact of each argument varies. The difference between Arguments 1 and 2, most of our students report, is the greater emotional power of 2. Whereas Argument 1 refers only to the abstraction "cruelty to animals," Argument 2 paints a vivid picture of chickens with their beaks cut off to prevent their pecking each other blind. Argument 2 makes a stronger appeal to *pathos* (not necessarily a stronger argument), stirring feelings by appealing simultaneously to the heart and to the head.

The difference between Arguments 1 and 3 concerns both *ethos* and *pathos*. Argument 3 appeals to the emotions through highly charged words like *torture*, *sadists*, and *tyranny*. But Argument 3 also draws attention to its writer, and most of our students report not liking that writer very much. His stance is self-righteous and insulting. In contrast, Argument 4's author establishes a more positive *ethos*. He establishes rapport with members of his audience by assuming they are committed to justice and by qualifying his argument with conditional terms such as *might* and *perhaps*. He also invites sympathy for his problem—an appeal to *pathos*—by offering a specific description of chickens crammed into tiny coops.

Which of these arguments is best? They all have appropriate uses. Arguments 1 and 4 seem aimed at receptive audiences reasonably open to exploration of the issue. Arguments 2 and 3 seem designed to shock complacent audiences or to rally a group of True Believers. Even Argument 3, which is too abusive to be effective in most instances, might work as a rallying speech at a convention of animal liberation activists.

Our point thus far is that *logos*, *ethos*, and *pathos* are different aspects of the same whole, different lenses for intensifying or softening the light beam you project onto the screen. Every choice you make as a writer affects in some way each of the three appeals. The rest of this chapter examines these choices in more detail.

How to Create an Effective *Ethos:* The Appeal to Credibility

The ancient Greek and Roman rhetoricians recognized that an argument will be more persuasive if the audience trusts the speaker. Aristotle argued that such trust resides within the speech itself, not in the prior reputation of the speaker. In the speaker's manner and delivery; in tone, word choice, and arrangement of reasons; and in the sympathy with which the speaker treats alternative views, he or she creates a trustworthy persona. Aristotle called the impact of the speaker's credibility the appeal from *ethos.* How does a writer create credibility? We will suggest three ways.

Be Knowledgeable About Your Issue

The first way to gain credibility is to *be* credible—that is, to argue from a strong base of knowledge, to have at hand the examples, personal experiences, statistics, and other empirical data needed to make a sound case. If you have done your homework, you will command the attention of most audiences.

Be Fair

Besides being knowledgeable about your issue, you need to demonstrate fairness and courtesy to alternative views. Because true argument can occur only where persons may reasonably disagree with one another, your *ethos* will be strengthened if you demonstrate that you understand and empathize with other points of view. There are times, of course, when you may appropriately scorn an opposing view. But these times are rare, and they mostly occur when you address audiences predisposed to your view. Demonstrating empathy to alternative views is generally the best strategy.

Build a Bridge to Your Audience

A third means of establishing credibility—building a bridge to your audience—has been treated at length in our earlier discussion of audience-based reasons. By grounding your argument in shared values and assumptions, you demonstrate your goodwill and enhance your image as a trustworthy person respectful of your audience's views. We mention audience-based reasons here to show how this aspect of *logos*—finding the reasons that are most rooted in the audience's values—also affects your *ethos* as a person respectful of your readers' views.

How to Create *Pathos:* The Appeal to Beliefs and Emotions

Although commonly defined as an "appeal to the emotions," *pathos* evokes effects that are subtler and more complex than the word *emotions* suggests. Because our understanding of something is a matter of feeling as well as perceiving, *pathos* can evoke nonlogical, but not necessarily nonrational, ways of knowing. When used effectively, pathetic appeals reveal the fullest human meaning of an issue, helping us walk in the writer's shoes. That is why arguments are often improved through the use of sensory details that allow us to see the reality of a problem or through stories that make specific cases and instances come alive. *Pathos* touches the heart and mind simultaneously.

Although it is difficult to classify all the ways that writers can create appeals from *pathos,* we will focus on five strategies: concrete language; specific examples and illustrations; narratives; word connotations, metaphors, and analogies; and visual images.

Use Concrete Language

Concrete language can increase the liveliness, interest level, and personality of one's prose and typically heightens *pathos* in an argument. Consider the differences between the first and second drafts of the following student argument:

> *First draft:* People who prefer driving a car to taking a bus think that taking the bus will increase the stress of the daily commute. Just the opposite is true. Not being able to find a parking spot when in a hurry to work or school can cause a person stress. Taking the bus gives a person time to read or sleep, etc. It could be used as a mental break.
>
> *Second draft:* Taking the bus can be more relaxing than driving a car. Having someone else behind the wheel gives people time to chat with friends or cram for a test. They can balance their checkbooks, do homework, doze off, read the daily newspaper, or get lost in a novel rather than foaming at the mouth looking for a parking space.

In the second draft, specific details enliven the prose by creating images that trigger positive feelings. Who wouldn't want some free time to doze off or to get lost in a novel?

Use Specific Examples and Illustrations

Specific examples and illustrations serve two purposes in an argument: They provide evidence that supports your reasons; simultaneously, they give your argument presence and emotional resonance. Note the flatness of the following draft arguing for the value of multicultural studies in a university core curriculum:

> *Early draft:* Another advantage of a multicultural education is that it will help us see our own culture in a broader perspective. If all we know is our own heritage, we might not be inclined to see anything bad about this heritage because we won't know anything else. But if we study other heritages, we can see the costs and benefits of our own heritage.

Now note the increase in "presence" when the writer adds a specific example.

Revised draft: Another advantage of multicultural education is that it raises questions about traditional Western values. For example, owning private property (such as buying your own home) is part of the American dream and is a basic right guaranteed in our Constitution. However, in studying the beliefs of American Indians, students are confronted with a very different view of private property. When the U.S. government sought to buy land in the Pacific Northwest from Chief Sealth, he is alleged to have replied:

> The president in Washington sends words that he wishes to buy our land. But how can you buy or sell the sky? The land? The idea is strange to us. If we do not own the freshness of the air and the sparkle of the water, how can you buy them? . . . We are part of the earth and it is part of us. . . . This we know: The earth does not belong to man, man belongs to the earth.

Our class was shocked by the contrast between traditional Western views of property and Chief Sealth's views. One of our best class discussions was initiated by this quotation from Chief Sealth. Had we not been exposed to a view from another culture, we would have never been led to question the "rightness" of Western values.

The writer begins his revision by evoking a traditional Western view of private property, which he then questions by shifting to Chief Sealth's vision of land as open, endless, and unobtainable as the sky. Through the use of a specific example, the writer brings to life his previously abstract point about the benefit of multicultural education.

Use Narratives

A particularly powerful way to evoke *pathos* is to tell a story that either leads into your claim or embodies it implicitly and that appeals to your readers' feelings and imagination. Brief narratives—whether real or hypothetical—are particularly effective as opening attention grabbers for an argument. To illustrate how an introductory narrative (either a story or a brief scene) can create pathetic appeals, consider the following first paragraph to an argument opposing jet skis:

> I dove off the dock into the lake, and as I approached the surface I could see the sun shining through the water. As my head popped out, I located my cousin a few feet away in a rowboat waiting to escort me as I, a twelve-year-old girl, attempted to swim across the mile-wide, pristine lake and back to our dock. I made it, and that glorious summer day is one of my most precious memories. Today, however, no one would dare attempt that swim. Jet skis have taken over this small lake where I spent many summers with my grandparents. Dozens of whining jet skis crisscross the lake, ruining it for swimming, fishing, canoeing, rowboating, and even waterskiing. More stringent state laws are needed to control jetskiing because it interferes with other uses of lakes and is currently very dangerous.

This narrative makes a case for a particular point of view toward jet skis by winning our identification with the writer's experience. She invites us to relive that experience with her while she also taps into our own treasured memories of summer experiences that have been destroyed by change.

Opening narratives to evoke *pathos* can be powerfully effective, but they are also risky. If they are too private, too self-indulgent, too sentimental, or even too dramatic and forceful, they can backfire on you. If you have doubts about an opening narrative, read it to a sample audience before using it in your final draft.

Choose Words, Metaphors, and Analogies with Appropriate Connotations

Another way of appealing to *pathos* is to select words, metaphors, or analogies with connotations that match your aim. We have already described this strategy in Chapter 6 in our discussion of the "framing" of evidence (pp. 101–103). By using words with particular connotations, a writer guides readers to see the issue through the writer's angle of vision. Thus if you want to create positive feelings about a recent city council decision, you can call it "bold and decisive"; if you want to create negative feelings, you can call it "haughty and autocratic." Similarly, writers can use favorable or unfavorable metaphors and analogies to evoke different imaginative or emotional responses. A tax bill might be viewed as a "potentially fatal poison pill" or as "unpleasant but necessary economic medicine." In each of these cases, the words create an emotional as well as intellectual response.

For Class Discussion

Outside class rewrite the introduction to one of your previous papers (or a current draft) to include more appeals to *pathos*. Use any of the strategies for giving your argument presence: concrete language, specific examples, narratives, metaphors, analogies, and connotative words. Bring both your original and your rewritten introductions to class. In pairs or in groups, discuss the comparative effectiveness of these introductions in trying to reach your intended audience.

Use Visual Arguments for Emotional Appeal

One of the most powerful ways to engage an audience emotionally is to use photos or other visual images. If you think of any news event that has captured wide media attention, you will probably recall memorable photos. Many of us are shaken to the core simply by recalling a still photograph of the hijacked airliner about to crash into the second tower of the World Trade Center, or subsequent photos of heroic firefighters, of posters from loved ones attached to the fence around St. Paul's Chapel, of mayor Rudy Giuliani wearing a NYFD hat (or a Yankees hat), and of Osama bin Laden.

Sometimes photographs create more than an emotional response to an event; they shape our perception of the event in subtle ways. Consider the image most frequently used to accompany stories of the U.S. women's soccer team's winning the world championship in 1999—not the great goal-keeping photo of African

American Briana Scurry blocking the last penalty kick, but of Brandi Chastain removing her jersey to reveal a black sports bra. Many analysts observed that the famous Brandi Chastain photograph shaped the public's emotional memory of that game by linking it with stereotypical views of women as sex objects rather than with women's athletic prowess. Sometimes we are only partially aware how the specific subject matter selected for a photo, its angle and cropping, the arrangement and posing of figures, and other details can encode an argument. Chapter 9 deals extensively with these aspects of visual arguments.

Because of the power of visual images, professional writers often try to use photographs or drawings to enhance their arguments. Visual images accompanying an argument can be particularly effective at grabbing viewers' attention, conveying the seriousness of an issue, and evoking strong emotions ranging from compassion to revulsion. While many written arguments do not lend themselves to visual illustrations, we suggest that when you construct arguments you consider the potential of visual support. Imagine that your argument were to appear in a newspaper or magazine where space would be provided for one or two visuals. What photographs or drawings might help persuade your audience toward your perspective?

When visual images work well, they are analogous to the verbal strategies of concrete language, specific illustrations, narratives, and connotative words. The challenge in using visuals is to find material that is straightforward enough not to require elaborate explanations, that is timely and relevant, and that clearly adds impact to a specific part of your argument. As an example, suppose you are writing an argument supporting fund-raising efforts to help third-world countries. To add a powerful appeal to *pathos*, you might consider incorporating into your argument the photograph shown in Color Plate D—a photograph of a Haitian woman walking on a rickety bridge over a vast garbage heap in a Haitian slum. This photograph, which appeared in the *New York Times* in summer 2002, creates an almost immediate emotional and imaginative response.

For Class Discussion

Working in small groups or as a whole class, share your responses to the following questions:

1. How would you describe the emotional/imaginative impact of Color Plate D (the photograph of Haitian poverty)?

2. Many appeals for helping third-world countries show pictures of big-bellied, starving children during a famine, often in Africa. How is your response to Color Plate D similar to or different from the commonly encountered pictures of starving children? How is Color Plate D's story about the ravages of poverty different from the stories of starving children?

3. Figures 7.1 and 7.2 show two photographs of John Lindh, the "American Taliban" captured in Afghanistan as part of the U.S. military response to

FIGURE 7.1 *Sheriff's office photograph of John Walker Lindh*

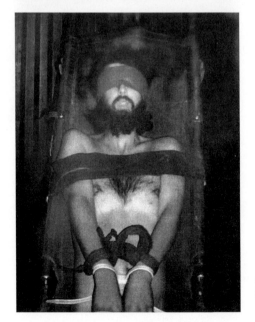

FIGURE 7.2 *Photograph of Lindh during incarceration in Afghanistan*

the September 11 terrorist attacks in 2001. Figure 7.1 shows the photograph of Lindh taken by the Alexandria County Sheriff's Department after Lindh was incarcerated in the United States, shaved, and placed in a prisoner's uniform. This photograph was widely reproduced in arguments calling for Lindh's prosecution as a traitor. In late March 2002, the U.S. government was forced to release a photograph of Lindh (Figure 7.2) taken while he was held captive in Afghanistan before being transferred to the United States. This photograph was immediately used by Lindh's defense attorneys and by groups seeking Lindh's release.

a. How would you describe the emotional and intellectual impact of Figure 7.2? As a visual argument, what claim does it make?

b. Why would prosecuting attorneys favor Figure 7.1 while defense attorneys favor Figure 7.2?

Conclusion

In this chapter, we have explored ways that writers can strengthen the persuasiveness of their arguments by creating appeals to *ethos* and *pathos*. Arguments are more persuasive if readers trust the credibility of the writer and if the argument appeals to readers' hearts and imaginations as well as to their intellects. Sometimes visual images may reinforce the argument by evoking strong emotional responses, thus enhancing *pathos*.

8 Accommodating Your Audience

Treating Differing Views

In the previous chapter we discussed the appeals of *ethos* and *pathos* as means of persuasion. In this chapter we focus on strategies for accommodating different kinds of audiences. Particularly, we discuss the problem of addressing opposing or alternative views—whether to omit them, refute them, concede to them, or incorporate them through compromise and conciliation. We show you how your choices about structure, content, and tone may differ depending on whether your audience is sympathetic, neutral, or strongly resistant to your views. The strategies explained in this chapter will increase your flexibility as an arguer and enhance your chance of persuading a wide variety of audiences.

One-Sided versus Multisided Arguments

Arguments are sometimes said to be one-sided or multisided. A *one-sided* argument presents only the writer's position on the issue without summarizing and responding to opposing viewpoints. A *multisided* argument presents the writer's position but also summarizes and responds to possible objections that an audience might raise. Which kind of argument is more persuasive to an audience?

According to some researchers, if people already agree with a writer's thesis, they usually find one-sided arguments more persuasive. A multisided argument appears wishy-washy, making the writer seem less decisive. But if people initially disagree with a writer's thesis, a multisided argument often seems more persuasive because it shows that the writer has listened to other views and thus seems more open-minded and fair. An especially interesting effect has been documented for neutral audiences. In the short run, one-sided arguments seem more persuasive to neutral audiences, but in the long run multisided arguments seem to have more staying power. Neutral audiences who have heard only one side of an issue tend to change their minds when they hear alternative arguments. By anticipating and in some cases refuting opposing views, the multisided argument diminishes the surprise and force of subsequent counterarguments and also exposes their weaknesses. In the rest of this chapter we will show you how your choice of writing one-sided or multisided arguments is a function of how you perceive your audience's resistance to your views.

Determining Your Audience's Resistance to Your Views

When you write an argument, you must always consider your audience's point of view. One way to imagine your relationship to members of your audience is to place them on a scale of resistance ranging from "strongly supportive" of your position to "strongly opposed" (see Figure 8.1). At the "accord" end of this scale are like-minded people who basically agree with your position on the issue. At the "resistance" end are those who strongly disagree with you, perhaps unconditionally, because their values, beliefs, or assumptions sharply differ from your own. In between lies a range of opinions. Close to your position will be those leaning in your direction but with less conviction than you. Close to the resistance position will be those basically opposed to your view but willing to listen to your argument and perhaps willing to acknowledge some of its strengths. In the middle are those undecided people who are still sorting out their feelings, seeking additional information, and weighing the strengths and weaknesses of alternative views.

Seldom, however, will you encounter an issue in which the range of disagreement follows a simple line from accord to resistance. Resistant views often fall into different categories so that no single line of argument appeals to all those whose views are different from your own. You have to identify not only your audience's resistance to your ideas but also the causes of that resistance.

Consider, for example, an issue that divided the state of Washington when the Seattle Mariners baseball team demanded a new stadium. A ballot initiative asked citizens to raise taxes to build a new retractable-roof stadium for the Mariners. Supporters of the initiative faced a complex array of resisting views (see Figure 8.2). Opponents of the initiative could be placed into four different categories. The first group simply had no interest in sports, cared nothing about baseball, and saw no benefit in building a huge sports facility in downtown Seattle. The second group loved baseball, perhaps followed the Mariners passionately, but was philosophically opposed to subsidizing rich players and owners with taxpayer money. Members of this group argued that the whole sports industry needed to be restructured so that stadiums were paid for out of

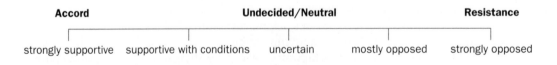

FIGURE 8.1   *Scale of resistance*

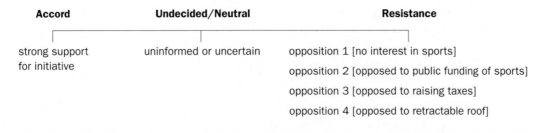

FIGURE 8.2   *Scale of resistance, baseball stadium issue*

sports revenues. The third group was opposed to tax hikes in general. This group's members focused on the principle of reducing the size of government and using tax revenues only for essential services. The fourth group supported baseball and supported the notion of public funding of a new stadium but opposed the kind of retractable-roof stadium specified in the initiative, preferring instead an old-fashioned, open-air stadium like Baltimore's Camden Yards or Cleveland's Jacobs Field.

Writers supporting the initiative found it impossible to address all these resisting audiences at once. A supporter of the initiative who wanted to aim an argument at sports haters could stress the spin-off benefits of a new ballpark (the new ballpark would attract tourist revenue, renovate the deteriorating Pioneer Square neighborhood, create jobs, make sports lovers more likely to vote for public subsidies of the arts, and so forth). But these arguments were irrelevant to those who wanted an open-air stadium, who opposed tax hikes categorically, or who objected to public subsidy of millionaires.

The Mariners example illustrates that it is not always easy to adapt your argument to your audience's position on the scale of resistance. Yet identifying your audience is important because writers need a stable vision of their audience before they can determine an effective content, structure, and tone for an argument. Sometimes as a writer you will simply need to "invent" your audience—that is, to assume that a certain category of readers will be your primary audience. Making this decision gives you a stable base from which to create audience-based reasons and to craft an appropriate tone and structure. The next sections show how you can adjust your arguing strategy depending on whether you imagine your audience as supportive, neutral, or hostile.

Appealing to a Supportive Audience: One-Sided Argument

Although arguing to a supportive audience might seem like preaching to the choir, such arguments are common. Usually, the arguer's goal is to convert belief into action—to inspire a party member to contribute to a senator's campaign or a bored office worker to sign up for a change-your-life weekend seminar.

Typically, appeals to a supportive audience are structured as one-sided arguments that either ignore opposing views or reduce them to "enemy" stereotypes. Filled with motivational language, these arguments list the benefits that will ensue from your donations to the cause and the horrors just around the corner if the other side wins. One of the authors of this text received a fund-raising letter from an environmental lobbying group declaring, "It's crunch time for the polluters and their pals on Capitol Hill." The "corporate polluters" and "anti-environment politicians," the letter continues, have "stepped up efforts to roll back our environmental protections—relying on large campaign contributions, slick PR firms and well-heeled lobbyists to get the job done before November's election." This letter makes the reader feel part of an in-group of good guys fighting big business "polluters." Nothing in the letter examines environmental issues from a business perspective or attempts to examine alternative views fairly. Since the intended audience already believes in the cause, nothing in the letter invites readers to consider the issues more complexly. Rather, the goal is to solidify support, increase the fervor of belief, and inspire action. Most appeal arguments make it easy to act, ending with an 800 phone number to call, a tear-out postcard to send in, or a congressperson's address to write to.

Appealing to a Neutral or Undecided Audience: Classical Argument

The in-group appeals that motivate an already supportive audience can repel a neutral or undecided audience. Because undecided audiences are like jurors weighing all sides of an issue, they distrust one-sided arguments that caricature other views. Generally the best strategy for appealing to undecided audiences is the classical argument described in Chapter 3 (pp. 55–57). What characterizes the classical argument is the writer's willingness to summarize opposing views fairly and to respond to them openly—either by trying to refute them or by conceding to their strengths and then shifting to a different field of values. Let's look at these strategies in more depth.

Summarizing Opposing Views

The first step toward responding to opposing views in a classical argument is to summarize them fairly. Follow the *principle of charity*, which obliges you to avoid loaded, biased, or "straw man" summaries that oversimplify or distort opposing arguments, making them easy to knock over.

Consider the difference between an unfair and a fair summary of Lisa Turner's "Playing with Our Food" (p. 21), which we examined in Chapter 2.

UNFAIR SUMMARY

In a biased article totally lacking in scientific understanding of biotechnology, natural foods huckster Lisa Turner parrots the health food industry's party line that genetically altered crops are Frankenstein's monsters run amuck. She ignorantly claims that consumption of biotech foods will lead to worldwide destruction, disease, and death, ignoring the wealth of scientific literature showing that genetically modified foods are safe. Her misinformed attacks are scare tactics aimed at selling consumers on overpriced "health food" products to be purchased at boutique organic food stores.

This summary distorts and oversimplifies Turner's argument while continually interjecting the writer's own views rather than fairly summarizing Turner's views. It uses loaded phrases ("huckster," "parrots the health food industry's party line," "ignorantly," "scare tactics") and creates an *ad hominem* attack (see Appendix One for a definition of this reasoning fallacy) by implying that Turner is motivated by health food industry profits rather than genuine concern. The writer thus sets up a straw man that is easier to knock over than is Turner's original argument.

In contrast, consider the following more fair summary, which follows the principle of charity and tries to represent Turner's views as justly and accurately as possible. (For a longer summary of Turner's article, see Chapter 2, p. 26.)

FAIR SUMMARY

In an article appearing in a nutrition magazine, health food advocate Lisa Turner warns readers that much of our food today is genetically modified using gene-level techniques that differ completely from ordinary crossbreeding. She argues that the potential, unforeseen, harmful consequences of genetic engineering offset the possible benefits of increasing the food supply, reducing the use of pesticides, and boosting the nutritional value of foods. Turner asserts that genetic engineering is imprecise, untested, unpredictable, irreversible, and also uncontrollable due to animals, insects, and winds.

Refuting Opposing Views

Once you have summarized an opposing view, you can either refute it or concede to its strengths. In refuting an opposing view, you attempt to convince readers that its argument is logically flawed, inadequately supported, or based on erroneous assumptions or wrong values. In Toulmin's terms, you can refute (1) the writer's stated reason and grounds, (2) the writer's warrant and backing, or (3) both.

For example, suppose you want to refute the following argument: "We shouldn't elect Joe as chairperson because he is too bossy." Displayed in Toulmin terms, the argument looks like this:

CLAIM: We shouldn't elect Joe as chairperson.

STATED REASON: because he is too bossy

GROUNDS: evidence that Joe is bossy

WARRANT: Bossy people make bad chairpersons.

One way to refute this argument is to rebut the stated reason and grounds:

> I disagree with you that Joe is bossy. In fact, Joe is very unbossy. He's a good listener who is willing to compromise, and he involves others in decisions. The example you cite for his being bossy wasn't typical. It was a one-time circumstance that doesn't represent his normal behavior. [The writer could then provide examples of Joe's cooperative nature.]

Or you could concede that Joe is bossy but rebut the argument's warrant that bossiness is a bad trait:

> I agree that Joe is bossy, but in this circumstance bossiness is just the trait we need. This committee hasn't gotten anything done for six months, and time is running out. We need a decisive person who can come in, get the committee organized, assign tasks, and get the job done.

Let's now illustrate these strategies in a more complex situation. For an example, we'll look at the issue of whether recycling is an effective strategy for saving the environment. A controversial subissue of recycling is whether the United States is running out of space for sanitary landfills. Here is how environmental writers George C. Lodge and Jeffrey F. Rayport argue that there are no places left to dump our garbage:

> Because the United States is running out of landfill space, Americans will simply not be able to put the 180 million tons of solid waste they generate each year into landfills, where 70 percent of it now goes. Since 1979, the United States has exhausted more than two-thirds of its landfills; projections indicate that another one-fifth will close over the next five years. Between 1983 and 1987, for example, New York closed 200 of its 500 landfills; this year Connecticut will exhaust its landfill capacity. If the problem seemed abstract to Americans, it became odiously real in the summer of 1989 as most of the nation watched the notorious garbage barge from Islip, New York, wander 6,000 miles, searching for a place to dump its rancid 3,100-ton load.

This passage tries to persuade us that the United States is running out of landfill space. Now watch how writer John Tierney attempts to refute this argument in an influential 1996 *New York Times Magazine* article entitled "Recycling Is Garbage":

> [Proponents of recycling believe that] our garbage will bury us. The *Mobro's** saga was presented as a grim harbinger of future landfill scarcity, but it actually represented a short-lived scare caused by new environmental regulations. As old municipal dumps were forced to close in the 1980's, towns had to send their garbage elsewhere and pay higher prices for scarce landfill space. But the higher prices predictably encouraged companies to open huge new landfills, in some regions creating a glut that set off

---

*Mobro is the name of the "notorious garbage barge" from Islip, New York, referred to at the end of the previous quotation.

price-cutting wars. Over the past few years, landfills in the South and Middle West have been vying for garbage from the New York area, and it has become cheaper to ship garbage there than to bury it locally.

America has a good deal more landfill space available than it did 10 years ago. . . . A. Clark Wiseman, an economist at Gonzaga University in Spokane, Wash., has calculated that if Americans keep generating garbage at current rates for 1,000 years, and if all their garbage is put in a landfill 100 yards deep, by the year 3000 this national garbage heap will fill a square piece of land 35 miles on each side.

This doesn't seem a huge imposition in a country the size of America. The garbage would occupy only 5 percent of the area needed for the national array of solar panels proposed by environmentalists. The millennial landfill would fit on one-tenth of 1 percent of the range land now available for grazing in the continental United States.

In this case, Tierney uses counterevidence to rebut the reason and grounds of the original enthymeme: "Recycling is needed because the United States is running out of landfill space." Tierney attacks this argument by disagreeing with the stated reason that the United States is running out of landfill space.

But writers are also likely to question the underlying assumptions (warrants) of an opposing view. For an example, consider another recycling controversy: From an economic perspective, is recycling cost-effective? In criticizing recycling, Tierney argues that recycling wastes money; he provides evidence that "every time a sanitation department crew picks up a load of bottles and cans from the curb, New York City loses money." The warrant of this argument is that "we should dispose of garbage in the most cost-effective way."

In rebutting Tierney's argument, proponents of recycling typically accepted Tierney's figures on recycling costs in New York City (that is, they agreed that in New York City recycling was more expensive than burying garbage). But in various ways they attacked his warrant. Typically, proponents of recycling said that even if the costs of recycling were higher than burying wastes in a landfill, recycling still benefited the environment by reducing the amount of virgin materials taken from nature. This argument says, in effect, that saving virgin resources takes precedence over economic costs.

These examples show how a refutation can focus on either the stated reasons and grounds of an argument or on the warrants and backing.

For Class Discussion

Imagine how each of the following arguments might be fleshed out with grounds and backing. Then attempt to refute each argument by suggesting ways to rebut the reason and grounds, the warrant and backing, or both.

1. Writing courses should be pass/fail because the pass/fail system would encourage more creativity.
2. The government should make cigarettes illegal because cigarettes cause cancer and heart disease.

3. Majoring in engineering is better than majoring in music because engineers make more money than musicians.

4. People should not eat meat because doing so causes needless pain and suffering to animals.

5. The endangered species law is too stringent because it seriously hampers the economy.

Strategies for Rebutting Evidence

Whether you are rebutting an argument's reasons and grounds or its warrant and backing, you will frequently need to question a writer's use of evidence. Here are some strategies that you can use.

Deny the Accuracy of the Data   What one writer considers a fact another may consider a case of wrong information. If you have reason to doubt a writer's facts, then call them into question.

Cite Counterexamples or Countertestimony   One of the most effective ways to counter an argument based on examples is to cite a counterexample. The effect of counterexamples is to deny the conclusiveness of the original data. Similarly, citing an authority whose testimony counters other expert testimony is a good way to begin refuting an argument based on testimony.

Cast Doubt on the Representativeness or Sufficiency of Examples   Examples are powerful only if the audience feels them to be representative and sufficient. Many environmentalists complained that John Tierney's attack on recycling was based too largely on data from New York City and that it didn't accurately take into account the more positive experiences of other cities and states. When data from outside New York City were examined, the cost-effectiveness and positive environmental impact of recycling seemed more apparent.

Cast Doubt on the Relevance or Recency of Examples, Statistics, or Testimony
The best evidence is up-to-date. In a rapidly changing universe, data that are even a few years out-of-date are often ineffective. For example, as the demand for recycled goods increases, the cost of recycling will be reduced. Out-of-date statistics will skew any argument about the cost of recycling. Another problem with data is their occasional lack of relevance. For example, in arguing that an adequate ozone layer is necessary for preventing skin cancer, it is not relevant to cite statistics on the alarming rise of lung cancer.

Call into Question the Credibility of an Authority   If an opposing argument is based on testimony, you can undermine its persuasiveness if you show that a person being cited lacks up-to-date or relevant expertise in the field. (This procedure is different from the *ad hominem* fallacy discussed in Appendix One because it attacks not the personal character of the authority but the authority's expertise on a specific matter.)

Question the Accuracy or Context of Quotations   Evidence based on testimony is frequently distorted by being either misquoted or taken out of context. Often scientists will qualify their findings heavily, but these qualifications will be omitted by the popular media. You can thus attack the use of a quotation by putting it in its original context or by restoring the qualifications accompanying the quotation in its original source.

Question the Way Statistical Data Were Produced or Interpreted   Chapter 9 provides fuller treatment of how to question statistics. In general, you can rebut statistical evidence by calling into account how the data were gathered, treated mathematically, or interpreted. It can make a big difference, for example, whether you cite raw numbers or percentages or whether you choose large or small increments for the axes of graphs.

Conceding to Opposing Views

In writing a classical argument, a writer must sometimes concede to an opposing argument rather than refute it. Sometimes you encounter portions of an argument that you simply can't refute. For example, suppose you support the legalization of hard drugs such as cocaine and heroin. Adversaries argue that legalizing hard drugs will increase the number of drug users and addicts. You might dispute the size of their numbers, but you reluctantly agree that they are right. Your strategy in this case is not to refute the opposing argument but to concede to it by admitting that legalization of hard drugs will promote heroin and cocaine addiction. Having made that concession, your task is then to show that the benefits of drug legalization still outweigh the costs you have just conceded.

As this example shows, the strategy of a concession argument is to switch from the field of values employed by the writer you disagree with to a different field of values more favorable to your position. You don't try to refute the writer's stated reason and grounds (by arguing that legalization will *not* lead to increased drug usage and addiction) or his warrant (by arguing that increased drug use and addiction is not a problem). Rather, you shift the argument to a new field of values by introducing a new warrant, one that you think your audience can share (that the benefits of legalization—eliminating the black market and ending the crime and violence associated with procurement of drugs—outweigh the costs of increased addiction). To the extent that opponents of legalization share your desire to stop drug-related crime, shifting to this new field of values is a good strategy. Although it may seem that you weaken your own position by conceding to an opposing argument, you may actually strengthen it by increasing your credibility and gaining your audience's goodwill. Moreover, conceding to one part of an opposing argument doesn't mean that you won't refute other parts of that argument.

Appealing to a Resistant Audience: Delayed-Thesis or Rogerian Argument

Classical argument is effective for neutral or undecided audiences, but it is often less effective for audiences strongly opposed to the writer's position. Because resisting audiences often hold values, assumptions, or beliefs widely different from the writer's, they are unswayed by classical argument, which attacks their worldview too directly. On many values-laden issues such as abortion, gun control, gay rights, and welfare reform the distance between a writer and a resisting audience can be so great that dialogue hardly seems possible.

Because of these wide differences in basic beliefs and values, a writer's goal is seldom to convert resistant readers to the writer's position. The best that the writer can hope for is to reduce somewhat the level of resistance, perhaps by opening a channel of conversation, increasing the reader's willingness to listen, and preparing the way for future dialogue. If you can get a resistant audience to say, "Well, I still don't agree with you, but I now understand you better and respect your views more," you will have been highly successful.

Delayed-Thesis Argument

In many cases you can reach a resistant audience by using a *delayed-thesis* structure in which you wait until the end of your argument to reveal your thesis. Classical argument asks you to state your thesis in the introduction, support it with reasons and evidence, and then summarize and refute opposing views. Rhetorically, however, it is not always advantageous to tell your readers where you stand at the start of your argument or to separate yourself so definitively from alternative views. For resistant audiences, it may be better to keep the issue open, delaying the revelation of your own position until the end of the essay.

To illustrate the different effects of classical versus delayed-thesis arguments, we invite you to read a delayed-thesis argument by nationally syndicated columnist Ellen Goodman. The article appeared shortly after the nation was shocked by a brutal gang rape in New Bedford, Massachusetts, in which a woman was raped on a pool table by patrons of a local bar.*

Minneapolis Pornography Ordinance
Ellen Goodman

1   Just a couple of months before the pool-table gang rape in New Bedford, Mass., *Hustler* magazine printed a photo feature that reads like a blueprint for the actual

---

*The rape occurred in 1985 and was later made the subject of an Academy Award–winning movie, *The Accused*, starring Jodie Foster.

crime. There were just two differences between *Hustler* and real life. In *Hustler,* the woman enjoyed it. In real life, the woman charged rape.

There is no evidence that the four men charged with this crime had actually 2 read the magazine. Nor is there evidence that the spectators who yelled encouragement for two hours had held previous ringside seats at pornographic events. But there is a growing sense that the violent pornography being peddled in this country helps to create an atmosphere in which such events occur.

As recently as last month, a study done by two University of Wisconsin re- 3 searchers suggested that even "normal" men, prescreened college students, were changed by their exposure to violent pornography. After just ten hours of viewing, reported researcher Edward Donnerstein, "the men were less likely to convict in a rape trial, less likely to see injury to a victim, more likely to see the victim as responsible." Pornography may not cause rape directly, he said, "but it maintains a lot of very callous attitudes. It justifies aggression. It even says you are doing a favor to the victim."

If we can prove that pornography is harmful, then shouldn't the victims have 4 legal rights? This, in any case, is the theory behind a city ordinance that recently passed the Minneapolis City Council. Vetoed by the mayor last week, it is likely to be back before the Council for an overriding vote, likely to appear in other cities, other towns. What is unique about the Minneapolis approach is that for the first time it attacks pornography, not because of nudity or sexual explicitness, but because it degrades and harms women. It opposes pornography on the basis of sex discrimination.

University of Minnesota Law Professor Catherine MacKinnon, who co-authored 5 the ordinance with feminist writer Andrea Dworkin, says that they chose this tactic because they believe that pornography is central to "creating and maintaining the inequality of the sexes. . . . Just being a woman means you are injured by pornography."

They defined pornography carefully as, "the sexually explicit subordination of 6 women, graphically depicted, whether in pictures or in words." To fit their legal definition it must also include one of nine conditions that show this subordination, like presenting women who "experience sexual pleasure in being raped or . . . mutilated. . . ." Under this law, it would be possible for a pool-table rape victim to sue *Hustler.* It would be possible for a woman to sue if she were forced to act in a pornographic movie. Indeed, since the law describes pornography as oppressive to all women, it would be possible for any woman to sue those who traffic in the stuff for violating her civil rights.

In many ways, the Minneapolis ordinance is an appealing attack on an ap- 7 palling problem. The authors have tried to resolve a long and bubbling conflict among those who have both a deep aversion to pornography and a deep loyalty to the value of free speech. "To date," says Professor MacKinnon, "people have identified the pornographer's freedom with everybody's freedom. But we're saying that the freedom of the pornographer is the subordination of women. It means one has to take a side."

But the sides are not quite as clear as Professor MacKinnon describes them. 8 Nor is the ordinance.

9   Even if we accept the argument that pornography is harmful to women—and I do—then we must also recognize that anti-Semitic literature is harmful to Jews and racist literature is harmful to blacks. For that matter, Marxist literature may be harmful to government policy. It isn't just women versus pornographers. If women win the right to sue publishers and producers, then so could Jews, blacks, and a long list of people who may be able to prove they have been harmed by books, movies, speeches or even records. The Manson murders, you may recall, were reportedly inspired by the Beatles.

10   We might prefer a library or book store or lecture hall without *Mein Kampf* or the Grand Whoever of the Ku Klux Klan. But a growing list of harmful expressions would inevitably strangle freedom of speech.

11   This ordinance was carefully written to avoid problems of banning and prior restraint, but the right of any woman to claim damages from pornography is just too broad. It seems destined to lead to censorship.

12   What the Minneapolis City Council has before it is a very attractive theory. What MacKinnon and Dworkin have written is a very persuasive and useful definition of pornography. But they haven't yet resolved the conflict between the harm of pornography and the value of free speech. In its present form, this is still a shaky piece of law.

Consider now how this argument's rhetorical effect would be different if Ellen Goodman had revealed her thesis in the introduction, using the classical argument form. Here is how this introduction might have looked:

GOODMAN'S INTRODUCTION REWRITTEN IN CLASSICAL FORM

Just a couple of months before the pool-table gang rape in New Bedford, Mass., *Hustler* magazine printed a photo feature that reads like a blueprint for the actual crime. There were just two differences between *Hustler* and real life. In *Hustler*, the woman enjoyed it. In real life, the woman charged rape. Of course, there is no evidence that the four men charged with this crime had actually read the magazine. Nor is there evidence that the spectators who yelled encouragement for two hours had held previous ringside seats at pornographic events.

But there is a growing sense that the violent pornography being peddled in this country helps to create an atmosphere in which such events occur. One city is taking a unique approach to attack this problem. An ordinance recently passed by the Minneapolis City Council outlaws pornography not because it contains nudity or sexually explicit acts, but because it degrades and harms women. Unfortunately, despite the proponents' good intentions, the Minneapolis ordinance is a bad law because it has potentially dangerous consequences.

Even though Goodman's position can be grasped more quickly in this classical form, our students generally find the original delayed-thesis version more effective. Why is this? Most people point to the greater sense of complexity and surprise in the delayed-thesis version, a sense that comes largely from the delayed discovery of the writer's position. The classical version immediately labels the ordinance a "bad law," but the original version withholds judgment, inviting the reader to examine the law more sympathetically and to identify with the position of those who drafted it. Rather than distancing herself from those who see pornography as a violation of women's rights, Goodman shares with her readers her own struggles to think through these issues, thereby persuading us of her genuine sympathy for the ordinance and for its feminist proponents. In the end, her delayed thesis renders her final rejection of the ordinance not only more surprising but more convincing.

Clearly, then, a writer's decision about when to reveal her thesis is critical. Revealing the thesis early makes the writer seem more hard-nosed, more sure of her position, more confident about how to divide the ground into friendly and hostile camps, more in control. Delaying the thesis, in contrast, complicates the issues, increases reader sympathy for more than one view, and heightens interest in the tension among alternative views and in the writer's struggle for clarity.

Rogerian Argument

An even more powerful strategy for addressing resistant audiences is a conciliatory strategy often called *Rogerian argument,* named after psychologist Carl Rogers, who used this strategy to help people resolve differences.* Rogerian argument emphasizes "empathic listening," which Rogers defined as the ability to see an issue sympathetically from another person's perspective. He trained people to withhold judgment of another person's ideas until after they listened attentively to the other person, understood that person's reasoning, appreciated that person's values, respected that person's humanity—in short, walked in that person's shoes. Before disagreeing with another person, Rogers told his clients, you must be able to summarize that person's argument so accurately that he or she will say, "Yes, you understand my position."

What Carl Rogers understood is that traditional methods of argumentation are threatening. When you try to persuade people to change their minds on an issue, Rogers claimed, you are actually demanding a change in their worldview—to get other people, in a sense, to quit being their kinds of persons and start being your kind of person. Research psychologists have shown that individuals are often not swayed by a logical argument if it somehow threatens their own view of the world. Carl Rogers was therefore interested in finding ways to make arguments less threatening. In Rogerian argument the writer typically waits until the end of the essay to present his position, and that position is often a compromise between the writer's original views and those of the resisting audience. Because Rogerian argument stresses the psychological as well as logical dimensions of argument, and because it emphasizes reducing threat and building bridges rather than winning an argument, it is particularly effective for dealing with emotionally laden issues.

---

*See Carl Rogers's essay "Communication: Its Blocking and Its Facilitation" in his book *On Becoming a Person* (Boston: Houghton, 1961), 329–37. For a fuller discussion of Rogerian argument, see Richard Young, Alton Becker, and Kenneth Pike, *Rhetoric: Discovery and Change* (New York: Harcourt, 1972).

Under Rogerian strategy, the writer reduces the sense of threat in her argument by showing that *both writer and resistant audience share many basic values.* Instead of attacking the audience as wrongheaded, the Rogerian writer respects her audience's intelligence and humanity and demonstrates an understanding of the audience's position before presenting her own position. Finally, the Rogerian writer never asks the audience to capitulate entirely to the writer's side—just to shift somewhat toward the writer's views. By acknowledging that she has already shifted toward the audience's views, the writer makes it easier for the audience to accept compromise. All of this negotiation ideally leads to a compromise between—or better, a synthesis of—the opposing positions.

The key to successful Rogerian argument, besides the art of listening, is the ability to point out areas of agreement between the writer's and reader's positions. For example, if you support a woman's right to choose abortion and you are arguing with someone completely opposed to abortion, you're unlikely to convert your reader but you might reduce the level of resistance. You begin this process by summarizing your reader's position sympathetically, stressing your shared values. You might say, for example, that you also value babies; that you also are appalled by people who treat abortion as a form of birth control; that you also worry that the easy acceptance of abortion diminishes the value society places on human life; and that you also agree that accepting abortion lightly can lead to lack of sexual responsibility. Building bridges like these between you and your readers makes it more likely that they will listen to you when you present your own position.

In its emphasis on establishing common ground, Rogerian argument has much in common with recent feminist theories of argument. Many feminists criticize classical argument as rooted in a male value system and tainted by metaphors of war and combat. Thus, classical arguments, with their emphasis on assertion and refutation, are typically praised for being "powerful," "forceful," or "disarming." The writer "defends" his position and "attacks" his "opponent's" position using facts and data as "ammunition" and reasons as "big guns" to "blow away" his opponent's claim. According to some feminists, viewing argument as war can lead to inauthenticity, posturing, and game playing. The traditional pro-con debate—defined in one desk dictionary as "a formal contest of argumentation in which two opposing teams defend and attack a given proposition"—treats argument as verbal jousting, more concerned to determine a winner than to clarify an issue.

One of our woman students, who excelled as a debater in high school and received straight A's in argument classes, recently explained in an essay her growing alienation from male rhetoric: "Although women students are just as likely to excel in 'male' writing . . . we are less likely to feel as if we were saying something authentic and true." Later the student elaborated on her distrust of "persuasion":

What many writing teachers have told me is that "the most important writing/speaking you will ever do will be to persuade someone." My experience as a person who has great difficulty naming and expressing emotions is that the most important communication in my life is far more likely to be simply telling someone how I feel. To say

"I love you," or "I'm angry with you," will be far more valuable in most relationship contexts than to say "These are the three reasons why you shouldn't have done what you did. . . ."*

Writers who share this woman's distrust of classical argumentation often find Rogerian argument appealing because it stresses self-examination, clarification, and accommodation rather than refutation. Rogerian argument is more in tune with win-win negotiation than with win-lose debate.

To illustrate a conciliatory or Rogerian approach to an issue, we show you a letter to a friend written as a class assignment. The student writer, Rebekah Taylor, is a member of PETA (People for the Ethical Treatment of Animals) and an outspoken advocate for animal rights on her campus. Note how Rebekah "listens" empathically to her friend and proposes a compromise action.

A Letter to Jim
Rebekah Taylor (student)

Dear Jim,

I decided to write you a letter today because I miss our long talks. Now that I   1
have transferred colleges, we haven't had nearly enough heated discussions to satisfy either of us. I am writing now to again take up one of the issues we vehemently disagreed on in the past—meat-based diets.

First, I must express to you that I have listened to and understood your opposi-   2
tion to my argument in the past. For you, eating meat has been a normal, unquestioned part of life. Through observation of your parents, you came to understand and accept that humans eat animals just as humans drink water, sleep, and defecate. This view was reinforced at school. All of the children around you ate meat; your school did not offer—and probably had never heard of—any vegetarian options. The image of a "food pyramid" based on meat protein was burned into your mind. Also, having been raised in a conservative Christian household, you were taught that God intended for humans to have ultimate dominion over all creatures of the earth, sea, and sky. You were taught that God made us fleshly creatures who feed off other living organisms just as do bears, cats, and birds. For humans, eating meat is part of the cycle of nature.

I understand, then, that our life histories have created for us very different   3
views about eating meat. You were raised in a family and community that accepted meat-based diets as normal, healthy, and ethically justifiable. I was raised in a family that cared very deeply for animals and attended a church that frequently

---

*Our thanks to Catherine Brown for this paragraph from an unpublished paper written at Seattle University.

4 entertained a vegan as a guest speaker. The conditions in which we were raised allowed us to become the people we are today and to shape the beliefs that we hold.

4 Let me now briefly reiterate for you my own basic beliefs about eating animals. As I have shared with you, my personal health is important to me, and I, along with other vegetarians and vegans, believe that a vegetarian diet is much more healthy than a meat diet. But my primary motivation is my deep respect for animals. I have always felt an overpowering sense of compassion for animals and forceful sorrow and regret for the injuries that humans inflict upon them. I detest suffering, especially when it is forced upon creatures that cannot speak out against it. These deep feelings led me to become a vegetarian at the age of 5. While lying in bed one night, I looked up at the poster of a silky-white harbor seal that had always hung on my wall. As I looked at the face of that seal, I made a connection between that precious animal on my wall and the animals that had been killed for the food I ate every day. In the dim glow of my Strawberry Shortcake night-light, I promised those large, dark seal eyes that I would never eat animals again. Seventeen years have passed now and that promise still holds true. Every day I feel more dedicated to the cause of animal rights around the world.

5 I know very well that my personal convictions are not the same as yours. However, I believe that we might possibly agree on more aspects of this issue than we realize. Although we would not be considered by others as allies on the issue of eating meat, we do share a common enemy—factory farms. Although you eat animal products and I do not, we both share basic common values that are threatened by today's factory farms. We both want the food we eat to be healthy, we both care about people, and we both disapprove of the unnecessary suffering of animals.

6 Let me briefly relate to you the ways in which factory farms threaten our common values. Widespread global implementation of factory farming has made food more dangerous for humans to eat. At factory farms, pigs, cows, and chickens eat foods laden with pesticides, receive injections of dangerous hormones, and are raised in unsanitary, crowded, and stressful conditions. All of these elements of life at a factory farm combine to make many of the food products that humans eat extremely unhealthy. In fact, most instances of meat-borne illnesses in humans, such as e-coli, salmonella, and mad cow disease, come about because of the horrible conditions at factory farms.

7 Also, factory farms cause the needless suffering of animals. Though we might disagree on the morality of using animals for food at all, we do agree that such animals should not be made to suffer. Yet at factory farms, billions of animals across the world are born, live, and die in horribly cramped, dark, and foul-smelling barns. Most receive only about five hours of human contact in their entire lives, and those that receive more are often brutally abused. None of these animals know the feeling of fresh air, or of warm, blessed sunlight on their backs. Most do not move out of their tight, uncomfortable pens until the day that they are to be slaughtered. At these factory farms, animals are processed as if they were inanimate objects, with no regard for the fact that they do feel fear and pain.

8 I hope it is evident now that although we may disagree on whether or not humans should eat meat and other animal products, we do agree that the way these

products are derived at factory farms is unnecessarily unhealthy, potentially destructive to humans, and cruel to animals. I am optimistic that our shared dislike of factory farms will help us take a crucial first step towards recognizing and understanding each other's views. This common ground shows me that though we will always disagree about many things, we are not that different, you and I.

It is because of our shared values that I ask you to consider making an effort to buy meat from small, independent local farmers. I am told by friends that all supermarkets offer such meat options. This would be an easy and effective way to fight factory farms. I know that I could never convince you to stop eating meat, and I will never try to force my beliefs on you. As your friend, I am grateful simply to be able to write to you so candidly about my beliefs. I trust that regardless of what your ultimate reaction is to this letter, you will thoughtfully consider what I have written, as I will thoughtfully consider what you write in return.

Sincerely,

Rebekah

For Class Discussion

1. In this letter, what shared values between writer and reader does the writer stress?

2. Imagine this letter rewritten as a classical argument. How would it be different?

Conclusion

This chapter has shown you the difference between one-sided and multisided arguments and explained why multisided arguments are likely to be more persuasive to neutral or resisting audiences. A multisided argument generally includes a fair summary of differing views, followed by refutation, concession, or Rogerian synthesis. The strategies you use for treating resistant views depend on the audience you are trying to reach and your purpose. We explained how audiences can be placed on a scale of resistance ranging from "strongly supportive" to "strongly opposed." In addressing supportive audiences, writers typically compose one-sided arguments with strong motivational appeals to action. Neutral or undecided audiences generally respond most favorably to classical arguments that set out strong reasons in support of the writer's position and yet openly address alternative views, which are first summarized and then either rebutted or conceded to. When the audience is strongly resistant, a delayed-thesis or Rogerian strategy is most effective at reducing resistance and helping move the audience slightly toward the writer's views.

WRITING ASSIGNMENT
FOR CHAPTERS 7 AND 8

The assignment for Chapters 7 and 8 has two parts. Part One is an argumentive essay that you will write. Part Two is your own self-reflective analysis on how you chose to appeal to and accommodate your audience.

PART ONE: For this assignment, argue against a popular cultural practice or belief that you think is wrong, or argue for an action or belief that you think is right even though it will be highly unpopular. Your claim, in other words, must be controversial—going against the grain of popular actions, values, and beliefs—so that you can predict considerable resistance to your views. This essay invites you to stand up for something you believe in even though your view will be highly contested. Your goal is to persuade your audience toward your position.

In writing and revising your argument, draw on appropriate strategies from Chapters 7 and 8. From Chapter 7 consider strategies for increasing your appeals to *ethos* and *pathos*. From Chapter 8 consider strategies for appealing to audiences according to their level of resistance. Choose the most resistant audience that you think you can sway to your point of view. Whether you use a refutation strategy, a delayed-thesis strategy, a Rogerian strategy, or some combination of these approaches is up to you.

PART TWO: Attach to your argument a self-reflective letter to your instructor and classmates explaining and justifying the choices you made for appealing to your audience and accommodating their views. In your letter address questions such as the following:

1. At the most "resistant" end of the spectrum, why are people opposed to your claim? How does your claim challenge their views and perhaps threaten their own value system?

2. Whom did you picture as the audience you were trying to sway? Where on the spectrum from "accord" to "resistance" did you address your argument? Why?

3. What strategies did you use for appealing to that audience?

4. What choices did you make in trying to accommodate differing views?

5. What challenges did this assignment present for you? How successful do you think you were in meeting those challenges?

9 Conducting Visual Arguments

In today's visually oriented culture, arguments increasingly use photographs, drawings, graphics, and innovative page and text design for persuasive effect. As we shall see, visuals can enhance the *logos, pathos,* and *ethos* of an argument by supporting or clarifying an argument's logical core, moving audiences imaginatively and emotionally, or enhancing the writer's credibility and authority. They can also substantially enliven a writer's argument, keeping readers hooked and engaged. In this chapter, we ask you to explore with us the enormous rhetorical potential of visual elements in arguments, particularly the way that visual and verbal elements can collaborate to achieve persuasive effects.

Using visuals in arguments also poses challenges. Visuals can imply unstated ideas and powerfully shape the audience's thinking. For example, in July 2002, Fox News and MSNBC evoked angry responses from the White House when they used a split screen to televise President Bush's speech on the economy, expanding their stock market tickers to take up most of the screen and reducing the president to a small box. As Bush talked about improvement in the economy, the larger portion of the screen showed stock market numbers falling. White House representatives objected that the split screen and the emphasis on the size of the stock market tickers suggested to viewers that Bush's speech had a causal connection with the shifts in the stock market.

Also realizing the power of visuals, the Humane Society of the United States has warned local Humane Society chapters against the careless use in their newsletters of drawings and photos that can undermine the organization's goals. To foster appropriate attitudes toward pets, local chapter newsletters must show dogs and cats wearing collars and must show older animals as well as adorable puppies and kittens. These examples illustrate the suggestive power of visual elements and the challenge of planning exactly how visuals should function in your argument. Using visuals places on arguers an even greater burden to understand their audience, to think through the effect visuals will have on that audience, and to make sure that the verbal and visual parts of an argument work together.

With this background in mind, we turn now to explaining some basic components of visual design. We then examine several genres of visual argument such as posters and fliers, public affairs advocacy ads, political cartoons, and Web pages. The third section of the chapter explains how you can use visual elements in your own arguments and invites you to create your own poster or advocacy advertisement. In the final section, we explain how you can display numerical data graphically for rhetorical effect.

Understanding Design Elements in Visual Argument

To understand how visual images can produce an argument, you need to understand the design elements that work together to create a visual text.

The Components of Visual Design

There are four basic components of visual design: use of type, use of space and layout, use of color, and use of images. The most important considerations in using these design components are shown in Table 9.1.

As Table 9.1 suggests, in arguments that don't use images and graphics the writer's primary visual concern is document design. In planning how the document will look, the writer hopes to make the document easy to read (choosing plain, conventional typefaces), to meet the readers' expectations for format (double-spacing manuscripts, following expected genre conventions if the argument is to be desktop published), and to provide appropriate structural cues that highlight points and guide the reader through the argument (using headings, paragraph breaks, bulleted lists). But in moving from verbal-only arguments to visual arguments that use visual elements for direct persuasive effect—for example in producing a flier, poster, or one-page newspaper advertisement—the writer can make creative use of all the elements of visual design.

Because using images and graphics effectively is especially challenging, we devote the rest of this chapter to explaining how images and graphics can be incorporated into visual arguments. We treat the use of photographs and drawings in the next main section and the use of quantitative graphics in the final section.

Analysis of a Visual Argument Using Type and Spatial Elements

To illustrate the persuasive power of type and layout, we ask you to consider Figure 9.1, which shows an advocacy ad sponsored by a coalition of organizations aimed at fighting illegal drugs.

This ad, warning about the dangers of the drug Ecstasy, uses different sizes of type and layout to present its argument. The huge word "Ecstasy" first catches the reader's attention. The first few words at the top of the ad, exuding pleasure, lull the reader with the congruence between the pleasurable message and the playful type. Soon, however, the reader encounters a dissonance

TABLE 9.1   *Components of Visual Design*

Design Component	Key Variables	Key Principles
Use of type	• Font style ranging from conservative (Times New Roman, Courier) to playful and decorative (*Monotype Corsiva* and other specialty fonts) • Font size • Variables for emphasis (**boldface,** *italics,* <u>underlining</u>, ALL CAPS)	• Choose *display type* (sans serif—without the little extensions on letters—like Century Gothic and Ariel) for headings, titles, and slogans. • Choose *body type* (serif—with the little extensions on letters—like Times New Roman and Courier New) for long documents and main text. • Make type functional and appealing by using only two or three typestyles per document. • Use consistent patterns of type to indicate relationships among items. • Choose type to project a specific impression. To create a formal, businesslike impression, as in scholarly publications, use a structured combination of serif and sans serif type. To create an informal look, as in popular magazine publications and highly visual posters and fliers, use sans serif and specialty type.
Use of space and layout	• Page size and type of paper • Proportion of text to white space • Arrangement of text on page (space, margins, columns, size of paragraphs, spaces between paragraphs, justification of margins) • Use of highlighting elements such as bulleted lists, tables, sidebars, boxes • Use headings and other means of breaking text into visual units	• Use layout to make documents highly readable and to guide readers with structural clues (headings, paragraph breaks, and bulleted lists). • Focus on creating meaning and coherence with layout. • For academic arguments, use simple, functional layouts. For popular magazine arguments and visual arguments, vary the layout and make the page visually attractive. However, for visual arguments, avoid clutter and confusion by limiting the amount of text and the number of visual items on a page.
Use of color	• Variations in font color for effect • Use of color in images and graphics • Use of background tints and colored shading	• Use color to meet audience and genre expectations (minimal use of color in academic arguments and often lavish color in popular magazines). • For visual arguments, use color functionally (to indicate relationships) or decoratively (to create visual appeal). • For visual arguments, decide whether color will be used to make images look documentary-like (realistic), to create symbolic associations (for example, psychedelic colors and the 1960s), or to create a specific aesthetic effect (for example, pleasing, disturbing, or soothing).
Images and graphics	• Photographs • Drawings • Numeric graphics	• For visual arguments, consider how the image will work in the argument: to convey an idea, illustrate a point, evoke an emotional response. • For all arguments, consider how to establish the relationship between the image or graphic and the verbal text. (Images and graphics are described in detail later in this chapter.)

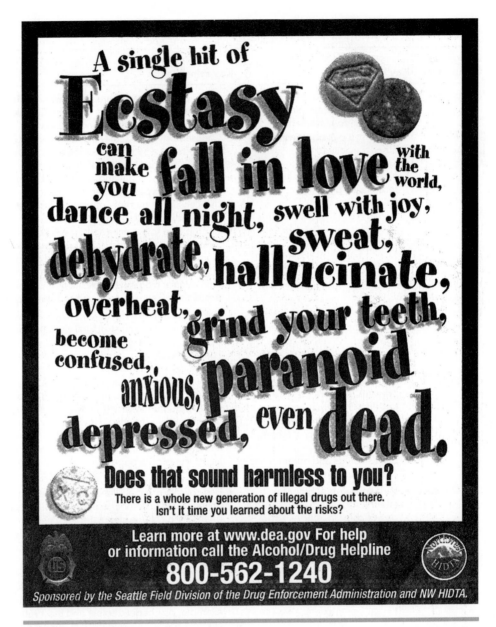

FIGURE 9.1   *Advocacy advertisement warning against Ecstasy*

between the playful type and the meaning of the words: "dehydrate," "halluci-
nate," "paranoid," and "dead" name unpleasant ideas. By the end of the ad,
readers realize they have been led through a downward progression of ideas
beginning with the youth culture's belief that Ecstasy creates wonderfully positive feelings and ending with the ad's thesis that Ecstasy leads to paranoia,

depression, and death. The playful informality of the font styles and the un-evenly scattered layout of the type convey the seductiveness and unpredictability of the drug. The ad concedes that the first effects are falling "in love with the world" but implies that what comes next is increasingly dark and dangerous. At the end of the ad, in the lines of type near the bottom, the message and typestyle are congruent again. The question "Does that sound harmless to you?" marks a shift in type design and layout. The designer composed this section of the ad in conventional fonts centered on the page in a rational, businesslike fashion. This type design signals a metaphoric move from the euphoria of Ecstasy to the or-dered structure of everyday reality, where the reader can now consider ratio-nally the drug's harm. The information at the bottom of the ad identifies the ad's sponsors and gives both a Web address and a telephone number to call for more information about Ecstasy and other illegal drugs.

The Compositional Features of Photographs and Drawings

Now that we have introduced you to the four major elements of visual design—type, layout, color, and images—we turn to an in-depth discussion of photo-graphic images and drawings. Used with great calculation in product adver-tisements, photos and drawings can be used with equal shrewdness in posters, fliers, advocacy ads, and Web sites. Although such images are often made to seem spontaneous and "natural," they are almost always composed: Designers consciously select the details of staging and composition as well as manipulate camera techniques (filters, camera angle, lighting), and digital or chemical devel-opment techniques (airbrushing, merging of images). For example, public officials often try to control the effect of photographs by creating "photo-ops" (photographing opportunities), wherein news photographers are allowed to photograph an event only during certain times and from certain angles. Political photographs appearing in newspapers are often press releases officially ap-proved by the politician's staff. (See the photographs of President Bush, later in this chapter on pp. 145–146.)

To analyze a photograph or drawing, or to create visual images for your own arguments, you need to think both about the composition of the image and about the camera's relationship to the subject. Since drawings produce a perspective on a scene analogous to that of a camera, design considerations for photographs can be applied to drawings as well. The following list of questions can guide your analysis of any persuasive image.

- *Type of photograph or drawing*: Is the image documentary-like (representing a real event), fictionlike (intended to tell a story or dramatize a scene), or concep-tual (illustrating or symbolizing an idea or theme)? The photo of a girl crowd surfing in a mosh pit in Color Plate C is a documentary photo capturing a real event in action. The drawing of the lizards in Color Plate F is both a fictional narrative telling a story and a conceptual drawing illustrating a theme.

- *Distance from the subject:* Is the image a close-up, medium shot, or long shot? Close-ups tend to increase the intensity of the image and suggest the importance of the subject; long shots tend to blend the subject into the background. The photograph of the girl with a kitten in Color Plate H is an extreme close-up. In contrast, the photograph of the young woman crossing the bridge in the Haiti photograph (Color Plate D) is a long-range shot showing her blending into the poverty-stricken background, suggesting the devastating effect of poverty.

- *Orientation of the image and camera angle:* Is the camera (or artist) positioned in front of or behind the subject? Is it positioned below the subject, looking up (a low-angle shot)? Or is it above the subject, looking down (a high-angle shot)? Front-view shots, such as the one of Albanian refugees in Figure 1.1 (p. 5), tend to emphasize the persons being photographed. In contrast, rear-view shots often emphasize the scene or setting. A low-angle perspective tends to make the subject look superior and powerful, whereas a high-angle perspective can reduce the size—and by implication—the importance of the subject. A level angle tends to imply equality. The high-angle shot of the "American Taliban" John Lindh strapped naked to a stretcher (Figure 7.2, p. 117) emphasizes the superiority of the camera and the helplessness of Lindh. In contrast, the low-angle perspective of the lizards in Color Plate F emphasizes the power of the lizards and the inferiority of the viewer.

- *Point of view:* Does the camera or artist stand outside the scene and create an objective effect as in the Haiti photograph in Color Plate D? Or is the camera or artist inside the scene as if the photographer or artist is an actor in the scene, creating a subjective effect as in the drawing of the lizards in Color Plate F?

- *Use of color:* Is the image in color or in black and white? Is this choice determined by the restrictions of the medium (the publication can't afford color, as in many newspaper photographs) or is it the conscious choice of the photographer or artist? Are the colors realistic or muted? Have special filters been used (a photo made to look old through the use of brown tints)? The bright colors in the lizard and Goldilocks drawing in Color Plate F and in the forest scene in Color Plate G resemble illustrations in books for children. The subdued colors in the soybean ad in Color Plate B are intended to look realistically natural and neutral.

- *Compositional special effects:* Is the entire image clear and realistic? Is any portion of it blurred? Is it blended with other realistic or nonrealistic images (a car ad that blends a city and a desert; a body lotion ad that merges a woman and a cactus)? Is the image an imitation of some other famous image such as a classic painting (as in parodies)? Both the Earthjustice ad in Color Plate F and the Saturn VUE ad in Color Plate G are conscious imitations of children's picture books.

- *Juxtaposition of images:* Are several different images juxtaposed, suggesting relationships between them? Juxtaposition can suggest sequential or causal relationships or can metaphorically transfer the identity of a nearby image or background to the subject (as when a bath soap is associated with a meadow). This technique is frequently used in public relations to shape viewers' perceptions of political figures as when President Bush is positioned in front of Mount Rushmore in Figure 9.4, page 146.

- *Manipulation of images:* Are images that are staged made to appear real, natural, documentary-like? Are images altered with airbrushing? Are images actually composites of a number of images (for instance, using images of different women's bodies to create one perfect model in an ad or film)? Are images cropped for emphasis? What is left out? Are images downsized or enlarged? For an example of a staged photo that is intended to look natural, see the "Save the Children" advocacy ad in Color Plate E. Note too how the figures in the "Save the Children" ad are isolated from any background.

- *Settings, furnishings, props:* Is the photo or drawing an outdoor or indoor scene? What is in the background and foreground? What furnishings and props, such as furniture, objects in a room, pets, and landscape features, help create the scene? What social associations of class, race, and gender are attached to these settings and props? The white girl holding a cat in the Center for Consumer Freedom ad in Color Plate H is a calculated choice. The ad maker could have used an African American boy with a dog or an Asian girl with a rabbit but selected the girl-and-cat photograph for a rhetorical purpose.

- *Characters, roles, actions:* Does the photo or drawing tell a story? Are the people in the scene models? Are the models instrumental (acting out real-life roles) or are they decorative (extra and included for visual or sex appeal)? What are the facial expressions, gestures, and poses of the people? What are the spatial relationships of the figures? (Who is in the foreground, center, and background? Who is large and prominent?) What social relationships are implied by these poses and positions? In the "Save the Children" advocacy ad shown in Color Plate E, the pose of the mother and child—each completely absorbed in adoration of the other—tells the story of the bonds of love between mothers and babies.

- *Presentation of images:* Are there multiple separate images, and if so, how are they related? Are the images large in proportion to verbal text? How are images labeled? How does the text relate to the image(s)? Does the image illustrate the text? Does the text explain or comment on the image? For example, the image of the soybean plant in Color Plate B dominates the right side of the advocacy ad, while attractively designed type dominates the left side of the ad. (You might consider why the ad maker places text on the left and image on the right instead of reversing the order or placing text on top and image on the bottom.)

An Analysis of a Visual Argument Using Images

To show you how images can be analyzed, let's examine the advertisement for a Saturn VUE sport-utility vehicle (Color Plate G). At one level, the persuasive intent of this ad is to urge viewers to buy a Saturn VUE. But at a more subtle level, this advertisement participates in an international debate about SUVs and the environment. Whereas Europeans are buying smaller, more fuel-efficient cars, Americans are buying SUVs that guzzle gas like trucks. Among their opponents,

SUVs—whether fairly or unfairly—have become a worldwide symbol of Americans' greed for oil and their disdain for the environment.

How do car manufacturers fight back? Clearly, they can't make a logical argument that owning an SUV is good for the environment. But they can use psychological strategies that urge consumers to associate SUVs with pro-environment sentiments. So in this ad Saturn turns to visual argument. Using a carefully designed drawing, the advertisement shows the Saturn VUE blending into an "evergreen forest" scene. Surrounded by a moose, a porcupine, a bear, a squirrel, and other forest birds and animals, the SUV seems to belong in its forest home. The brilliance of the ad is the insert legend at the bottom left, where the forest creatures are identified by name. The ad teaches city dwellers who buy SUVs the names of the forest animals—not just "bird" but "Black-Capped Chickadee," not just "rabbit" but "Snowshoe Hare." (Because the ad was designed as a two-page magazine spread, we have had to reduce its size in Color Plate G, making the animal names tiny. They are easily readable in the original.) The ad becomes a mini-lesson in identifying and naming the "Creatures of the evergreen forest"—creature number one, of course, being the Saturn VUE.

To make the Saturn VUE blend harmoniously with the forest, this ad cleverly de-emphasizes the size of the vehicle, even though the dominant size of SUVs is part of their appeal to urban consumers. To compensate for this choice, the typical appeals of SUVs are rendered symbolically. For example, the VUE's power and agility, hinted at in the brief copy at the bottom right of the ad, are conveyed metaphorically in the image of the puma, "poised" like the Saturn, crouching and oriented in the same direction, like the car's guiding spirit. It enters the scene from the outside, the predator, silent and powerful—the main animal to be identified with the car itself. Other animals close to the car and facing the same direction as the car each stand for one of the car's attributes so that the VUE also possesses the speed of the hare, the brute size and strength of the bear, and the soaring freedom of the goshawk.

The whole ad works by association. The slogan "At home in almost any environment" means literally that the car can go from city to country, from desert to mountains, from snow to tropic heat. But so can any car. The slogan's purpose is to associate the car with the words "home" and "environment"—words that connote all the warm, fuzzy feelings that make you feel good about owning a Saturn VUE. In addition, the use of drawings and the identification of animals by numbers conjure up the delightful, instructive innocence of children's books: this car must be a good thing. And in its own special way, this ad has skillfully shifted consumers' attention away from global warming and environmental degradation.

For Class Discussion

1. The techniques for constructing photos come into play prominently in news photography. In this exercise, we ask you to examine three photographs of President Bush that accompanied news articles appearing

in the *New York Times* in summer 2002. These photographs were taken at photo-ops carefully staged by White House staff. Working individually or in groups, study Figures 9.2, 9.3, and 9.4 and then answer the following questions:

a. What are the most noticeable features of each photo?

b. What do you think is the dominant impression of Bush that each photo seeks to convey? In other words, what is the implicit argument?

c. What camera techniques and compositional features do you see in each photo?

d. What image of President Bush do these photographs attempt to create for citizens and voters?

2. The image on the opening page of Part Three (p. 163) is a photograph of the suffragettes' campaign for the vote for women in the early twentieth century. What is the rhetorical effect or impact of this photograph?

a. What features of the composition of the photo and its type suggest that this is an old photo? What features most stand out in this photo?

FIGURE 9.2   *President Bush clearing brush from Texas ranch*

FIGURE 9.3   *President Bush greeting a crowd*

FIGURE 9.4   *President Bush delivering speech at Mount Rushmore*

    b. What is the dominant impression of this photo?

    c. What image of women does this photo project?

3. Examine carefully the advertisement sponsored by the Center for Consumer Freedom in Color Plate H and then, working individually or in groups, answer the following questions:

    a. What camera techniques and compositional features do you see in this ad?

    b. What is the proportion of verbal text to image? How would you describe the layout of this ad? How does the text relate to the image?

    c. We think of most ads as *for* some product or organization, yet this ad focuses on what it is *against.* How does the cropping of the image and the intrusiveness of the verbal text help to convey the argument of the ad? How would you summarize the ad's argument?

    d. This ad appeared in *Newsweek,* a news commentary magazine with a general readership. How does the ad use its visual design to reach its audience?

The Genres of Visual Arguments

We have already mentioned that verbal arguments today are frequently accompanied by photographs or drawings that contribute to the text's persuasive appeal. For example, a verbal argument promoting United Nations action to help AIDS victims in Africa might be accompanied by a photograph of a dying mother and child. However, some genres of argument are dominated by visual elements. In these genres, the visual design carries most of the argumentative weight; verbal text is used primarily for labeling, for focusing the argument's claim, or for commenting on the images. In this section we describe specifically these highly visual genres of argument.

Posters and Fliers

To persuade audiences, an arguer might create a poster designed for placement on walls or kiosks or a flier to be passed out on street corners. Posters dramatically attract and direct viewers' attention toward one subject or issue. They often seek to rally supporters, promote a strong stance on an issue, and call people to action. For example, during World War II, posters asked Americans to invest in war bonds and urged women to join the workforce to free men for active combat. During the Vietnam War, famous posters used slogans such as "Make Love Not War" or "Girls say yes to boys who say no" to increase national resistance to the war.

The hallmark of an effective poster is the way it focuses and encodes a complex meaning in a verbal-visual text, often with one or more striking images. These images are often symbolic—for example, using children to symbolize family and home, a soaring bird to symbolize freedom, or three firefighters raising the American flag over the World Trade Center rubble in September 2001 to symbolize American heroism, patriotism, and resistance to terrorism. These symbols derive potency from the values they share with their target audience. Posters tend to use words sparingly, either as slogans or as short, memorable directives. This terse verbal text augments the message encoded in an eye-catching, dominant image.

As an example of a classic poster, consider the Part Opener on page 63, which promotes bicycle riding as an alternative to cars. Note how the drawing of the tortured figures captures imaginatively both the physical damage of air pollution and the psychological damage of being trapped in traffic—ideas also captured in the carefully chosen words, which are charged with double meanings: "Exhausted" denotes both "exhaust" from cars and "exhaustion" from the snarled traffic and the hectic pace of an automobile-dominated life. "Get a Life" alludes both to improving your health and to improving the quality of your lived experience through the exercise, simplicity, and freedom of a bicycle.

Fliers and brochures often use visual elements similar to those in posters. An image might be the top and center attraction of a flier or the main focus of the front cover of a brochure. However, unlike posters, fliers and brochures offer additional space for verbal arguments, which often present the writer's claim supported with bulleted lists of reasons. Sometimes pertinent data and statistics, along with testimony from supporters, are placed in boxes or sidebars.

Public Affairs Advocacy Advertisements

Public affairs advocacy advertisements share with posters an emphasis on visual elements, but they are designed specifically for publication in newspapers and magazines and, in their persuasive strategies, are directly analogous to product advertisements. Public affairs advocacy ads are usually sponsored by a corporation or an advocacy organization and often have a more time-sensitive message than do posters and a more immediate and defined target audience. Designed as condensed arguments aimed at influencing public opinion on civic issues, these ads are characterized by their brevity, audience-based appeals, and succinct, sound bite style. Often, in order to sketch out their claim and reasons clearly and concisely, they employ headings and subheadings, bulleted lists, different sizes and styles of type, and a clever, pleasing layout on the page. They usually have some attention-getting slogan or headline like "MORE KIDS ARE GETTING BRAIN CANCER. WHY?" or "STOP THE TAX REVOLT JUGGERNAUT!"

The balance between verbal and visual elements in an advocacy advertisement varies. Some advocacy ads are verbal only with visual concerns focused on document design (for example, an "open letter" from the president of a corporation appearing as a full-page newspaper ad). Other advocacy ads are primarily visual, using images and other design elements with the same shrewdness as product advertisements. We looked closely at advocacy ads in Chapter 2, where we referred to ads opposing and supporting genetically modified foods (Color Plate A and Color Plate B), and in this chapter in the ad on Ecstasy.

As an example of a public affairs advocacy ad, consider "Save the Children," appearing as Color Plate E. This advocacy ad combines type, layout, color, and image skillfully and harmoniously through its dominant image complemented by verbal text that interprets and applies the ideas conveyed by the image. The layout of the ad divides the page into three main parts, giving central focus to the image of the mother standing and looking into the eyes of the child she is holding in her arms. The blank top panel leads readers to look at the image. Two color panels, mauve behind the child and rose behind the mother, also highlight the two figures, isolate them in time and space, and concentrate the readers' attention on them. The large type in the black borders ("SHE'S THE BEST QUALIFIED TEACHER FOR HER CHILDREN" and "IMAGINE IF SHE HAD AN EDUCATION") frames the image, attracts readers' eyes, and plants the main idea in readers' minds: mothers should be equipped to teach their children.

This advocacy ad, which appeared in *Newsweek,* skillfully blends familiar, universal ideas—a mother's love for her child and the tenderness and strength of this bond—with unfamiliar, foreign associations—a mother and child from a third-world country, wearing the traditional clothing of their country depicted by the head scarf the mother is wearing and the elaborate design on her sleeve. In addition to the familiar-unfamiliar dynamic, a universal-particular dynamic also operates in this ad. This woman and baby are *every* mother and child (after all, we don't know exactly where she is from), but they are also from some specific third-world country. The two figures have been posed to conjure up Western paintings and statues of the Madonna and Christ child. With this pose, the ad intends that readers will connect with this image of motherly love and devotion and respond by supporting the "Every Mother/Every Child" campaign. Color in this ad also accents the warm, cozy, hopeful impression of the image; pink in Western culture is a feminine color often associated with women and babies. In analyzing the photographic image, you should note what is *not* shown: any surroundings, any indication of housing or scenery, any concrete sense of place or culture. The text of the ad interprets the image, provides background information, and seeks to apply the ideas and feelings evoked by the image to urging readers to action. The image, without either the large type or the smaller type, does convey an idea as well as elicit sympathy from readers, but the text adds meaning to the image and builds on those impressions and applies them.

The ad designer could have focused on poverty, illiteracy, hunger, disease, and high mortality rates but instead has chosen to evoke positive feelings of identification and to convey hopeful ideas. While acknowledging their cultural difference from this mother and child, readers recognize their common humanity and are moved to "give mothers and children the best chance to survive and thrive." The large amounts of blank space in this ad help to convey that the main points here are important, serious, elemental, but also simple—as if the ad has gotten to the heart of the matter. The bottom panel of the ad gives readers the logo and name of the organization "Save the Children" and a phone number and Web address to use to show their support.

For Class Discussion

Examine the public affairs advocacy ad shown in Color Plate F. This ad, sponsored by Earthjustice, defends the presence of grizzly bears in Yellowstone National Park as well as other wilderness areas in the Rocky Mountains. In our classes, this ad has yielded lively discussion of its ingenuity and complexity.

Working individually or in groups, conduct your own examination of this ad using the following questions:

1. What visual features of this ad immediately attract your eyes? What principles for effective use of type, layout, color, and image does this ad exemplify?

2. What is the core argument of this ad?

3. Why did Earthjustice use the theme of Goldilocks? How do the lizards function in this ad? Why does the ad *not* have any pictures of grizzlies or bears of any kind?

4. How would you design an advocacy ad for the preservation of grizzly bears? What visuals would you use?

Cartoons

An especially charged kind of visual argument is the political cartoon. Although you are perhaps not likely to create your own political cartoons, it is useful to understand how cartoonists use visual and verbal elements to convey their message. Political cartoons are often mini-narratives, portraying an issue dramatically, compactly, and humorously. They employ images and a few well-chosen words to dramatize conflicts and problems. Using caricature, exaggeration, and distortion, cartoonists distill an issue down to an image that boldly reveals the creator's perspective and subsequent claim on a civic issue. The purpose of political cartoons is usually satirical. Because they are so condensed and often connected to current affairs, political cartoons are particularly dependent on the audience's background knowledge of cultural and political events When political cartoons work well, through their perceptive combination of image and words, they flash a brilliant, clarifying light on a perspective or provide a new lens on an issue, often giving readers a shock of insight.

As an illustration, note the Dana Summers cartoon in Figure 9.5, which first appeared in the *Orlando Sentinel* during a period of national debate on the right of music lovers to download free songs and CDs from the Internet. Media opinion often sided with the music industry, which held that free downloading of

FIGURE 9.5   *Political cartoon supporting music industry in dispute about down-loaded music*

Source: © Tribune Media Services, Inc. All Rights Reserved. Reprinted with permission.

music constituted theft of intellectual property. A defense often made by music lovers was that the music industry was gouging the market with overpriced CDs. Dana Summers' cartoon constitutes his needle-sharp rebuttal of this common argument.

For Class Discussion

Cartoons can often sum up a worldview in a single image. Working individually or in groups, use the following questions to analyze the argument in the political cartoon on genetically engineered food on the opening page of Part One (p. 1) and in a cartoon chosen by you or your instructor:

1. What mini-narrative or conflict does the cartoon portray?
2. What is the cartoon arguing?
3. How does the cartoon use caricature, exaggeration, or distortion to convey its perspective?

Web Pages

So far we have only hinted at the influence of the World Wide Web in accelerating use of visual images in argument. Because reproducing high-quality images (especially color images) is expensive in a print medium, writers of argument prior to the Web often relied mainly on verbal text. But the Web has now made it possible to publish arguments incorporating powerful color images. The hypertext design of Web pages, along with their complex intermixture of text and image, has changed the way many writers think of argument. The home page of an advocacy site, for example, often has many features of a poster argument with hypertext links to galleries of images on the one hand, and to verbal arguments on the other. These verbal arguments themselves often contain photographs, drawings, and graphics. The strategies discussed in this chapter for analyzing and interpreting visual texts also apply to Web pages. Consider, for example, the home page of "50 Years Is Enough: The U.S. Network for Global and Economic Justice" (Color Plate I). This organization is opposed to the economic policies of the International Monetary Fund and the World Bank Group, which, the organization claims, have caused widespread suffering and poverty over its fifty-year history. The site's design uses colorful posters as "buttons" for its hyperlinks to "About Us," "Take Action," and so forth. How does the home page design and its use of images contribute to the *ethos* of the organization and the *pathos* of its appeal for grassroots action against the World Bank?

Because the Web is such an important tool in research, we have placed our main discussion of Web sites in Appendix Two, pages 284–288. On these pages you will find our explanations for reading, analyzing, and evaluating Web sites.

Constructing Your Own Visual Argument

The most common visual arguments you are likely to create are posters and fliers, public affairs advocacy ads, and possibly Web pages. You may also decide that in longer verbal arguments the use of visuals or graphics could clarify your points while adding visual variety to your paper. The following guidelines will help you apply your understanding of visual elements in the construction of your own visual arguments.

Guidelines for Creating Visual Arguments

1. *Genre*: Determine where this visual argument is going to appear (bulletin board, passed out as a flier, a one-page magazine or newspaper spread, or as a Web page).

2. *Audience-based appeals*: Determine who your target audience is.

   - What values and background knowledge of your issue can you assume that your audience has?
   - What specifically do you want your audience to think or do after reading your visual argument?
   - If you are promoting a specific course of action (sign a petition, send money, vote for or against a bill, attend a meeting), how can you make that request clear and direct?

3. *Core of your argument*: Determine what clear claim and reasons will form the core of your argument; decide if this claim and these reasons will be explicitly stated or implicit in your visuals and slogans.

   - How much verbal text will you use?
   - If the core of your argument will be largely implicit, how can you still make it readily apparent and clear for your audience?

4. *Visual design*: What visual design and layout will grab your audience's attention and be persuasive?

   - How can font sizes and styles, layout, and color be used in this argument to create a strong impression?
   - What balance and harmony can you create between the visual and verbal elements of your argument? Will your verbal element be a slogan, express the core of the argument, or summarize and comment on the image(s)?

5. *Use of images*: If your argument lends itself to images, what photo or drawing would support your claim or have emotional appeal? (If you want to use more than one image, be careful that you don't clutter your page and confuse your message. Simplicity and clarity are important.)

WHAT IF EVERYTHING WAS LABELED LIKE GENETICALLY ENGINEERED FOODS?

Genetically engineered (GE) fruits, vegetables and meats are on your dinner plate. Up to 70% of processed foods now contain GE ingredients. Yet, despite the fact that most Americans have indicated in national polls that they want to be able to identify these products, there is no label for GE foods, and no way for consumers to know whether the food they eat contains them.

Because the government doesn't require rigorous independent safety testing, no one can predict the long-term effects of these foods on our health, the environment, the economy, or the future of farming.

We believe that consumers have the right to know if their food has been genetically engineered. Join with us in asking the Food and Drug Administration to better regulate GE foods by requiring mandatory labeling and safety testing.

Take Action Today!

KEEP NATURE NATURAL

Learn more! 800-357-2211
www.keepnatural.org

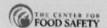

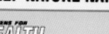

THE CENTER FOR
FOOD SAFETY

The Environmental Information Group

COLOR PLATE A   *"Keep Nature Natural" advocacy ad. This ad ran in* Vegetarian Times *and the* Utne Reader.

WOULD IT
SURPRISE YOU TO KNOW
THAT GROWING SOYBEANS CAN
HELP THE ENVIRONMENT?

Biotech soybeans have been widely
planted by American farmers and they
help preserve our natural resources.
Plant biotechnology makes it easier to
control weeds and plow soybean fields
less—which means less soil erosion.

But before those soybean seeds could
be planted, it took years of research and
testing to ensure that biotech crops
were safe for people and the environment. Extensive testing by scientists
shows foods derived from plant
biotechnology are as safe to eat as
traditional foods.

In fact, three government agencies
share the authority to evaluate the safety
of new biotech products from incep-
tion to approval—the U.S.
Department of Agriculture
(USDA), the Environmental Protection
Agency (EPA), and the Food and Drug
Administration (FDA). If you want to
learn more, we invite you to call or
visit our Web site.

WWW.WHYBIOTECH.COM
1-800-980-8660

Biotech
Soybean

COLOR PLATE B *Biotechnology advocacy ad*

COLOR PLATE C *Crowd-surfing at a rock concert* (TOM REESE/THE SEATTLE TIMES)

COLOR PLATE D *La Saline, a slum in Port-au-Prince, Haiti* (© 2002 Alex Quesada/Matrix)

SHE'S THE BEST QUALIFIED TEACHER FOR HER CHILDREN.

In a world where almost one-third of women are illiterate, improving access to education is urgent. Studies show that an educated mother is more likely to provide her children with adequate nutrition, seek needed health care, and send her girls, as well as boys, to school. Support the Every Mother/Every Child campaign, and give mothers and children the best chance to survive and thrive.

IMAGINE IF SHE HAD AN EDUCATION.

1-800-728-3843 • savethechildren.org

planet

Save the Children®

COLOR PLATE E   *Save the Children advocacy ad*

Just then, the three lizards came home and found Goldilocks eating their porridge...

IT'S JUST NOT THE SAME WITHOUT BEARS.

Once upon a time there were over 100,000 grizzly bears in the lower 48 states. Now, there are less than a thousand grizzly bears left. The health of the grizzly is dependent on vast, undisturbed, wild lands. When bears disappear, other species will follow. Bears are such an important part of our wilderness, history, and culture that it's hard to imagine a world without them in the picture.

Grizzly bears are a threatened species, protected by the Endangered Species Act. But some special interests are pushing the U.S. Fish and Wildlife Service to remove Yellowstone grizzlies from the endangered species list. Why? They want to open up wild lands around Yellowstone

National Park to destructive logging, mining, off-road vehicle use, and development.

You can help protect our wilderness and grizzly bears. Please take a moment to contact Secretary Bruce Babbitt, Department of Interior, 1849 C St. NW, Washington DC 20240, or email Bruce_Babbitt@os.doi.gov – Tell him to keep grizzly bears on the Endangered Species List and that grizzly bears need more protection, not less.

Earthjustice Legal Defense Fund is working tirelessly to protect the grizzly bears and the wilderness they stand for. If we all work together, the grizzly bears will live happily ever after.

HELP KEEP BEARS IN THE PICTURE
www.earthjustice.org

 EARTHJUSTICE
LEGAL DEFENSE FUND
1-800-584-6460

designed by **Sustain**

COLOR PLATE F   *Earthjustice advocacy ad*

COLOR PLATE G *Saturn VUE ad* (Used with permission of General Motors Corp.)

COLOR PLATE H *Center for Consumer Freedom advocacy ad*

HOME
ABOUT US
ECONOMIC JUSTICE
NEWS
THE ISSUES
THE INSTITUTIONS
CONFERENCES
TAKE ACTION
LINKS
PHOTOS
FACTSHEETS
PRESS
UPDATES
JOBS / INTERNSHIPS
FEEDBACK
DONATE

JOIN THE 50 YEARS
LISTSERV

Search
[   ] Go

SUPPORT THE
NETWORK

WELCOME TO

50 50 ENOUGH
YEARS IS

US Network for Global Economic Justice

ABOUT US

TAKE ACTION!

THE ISSUES

THE INSTITUTIONS

ECONOMIC JUSTICE NEWS

CONFERENCES

WHAT'S NEW

Join the Movement Demands of IMF & World Bank

International Day of Action Against Military and Economic Intervention in Latin America and the Caribbean

We call for the immediate suspension of the policies and practices of the International Monetary Fund (IMF) and World Bank Group which have caused widespread poverty, inequality, and suffering among the world's peoples and damage to the world's environment....

Job Announcement OFFICE COORDINATOR

Economic Justice News - December 2002

Read more from the 50 Years is Enough Network Platform

Rebuttal to World Bank Response to 4 Demands

Debt

As an April 2002 report prepared by the IMF and World Bank acknowledges, the institutions' debt management program (HIPC) is failing.

IMF/World Bank Debt Plan: Still Failing After All These Years

Talk Back!

Declaration on Africa's Development Challenges

Responding to "mainstream" attitudes on the IMF & World Bank

Tax the Bank!

COLOR PLATE I   *U.S. Network for Global Economic Justice web site*

- What image would be memorable and meaningful to your audience? Would a photo image or a drawing be most effective?
- Will your image(s) be used to provide evidence for your claim or illustrate a main idea, evoke emotions, or enhance your credibility and authority?

As an example of a poster argument created by a student, consider Leah Johnson's poster in Figure 9.6. Intended for bulletin boards and kiosks around her

Drink and Then Drive?
Jeopardize My Future?

- Arrest
  - Financial Problems (fines up to $8,125)
    - Increased Insurance Rates
      - License Suspension
        - Criminal Conviction
          - Incarceration
            - Serious Injury or Death

or
Designate a Driver?

It's a no-brainer.
Join your Senior Class at Thirsty Thursday, but
designate a driver.

FIGURE 9.6 *Student poster argument promoting designated drivers*

college campus, Johnson's work illustrates how a writer can use minimal but well-chosen verbal text, layout, and images to convey a rhetorically effective argument. (That is Leah herself in the photograph.) In this ad, Leah is joining a national conversation about alcohol abuse on college campuses and is proposing a safe way of handling her university's weekly social get-together for older students, "Thirsty Thursdays." Notice how Leah in this visual argument has focused on her claim and reasons without seeing the need to supply evidence.

For Class Discussion

This exercise asks you to do the thinking and planning for a poster argument to be displayed on your college or university campus. Choose an issue that is controversial on your campus (or in your town or city), and follow the Guidelines for Creating Visual Arguments on pages 152–154 to envision the view you want to advocate on that issue. What might the core of your argument be? Who is your target audience? Are you representing a group, club, or other organization? What image(s) might be effective in attracting and moving this audience? Possible topics for issues might be commuter parking; poor conditions in the computer lab; student reluctance to use the counseling center; problems with dorm life, financial aid programs, or intramural sports; ways to improve orientation programs for new students, work-study programs, or travel-abroad opportunities; or new initiatives such as study groups for the big lecture courses or new service-learning opportunities.

Using Graphics as Visual Arguments

Besides images in the form of photographs and drawings, writers often use quantitative graphics to support arguments using numbers. In Chapter 6 we introduced you to the use of quantitative data in arguments. We discussed the persuasiveness of numbers and showed you ways to use them responsibly in your arguments. (See pp. 102–103.) With the advent of spreadsheet and presentation programs, today's writers often create and import quantitative graphics into their documents. These visuals—such as tables, pie charts, and line or bar graphs—can have great rhetorical power by making numbers tell a story at a glance. In this section, we'll show you how quantitative graphics can make numbers speak. We'll also show you how to incorporate graphics into your text and reference them effectively.

How Tables Contain a Variety of Stories

Data used in arguments usually have their origins in raw numbers collected from surveys, questionnaires, observational studies, scientific experiments, and so forth. Through a series of calculations, the numbers are combined, sorted, and arranged in a meaningful fashion, often in detailed tables. Some of the tables published by the U.S. Census Bureau, for example, contain dozens of pages. The more dense the table, the more their use is restricted to statistical experts who pore over them to analyze their meanings. More useful to the general public are midlevel tables contained on one or two pages that report data at a higher level of abstraction.

Consider, for example, Table 9.2, published by the U.S. Census Bureau in its document "America's Families and Living Arrangements: Population Characteristics" based on the 2000 census. This table shows the marital status of people fifteen years of age and older, broken into gender and age groupings, in March 2000. It also provides comparative data on the "never married" percent of the population in March 2000 and March 1970.

Take a few moments to peruse the table and be certain you know how to read it. You read tables in two directions: from top to bottom and from left to right. Always begin with the title, which tells you what the table contains and includes elements from both the vertical and horizontal dimensions of the table. In this case the vertical dimension presents demographic categories for people "15 years old and over": for both sexes, for males, and for females. Each of these gender categories is subdivided into age categories. The horizontal dimension provides information about "marital status." Seven of the columns give total numbers (reported in thousands) for March 2000. The eighth column gives the "percent never married" for March 2000, while the last column gives the "percent never married" for March 1970. To make sure you know how to read the table, pick a couple of rows at random and say to yourself what each number means. For example, the first row under "Both sexes" gives total figures for the entire population of the United States ages 15 and older. In March 2000 there were 213,773,000 persons 15 and older (remember that the numbers are presented in thousands). Of these, 113,002,000 were married and living with their spouses. (If you have a pocket calculator handy, you can do your own arithmetic to determine that roughly 52 percent of people over 15 are married and living with their spouses.) As you continue across the columns, you'll see that 2,730,000 persons are married but not living with their spouses (a spouse might be stationed overseas or in prison; or a married couple might be maintaining a "commuter marriage" with separate households in different cities). Continuing across the columns, you'll see that 4,479,000 persons were separated from their spouses, 19,881,000 were divorced, 13,665,000 were widowed, and an additional 60,016,000 were never married. In the next-to-the-last column, the number of never-married persons is converted to a percentage: 28.1 percent (see for yourself that 60,016 divided by 213,773 is 28.1%). Finally, the last column shows the percentage of never-married persons in 1970: 24.9%. These last two columns show us that the number of unmarried persons in the United States rose 3.2 percentage points since 1970.

Now that you know how to read the table, peruse it carefully to see the kinds of stories it tells. What does the table show you, for example, about the percentage of married persons ages 25–29 in 1970 versus 2000? What does it show about different age-related patterns of marriage in males and females? By showing you that Americans are waiting much later in life to get married, a table like this initiates many causal questions for analysis and argument. What happened in American culture between 1970 and 2000 to explain the startling difference in the

TABLE 9.2 Marital status of people 15 years and over: March 1970 and March 2000 (In thousands)

Characteristic	March 2000								March 1970 Percent never married[a]
	Number							Percent never married	
	Total	Married spouse present	Married spouse absent	Separated	Divorced	Widowed	Never married		
Both sexes									
Total 15 years old and over..	213,773	113,002	2,730	4,479	19,881	13,665	60,016	28.1	24.9
15 to 19 years old.........	20,102	345	36	103	64	13	19,541	97.2	93.9
20 to 24 years old.........	18,440	3,362	134	234	269	11	14,430	78.3	44.5
25 to 29 years old.........	18,269	8,334	280	459	917	27	8,255	45.2	14.7
30 to 34 years old.........	19,519	11,930	278	546	1,616	78	5,071	26.0	7.8
35 to 44 years old.........	44,804	29,353	717	1,436	5,967	399	6,932	15.5	5.9
45 to 54 years old.........	36,633	25,460	492	899	5,597	882	3,303	9.0	6.1
55 to 64 years old.........	23,388	16,393	308	441	3,258	1,770	1,218	5.2	7.2
65 years old and over......	32,620	17,827	485	361	2,193	10,484	1,270	3.9	7.6
Males									
Total 15 years old and over..	103,113	56,501	1,365	1,818	8,572	2,604	32,253	31.3	28.1
15 to 19 years old.........	10,295	69	3	51	29	3	10,140	98.5	97.4
20 to 24 years old.........	9,208	1,252	75	70	101	-	7,710	83.7	54.7
25 to 29 years old.........	8,943	3,658	139	170	342	9	4,625	51.7	19.1
30 to 34 years old.........	9,622	5,640	151	205	712	15	2,899	30.1	9.4
35 to 44 years old.........	22,134	14,310	387	585	2,775	96	3,981	18.0	6.7
45 to 54 years old.........	17,891	13,027	255	378	2,377	157	1,697	9.5	7.5
55 to 64 years old.........	11,137	8,463	158	188	1,387	329	612	5.5	7.8
65 years old and over......	13,885	10,084	197	171	849	1,994	590	4.2	7.5
Females									
Total 15 years old and over..	110,660	56,501	1,365	2,661	11,309	11,061	27,763	25.1	22.1
15 to 19 years old.........	9,807	276	33	52	35	10	9,401	95.9	90.3
20 to 24 years old.........	9,232	2,110	59	164	168	11	6,720	72.8	35.8
25 to 29 years old.........	9,326	4,676	141	289	575	18	3,627	38.9	10.5
30 to 34 years old.........	9,897	6,290	127	341	904	63	2,172	21.9	6.2
35 to 44 years old.........	22,670	15,043	330	851	3,192	303	2,951	13.0	5.2
45 to 54 years old.........	18,742	12,433	237	521	3,220	725	1,606	8.6	4.9
55 to 64 years old.........	12,251	7,930	150	253	1,871	1,441	606	4.9	6.8
65 years old and over......	18,735	7,743	288	190	1,344	8,490	680	3.6	7.7

[a]The 1970 percentages include 14-year-olds, and thus are for 14+ and 14–19.
Represents zero or rounds to zero.
Source: U.S. Census Bureau, Current Population Survey, March 2000.

percentage of married persons within, say, the 20–24 age bracket? In 2000 only 22 percent of persons in this age bracket were married (we converted "unmarried" to "married" by subtracting 78.3 from 100). However, in 1970, 55 percent of persons in this age bracket were married.

Using a Graphic to Tell a Story

Table 9.2, as we have seen, tells the story of how Americans are postponing marriage until later in life. However, one has to peruse the table carefully, poring over it like a sleuth, to tease out the story from the dense columns of numbers. To focus on a key story and make it powerfully immediate, you can create a graphic.

Bar Graphs Suppose, for example, that you are writing an argument in which you want to show that the percentage of married women in age groups 20–29 has dropped significantly since 1970. You could tell this story through a simple bar graph (Figure 9.7).

Bar graphs use bars of varying length, extending either horizontally or vertically, to contrast two or more quantities. As with any graphic presentation, you must create a comprehensive title. In the case of bar graphs, titles tell readers what is being compared to what. Most bar graphs also have "legends," which explain what the different features on the graph represent. Bars are typically distinguished from each other by use of different colors, shades, or patterns of cross-hatching. The special power of bar graphs is that they can help readers make quick comparisons between different groups across a variable such as time.

Pie Charts Another vivid kind of graphic is a pie chart, which depicts different percentages of a total (the pie) in the form of slices. Pie charts are a favorite way of depicting noteworthy patterns in the way parts of a whole are divided up. Suppose, for example, that you wanted your readers to notice the high percentage

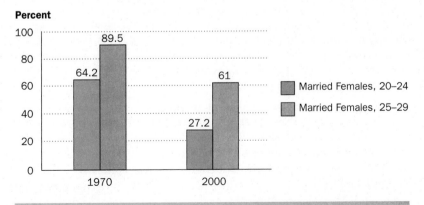

FIGURE 9.7 *Percentage of married females, ages 20–29, 1970 and 2000*

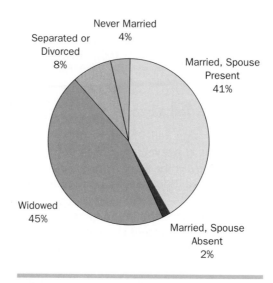

FIGURE 9.8   *Marital status of females, ages 65 and older, 2000*

of widows among women ages 65 and older. To do so, you could create a pie chart (Figure 9.8) based on the data in the last row of Table 9.2.

As you can see from Figure 9.8 a pie chart can demonstrate at a glance how the whole of something is divided into segments. The effectiveness of pie charts diminishes as you add more slices. In most cases, you'll begin to confuse readers if you include more than five or six slices.

Line Graphs   Another powerful quantitative graphic is a line graph, which converts numerical data into a series of points on a grid and connects them to create flat, rising, or falling lines. The result gives us a picture of the relationship between the variables represented on the horizontal and vertical axes.

Suppose you wanted to tell the story of the rising number of separated/divorced women in the U.S. population. Using Table 9.2, you can calculate the percent of separated/divorced females in 2000 by adding the number of separated females (2,661,000) and the number of divorced females (11,309,000) and dividing that sum by the total number of females (110,660,000). The result is 12.6 percent. You can make the same calculations for 1990, 1980, and 1970 by looking at U.S. census data from those years (available on the Web or in your library). The resulting line graph is shown in Figure 9.9.

To determine what this graph is telling you, you need to clarify what's represented on the two axes. By convention, the horizontal axis of a graph contains the predictable, known variable that has no surprises—what researchers call the "independent variable." In this case the horizontal axis represents the years 1970–2000 arranged predictably in chronological order. The vertical axis contains

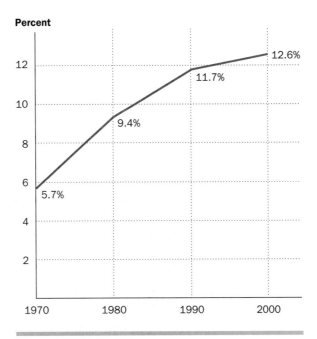

FIGURE 9.9   *Percentage of females age 15 and older who are separated or divorced, 1970–2000*

the unpredictable variable that forms the graph's story—what researchers call the "dependent variable"—in this case the percentage of divorced females. The ascending curve tells the story at a glance.

Note that with line graphs the steepness of a slope (and hence the rhetorical effect) can be manipulated by the intervals chosen for the vertical axis. Figure 9.9 shows vertical intervals of 2 percent. The slope could be made less dramatic by choosing intervals of, say, 10 percent and more dramatic by choosing intervals of 1 percent.

Incorporating Graphics into Your Argument

Today writers working with quantitative data usually use graphing software that automatically creates tables, graphs, or charts from data entered into the cells of a spreadsheet. (It is beyond the scope of this textbook to explain how to use these graphing utilities.) For college papers, some instructors may allow you to make your graphs with pencil and ruler and paste them into your document.

Designing the Graphic   When you design your graphic, your goal is to have a specific rhetorical effect on your readers, not to demonstrate all the bells and whistles available on your software. Adding extraneous data in the graph or chart or using such features as three-dimensional effects can often call attention away from the story you are trying to tell. Keep the graphic as uncluttered and simple as possible and design it so that it reinforces the point you are making in your text.

Numbering, Labeling, and Titling Graphics   In newspapers and popular magazines, writers often include graphics in boxes or sidebars without specifically referring to them in the text itself. However, in academic or workplace writing, graphics are always labeled, numbered, titled, and referred to directly in the text. By convention, tables are listed as "Tables," while line graphs, bar graphs, pie charts, or any other kind of drawings or photographs are labeled "Figures." Suppose you create a document that includes four graphics—a table, a bar graph, a pie chart, and an imported photograph. The table would be labeled Table 1. The rest of the graphics would be labeled Figure 1, Figure 2, and Figure 3.

In addition to numbering and labeling, every graphic needs a comprehensive title that explains fully what information is being displayed. Look back over the tables and figures in this chapter and compare their titles to the information in the graphics. In a line graph showing changes over time, for example, a typical title will identify the information on both the horizontal and vertical axes and the years covered. Bar graphs also have a "legend" explaining how the bars are coded, if necessary. When you import the graphic into your own text, be consistent in where you place the title—either above the graphic or below it.

Referencing the Graphic in Your Text   Academic and professional writers follow a referencing convention called *independent redundancy*. The general rule is this: The graphic should be understandable without the text; the text should be understandable without the graphic; the text should repeat the most important information in the graphic. Suppose, for example, that you are writing an argument saying that social services for the elderly is a women's issue as well as an age issue and you want to use a pie chart that you have constructed. In your text, you would reference this chart and then repeat its key information as shown in Figure 9.10.

Conclusion

In this chapter we have explained the challenge and power of using visuals in arguments. We have examined the components of visual design—use of type, layout, color, and images—and shown how these components can be used for persuasive effect in arguments. We have also described the argumentative genres that depend on effective use of visuals—posters and fliers, advocacy advertisements, cartoons, and Web pages—and invited you to produce your own visual argument. Finally, we showed you that graphics can tell a numeric story in a highly focused and dramatic way. Particularly we explained the functions of tables, bar graphs, pie charts, and line graphs, and showed you how to incorporate and reference graphics in your own prose.

Elderly women are likely to need more social services ⎤— *Writer's Point*
than men because they are more likely to live alone.
<u>As shown in Figure 1</u>, only 41 percent of women over—— *References the figure*
sixty-five live with their spouses. Of those without⎤   *Repeats the key*
spouses, 45 percent are widowed. In contrast, 74 per- ⎬— *information shown in*
cent of men over sixty-five live with their spouses⎦   *the figure*
while only 14 percent are widowed. These differences-
caused largely by the longer life expectancy of women⎤
and by men's tendency to marry women younger than ⎬— *Connects the*
themselves—mean that women are more apt than men to⎦   *information to the*
face old age alone.   *point*

Figure 1: Marital Status of Males and Females, Ages 65 and Older, 2000 —— *Title*

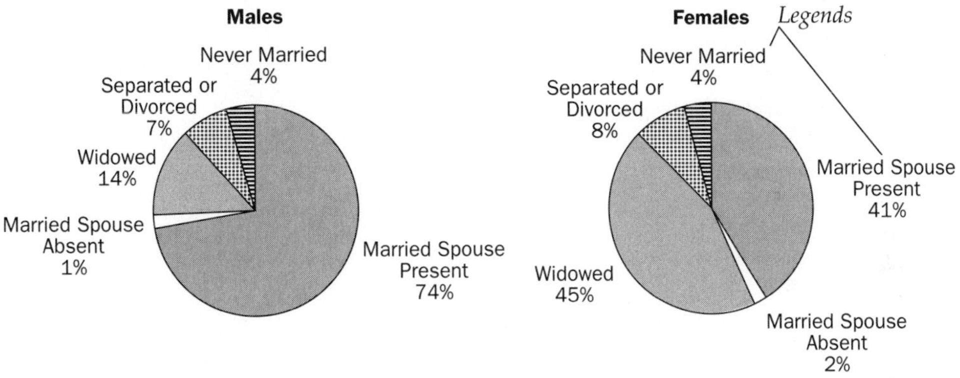

Source: "America's Families and Living Arrangements: Population Characteristics," U.S. Census —*Source*
Bureau, 2000

FIGURE 9.10   *Example of a student text with referenced graphic*

WRITING ASSIGNMENTS
FOR CHAPTER 9

Option 1: A Poster Argument   Working with the idea for a poster argument that you explored in the For Class Discussion on page 149, use the visual design concepts and principles presented on pages 147 in this chapter, your understanding of the visual argument and the genre of poster arguments, and your own creativity to produce a poster argument that can be displayed on your campus or in your town or city. Try out the draft of your poster argument on people who are part of your target audience. Based on these individuals' suggestions for improving the clarity and impact of this visual argument, prepare a final version of your poster argument.

Option 2: A Microtheme   Write a short microtheme that tells a story based on data you select from Table 9.2 or from some other table provided by your instructor or located by you. Include in your microtheme at least one quantitative graphic (table, line graph, bar graph, pie chart), which should be labeled and referenced according to standard conventions. Use as a model the short piece shown in Figure 9.10 on page 161.

Claim Types in Argument

This photograph of suffragettes in Asbury Park, New Jersey, taken between 1914 and 1920, depicts a major historical political issue: women campaigning for the vote.

10 An Introduction to the Types of Claims

In Part One we discussed the reading and writing of arguments, linking argument to both persuasion and inquiry. In Part Two we examined the internal structure of arguments and showed how persuasive writers link their arguments to the beliefs and values of their audiences. We also showed how writers can vary their content, structure, and style to reach audiences offering varying degrees of resistance to the writers' views.

Now in Part Three we examine arguments in depth by explaining six types of claims and by showing how each type has its own characteristic patterns of development and support. Because almost all arguments use one or more of these types of claims as basic argumentative "moves" or building blocks, knowing how to develop each claim type will advance your skills in argument. The types of claims to be examined in Part Three are related to an ancient rhetorical concept called *stasis*, from a Greek term meaning "stand" as in "to take a *stand* on something." There are many competing theories of stasis, so no two rhetoricians discuss stasis in exactly the same way. But all the theories have valuable components in common.

In Part Three we present our own version of stasis theory or, to use more ordinary language, our own approach to argument based on the types of claims. The payoff for you will be twofold. First, understanding the types of claims will help you to focus an argument and generate ideas for it. Second, a study of claim types teaches you characteristic patterns of support for each type, thereby helping you organize and develop your arguments.

An Overview of the Types of Claims

To appreciate what a study of claim types can do, imagine one of those heated but frustrating arguments—let's suppose it's about gun control—where the question at issue keeps shifting. Everyone talks at cross-purposes, voice levels rising. No speaker's point seems to relate clearly to the previous speaker's. Rational discussion turns into a shouting match. Sometimes you can get such a discussion back on track if one person says, "Hold it for a moment. What are we actually disagreeing about here? Are we arguing about all guns or just handguns? Do we agree that gun ownership prevents crimes or not? Do we think that getting a gun license would be like getting a driver's license? Let's figure out what we agree on and where we disagree, because we can't debate all these questions at once." Whether she recognizes it or not, this person is applying the concept of claim types to get the argument focused.

To understand how claim types work, let's return to the concept of stasis. A *stasis* is an issue or question that focuses a point of disagreement. You and your audience might agree on the answer to Question A and so have nothing to argue about. Likewise you might agree on the answer to Question B. But on Question C you disagree. Question C constitutes a stasis where you and your audience diverge. It is the place where disagreement begins, where as an arguer you take a stand against another view. Thus you and your audience might agree that handgun ownership is legal. You might agree further that widespread ownership of handguns reduces crime. But if you ask the question "Is widespread handgun ownership a good thing?" you and your audience might disagree. This last question constitutes a stasis, the point where you and your audience part company.

Rhetoricians have discovered that the kinds of questions that divide people have classifiable patterns. In this text we identify six broad types of claims—each type originating in a different kind of question. To emphasize the structural pattern of each type, we will first use the letters X and Y to represent slots so that you can focus on the structure rather than the content of the claim type. Then we'll move quickly to actual examples. Here is a brief overview of the six claim types.

Type 1: Simple Categorical Arguments (Is X a Y?, Where You and Your Audience Agree on the Meaning of Y)

A categorical argument occurs when persons disagree about the category (Y) that a given thing (X) belongs to. A categorical question is said to be simple if there is no dispute about the meaning of the Y term. Here are three examples of questions leading to simple categorical arguments:

> Is *Sesame Street* a sexist program?
>
> Is surfing the Internet a new kind of addiction?
>
> Was Senator Weasel's vote for increased military spending politically motivated?

In these examples, we assume that writer and audience agree on the meaning of "sexist program," "addiction," and "politically motivated." At issue is whether *Sesame Street*, surfing the Internet, and Senator Weasel's vote for military spending belong to these categories.

The strategy for conducting a simple categorical argument is to provide examples or other evidence to show that X does or does not belong to category Y.

Yes, *Sesame Street* is a sexist program (provide examples). Yes, surfing the Internet is a new kind of addiction (provide examples, testimony from psychologists). No, Senator Weasel's support for new weapons funding was not politically motivated (provide evidence that Weasel has a long record of pro-military spending). Simple categorical arguments are discussed in the first part of Chapter 11.

Type 2: Definitional Arguments (Is X a Y?, Where the Definition of Y Is Contested)

A categorical argument becomes more complex if you and your audience disagree about the meaning of the Y term. In this second type of claim, you have to define the Y term and defend your definition against objections and alternative definitions. Suppose, for example, you want to argue that using animals for medical research constitutes cruelty to animals. You would have to define what you mean by "cruelty to animals" and show how using animals for medical research fits your definition. Almost all legal disputes require definitional arguing because courts must determine whether an action meets or does not meet the criteria for a crime or civil tort as defined by a law, statute, or series of previous court rulings. Here are three examples of questions leading to definitional arguments:

> Is the occasional telling of off-color jokes in the workplace an instance of sexual harassment?
>
> Is e-mail spam constitutionally protected free speech?
>
> Is Pluto a planet or an asteroid?

The general strategy for conducting a definitional argument is to define the second term and then argue whether the first term meets or does not meet the definition. We call this strategy *criteria-match arguing* because to define the second term you must specify the criteria that something must meet to fit the category, and then you must argue that your first term does or does not match these criteria. Definitional arguments are treated in depth in Chapter 11.

Type 3: Cause/Consequence Arguments (Does X Cause Y? Is Y a Consequence of X?)

Another major argument type entails cause-and-effect reasoning. Such arguments often arise from disagreements about the cause of an event or a trend: "What caused the stock market crash in summer 2002?" or "What causes teenage males to become violent?" Just as frequently, causal arguments arise from speculations about the possible consequences of an action: "What will be the environmental consequences of growing genetically engineered food?" "Will gun control legislation reduce violence in the schools?"

The general strategy for conducting causal arguments is to describe the chain of events that lead from X to Y. If a causal chain cannot be directly established, you can argue indirectly, using inductive methods, statistical analyses, or analogies. Causal arguments are treated in detail in Chapter 12.

Type 4: Resemblance Arguments (Is X Like Y?)

A fourth argument type involves disputes about appropriate analogies or precedents. Suppose you disapproved of investing in the stock market and wanted to argue that stock market investing is like gambling. In showing the similarities between investing and gambling, you would be making a resemblance argument. Here are three examples of questions that lead to resemblance arguing:

Was Slobodan Milosevic's policy of "ethnic cleansing" in Kosovo like Hitler's "final solution" against the Jews?

Is killing starlings in your attic like killing rats in your attic? (Are starlings like rats?)

Does pornography disparage women the way neo-Nazi propaganda disparages people of color? (Is pornography like racist propaganda?)

The general strategy for resemblance arguments is to compare the first term to the second, pointing out similarities between them (if your goal is to make X like Y) or differences between them (if your goal is to make X unlike Y). Resemblance arguments are covered in Chapter 13.

Type 5: Evaluation Arguments (Is X Good or Bad? Is X a Good or Bad Y?)

Categorical, causal, and resemblance arguments (types 1–4) are often called reality or truth arguments. In such arguments, people question the way things are, were, or will be; they are disagreeing about the nature of reality. In contrast, evaluation and proposal arguments (types 5 and 6) deal with values, what people consider important, good, or worth doing. Although a person's values often begin as feelings founded on personal experience, they can nevertheless form the basis of reasonable argument in the public sphere if they are articulated and justified. When you articulate your values, explain their source (if necessary), and apply them consistently to specific cases, you make your values transpersonal and shareable, and you can use them to build coherent and reasonable arguments.

Evaluation arguments (type 5) ask questions about whether X is good or bad. Here are three examples of evaluation questions:

Is a European-style, single-payer health insurance system a good policy for the United States to enact?

Is acquiring job experience between college and graduate school a good career plan?

Is a sport-utility vehicle a good urban vehicle?

The general strategy for evaluation arguments uses criteria-match arguing similar to that used for definitional arguments: You first establish your criteria for "good" in the specific case and then show how your first term does or does not meet the criteria. A special category of evaluation arguments deals with ethical or moral issues (for example, "Is it morally justifiable to spank children?" or "Are human stem cell experiments ethical?"). Evaluation and ethical arguments are covered in Chapter 14.

Type 6: Proposal Arguments (Should We Do X?)

Whereas argument types 1–5 all involve changing your audience's beliefs about something—whether about reality (types 1–4) or about the value of something (type 5)—proposal arguments call for action. Proposals ask your audience to do something, to act in some way. Typically, proposals use words like *should, ought,* or *must* followed by an action of some kind. The following questions would all lead to proposal arguments:

Should the United States provide universal health care for its citizens?

Should teens who commit crimes receive the same sentences as adult criminals?

Should gay marriages be legalized?

The most typical strategy for making proposal arguments is to follow a problem-solution-justification structure: The opening section convinces the audience that a problem exists. The second section proposes a solution to solve the problem. The last section justifies the solution by demonstrating that the benefits of acting on the proposal outweigh the costs or that the inherent "rightness" of the solution (on moral grounds) compels action. Proposal arguments are covered in Chapter 15.

For Class Discussion

Working as a whole class or in small groups, decide which claim type is represented by each of the following questions. Sometimes the argument categories overlap or blend together. For example, the question "Is airline travel safe?" might be considered either a simple categorical question or an evaluation question.

1. Should violent video games be made illegal?
2. How effective is aspirin in reducing the risk of heart attacks and stroke?
3. Why is anorexia nervosa primarily a disease of white, middle-class females?
4. Is depression in the elderly common in Asian cultures?
5. Were the September 11, 2001, terrorist attacks like Pearl Harbor (an act of war) or like an earthquake (a natural disaster)?

6. Should professional baseball impose a salary cap on its superstar players?

7. Is this Web site racist?

8. Is tobacco a drug?

9. Are Nike's Asian shoe factories sweatshops?

10. Do American girls lose self-esteem when they reach puberty, as claimed by some researchers?

What Is the Value of Studying Claim Types?

Having provided an overview of the types of claims, we conclude this chapter by showing you two substantial benefits you will derive from knowing about each type: help in focusing and generating ideas for an argument and help in organizing an argument.

Help in Focusing an Argument and Generating Ideas

Knowing the different types of claims can help you focus an argument and generate ideas for it. Understanding claim types helps you focus by asking you to determine what's at stake between you and your audience. Where do you and your audience agree and disagree? What are the questions at issue? It helps you generate ideas by guiding you to pose questions that suggest lines of development.

To illustrate, let's take a hypothetical case—one Isaac Charles Little (affectionately known as I. C. Little), who desires to chuck his contact lenses and undergo the new lasik procedure to cure his nearsightedness. ("Lasik" is the common name for laser in-situ keratomileusis, a recent advance in surgical treatments for myopia. Sometimes known as "flap and zap" surgery, it involves using a laser to cut a layer of the corneal tissue thinner than a human hair and then flattening the cornea. It's usually not covered by insurance and is quite expensive.) I. C. has two different arguments he'd like to make: (1) He'd like to talk his parents into helping him pay for the procedure. (2) He'd like to convince insurance companies that the lasik procedure should be covered by standard medical insurance policies.

In the discussions that follow, note how the six types of claims can help I. C. identify points of disagreement for each audience and simultaneously suggest lines of argument for persuading each. Note too how the questions at issue vary for each audience.

First imagine what might be at stake in I. C.'s discussions with his parents:

Claim-Type Analysis: Parents as Audience

- *Simple categorical argument:* I. C.'s parents will be concerned about the safety and effectiveness of this procedure. Is lasik safe? Is it effective? (These are the first questions at issue. I. C.'s mom has heard a horror story about an earlier surgical procedure for myopia, so I. C. knows he will have to persuade her that lasik is safe and effective.)

- *Definitional argument:* With parents as audience, I. C. will have to define what lasik surgery is so they won't have misconceptions about what is involved. However, he can't think of any arguments that would ensue over this definition, so he proceeds to the next claim type.

- *Causal argument:* Both parents will question I. C.'s underlying motivation for seeking this surgery. "What causes you to want this lasik procedure?" they will ask. (I. C.'s dad, who has worn eyeglasses all his adult life, will not be swayed by cosmetic desires. "If you don't like contacts," he will say, "just wear glasses.") Here I. C. needs to argue that permanently correcting his nearsightedness will improve his quality of life. I. C. decides to emphasize his desire for an active, outdoor life, and especially his passion for water sports including swimming and scuba diving, where his need for contacts or glasses is a serious handicap. Also, I. C. says that if he doesn't have to wear contacts he can get a summer job as a lifeguard.

- *Resemblance argument:* I. C. can't think of any resemblance questions at issue.

- *Evaluation argument:* When the pluses and minuses are weighed, is lasik a good thing? Would the results of the surgery be beneficial enough to justify the cost and the risks? In terms of costs, I. C. might argue that even though the procedure is initially expensive (from $1,000 to $4,000), over the years he will save money by not needing contacts or glasses. The pleasure of seeing well in the water and not being bothered by contacts or glasses while hiking and camping constitutes a major psychological benefit. (He decides to leave out the cosmetic benefits—I. C. thinks he'll look cooler without glasses—because his dad thinks wearing glasses is fine.)

- *Proposal argument:* Should I. C. (or a person in general) get this operation for treatment of myopia? (All the previous points of disagreement are subissues related to this overarching proposal issue.)

What this example should help you see is that the values arguments in the last two claim types (evaluation and proposal) depend on the writer's resolving related reality/truth questions in one or more of the first four types (simple categorical, definitional, cause, resemblance). In this particular case, before convincing his parents that they should help him pay for the lasik procedure (I. C.'s proposal claim), I. C. would need to convince them that the procedure is safe and effective (simple categorical arguments), that having the surgery would significantly improve the quality of I. C.'s life (causal argument), and that the benefits outweigh the costs (evaluation argument). Almost all arguments combine subarguments in this way so that lower-order claims provide supporting materials for addressing higher-order claims.

The previous illustration focused on parents as audience. If we now switch audiences, we can use our theory of claim types to identify different questions at issue. Let's suppose I. C. wants to persuade insurance companies to cover the lasik procedure. He imagines insurance company decision makers as his primary audience, along with the general public and state legislators who may be able to influence them.

Claim-Type Analysis: Insurance Decision Makers as Audience

- *Simple categorical argument:* No disagreements come immediately to mind. (This audience shares I. C.'s belief that lasik is safe and effective.)

- *Definitional argument:* Should lasik be considered "cosmetic surgery" (as insurance companies contend) or "medically justifiable surgery" (as I. C. contends)? This definitional question constitutes a major stasis. I. C. wants to convince his audience that lasik belongs in the category "medically justifiable surgery" rather than "cosmetic surgery." He will need to define "medically justifiable surgery" in such a way that lasik can be included.

- *Causal argument:* What will be the consequences to insurance companies and to the general public of making insurance companies pay for lasik? For this audience, consequence issues are crucial. Will insurance companies be deluged with claims? What will happen to insurance rates? Will optometrists and eyeglass manufacturers go out of business?

- *Resemblance argument:* Does lasik more resemble a face-lift (not covered by insurance) or plastic surgery to repair a cleft palate (covered by insurance)?

- *Evaluation argument:* Would it be good for society as a whole if insurance companies had to pay for lasik?

- *Proposal argument:* Should insurance companies be required to cover lasik?

As this analysis shows, the questions at issue change when you consider a different audience. Now the chief question at issue is definition: Is lasik cosmetic surgery or medically justifiable surgery? I. C. needs to spend no time arguing that the surgery is safe and effective (major concerns for his parents); instead he must establish criteria for "medically justifiable surgery" and then argue that lasik meets these criteria. Again note how the higher-order issues of value depend on resolving one or more lower-order issues of reality/truth.

So what can a study of claim types teach you about focusing an argument and generating ideas? First it teaches you to analyze what's at stake between you and your audience by determining major points of disagreement. Second, it shows you that you can make any of the claim types your argument's major focus. Rather than tackle a values issue, you might tackle only a reality/truth issue. You could, for example, focus an entire argument on the simple categorical question "Is lasik safe?" (an argument requiring you to research the medical literature). Likewise you could write a causal argument focusing on what might happen to optometrists and eyeglass manufacturers if the insurance industry decided to cover lasik. Often arguers jump too quickly to issues of value without first resolving issues of reality/truth. Finally, a study of claim types helps you pose questions that generate ideas and suggest lines of reasoning. Later in Part Three we will show you a particularly powerful way of using lower-order questions about reality/truth to generate supporting ideas for a proposal argument (see Chapter 15, pp. 256–259).

For Class Discussion

Select an issue familiar to most members of the class—perhaps a current campus issue, an issue prominent in the local or national news, or an issue that the class has recently discussed—and analyze it using our sequence of claim types. Consider how a writer or speaker might address two different audiences on this issue. Hypothesizing the writer/speaker's perspective and claim, make a list of points of agreement and disagreement for both audiences, using as a pattern our claim type analyses for lasik.

Help in Organizing and Developing an Argument

The second main benefit of studying claim types will become clearer as you read the chapters in Part Three. Because each type of claim has its own characteristic pattern of development, learning these patterns will help you organize and develop your arguments. Studying claim types shows you how different arguments are typically structured, teaching you generic moves needed in many different kinds of argumentative situations. If, for example, you make a proposal claim, a study of claim types will show you the generic moves typically needed in proposal arguments. If one of your supporting reasons is a definitional claim or an evaluation claim, study of claim types will show you how to do the criteria-match arguing typical of such claims. Likewise such a study shows you how to develop each of the other claim types to help you construct arguments that tap into your audience's values and that include strong support to overcome your audience's resistance. In the following chapters in Part Three, we discuss each claim type in depth.

11 Categorical and Definitional Arguments

X Is (Is Not) a Y

EXAMPLE CASE

Following the terrorist attacks of September 11, 2001, the capture of Taliban and Al Qaeda fighters in Afghanistan gave rise to wrenching definitional questions. Was a captured Afghan fighter a "prisoner of war," in which case he was guaranteed certain rights by the Geneva Conventions, including a right to a standard of food, health care, and shelter equivalent to that of U.S. troops and the right to be released and returned to his native country when the war was over? Or was a captured fighter an "unlawful combatant" still guaranteed humane treatment under the Geneva Conventions but with fewer rights than a POW? Or was a captured fighter a "suspected terrorist" not entitled to any protection under the Geneva Conventions? The U.S. executive branch argued that the Geneva Conventions do not apply to a war against terrorism. The Human Rights Watch, an organization that opposed the U. S. treatment of prisoners in Guantánamo Bay, argued that the prisoners were captured in a war against Afghanistan (rather than against "terrorism" in general) and that most of the detainees met the four criteria for POW status: (1) be under the control of a responsible commander; (2) carry arms openly; (3) wear uniforms with distinct insignia; and (4) conduct their operations in accordance with the laws and customs of war. These definitional issues were bitterly debated in the media.

An Overview of Categorical Arguments

Categorical arguments are among the most common argument types you will encounter. They occur whenever you claim that any given X belongs in category Y. Does skateboarding belong in the category "true sport"? Should this forthcoming movie be placed in the category PG-13 or the category R? Is graffiti "art" or "vandalism"? Does my swerving across the center lane while trying to slap a bee on my windshield belong in the category "reckless driving"?

We place items in categories all the time, and the categories we choose can have subtle but powerful rhetorical effects, creating implicit mini-arguments. For example, if you don't like unsolicited e-mail, you might place it in the category "spam" and support legislation to make spam illegal. But people who make their livings through e-mail advertising place the same messages in the category "constitutionally protected free speech." If you favor biotech corn, you want to place it in the broad category "corn" and keep the term "biotech" off labels on cans. If you oppose it, you want to classify it as "frankenfood." Or consider the competing categories proposed for whales in an international whaling controversy accelerated by the recent desires of whaling nations such as Japan to resume commercial whaling. What category does a whale belong to? Some arguers place whales in the category "sacred animals" that should never be killed because of their intelligence, beauty, grace, and power. Others group whales with tuna, crabs, cattle, and chickens in the category "renewable food resource." Others worry whether the specific kinds of whales being hunted are "an endangered species"—a concept that argues for the preservation of whale stocks but not necessarily for a ban on controlled hunting of individual whales once population numbers rise sufficiently. Each of these whaling arguments places whales within a different category that implicitly urges the reader to adopt that category's perspective on whaling.

Categorical claims shift from implicit to explicit arguments whenever the arguer supplies reasons and evidence to persuade us that X does or does not belong in category Y. In the rest of this chapter we discuss two kinds of categorical arguments: (1) simple categorical arguments in which writer and an audience agree on the meaning of the Y term and (2) definitional arguments in which the meaning of the Y term itself is controversial.

Simple Categorical Arguments

A categorical argument can be said to be "simple" if there is no disagreement about the meaning of the Y term. For example, suppose you are discussing with fellow committee members whom to select as committee chairperson. You want to make the case that "David won't make a good committee chair because he is too bossy." Your supporting reason ("David is too bossy") is a simple categorical claim. You assume that everyone agrees what "bossy" means; the point of contention is whether David is or is not bossy. To support your claim, you would supply examples of David's bossiness; to refute it, someone else might supply counterexamples of David's cooperative and kind nature. As this example suggests, the basic procedural rule for developing a simple categorical claim is to supply examples and other data that show how X is or is not a member of category Y.

Difference Between Facts and Simple Categorical Claims

Simple categorical claims are interpretive statements about reality. They claim that something does or does not exist or that something does or does not possess the qualities of a certain category. Often simple categorical claims look like facts, so it is important to distinguish between a fact and a simple categorical claim.

A *fact* is a statement that can be verified in some way, either by empirical observation or by reference to a reliable source (say, an encyclopedia) trusted by you and your audience. Here are some facts: Water freezes at thirty-two degrees. Boise is in Idaho, not Montana. The bald eagle is no longer on the EPA's endangered species list. These are all facts because they can be verified; no supporting arguments are needed or called for.

In contrast, a *simple categorical claim* is a contestable interpretation of facts. Consider the difference between these two sentences:

Fact: The bald eagle is no longer on the EPA's endangered species list.

Simple categorical claim: The bald eagle is no longer an endangered species.

We can verify the factual statement by looking at the list of endangered species published by the Environmental Protection Agency. We can see the date on which the bald eagle was placed on the list (1973) and the date it was removed (1995). The second statement is a claim. Imagine all the debates and arguments that EPA scientists had as they pored over statistical data about eagle population numbers and over field reports from observers of eagles before they decided to remove the bald eagle from the list.

For Class Discussion

Working individually or in small groups, determine which of the following statements are facts and which are categorical claims. If you think a statement could be a "fact" for some audiences and a "claim" for others, explain your reasoning.

1. State sales taxes are not deductible on your federal income tax form.
2. State sales taxes are annoying to both buyers and sellers.
3. State sales taxes are a hardship on low-income families.
4. Nelly is a recording artist.
5. Nelly is a gangsta rapper.

Variations in the Wording of Simple Categorical Claims

Simple categorical claims typically take the grammatical structure "X is a Y." Grammarians describe this structure as a subject followed by a linking verb (such as "to be" or "to seem") followed by a predicate noun or adjective.

David is bossy.

State sales taxes are annoying.

Eleanor Roosevelt sometimes seemed anti-Semitic.

But other grammatical constructions can be used to make the same categorical claims.

> David frequently bosses people around. (He belongs to the category "people who are bossy.")
>
> Sales taxes really annoy people. (Sales taxes belong to the category "things that are annoying.")
>
> On occasion, Eleanor Roosevelt made anti-Semitic remarks. (Eleanor Roosevelt belongs to the category "people who occasionally seem anti-Semitic.")

Almost any kind of interpretive statement about reality (other than causal statements, which are covered in Chapter 12) is a categorical claim of some kind. Whether they are worded directly as "X is Y" statements or disguised in different grammatical structures, they assert that item X belongs in category Y or possesses the features of category Y.

Supporting Simple Categorical Claims: Supply Examples

The basic strategy for supporting a simple categorical claim is to give examples or other data showing how X belongs in category Y. If you want to argue that Sam is a party animal, provide examples of his partying behavior. If you want to argue that Eleanor Roosevelt sometimes seemed anti-Semitic, quote excerpts of anti-Semitic statements from her personal correspondence.* Because simple categorical arguments are common building blocks for longer, more complex arguments, they often take no more than one or two paragraphs inside a longer piece. But a simple categorical claim can also be the thesis for a whole argument. We provide such an example in the letter to the editor (pp. 190–191) by the director general of the Taipei Economic and Cultural Office asserting that Taiwan meets the criteria for admission to the United Nations.

Refuting Simple Categorical Claims

If you wish to challenge or question someone else's simple categorical claim, you have three common strategies at your disposal:

- *Deny the accuracy or truth of the examples and data.* "You say that David is bossy. But you are remembering incorrectly. That wasn't David who did those bossy things; that was Paul."

---

*Roosevelt's biographer Blanche Wiesen Cook deals sensitively with this complex issue, largely exonerating Roosevelt from the charge of anti-Semitism. See *Eleanor Roosevelt*, vol. 2, *1933–38* (New York: Viking, 1999).

■ *Provide counterexamples that place X in a different category.* "Well, maybe David acted bossy on a few occasions. But more often he is kind and highly cooperative. For example . . . ."

■ *Raise definitional questions about the Y term.* "Well, that depends on what you mean by 'bossy.' What you call bossiness, I call decisiveness."

The last of these strategies shows how easily a simple categorical claim can slip into a definitional dispute. In the rest of this chapter we turn our attention to definitional arguments.

For Class Discussion

Working as a whole class or in small groups, prepare brief arguments in support of each of the following categorical claims. Then discuss ways in which you might call these claims into question.

1. Americans today are obsessed with their appearance.
2. Professional athletes are overpaid.
3. The video games most enjoyed by children are extremely violent.

An Overview of Definitional Arguments

As we turn now to definitional arguments, it is important to distinguish between cases where definitions are *needed* and cases where definitions are *disputed.* Many arguments require a definition of key terms. If you are arguing, for example, that after-school jobs are harmful to teenagers because they promote materialism, you will probably need to define *materialism* somewhere in your argument. Writers regularly define key words for their readers by providing synonyms, by citing a dictionary definition, by stipulating a definition, or by some other means.

In the rest of this chapter, we focus on arguments in which the meaning of a key term is disputed. Consider, for example, the environmental controversy over the definition of *wetland.* Section 404 of the federal Clean Water Act provides for federal protection of wetlands but leaves the task of defining *wetland* to administrative agencies and the courts. Currently about 5 percent of the land surface of the contiguous forty-eight states is potentially affected by the wetlands provision, and 75 percent of this land is privately owned. Efforts to define *wetland* have created a battleground between pro-environment and pro-development (or pro–private property rights) groups. Farmers, homeowners, and developers often want a narrow definition so that more property is available for commercial or private use. Environmentalists favor a broad definition in order to protect different habitat types and maintain the environmental safeguards that wetlands provide (control of water pollution, spawning grounds for aquatic species, floodwater containment, and so forth).

The problem is that defining *wetland* is tricky. For example, one federal regulation defines a wetland as any area that has a saturated ground surface for twenty-one consecutive days during the year. But how would you apply this law to a pine flatwood ecosystem that was wet for ten days this year but thirty days last year? And how should the courts react to lawsuits claiming that the regulation itself is either too broad or too narrow? It is easy to see why the wetlands controversy provides hefty incomes for lawyers and congressional lobbyists.

The Criteria-Match Structure of Definitional Arguments

As the wetlands example suggests, definitional arguments usually have a two-part structure—a definition part that tries to establish the meaning of the Y term (What do we mean by *wetland*?) and a match part that argues whether a given X meets that definition (Does this thirty-acre parcel of land meet the criteria for wetlands?) We use the term *criteria-match* to describe this structure, which occurs regularly not only in definitional arguments but also in evaluation arguments of the type "X is (is not) a good Y" (see Chapter 14). The "criteria" part of the structure defines the Y term by setting forth the criteria that must be met for something to be considered a Y. The "match" part examines whether the X term meets these criteria.

Let's consider another example. Suppose you work for a consumer information group that wishes to encourage patronage of socially responsible companies while boycotting irresponsible ones. Your group's first task is to define *socially responsible company*. After much discussion and research, your group establishes three criteria that a company must meet to be considered socially responsible:

> *Your definition:* A company is socially responsible if it (1) avoids polluting the environment, (2) sells goods or services that contribute to the well-being of the community, and (3) treats its workers justly.

The criteria section of your argument would explain and illustrate these criteria. The match part of the argument would then try to persuade readers that a specific company does or does not meet the criteria. A typical thesis statement might be as follows:

> *Your thesis statement:* Although the Hercules Shoe Company is nonpolluting and provides a socially useful product, it is *not* a socially responsible company because it treats workers unjustly.

Here is how the core of the argument could be displayed in Toulmin terms (note how the criteria established in your definition serve as warrants for your argument):

INITIAL ENTHYMEME: The Hercules Shoe Company is not a socially responsible company because it treats workers unjustly.

CLAIM: The Hercules Shoe Company is *not* a socially responsible company.

STATED REASON: because it treats workers unjustly

GROUNDS: evidence that the company manufactures its shoes in East Asian sweatshops; evidence of the inhumane conditions in these shops; evidence of hardships imposed on displaced American workers

WARRANT: Socially responsible companies treat workers justly.

BACKING: arguments showing that just treatment of workers is right in principle and also benefits society; arguments that capitalism helps society as a whole only if workers achieve a reasonable standard of living, have time for leisure, and are not exploited

POSSIBLE CONDITIONS OF REBUTTAL: Opponents of this thesis might argue that justice needs to be considered from an emerging nation's standpoint: The wages paid workers are low by American standards but are above average by East Asian standards. Displacement of American workers is part of the necessary adjustment of adapting to a global economy and does not mean that a company is unjust.

As this Toulmin schema illustrates, the writer's argument needs to contain a criteria section (warrant and backing) showing that just treatment of workers is a criterion for social responsibility and a match section (stated reason and grounds) showing that the Hercules Shoe Company does not treat its workers justly. The conditions of rebuttal help the writer imagine alternative views and see places where opposing views need to be acknowledged and rebutted.

For Class Discussion

Consider the following definitional claims. Working as individuals or in small groups, identify the criteria issue and the match issue for each of the following claims.

EXAMPLE: A Honda assembled in Ohio is (is not) an American-made car.

CRITERIA PART: What criteria have to be met before a car can be called "American made"?

MATCH PART: Does a Honda assembled in Ohio meet these criteria?

1. Enron's accounting practices did (did not) constitute an illegal pyramid scheme.
2. Writing graffiti on subways is (is not) vandalism.
3. American Sign Language is (is not) a "foreign language" for purposes of a college graduation requirement.
4. Beauty contests are (are not) sexist events.
5. Bungee jumping from a crane is (is not) a "carnival amusement ride" subject to state safety inspections.

Conceptual Problems of Definition

Before moving on to discuss ways of defining the Y term in a definitional argument, we should explore briefly some of the conceptual difficulties of definition. Language, for all its wonderful powers, is an arbitrary system that requires agreement among its users before it can work. And it's not always easy to get that agreement. In fact, the task of defining something can be devilishly complex.

Why Can't We Just Look in the Dictionary?

What's so hard about defining? you might ask. Why not just look in a dictionary? To get a sense of the complexity of defining something, consider again the word *wetland.* A dictionary can tell us the ordinary meaning (the way a word is commonly used), but it can't resolve a debate about competing definitions when different parties have interests in defining the word in different ways. For example, *Webster's Seventh New Collegiate Dictionary* defines *wetland* as "land containing much soil moisture"—a definition that is hardly helpful in determining whether the federal government can prevent the development of a beach resort on some landowner's private property. Moreover, dictionary definitions rarely tell us such things as *to what degree* a given condition must be met before something qualifies for class membership. How wet does land have to be before it is *legally* a wetland? How long does this wetness have to last? When is a wetland a mere swamp that ought to be drained rather than protected?

Definitions and the Rule of Justice: At What Point Does X Stop Being a Y?

For some people, all this concern about definition may seem misplaced. How often, after all, have you heard people accuse each other of getting bogged down in "mere semantics"? But how you define a given word can have significant implications for people who must either use the word or have the word used on them. Take, for example, what some philosophers refer to as the *rule of justice*. According to this rule, "beings in the same essential category should be treated in the same way." Should an insurance company, for example, treat anorexia nervosa as a physical illness like diabetes (in which case treatment is paid for by the insurance company) or as a mental illness like paranoia (in which case insurance payments are minimal)? Or, to take another example, if a company gives "new baby" leave to a mother, should it also give "new baby" leave to a father? In other words, is this kind of leave "new mother" leave or is it "new parent" leave? And what if a couple adopts an infant? Should "new mother" or "new parent" leave be available to adoptive parents also? These questions are all definitional issues involving arguments about what class of beings an individual belongs to and about what actions to take to comply with the rule of justice, which demands that all members of that class be treated equally.

The rule of justice becomes even harder to apply when we consider X's that grow, evolve, or otherwise change through time. When Young Person back in Chapter 1 argued that she could set her own curfew because she was mature, she raised the question "What are the attributes or criteria of a 'mature' person?" In this case, a categorical distinction between two separate kinds of things ("mature" versus "not mature") evolves into a distinction of degree ("mature enough"). So perhaps we should ask not whether Young Person is mature but whether she is "mature enough." At what point does a child become an adult? (When does a fetus become a human person? When does a social drinker become an alcoholic?)

Although we may be able arbitrarily to choose a particular point and declare, through stipulation, that "mature" means eighteen years old or that "human person" includes a fetus at conception, or at three months, or at birth, in the everyday world the distinction between child and adult, between egg and person, between social drinking and alcoholism seems an evolution, not a sudden and definitive step. Nevertheless, our language requires an abrupt shift between classes. In short, applying the rule of justice often requires us to adopt a digital approach to reality (switches are either on or off, either a fetus is a human person or it is not), whereas our sense of life is more analogical (there are numerous gradations between on and off; there are countless shades of gray between black and white).

As we can see by the preceding examples, the promise of language to fix what psychologist William James called "the buzz and confusion of the world" into an orderly set of categories turns out to be elusive. In most definitional debates, an argument, not a quick trip to the dictionary, is required to settle the matter.

Kinds of Definitions

In this section we discuss two methods of definition commonly used in definitional arguments: Aristotelian and operational.

Aristotelian Definition

Aristotelian definitions, regularly used in dictionaries, define a term by placing it within the next larger class or category and then showing the specific attributes that distinguish the term from other terms within the same category. For example, a *pencil* is a "writing implement" (next larger category) that differs from other writing implements in that it makes marks with lead or graphite rather than ink. You could elaborate this definition by saying, "Usually the lead or graphite is a long, thin column embedded in a slightly thicker column of wood with an eraser on one end and a sharpened point, exposing the graphite, on the other." You could even distinguish a wooden pencil from a mechanical pencil, thereby indicating again that the crucial identifying attribute is the graphite, not the wooden column.

As you can see, an Aristotelian definition of a term identifies specific attributes or criteria that enable you to distinguish it from other members of the next larger class. We created an Aristotelian definition in our example about socially responsible companies. A *socially responsible company,* we said, is any company (next larger class) that meets three criteria: (1) It doesn't pollute the environment, (2) it creates goods/services that promote the well-being of the community, and (3) it treats its workers justly.

Operational Definition

In some rhetorical situations, particularly those arising in the physical and social sciences, writers need *operational definitions*—precise definitions that can be measured empirically and are not subject to problems of context and disputed criteria. Consider, for example, an argument involving the concept "aggression": "Do violent television programs increase the incidence of aggression in children?" To do research on this issue, a scientist needs a precise, measurable definition of *aggression.* Typically, a scientist might measure "aggression" by counting the number of blows or kicks a child gives to an inflatable bozo doll over a fifteen-minute period when other play options are available. The scientist might then define "aggressive behavior" as six or more blows to the bozo doll.

In our wetlands example, a federal authority created an operational definition of *wetland*: A wetland is a parcel of land that has a saturated ground surface for twenty-one consecutive days during the year. Such definitions are useful because they are precisely measurable, but they are also limited because they omit criteria that may be unmeasurable but important. Many scientists, for example, object to definitions of *wetland* based on consecutive days of wetness. What is more relevant, they argue, is not the duration of wetness in any parcel of land, but the kind of plants and animals that depend on the wetland as a habitat. As another example, we might ask whether it is adequate to define a "superior student" as someone with a 3.5 GPA or higher or a "successful sex education program" as one that results in a 25 percent reduction in teenage pregnancies. What important aspects of a superior student or a successful sex education program are not considered in these operational definitions?

Strategies for Defining the Contested Term in a Definitional Argument

In constructing criteria to define your contested term, you can take two basic approaches—what rhetoricians call reportive and stipulative definitions. A *reportive definition* cites how others have used the term. A *stipulative definition* cites how you define the term. You can take a reportive approach by turning to standard or specialized dictionaries, judicial opinions, or expert testimony to establish a definition based on the authority of others. A lawyer defining *wetland* as land with twenty-one consecutive days of saturated ground surface would be using a reportive definition with a federal regulation as her source. The other approach requires you to use your own critical thinking to stipulate a definition, thereby defining the contested term yourself. Our definition of *socially responsible company*, specifying three criteria, is a stipulative definition. This section explains these approaches in more detail.

Reportive Approach: Research How Others Have Used the Term

When you take a reportive approach, you research how others have used the term, searching for authoritative definitions acceptable to your audience yet favorable to your case. Student writer Kathy Sullivan uses this approach in her argument that photographs displayed at the Oncore Bar are not obscene (see pp. 191–193). To define *obscenity*, she turns to *Black's Law Dictionary* and Pember's *Mass Media Laws*. (Specialized dictionaries are a standard part of the reference section of any library—see your reference librarian for assistance.) Other sources of specialized definitions are state and federal appellate court decisions, legislative and administrative statutes, and scholarly articles examining a given definitional conflict. Lawyers use this research strategy exhaustively when preparing court briefs. They begin by looking at the actual text of laws as passed by legislatures or written by administrative authorities. Then they look at all the court cases in which the laws have been tested, and they examine the ways courts have refined legal definitions and applied them to specific cases. Using these refined and elaborated definitions, lawyers then apply them to their own case at hand.

When research fails to uncover a definition favorable to the arguer's case, the arguer can sometimes adopt an *original intentions strategy*. For example, if a scientist is dissatisfied with definitions of *wetland* based on consecutive days of saturated ground surface, she might proceed as follows: "The original intention of the Congress in passing the Clean Water Act was to preserve the environment." What members of Congress intended, she could then claim, was to prevent development of those wetland areas that provide crucial habitat for wildlife or that inhibit water pollution. She could then propose an alternative definition (either a stipulative one that she develops herself or a reportive one that she uncovers in research) based on criteria other than consecutive days of ground saturation. (Of course, original intentions arguments can often be refuted by a "times have changed" strategy or by a "we can't know what they originally intended; we can only know what they wrote" strategy.)

Another way to make a reportive definition is to employ a strategy based on etymology, the *earlier meaning strategy.* Using an etymological dictionary or the *Oxford English Dictionary* (which traces the historical evolution of a word's meaning), an arguer can often unveil insights favorable to the writer's case. For example, if you wanted to argue that portrayal of violence in films is obscene, you could point to the etymology of the word *obscene,* which literally means "offstage." The word derives from classical Greek tragedy, in which violent acts occurred offstage and were only reported by a messenger. This strategy allows you to show how the word originally applied to violence rather than to sexual explicitness.

Stipulative Approach: Create Your Own Definition*

Often, however, you need to create your own definition of the contested term. An effective strategy is to establish initial criteria for your contested term by thinking of hypothetical cases that obviously fit the category you are trying to define and then thinking of hypothetical cases that obviously don't fit the category. You can then test and refine your criteria by applying them to borderline cases. For example, suppose you work at a homeless agency where you overhear street people discuss an incident that strikes you potentially as "police brutality." You wonder whether you should write to your local paper to bring attention to the incident.

CONTESTED CASE REGARDING POLICE BRUTALITY

Two police officers confront an inebriated homeless man who is shouting obscenities on a street corner. The officers tell the man to quiet down and move on, but he keeps shouting obscenities. When the officers attempt to put the man into the police car, he resists and takes a wild swing at one of the officers. As eyewitnesses later testified, this officer shouted obscenities back at the drunk man, pinned his arms behind his back in order to handcuff him, and lifted him forcefully by the arms. The man screamed in

---

*The defining strategies and collaborative exercises in this section are based on the work of George Hillocks and his research associates at the University of Chicago. See George Hillocks Jr., Elizabeth A. Kahn, and Larry R. Johannessen, "Teaching Defining Strategies as a Mode of Inquiry: Some Effects on Student Writing," *Research in the Teaching of English* 17 (Oct. 1983): 275–84. See also Larry R. Johannessen, Elizabeth A. Kahn, and Carolyn Calhoun Walter, *Designing and Sequencing Prewriting Activities* (Urbana: NCTE, 1982).

pain and was later discovered to have a dislocated shoulder. Is this officer guilty of police brutality?

To your way of thinking, this officer seems guilty: An inebriated man is too uncoordinated to be a threat in a fight, and two police officers ought to be able to arrest him without dislocating his shoulder. But a friend argues that because the man took a swing at the officer, the police were justified in using force. The dislocated shoulder was simply an accidental result of using justified force.

To make your case, you need to develop a definition of "police brutality." You can begin by creating a hypothetical case that is obviously an instance of "police brutality":

CLEAR CASE OF POLICE BRUTALITY

A police officer confronts a drunk man shouting obscenities and begins hitting him in the face with his police baton. *[This is an obvious incidence of police brutality because the officer intentionally tries to hurt the drunk man without justification; hitting him with the baton is not necessary for making an arrest or getting the man into a police car.]*

You could then vary the hypothetical case until it is clearly *not* an instance of police brutality.

CASES THAT ARE CLEARLY NOT POLICE BRUTALITY

Case 1: The police officer handcuffs the drunk man, who, in being helped into the police car, accidentally slips on the curb and dislocates his arm while falling. *[Here the injury occurs accidentally; the police officer does not act intentionally and is not negligent.]*

Case 2: The police officer confronts an armed robber fleeing from a scene and tackles him from behind, wrestling the gun away from him. In this struggle, the officer pins the robber's arm behind his back with such force that the robber's shoulder is dislocated. *[Here aggressive use of force is justified because the robber was armed, dangerous, and resisting arrest.]*

Using these hypothetical cases, you decide that the defining criteria for police brutality are (1) *intention* and (2) use of *excessive force*—that is, force beyond what was required by the immediate situation. After more contemplation, you are convinced that the officer was guilty of police brutality and have a clearer idea of how to make your argument. Here is how you might write the "match" part of your argument.

MATCH ARGUMENT USING YOUR STIPULATED DEFINITION

If we define police brutality as the *intentional* use of *excessive* force, then the police officer is guilty. His action was intentional because he was purposefully responding to the homeless man's drunken swing and was angry enough to be shouting obscenities back at the drunk (according to the eyewitnesses). Second, he used excessive force in applying the handcuffs. A drunk man taking a wild swing hardly poses a serious danger to two police officers. Putting handcuffs on the drunk may have been justified, but lifting the man's arm violently enough to dislocate a shoulder indicates excessive force. The officer lifted the man's arms violently not because he needed to but because he was angry, and acting out of anger is no justification for that violence. In fact, we can charge police officers with "police brutality" precisely to protect us from being victims of police anger. It is the job of the court system to punish us, not the police's job. Because this officer acted intentionally and applied excessive force out of anger, he should be charged with police brutality.

The strategy we have demonstrated—developing criteria by imagining hypothetical cases that clearly do and do not belong to the contested category—gives you a systematic procedure for developing a stipulated definition for your argument.

For Class Discussion

1. Suppose you wanted to define the concept "courage." Working in groups, try to decide whether each of the following cases is an example of courage:

    a. A neighbor rushes into a burning house to rescue a child from certain death and emerges, coughing and choking, with the child in his arms. Is the neighbor courageous?

    b. A firefighter rushes into a burning house to rescue a child from certain death and emerges with the child in her arms. The firefighter is wearing protective clothing and a gas mask. When a newspaper reporter calls her courageous, she says, "Hey, this is my job." Is the firefighter courageous?

    c. A teenager rushes into a burning house to recover a memento given to him by his girlfriend, the first love of his life. Is the teenager courageous?

    d. A parent rushes into a burning house to save a trapped child. The fire marshal tells the parent to wait because there is no chance the child can be reached from the first floor. The fire marshal wants to try cutting a hole in the roof to reach the child. The parent rushes into the house anyway and is burned to death. Was the parent courageous?

2. As you make your decisions on each of these cases, create and refine the criteria you use.

3. Make up your own series of controversial cases, like those above for "courage," for one or more of the following concepts:

    a. cruelty to animals

    b. child abuse

    c. true athlete

    d. sexual harassment

    e. free speech protected by the First Amendment

Based on your controversial cases, construct a definition of your chosen term. Follow the strategy demonstrated in the "police brutality" example (pp. 185–187) of using a clear case that meets the criteria and then negative cases that do not meet the criteria.

Conducting the Match Part of a Definitional Argument

In conducting a match argument, you need to show that your contested case does or does not meet the criteria you established in your definition, supplying evidence and examples showing why the case meets or does not meet the criteria. In essence, you support the match part of your argument in much the same way you would support a simple categorical claim.

For example, if you were developing the argument that the Hercules Shoe Company is not socially responsible because it treats its workers unjustly, your match section would provide evidence of this injustice. You might supply data about the percentage of shoes produced in East Asia, about the low wages paid these workers, and about the working conditions in these factories. You might also describe the suffering of displaced American workers when Hercules closed its American factories and moved operations to Asia, where the labor was non-union and cheap. The match section should also summarize and respond to opposing views.

Organizing a Definitional Argument

As you compose a first draft of your essay, you may find it helpful to know a prototypical structure for definitional arguments. Here are several possible plans.

Plan 1 (Criteria and Match in Separate Sections)

- Introduce the issue by showing disagreements about the definition of a key term or about the application of a key term to a problematic case.
- State your claim.
- Present your definition of the key term.
  State and develop Criterion 1.
  State and develop Criterion 2.
  Continue with the rest of your criteria.
- Summarize and respond to possible objections to your definition.
- Restate your claim about the contested case (it does or does not meet your definition).
  Apply Criterion 1 to your case.
  Apply Criterion 2 to your case.
  Continue the match argument.

- Summarize and respond to possible objections to your match argument.
- Conclude your argument.

Plan 2 (Criteria and Match Interwoven)

- Introduce the issue by showing disagreements about the definition of a key term or about the application of a key term to a problematic case.
- Present your claim.

   State Criterion 1 and argue that the contested case meets or does not meet the criterion.

   State Criterion 2 and argue that the contested case meets or does not meet the criterion.

   Continue with criteria-match sections for additional criteria.

- Summarize opposing views.
- Refute or concede to opposing views.
- Conclude your argument.

Questioning and Critiquing a Definitional Argument

In refuting a definitional argument, you need to appreciate its criteria-match structure. Your refutation can question the argument's criteria, the argument's match, or both.

Questioning the Criteria

Might a skeptic claim that your criteria are not the right ones? This is the most common way to attack a definitional argument. Skeptics might say that one or more of your argument's criteria are irrelevant or too narrow or too broad. Or they might argue for different criteria or point out crucial missing criteria.

   Might a skeptic point out possible bad consequences of accepting your argument's criteria? Here a skeptic could raise doubts about your definition by showing how it would lead to unintended bad consequences.

   Might a skeptic cite extraordinary circumstances that weaken your argument's criteria? Skeptics might argue that your criteria are perfectly acceptable in ordinary circumstances but are rendered unacceptable by extraordinary circumstances.

   Might a skeptic point out a bias or slant in your definition? Writers create definitions favorable to their case. By making this slant visible, a skeptic may be able to weaken the persuasiveness of your definition.

Questioning the Match

A match argument usually uses examples and other evidence to show that the contested case meets or does not meet the criteria in the definition. The standard methods of refuting evidence thus apply (see pp. 126–127). Thus skeptics might ask one or more of the following questions:

> Are your examples out-of-date or too narrow and unrepresentative?
>
> Are your examples inaccurate?
>
> Are your examples too extreme?
>
> Are there existing counterexamples that alter the case?

By using the questions to test your own argument, you can reshape and develop your argument to make it thought provoking and persuasive for your audience.

Readings

Our first reading makes a simple categorical claim that Taiwan meets the criteria for membership in the United Nations. In this letter to the editor of a major newspaper, Jack K. C. Chiang, director general of the Taipei Economic and Cultural Office, cites factual evidence about Taiwan related to the U.N.'s criteria for membership. What prevents Taiwan's membership in the U.N.—Chiang notes—is the veto of mainland China (the People's Republic of China), which refuses to grant recognition to Taiwan. It claims that Taiwan legitimately belongs to the People's Republic.

Why Not Taiwan?

Jack K. C. Chiang

1   Switzerland recently voted to join the United Nations and will become the U.N.'s 190th member this September ("Neutral Swiss vote to join United Nations," Times, March 4). A question raised among the people in Taiwan (The Republic of China) and all Taiwanese Americans is: If Switzerland is qualified for U.N. membership, why not Taiwan? Consider Taiwan's list of qualifications for U.N. membership:

- A defined territory covering some 14,000 square miles.
- A population of some 23 million people, which is the 46th largest in the world, more than the population of two-thirds of U.N. member nations.
- A fully democratically elected government through two popular presidential elections since 1996.
- A vibrant economy marking the world's 16th largest, and third-largest holder of foreign exchange.

2   As a sovereign state, Taiwan absolutely meets all the criteria the U.N. uses to judge a country. Unfortunately, Taiwan has failed to be accepted by the U.N. merely because the People's Republic of China (PRC) opposes it. PRC claims that Taiwan is part

of its territory so that Taiwan cannot have its delegates in the U.N. But the facts are, since 1949, the government of the Republic of China has exercised effective control and jurisdiction over Taiwan, while PRC government has over the mainland during the same time. In other words, PRC has never ruled Taiwan, even for a single day.

U.N. Secretary-General Kofi Annan welcomed the vote in Switzerland, saying it   3
brought the United Nations closer to universality. Mr. Annan is perfectly right. Universality is the essence of the U.N.'s goal to world peace. So, why not Taiwan? With the participation of Taiwan, the U.N. can live up to its principle of universality, achieve its goal of preventive diplomacy, and facilitate the cross-Taiwan-strait reconciliation and peace process.

If the United Nations accepts Switzerland, then it should also welcome Taiwan.   4

Our second reading, by student Kathy Sullivan, was written for the definition assignment on page 193. The definitional issue that she addresses—"Are the Menasee photographs obscene?"—became a local controversy in the state of Washington when the state liquor control board threatened to revoke the liquor license of a Seattle gay bar, the Oncore, unless it removed a series of photographs that the board deemed obscene.

Oncore, Obscenity, and the Liquor Control Board
Kathy Sullivan (student)

In early May, Geoff Menasee, a Seattle artist, exhibited a series of photographs   1
with the theme of "safe sex" on the walls of an inner-city, predominantly homosexual restaurant and lounge called the Oncore. Before hanging the photographs, Menasee had to consult with the Washington State Liquor Control Board because, under the current state law, art work containing material that may be considered indecent has to be approved by the board before it can be exhibited. Of the almost thirty photographs, six were rejected by the board because they partially exposed "private parts" of the male anatomy. Menasee went ahead and displayed the entire series of photographs, placing Band-Aids over the "indecent" areas, but the customers continually removed the Band-Aids.

The liquor control board's ruling on this issue has caused controversy in the   2
Seattle community. The *Seattle Times* has provided news coverage, and a "Town Meeting" segment was filmed at the restaurant. The central question is this: Should an establishment that caters to a predominantly homosexual clientele be enjoined from displaying pictures promoting "safe sex" on the grounds that the photographs are obscene?

Before I can answer this question, I must first determine whether the art work   3
should truly be classified as obscene. To make that determination, I will use the definition of *obscenity* in *Black's Law Dictionary:*

Material is "obscene" if to the average person, applying contemporary community standards, the dominant theme of material taken as a whole appeals to prurient interest, if it is utterly without redeeming social importance, if it goes substantially beyond customary limits of candor in description or representation, if it is characterized by patent offensiveness, and if it is hard core pornography.

4   An additional criterion is provided by Pember's *Mass Media Laws:* "A work is obscene if it has a tendency to deprave and corrupt those whose minds are open to such immoral influences (children for example) and into whose hands it might happen to fall" (394). The art work in question should not be prohibited from display at predominantly homosexual establishments like the Oncore because it does not meet the above criteria for obscenity.

5   First of all, to the average person applying contemporary community standards, the predominant theme of Menasee's photographs is not an appeal to prurient interests. The first element in this criterion is "average person." According to Rocky Breckner, manager of the Oncore, 90 percent of the clientele at the Oncore is made up of young white homosexual males. This group therefore constitutes the "average person" viewing the exhibit. "Contemporary community standards" would ordinarily be the standards of the Seattle community. However, this art work is aimed at a particular group of people—the homosexual community. Therefore, the "community standards" involved here are those of the gay community rather than the city at large. Since the Oncore is not an art museum or gallery, which attracts a broad spectrum of people, it is appropriate to restrict the scope of "community standards" to that group who voluntarily patronize the Oncore.

6   Second, the predominant theme of the photographs is not "prurient interest" nor do the photographs go "substantially beyond customary limits of candor." There are no explicit sexual acts found in the photographs; instead, their theme is the prevention of AIDS through the practice of safe sex. Homosexual displays of affection could be viewed as "prurient interest" by the larger community, but same-sex relationships are the norm for the group at whom the exhibit is aimed. If the exhibit were displayed at McDonald's or even the Red Robin it might go "substantially beyond customary limits of candor," but it is unlikely that the clientele of the Oncore would find the art work offensive. The manager stated that he received very few complaints about the exhibit and its contents.

7   Nor is the material pornographic. The liquor control board prohibited the six photographs based on their visible display of body parts such as pubic hair and naked buttocks, not on the basis of sexual acts or homosexual orientation. The board admitted that the photographs depicted no explicit sexual acts. Hence, it can be concluded that they did not consider the suggestion of same-sex affection to be hard-core pornography. Their sole objection was that body parts were visible. But visible genitalia in art work are not necessarily pornographic. Since other art work, such as Michelangelo's sculptures, explicitly depicts both male and female genitalia, it is arguable that pubic hair and buttocks are not patently offensive.

It must be conceded that the art work has the potential of being viewed by 8
children, which would violate Pember's criterion. But once again the incidence of
minors frequenting this establishment is very small.

But the most important reason for saying these photographs are not obscene is 9
that they serve an important social purpose. One of Black's criteria is that obscene
material is "utterly without redeeming social importance." But these photographs
have the explicit purpose of promoting safe sex as a defense against AIDS. Recent
statistics reported in the *Seattle Times* show that AIDS is now the leading cause of
death of men under forty in the Seattle area. Any methods that can promote the
message of safe sex in today's society have strong redeeming social significance.

Those who believe that all art containing "indecent" material should be banned 10
or covered from public view would most likely believe that Menasee's work is obscene. They would disagree that the environment and the clientele should be the
major determining factors when using criteria to evaluate art. However, in the case
of this exhibit I feel that the audience and the environment of the display are factors
of overriding importance. Therefore, the exhibit should have been allowed to be displayed because it is not obscene.

WRITING ASSIGNMENT
FOR CHAPTER 11

Write an argument that develops a definitional claim of the form "X is (is not) a
Y," where Y is a controversial term with a disputed definition. Typically your argument will have a criteria section in which you develop an extended definition
of your Y term and a match section in which you argue that your X does or does
not meet the criteria for Y.

12 Causal Arguments
X Causes (Does Not Cause) Y

EXAMPLE CASE

A world haunted by terrorism is also haunted by outbreaks of appalling teenage violence. On April 22, 2002, a nineteen-year-old student in Erfurt, Germany, opened fire on his classmates, shooting sixteen victims at close range before he was stopped by a courageous, unarmed teacher. In trying to understand the causes of this event, German sociologists turned to the causal debate in America following the Columbine High School massacre in Littleton, Colorado, where two male students killed twelve of their classmates and wounded twenty-three before killing themselves. Among the causes of teenage violence proposed by social scientists and media commentators were the following: violent movies, violent video games, violent TV, the music of Marilyn Manson, easy access to guns, breakdown of the traditional family, absence of parental involvement in teen lives, erosion of school discipline, inadequate school counseling, Internet neo-Nazi chat rooms, Internet lessons on how to make bombs, and the irresponsible prescribing of antidepressants to teenagers (one of the Columbine assailants was on Prozac). For each proposed cause, the arguer suggested a different approach for reducing teen violence.

An Overview of Causal Arguments

We encounter causal issues all the time. What caused the massacres in Erfurt, Germany, and Littleton, Colorado? What is the effect of rap music on teenagers? What caused the corporate greed leading to the Enron and WorldCom scandals in 2002? What will be the consequences of curtailing human rights in the fight against terrorism? Will opening up national forests to more logging (the proposed federal policy under the Bush administration) help prevent forest fires?

Sometimes an argument can be devoted entirely to a causal issue. Just as frequently, causal arguments support proposal arguments in which the writer argues that we should (should not) do X because doing X will lead to good (bad) consequences. Convincing readers how X will lead to these consequences—a causal argument—thus bears on the success of many proposal arguments.

Because causal arguments require close analysis of phenomena, effective causal arguing is closely linked to critical thinking. Studies of critical thinking show that good problem solvers systematically explore the causes of a problem before proposing a solution. Equally important, before making a decision, good problem solvers predict and weigh the consequences of alternative solutions to a problem, trying to determine a solution that produces the greatest benefits with the least cost. Adding to the complexity of causal arguing is the way a given event can have multiple causes and multiple consequences. In an effort to save salmon, for example, environmentalists have proposed the elimination of several dams on the Snake River above Lewiston, Idaho. Will the removal of these dams save the salmon? Nobody knows for sure, but three universally agreed-on consequences of removing the dams will be the loss of several thousand jobs in the Lewiston area, the loss of some hydroelectric power, and the shift in wheat transportation from river barges to overland trucks and trains. So the initial focus on consequences to salmon soon widens to include consequences to jobs, to power generation, and to agricultural transportation.

The Nature of Causal Arguing

Typically, causal arguments try to show how one event brings about another. On the surface, causal arguments may seem a fairly straightforward matter—more concrete, to be sure, than the larger moral issues in which they are often embedded. But consider for a moment the classic illustration of causality—one billiard ball striking another on a pool table. Surely we are safe in saying that the movement of the second ball was "caused" by a transfer of energy from the first ball at the moment of contact. Well, yes and no. British philosopher David Hume (among others) argued long ago that we don't really perceive "causality"; what we perceive is one ball moving and then another ball moving. We infer the notion of causality, which is a human construct, not a property of billiard balls.

When humans become the focus of a causal argument, the very definition of causality is immediately vexed. When we say, for example, that a given factor X "caused" a person to do Y, we might mean that X "forced her to do Y," thereby negating her free will (for example, the presence of a brain tumor caused my erratic behavior, which caused me to lose my job). But we might simply mean that factor X "motivated" her to do Y, in such a way that doing Y is still an expression of freedom (for example, my love of the ocean caused me to give up my job as a Wal-Mart greeter and become a California surf bum).

When we argue about causality in human beings, we must guard against confusing these two senses of "cause" or assuming that human behavior can be predicted or controlled in the same way that nonhuman behavior can. A rock dropped from a roof will always fall to the ground at thirty-two feet per second squared; and a rat zapped for making left turns in a maze will always quit making left turns. But if we raise interest rates, will consumers save more? If so, how much? This is the sort of question we debate endlessly.

Fortunately, most causal arguments can avoid the worst of these scientific and philosophic quagmires. As human beings, we share a number of assumptions about what causes events in the observable world, and we can depend on the goodwill of our audiences to grant us most of these assumptions. Most of us, for example, would be satisfied with the following explanation for why a car went into a skid: "In a panic the driver locked the brakes of his car, causing the car to go into a skid."

> panic → slamming brake pedal → locking brakes → skid

We probably do not need to defend this simple causal chain because the audience will grant the causal connections between events A, B, C, and D. The sequence seems reasonable according to our shared assumptions about psychological causality (panic leads to slamming brake pedal) and physical causality (locked brakes lead to skid).

But if you are an attorney defending a client whose skidding car caused considerable damage to an upscale boutique, you might see all sorts of additional causal factors. ("Because the stop sign at that corner was obscured by an untrimmed willow tree, my client innocently entered what he assumed was an open intersection only to find a speeding beer truck bearing down on him. When my client took immediate decelerating corrective action, the improperly maintained, oil-slicked roadway sent his car into its near-fatal skid and into the boutique's bow windows—windows that extrude into the walkway eleven full inches beyond the limit allowed by city code.") Okay, now what's the cause of the crash and who's at fault?

As the previous example shows, explaining causality entails creating a plausible chain of events linking a cause to its effect. Let's take another example—this time a real rather than hypothetical one. Consider an argument put forward by syndicated columnist John Leo as an explanation for the Columbine High School massacre.[*] Leo attributes part of the cause to the desensitizing effects of violent video games. After suggesting that the Littleton killings were partly choreographed on video game models, Leo suggests the following causal chain:

> Many youngsters are left alone for long periods of time → they play violent video games obsessively → their feelings of resentment and powerlessness "pour into the killing games" → the video games break down a natural aversion to killing, analogous to psychological techniques employed by the military → realistic touches in modern video games blur the "boundary between fantasy and reality" → youngsters begin identifying not with conventional heroes but with sociopaths who get their kicks from blowing away ordinary people ("pedestrians, marching bands, an elderly woman with a walker") → having enjoyed random violence in the video games, vulnerable youngsters act out the same adrenaline rush in real life.

---

*John Leo, "Kill-for-Kicks Video Games Desensitizing Our Children," *Seattle Times*, 27 Apr. 1999: B4.

Describing a Causal Argument in Toulmin Terms

Because causal arguments can involve lengthy or complex causal chains, they are often harder to summarize in *because* clauses than are other kinds of arguments. Likewise, they are not as likely to yield quick analysis through Toulmin's schema. Nevertheless, a causal argument can usually be stated as a claim with *because* clauses. Typically, a *because* clause for a causal argument pinpoints one or two key elements in the causal chain rather than trying to summarize every link. Leo's argument could be summarized in the following claim with *because* clause:

> Violent video games may have been a contributing cause to the Littleton massacre because playing these games can make random, sociopathic violence seem pleasurable.

Once stated as an enthymeme, the argument can be analyzed with Toulmin's schema. (It is easiest to apply Toulmin's schema to causal arguments if you think of the grounds as the observable phenomena at any point in the causal chain and the warrants as the shareable assumptions about causality that join links together.)

CLAIM: Violent video games may have been a contributing cause to the Littleton massacre.

STATED REASON: because playing these games can make random, sociopathic violence seem pleasurable

GROUNDS: evidence that the killers, like many young people, played violent video games; evidence that the games are violent; evidence that the games involve random, sociopathic violence (not heroic cops against aliens or gangsters, but a killer blowing away ordinary people—marching bands, little old ladies, etc.); evidence that young people derive pleasure from these games

WARRANT: If youngsters derive pleasure from random, sociopathic killing in video games, they can transfer this pleasure to real life, thus leading to the Littleton massacre.

BACKING: testimony from psychologists; evidence that violent video games desensitize persons to violence; analogy to military training where video game strategies are used to "make killing a reflex action"; evidence that the distinction between fantasy and reality becomes especially blurred for unstable children

CONDITIONS OF REBUTTAL: *Questioning the reason and grounds:*   Perhaps the killers didn't play video games. Perhaps the video games are no more violent than traditional kids' games (such as cops and robbers). Perhaps the video games do not feature sociopathic killing.

Questioning the warrant and backing: Perhaps kids are fully capable of distinguishing fantasy from reality. Perhaps the games are just fun with no transference to real life. Perhaps these video games are substantially different from military training strategies.

QUALIFIER: (Claim is already qualified by may and contributing cause.)

For Class Discussion

1. Working individually or in small groups, create a causal chain to show how the item on the left could help lead to the item on the right.

   a. invention of the automobile   redesign of cities

   b. invention of the automobile   changes in sexual mores

   c. invention of the telephone   loss of sense of community
                                            in neighborhoods

   d. origin of rap in black urban   the popularity of rap spreads
      music scene   from urban black audiences to
                                           white middle-class youth culture

   e. development of a way to   liberalization of euthanasia laws
      prevent rejections in transplant
      operations

2. For each of your causal chains, compose a claim with an attached *because* clause summarizing one or two key links in the causal chain. For example, "The invention of the automobile helped cause the redesign of cities because automobiles made it possible for people to live farther away from their places of work."

Three Methods for Arguing That One Event Causes Another

One of the first things you need to do when preparing a causal argument is to note exactly what sort of causal relationship you are dealing with. Are you concerned with causes or consequences of a specific one-time event (such as a mysterious airplane crash, your college faculty's decision to institute a service-learning requirement, or a recent Supreme Court decision), of a recurring phenomenon (such as eating disorders, road rage, or spousal abuse), or of a puzzling trend (such as the rising popularity of extreme sports or of recent changes in women's clothes toward microskirts, belly shirts, and low-rider pants)?

With recurring phenomena or with trends, you have the luxury of being able to study multiple cases over long periods of time and establishing correlations between suspected causal factors and effects. In some cases you can even intervene in the process and test for yourself whether diminishing a suspected causal factor results in a lessening of the effect or whether increasing the causal factor results in a corresponding increase in the effect. Additionally, you can spend time exploring how the mechanics of causation might work.

But with a one-time occurrence your focus is on the details of the event and specific causal chains that may have contributed to the event. Sometimes evidence has disappeared or changed its nature. You often end up in the position more of a detective than of a scientific researcher, and your conclusion will have to be more tentative as a result.

Having briefly stated these words of caution, let's turn now to the various ways you can argue that one event causes another.

First Method: Explain the Causal Mechanism Directly

The most convincing kind of causal argument identifies every link in the causal chain, showing how X causes A, which causes B, which in turn causes C, which finally causes Y. In some cases, all you have to do is fill in the missing links. In other cases—when your assumptions about causality may seem questionable to your audience—you have to argue for the causal connection with more vigor.

A careful spelling out of each step in the causal chain is the technique used by science writer Robert S. Devine in the following passage from his article "The Trouble with Dams." Although the benefits of dams are widely understood (cheap, pollution-free electricity; flood control; irrigation; barge transportation), the negative effects are less commonly known and understood. In this article, Devine tries to persuade readers that dams have serious negative consequences. In the following passage, he explains how dams reduce salmon flows by slowing the migration of smolts (newly hatched young salmon) to the sea.

CAUSAL ARGUMENT DESCRIBING A CAUSAL CHAIN

Such transformations lie at the heart of the ongoing environmental harm done by dams. Rivers are rivers because they flow, and the nature of their flows defines much of their character. When dams alter flows, they alter the essence of rivers.

Consider the erstwhile river behind Lower Granite [a dam on Idaho's Snake River]. Although I was there in the springtime, when I looked at the water it was moving too slowly to merit the word "flow"—and Lower Granite Lake isn't even one of the region's enormous storage reservoirs, which bring currents to a virtual halt. In the past, spring snowmelt sent powerful currents down the Snake during April and May. Nowadays hydropower operators of the Columbia and Snake systems store the runoff behind the dams and release it during the winter, when demand—and the price—for electricity rises. Over the ages, however, many populations of salmon have adapted to the spring surge. The smolts used the strong flows to migrate, drifting downstream with the current. During the journey smolts' bodies undergo physiological changes that require them to reach salt water quickly. Before dams backed up the Snake, smolts coming down from Idaho got to the sea in six to twenty days; now it takes from sixty to ninety days, and few of the young salmon reach salt water in time. The emasculated current is the single largest reason that the number of wild adult salmon migrating up the Snake each year has crashed from predevelopment runs of 100,000–200,000 to what was projected to be 150–175 this year.*

This tightly constructed passage connects various causal chains to explain the decline of salmon runs:

Smolts use river flow to reach the sea → dams restrict flow of river → a trip that before development took 6–20 days now takes 60–90 days → migrating smolts undergo physiological changes that demand quick access to salt water → delayed migration time kills the smolts.

Describing each link in the causal chain—and making each link seem as plausible as possible—is the most persuasive means of convincing readers that X causes Y.

Second Method: Use Various Inductive Methods to Establish a High Probability of a Causal Link

If we can't explain a causal link directly, we often employ a reasoning strategy called *induction*. Through induction we infer a general conclusion based on a limited number of specific cases. For example, if on several occasions you got a headache after drinking red wine but not after drinking white wine, you would be likely to conclude inductively that red wine causes you to get headaches. However, because there are almost always numerous variables involved, because there are exceptions to most principles arrived at inductively, and because we can't be certain that the future will always be like the past, inductive reasoning gives only probable truths, not certain ones.

When your brain thinks inductively, it sorts through data looking for patterns of similarity and difference. But the inductive process does not explain the causal mechanism itself. Thus, through induction you know that red wine gives you a headache, but you don't know how the wine actually works on your nervous system—the causal chain itself.

In this section we explain three kinds of inductive reasoning: informal induction, scientific experimentation, and correlation.

Informal Induction   Informal induction is our term for the habitual kind of inductive reasoning people do all the time. Toddlers think inductively when they learn the connection between flipping a wall switch and watching the ceiling light come on. They hold all variables constant except the position of the switch and infer inductively a causal connection between the switch and the light.

---

*Robert S. Devine, "The Trouble with Dams," *Atlantic,* Aug. 1995: 64–75. The example quotation is from page 70.

According to the nineteenth-century philosopher John Stuart Mill, typical ways in which the mind infers causality include looking for a common element that can explain a repeated circumstance. For example, psychologists attempting to understand the causes of anorexia have discovered that many anorexics (but not all) come from perfectionistic, highly work-oriented homes that emphasize duty and responsibility. This common element is thus a suspected causal factor leading to anorexia. Another of Mill's methods involves looking for a single difference. When infant death rates in the state of Washington shot up in July and August 1986, one event stood out making these two months different: increased radioactive fallout from the Chernobyl nuclear meltdown in the Ukraine. This single difference thus led some researchers to suspect radiation as a possible cause of infant deaths. Informal induction typically proceeds from this kind of "common element" or "single difference" reasoning.

Largely because of its power, informal induction can often lead you to wrong conclusions. You should be aware of two common fallacies of inductive reasoning that can tempt you into erroneous assumptions about causality. (Both fallacies are treated more fully in Appendix One.)

The *post hoc, ergo propter hoc* fallacy ("after this, therefore because of this") mistakes precedence for cause. Just because event A regularly precedes event B does not mean that event A causes event B. The same reasoning that tells us that flipping a switch causes the light to go on can make us believe that low levels of radioactive fallout from the Chernobyl nuclear disaster caused a sudden rise in infant death rates in the state of Washington. The nuclear disaster clearly preceded the rise in death rates. But did it clearly *cause* it? Our point is that precedence alone is no proof of causality and that we are guilty of this fallacy whenever we are swayed to believe that X causes Y primarily because X precedes Y. We can guard against this fallacy by seeking plausible link-by-link connections showing how X causes Y.

The *hasty generalization* fallacy occurs when you make a generalization based on too few cases or too little consideration of alternative explanations: You flip the switch, but the lightbulb doesn't go on. You conclude—too hastily—that the power has gone off. (Perhaps the lightbulb has burned out or the switch is broken.) How many trials does it take before you can make a justified generalization rather than a hasty generalization? It is difficult to say. Both the *post hoc* fallacy and the hasty generalization fallacy remind us that induction requires a leap from individual cases to a general principle and that it is always possible to leap too soon.

Scientific Experimentation   One way to avoid inductive fallacies is to examine causal hypotheses as carefully as possible. When we deal with a recurring phenomenon such as cancer, we can create scientific experiments that give us inductive evidence of causality with a fairly high degree of certainty. If, for example, we were concerned that a particular food source such as spinach might contain cancer-causing chemicals, we could test our hypothesis experimentally. We could take two groups of rats and control their environment carefully so that the only difference between them (in theory, anyway) was that one group ate large quantities of spinach and the other group ate none. Spinach eating, then, is the one variable between the two groups that we are testing. After a specified period of time, we would check to see what percentage of rats in each group developed cancer. If twice as many spinach-eating rats contracted cancer, we could probably conclude that our hypothesis had held up.

Correlation   Still another method of induction is *correlation,* which expresses a statistical relationship between X and Y. A correlation between X and Y means that when X occurs, Y is likely to occur also, and vice versa. To put it another way, correlation establishes a possibility that an observed link between X and Y is a causal link rather than mere coincidence. The existence of a correlation, however, does not tell us whether X causes Y, whether Y causes X, or whether both are caused by some third phenomenon.

For example, there is a fairly strong correlation between nearsightedness and intelligence. (In a given sample of nearsighted people and people with normal eyesight, a higher percentage of the nearsighted people will be highly intelligent. Similarly, in a sample of high-intelligence people and people with normal intelligence, a higher percentage of the high-intelligence group will be nearsighted.) But the direction of causality isn't clear. It could be that high intelligence causes people to read more, thus ruining their eyes (high intelligence causes nearsightedness). Or it could be that nearsightedness causes people to read more, thus raising their intelligence (nearsightedness causes high intelligence). Or it could be that some unknown phenomenon inside the brain causes both nearsightedness and high intelligence.

In recent years, correlation studies have been made stunningly sophisticated through the power of computerized analyses. For example, we could attempt to do the spinach-cancer study without resorting to a scientific experiment. If we identified a given group that ate lots of spinach (for example, vegetarians) and another group that ate little if any spinach (Inuits) and then checked to see if their rates of cancer correlated to their rates of spinach consumption, we would have the beginnings of a correlation study. But it would have no scientific validity until we factored out all the other variables between vegetarians and Inuits that might skew the findings—variables such as lifestyle, climate, genetic inheritance, and differences in diet other than spinach. Factoring out such variables is one of the complex feats that modern statistical analyses attempt to accomplish. But the fact remains that the most sophisticated correlation studies still cannot tell us the direction of causality or even for certain that there is causality.

Conclusion about Inductive Methods   Induction, then, can tell us within varying degrees of certainty whether X causes Y. It does not, however, explain the causal mechanism itself. Typically, the *because* clause structure of an inductive argument would take one of the following three shapes: (1) "Although we cannot explain the causal mechanism directly, we believe that X and Y are very probably causally linked because we have repeatedly observed their conjunction"; (2) " . . . because we have demonstrated the linkage through controlled scientific

experiments"; or (3) " . . . because we have shown that they are statistically correlated and have provided a plausible hypothesis concerning the causal direction."

For Class Discussion

Working individually or in small groups, develop plausible causal chains that
might explain the correlations between the following pairs of phenomena:

a. A person who registers low stress   Does daily meditation
level on electrochemical stress
meter

b. White female teenager   Is seven times more likely to smoke
than black female teenager

c. Someone who grew up in a house   Is more likely to have higher SAT
with two bathrooms   scores than a person who grew up
in a one-bathroom home

d. A member of the National Rifle   Favors tough treatment of criminals
Association

Third Method: Argue by Analogy or Precedent

Another common method of causal arguing is through analogy or precedent. (See
also Chapter 13, which deals in more depth with the strengths and weaknesses of
this kind of arguing.) When you argue through resemblance, you try to find a case
that is similar to the one you are arguing about but is better known and less
controversial to the reader. If the reader agrees with your view of causality in the
similar case, you then try to transfer this understanding to the case at issue. In the
following example, the writer tries to explain the link between environmental and
biological factors in the creation of teen violence. In this analogy, the biological pre-
disposition for violent behavior is compared to some children's biological predis-
position for asthma. Cultural and media violence is then compared to air pollution.

CAUSAL ARGUMENT BY ANALOGY

To deny the role of these influences [bad parenting, easy access to guns, violence in the
media] is like denying that air pollution triggers childhood asthma. Yes, to develop
asthma a child needs a specific, biological vulnerability. But as long as some children
have this respiratory vulnerability—and some always will—then allowing pollution
to fill our air will make some children wheeze, and cough, and die. And as long as
some children have a neurological vulnerability [to violent behavior]—and some
always will—then turning a blind eye to bad parenting, bullying, and the gun culture
will make other children seethe, and withdraw, and kill.[*]

---

[*]Sharon Begley, "Why the Young Kill," *Newsweek,* 3 May 1999: 35.

Causal arguments by analogy and precedent are logically weaker than arguments based on causal chains or scientific induction. Although they can be powerfully persuasive, you should be aware of their limits. If any two things are alike in some ways (analogous), they are different in others (disanalogous), and these differences shouldn't be ignored. Consider the following example:

> A huckster markets a book called *30 Days to a More Powerful Brain*. The book contains logical puzzles and other brain-teasing exercises that he calls "weight training for the mind."

This argument depends on the warrant that the brain is like a muscle. Because the audience accepts the causal belief that weight training strengthens muscles, the marketers hope to transfer that same belief to the field of mental activity (mind exercises strengthen the brain). However, cognitive psychologists have shown that the brain does *not* work like a muscle, so the analogy is false. Although the argument seems powerful, you should realize that the warrant that says X is like Y is almost always vulnerable.

All resemblance arguments, therefore, are in some sense "false analogies." But some analogies are so misleading that logicians have labeled them fallacious—the fallacy of *false analogy*. The false analogy fallacy covers those truly blatant cases where the differences between X and Y are too great for the analogy to hold. An example might be the following: "Putting red marks all over students' papers causes great emotional distress just as putting knife marks over their palms would cause great physical distress." It is impossible to draw a precise line, however, between an analogy that has true clarifying and persuasive power and one that is fallacious. Whether the analogy works in a particular situation depends on the audience's shared assumptions with the arguer.

Glossary of Terms Encountered in Causal Arguments

Because causal arguments are often easier to conduct if writer and reader share a few specialized terms, we offer the following glossary for your convenience.

Fallacy of Oversimplified Cause: One of the greatest temptations when establishing causal relationships is to fall into the habit of looking for *the* cause of something. Most phenomena, especially the ones we argue about, have multiple causes. For example, scientists know that a number of different causes must work together to create a complex disease such as cancer. But though we know all this, we still long to make the world less complex by looking for *the* cause of cancer, thus attributing a single cause to puzzling effects.

Universal/Existential Quantifiers: Closely related to the fallacy of the single cause is the tendency to confuse what logicians call the universal quantifier (*all*) with the existential quantifier (*some*). The mixing up of universal and existential quantifiers can falsify an argument. For example, to argue that *all* the blame for recent school shootings comes from the shooters' playing violent video games is to claim that playing violent video games is the sole cause—a universal statement. An argument will be stronger and more accurate if the arguer makes an existential statement: *Some* of the blame for this violent behavior can be attributed to playing violent video games. Arguers sometimes deliberately mix up these quantifiers to misrepresent and dismiss opposing views. For example, someone might argue that because the violent video games are not totally and exclusively responsible for the students' violent behavior, they are not an influential factor at all. In this instance, arguers are attempting to dismiss potential causes by framing them as universal statements that can be rejected because they are too extreme and indefensible. Because something is not a sole or total cause does not mean that it could not be a partial cause.

Immediate/Remote Causes: Every causal chain links backward indefinitely into the past. An immediate cause is the closest in time to the event being examined. When John F. Kennedy Jr.'s plane crashed into the Atlantic Ocean south of Martha's Vineyard in July 1999, experts speculated that the *immediate cause* was Kennedy's becoming disoriented in the night haze, losing visual control of the plane, and sending the plane into a fatal dive. A slightly less immediate cause was his decision to make an overwater flight at night without being licensed for instrument flying. The cause of that decision was the need to get to Hyannis Port quickly to attend a wedding. Farther back in time were all the factors that made Kennedy the kind of risk taker who took chances with his own life. For example, several months earlier he had broken an ankle in a hang-gliding accident. Many commentators said that the numerous tragedies that befell the Kennedy family helped shape his risk-taking personality. Such causes going back into the past are considered *remote causes.* It is sometimes difficult to determine the relative significance of remote causes, which are not obviously linked to an event and often have to be dug out or inferred. It's difficult to know, for example, just how seriously to take Hillary Clinton's explanation for her husband's extramarital affairs with Monica Lewinsky and other women. Clinton's womanizing tendencies, she claimed, were caused by "a terrible conflict between his mother and grandmother" when Clinton was four years old. During this period, she said, he "was scarred by abuse."*

Precipitating/Contributing Causes: These terms are similar to *immediate* and *remote* causes but don't designate a temporal linking going into the past. Rather, they refer to a main cause emerging out of a background of subsidiary causes. The *contributing causes* are a set of conditions that give rise to the *precipitating cause,* which triggers the effect. If, for example, a husband and wife decide to separate, the precipitating cause may be a stormy fight over money, which itself is a symptom of their inability to communicate with each other any longer. All the factors that contribute to that inability to communicate—preoccupation with their respective careers, anxieties about

---

*"First Lady's Remarks Take White House by Surprise," *Seattle Times*, 2 Aug. 1999: A1.

money, in-law problems—may be considered contributing causes. Note that the contributing causes and precipitating cause all coexist simultaneously in time—none is temporally more remote than another. But the marriage might have continued had the contributing causes not finally resulted in frequent angry fighting, which doomed the marriage.

Constraints: Sometimes an effect occurs not because X happened but because another factor—a *constraint*—was removed. At other times a possible effect does not occur because a given constraint prevents it from happening. A constraint is a kind of negative cause that limits choices and possibilities. As soon as the constraint is removed, a given effect may occur. For example, in the marriage we have been discussing, the presence of children in the home might have been a constraint against divorce; as soon as the children graduate from high school and leave home, the marriage may dissolve.

Necessary/Sufficient Causes: A *necessary* cause is one that has to be present for a given effect to occur. For example, fertility drugs are necessary to cause the conception of septuplets. Every couple who has septuplets must have used fertility drugs. In contrast, a *sufficient* cause is one that always produces or guarantees a given effect. Smoking more than a pack of cigarettes per day is sufficient to raise the cost of one's life insurance policy. This statement means that if you are a smoker, life insurance companies will always place you in a higher risk bracket and charge you more for life insurance. In some cases, a single cause can be both necessary and sufficient. For example, lack of ascorbic acid is both a necessary and a sufficient cause of scurvy. (Think of all those old sailors who didn't eat fruit for months.) It is a necessary cause because you can't get scurvy any other way except through absence of ascorbic acid; it is a sufficient cause because the absence of ascorbic acid always causes scurvy.

For Class Discussion

The terms in the preceding glossary can be effective brainstorming tools for thinking of possible causes of an event. For the following events, try to think of as many causes as possible by brainstorming possible *immediate causes, remote causes, precipitating causes, contributing causes,* and *constraints.*

1. Working individually, make a list of different kinds of causes/constraints for one of the following:
   a. your decision to attend your present college
   b. an important event in your life or your family (a divorce, a major move, etc.)
   c. a personal opinion you hold that is not widely shared
2. Working as a group, make a list of different kinds of causes/constraints for one of the following:

  a. why women's fashion and beauty magazines are the most frequently purchased magazines in college bookstores

  b. why American students consistently score below Asian and European students in academic achievement

  c. why the number of babies born out of wedlock has increased dramatically in the last thirty years

Organizing a Causal Argument

At the outset, it is useful to know some of the standard ways to organize a causal argument. Later, you may decide on a different organizational pattern, but these standard ways will help you get started.

Plan 1

When your purpose is to describe and explain all the links in a causal chain:

- Introduce phenomenon to be explained and show why it is problematical.

- Present your thesis in summary form.

- Describe and explain each link in the causal chain.

Plan 2

When your purpose is to explore the relative contribution of several causes to a phenomenon or to explore multiple consequences of a phenomenon:

- Introduce the phenomenon to be explained and suggest how or why it is controversial.

- Devote one section to each possible cause/consequence and decide whether it is necessary, sufficient, contributory, remote, and so forth. (Arrange sections so that the causes most familiar to the audience come first and the most surprising ones come last.)

Plan 3

When your purpose is to argue for a cause or consequence that is surprising or unexpected to your audience:

- Introduce a phenomenon to be explained and show why it is controversial.

- One by one, examine and reject the causes or consequences your audience would normally assume or expect.

- Introduce your unexpected or surprising cause or consequence and argue for it.

Plans 2 and 3 are similar in that they examine numerous possible causes or consequences. Plan 2, however, tries to establish the relative importance of each cause or consequence, whereas plan 3 aims at rejecting the causes or consequences normally assumed by the audience and argues for an unexpected surprising cause or consequence.

Plan 4

When your purpose is to change your audience's mind about a cause or consequence:

- Introduce the issue and show why it is controversial.
- Summarize your opponent's causal argument and then refute it.
- Present your own causal argument.

Plan 4 is a standard structure for all kinds of arguments. This is the structure you would use if you were the attorney for the person whose car skidded into the boutique (p. 196). The opposing attorney would blame your client's reckless driving. You would lay blame on a poorly signed intersection, a speeding beer truck, and violation of building codes.

Questioning and Critiquing a Causal Argument

Because of the strenuous conditions that must be met before causality can be proven, causal arguments are vulnerable at many points. The following strategies will generally be helpful.

If you described every link in a causal chain, would skeptics point out weaknesses in any of the links?   Describing a causal chain can be a complex business. A skeptic can raise doubts about an entire argument simply by questioning one of the links. Your best defense is to make a diagram of the linkages and role-play a skeptic trying to refute each link in turn. Whenever you find possible arguments against your position, see how you can strengthen your own argument at that point.

If your argument is based on a scientific experiment, could skeptics question the validity of the experiment?   The scientific method attempts to demonstrate causality experimentally. If the experiment isn't well designed, however, the demonstration is less likely to be acceptable to skeptical audiences. Here are ways to question and critique a scientific argument:

- *Question the findings.*   Skeptics may have reason to believe that the data collected were not accurate or representative. They might provide alternative data or simply point out flaws in the way the data were collected.

- *Question the interpretation of the data.*   Many research studies are divided into a "findings" and a "discussion" section. In the discussion section the researcher analyzes and interprets the data. A skeptic might provide an alternative interpretation of the data or otherwise argue that the data don't support what the original writer claims.

- *Question the design of the experiment.*   A detailed explanation of research design is beyond the scope of this text, but we can give a brief example of how a typical experiment did go wrong. When home computers were first developed in the 1980s, a group of graduate students conducted an experiment to test the effect of word processors on students' writing in junior high school. They reported that students who used the word processors for revising all their essays did significantly better on a final essay than a control group of students who didn't use word processors. It turned out, however, that there were at least two major design flaws in the experiment. First, the researchers allowed students to volunteer for the experimental group. Perhaps these students were already better writers than the control group from the start. (Can you think of a causal explanation of why the better students might volunteer to use the computers?) Second, when the teachers graded essays from both the computer group and the control group, the essays were not retyped uniformly. Thus the computer group's essays were typed with "computer perfection," whereas the control group's essays were handwritten or typed on ordinary typewriters. Perhaps the readers were affected by the pleasing appearance of the computer-typed essays. More significantly, perhaps the graders were biased in favor of the computer project and unconsciously scored the computer-typed papers higher.

If you have used correlation data, could skeptics argue that the correlation is much weaker than you claim or that you haven't sufficiently demonstrated causality?   As we discussed earlier, correlation data tell us only that two or more phenomena are likely to occur together. They don't tell us that one caused the other. Thus, correlation arguments are usually accompanied by hypotheses about causal connections between the phenomena. Correlation arguments can often be refuted as follows:

- Find problems in the statistical methods used to determine the correlation.
- Weaken the correlation by pointing out exceptions.
- Provide an alternative hypothesis about causality.

If you have used an analogy argument, could skeptics point out disanalogies? Although among the most persuasive of argumentative strategies, analogy arguments are also among the easiest to refute. The standard procedure is to counter your argument that X is like Y by pointing out all the ways that X is *not* like Y. Once again, by role-playing an opposing view, you may be able to strengthen your own analogy argument.

Could a skeptic cast doubt on your argument by reordering your priority of causes? Up to this point we've focused on refuting the claim that X causes Y. However, another approach is to concede that X helps cause Y but argue that X is only one of several contributing causes and not the most significant one.

Readings

The following essay, by student writer Daeha Ko, appeared as an op-ed piece in the *University of Washington Daily* on May 9, 1999, several weeks after the Columbine High School massacre in Littleton, Colorado. Ko's motivation for writing is his anger at media attempts to explain the massacre—none of which focused on the cliquish social structure of high school itself.

The Monster That Is High School

Daeha Ko (student)

1   In the past weeks, intensive media coverage has surrounded the shooting incident in Littleton, Colorado, where 12 students and a teacher died, along with 23 wounded. Yet people forget the real victims of the Littleton massacre are Dylan Klebold and Eric Harris.

2   What they did was against the law, but let's face it—the incident was waiting to happen. And there's nothing surprising about it.

3   The social priorities of high school are to blame. In truth, high school is a place where jocks, cheerleaders and anyone associated with them can do whatever they want and get away with it. Their exploits are celebrated in pep rallies, printed in school papers and shown off in trophy cases. The popular cliques have the most clout, and are—in a sense—local celebrities. If they ever run into disciplinary problems with the school or police, they get let off the hook under the guise that they are just kids.

4   Public schools claim to support all students, but in reality choose to invest their priorities in activities associated with popular cliques. Schools are willing to go to any means necessary to support the sports teams, for example. They care less about students who don't belong to popular cliques, leaving them almost nothing. School becomes less about getting a good education, instead priding itself on the celebration of elite cliques.

5   The popular cliques are nice to their own but spit out extremely cruel insults to those who don't fit in. As noted in *Time,* jocks admitted they like to pick on unpopular kids "because it's just fun to do." Their insulting words create deep emotional wounds, while school authorities ignore the cruelty of the corrupt high-school social system.

6   Schools refuse to accept any accountability and point to parents instead. While it is the job of parents to condition their kids, it is impossible for them to supervise their kids 24 hours a day.

7   As an outcast, I was harassed on an everyday basis by jocks, and received no help from school authorities. It got so bad that I attempted suicide.

8   Yes, I did (and still do) wear all black, play Doom and listen to raucous heavy metal, punk and Goth music. I was into the occult and had extensive knowledge on guns and how to build bombs.

9   I got into several fights, including one where I kicked the shit out of a basketball player. The only reason why I didn't shoot him and his jock cronies is because I lacked access to guns. I would've blown every single one of them away and not cared.

10   To defend myself, I carried around a 7-inch blade. If anyone continued to mess with me, I sent them anonymous notes with a big swastika drawn on them. I responded to harassment with "Yeah, heil Hitler," while saluting.

11   They got the hint. Eventually, I found some friends who were also outcasts. We banded together and didn't judge each other by the way we looked or what we liked. But I still held contempt for jocks whom I believed should be shot and fed to the sharks.

Even in their deaths, Klebold and Harris are still treated like outcasts. How dare *Time* call them "The Monsters Next Door." News analysis poured over the "abnormal" world of "Goth" culture, Marilyn Manson, violent computer games and gun control. It also targeted other outcast students as trenchcoat-goth, submerged, socially challenged kids who fail to fit the "correct" image of American teens.

The popular cliques have their likeness reinforced through the images of trashy teen media as seen on MTV, *90210* and *Dawson's Creek.* It's heard in the bubble-gum pop of Britney Spears and Backstreet Boys, along with their imitators. Magazines like *YM* and *Seventeen* feature pretty-looking girls, offering advice on the latest trends in dress, makeup and dating.

Media coverage was saturated with memorials and funeral services of the deceased. Friends and family remembered them as "good kids." Not all those killed knew or made fun of Klebold or Harris. Obviously there were members of the popular cliques who made fun of them and escaped harm. But innocent people had to die in order to bring injustices to light that exist in our society.

It's tragic, but perhaps that's the price that had to be paid. Perhaps they are shocked by the fact that some "nerds" have actually defeated them for once because teasing isn't fun and games anymore.

With the last of the coffins being laid to rest, people are looking for retribution, someone to prosecute. Why? The two kids are dead—there is no sense in pursuing this problem any further. But lawyers are trying to go after those who they believe influenced Harris and Klebold: namely their parents, gun dealers, and the Trenchcoat Mafia. Police heavily questioned Harris' girlfriend about the guns she gave them and arrested one person.

The families of the deceased, lawyers and the police need to get a clue and leave the two kids' families and friends alone. They are dealing with just as much grief and do not need to be punished for someone else's choices. Filing lawsuits will drag on for years, burdening everyone and achieving little.

It's not like you can bring your loved ones back to life after you've won your case.

What we need is bigger emphasis on academic discipline and more financing toward academic programs. Counselors and psychiatrists need to be hired to attend to student needs. People need practical skills, not the pep-rally fluff of popular cliques.

The people of Littleton need to be at peace with the fate of their town and heal wounds instead of prying them open with lawsuits.

Our second reading is an advocacy advertisement seeking donations to the "Community Safety Net Fund" of the United Way organization in a major American city (Figure 12.1). What techniques of visual argument are used by this advocacy ad (see pp. 138–141)? What values does this ad appeal to? The cited statistic implies a cause-effect relationship between after-school activities and reduced likelihood of teenage parenthood. How might you argue that this statistic shows a correlation rather than a cause and effect?

Kids who do not participate
in after-school activities
are 37% more likely
to become teen parents
than kids who do.

Your gift to the Community Safety Net Fund helps bring together the people
and resources to identify and address the challenges that face our community.
Call (206) 461-GIVE or log on to unitedwayofkingcounty.org.

UNITED WAY
of KING COUNTY

BE PART OF THE ANSWER.

FIGURE 12.1   *United Way advocacy advertisement*

WRITING ASSIGNMENT
FOR CHAPTER 12

Choose an issue involving the causes or consequences of a trend, event, or other phenomenon. Write an argument that persuades an audience to accept your explanation of the causes or consequences of your chosen phenomenon. Within your essay you should examine alternative hypotheses or opposing views and explain your reasons for rejecting them. You can imagine your issue either as a puzzle or as a disagreement. If a puzzle, your task will be to create a convincing case to an audience that doesn't already have in mind an answer to your causal question. If a disagreement, your task will be more overtly persuasive because your goal will be to change your audience's views.

13 Resemblance Arguments
X Is (Is Not) Like Y

EXAMPLE CASE

To justify a possible invasion of Iraq during the national debate in summer 2002, media supporters of the Bush administration called Saddam Hussein an "Arab Hitler." A similar analogy was used when NATO began bombing Serbia during the Kosovo crisis. The Clinton administration, along with the U.S. media, likened Yugoslavian president Slobodan Milosevic to Adolf Hitler and compared the "ethnic cleansing" of Kosovo to the Nazi's "final solution" against the Jews. When justifying the bombing, Clinton frequently evoked the Holocaust and the lessons of World War II. "Never again," he said. Meanwhile, the Serbian community in the United States (and many Balkan scholars) criticized the Holocaust analogy. The Serbian community likened the Kosovo crisis not to the Nazi annihilation of the Jews but to a civil war in which Serbs were protecting their homeland against Albanian terrorists.

An Overview of Resemblance Arguments

Resemblance arguments support a claim by comparing one thing to another with the intention of transferring the audience's understanding of (or feelings about) the second thing back to the first. Sometimes an entire argument can be devoted to a resemblance claim. More commonly, brief resemblance arguments are pieces of larger arguments devoted to a different stasis. Thus cultural critic Susan Sontag, in arguing that the U.S. response to terrorism following the September 11, 2001, attacks was misguided, compared the war on terrorism to wars on cancer or poverty.

> Wars on such enemies as cancer, poverty and drugs are understood to be endless wars. There will always be cancer, poverty and drugs. And there will always be despicable terrorists . . . .*

---

*Susan Sontag, "Real Battles and Empty Metaphors," *New York Times*, 19 Sept. 2002: A31.

Her point is that terrorism does not constitute a one-time enemy that can be defeated (as in a war with Japan or Germany in World War II) but an endless war (as in the war against disease or poverty). Her goal is to resist the Bush administration's use of wartime rhetoric to rally Americans to military action and to the acceptance of reduced civil liberties. The strategy of resemblance arguments is to take the audience's understanding of the point made in the comparison (you shouldn't use actual wartime strategies to fight a metaphorical war like the war on poverty or drugs) and transfer it to the issue being debated (you shouldn't use actual wartime strategies to fight the war against terrorism).

Those who supported the Bush administration, in contrast, often compared the terrorist attacks on the World Trade Center and the Pentagon to Japan's attack on Pearl Harbor that initiated U.S. entry into World War II. The persuasive power of resemblance arguments comes from their ability to clarify an audience's conception of contested issues while conveying strong emotions. Resemblance arguments typically take the form "X is (is not) like Y." Resemblance arguments work best when the audience has a clear (and sometimes emotionally charged) understanding of the Y term. The writer then hopes to transfer this understanding, along with accompanying emotions, to the X term. The danger of resemblance arguments, as we shall see, is that the differences between the X and Y terms are often so significant that the resemblance argument collapses under close examination.

Like most other argument types, resemblance arguments can be analyzed using the Toulmin schema. Suppose, for example, that you want to awaken young women to the dangers of dieting by showing them how an obsession with weight is caused, at least partially, by a patriarchal construction of female beauty that keeps women submissive and powerless. You decide to make the resemblance claim that women's obsessive dieting is like foot-binding in ancient China. This argument can be displayed in Toulmin terms as follows:

ENTHYMEME: Women's obsessive dieting in America is like foot-binding in ancient China because both practices keep women childlike, docile, dependent, and unthreatening to men.

CLAIM: Women's obsessive dieting in America is like foot-binding in ancient China.

STATED REASON: because both practices keep women childlike, docile, dependent, and unthreatening to men.

GROUNDS: evidence that both obsessive dieting and foot-binding lead to childlike subordination: Both practices involve women's painful attempts to meet patriarchal standards of beauty in which men are powerful agents and women are beautiful objects; women, in attempting to imitate society's image of the "perfect woman," damage themselves (Chinese women are physically maimed; American women are psychologically maimed and often weakened by inadequate diet or constant worry about being fat); both practices make women childlike rather than grown-up (men call beautiful women "babes" or "dolls"; anorexia stops menstruation); women obsessed with beauty end up satisfied with less pay and subordinate positions in society so long as they are regarded as feminine and pretty.

WARRANT: We should reject practices that are like Chinese foot-binding.

BACKING: Arguments that the subordinate position of women evidenced in both foot-binding and obsession with weight are related to patriarchal construction of women's roles; further arguments for why women should free themselves from patriarchal views.

CONDITIONS OF REBUTTAL: All the ways that dieting and concern for weight are not like Chinese foot-binding. For example, skeptics might say that women who diet are concerned with health, not beauty; concern for healthy weight is "rational," not "obsessive"; thin women are often powerful athletes, not at all like Chinese victims of foot-binding, who can hardly walk; dieting does not cause crippling deformity; a concern for beauty does not make a woman subordinate or satisfied with less pay; dieting is a woman's choice— not something forced on her as a child.

QUALIFIER: Perhaps the writer should say, "*Under certain conditions* obsessive dieting can even seem like Chinese foot-binding."

For many audiences, the comparison of women's dieting to Chinese foot-binding will have an immediate and powerful emotional effect, perhaps causing them to see attitudes toward weight and food from a new, unsettling perspective. The analogy invites them to transfer their understanding of Chinese foot-binding— which seems instantly repulsive and oppressive of women—to their understanding of obsessive concern for losing weight. Whereas social controls in ancient China were overt, the modern practice uses more subtle kinds of social controls, such as the influence of the fashion and beauty industry and peer pressure. But in both cases women feel forced to mold their bodies to a patriarchal standard of beauty—one that emphasizes soft curves, tiny waists, and daintiness rather than strength and power.

But this example also illustrates the dangers of resemblance arguments, which often ignore important differences or *disanalogies* between the terms of comparison. As the "conditions of rebuttal" show, there are many differences between dieting and foot-binding. For example, the practice of foot-binding was not a conscious choice of young Chinese girls, who were forced to have their feet wrapped at an early age. Dieting, on the other hand, is something one chooses, and it may reveal a healthy and rational choice rather than an obsession with appearance. When the practice degenerates to anorexia or bulimia, it becomes a mental disease, not a physical deformity forced on a girl in childhood. Thus a resemblance argument is usually open to refutation if a skeptic points out important disanalogies.

We now turn to the two types of resemblance arguments: analogy and precedent.

Arguments by Analogy

The use of *analogies* can constitute the most imaginative form of argument. If you don't like your new boss, you can say that she's like a marine drill sergeant, a distraught captain of a sinking ship, or a mother hen. Each of these analogies suggests a different management style, clarifying the nature of your dislike through a comparison that grips your audience emotionally.

Of course, this power to make things clear comes at a price. Analogies often clarify one aspect of a relationship at the expense of other aspects. For example, in nineteenth-century America many commentators were fond of justifying certain negative effects of capitalism (such as the squalor of the poor) by comparing social and economic processes to Darwinian evolution—the survival of the fittest. In particular, they fastened on one aspect of evolution, competition, and spoke darkly of life as a cutthroat struggle for survival. Clearly the analogy clarified one aspect of human interaction: People and institutions do indeed compete for limited resources, markets, and territory; and the consequences of failure are often dire (the weak get eaten by the strong). But competition is only one aspect of evolution—albeit a particularly dramatic one. The ability to dominate an environment is less important to the long-term survival of a species than is the ability to adapt to that environment. Thus, the mighty dinosaur disappeared, but the lowly cockroach continues to flourish because of its uncanny ability to adjust to circumstance.

The use of the evolutionary analogies to account for the competitive nature of human existence fit the worldview (and served the interests) of those who were most fond of invoking them, in particular the so-called robber barons and conservative Social Darwinists. But in overlooking other dimensions of evolution, especially the importance of adaptation and cooperation to survival, the analogy created a great deal of mischief.

So analogies have the power to get an audience's attention like virtually no other persuasive strategy. But seldom are they sufficient in themselves to provide full understanding. At some point with every analogy you need to ask yourself, "How far can I legitimately go with this? At what point are the similarities between the two things I am comparing going to be overwhelmed by their dissimilarities?" Analogies are useful attention-getting devices; used carefully and cautiously, they can be extended to shape an audience's understanding of a complex situation. But they can conceal and distort as well as clarify. With this caveat, let's look at the uses of both undeveloped and extended analogies.

Using Undeveloped Analogies

Typically, writers use short, undeveloped analogies to drive home a point (and evoke an accompanying emotion) and then quickly abandon the analogy before the reader's awareness of disanalogies begins to set in. Thus columnist James Kilpatrick, in arguing that it is not unconstitutional to require drug testing of federal employees, compares giving a urine specimen when applying for a federal job to going through an airport metal detector when flying:

> The Constitution does not prohibit all searches and seizures. It makes the people secure in their persons only from "unreasonable" searches and seizures. . . . A parallel situation may be observed at every airport in the land. Individuals may have a right to fly, but they have no right to fly without having their persons and baggage inspected for weapons. By the same token, the federal worker who refuses a urine specimen [has no right to a federal job].*

Kilpatrick wants to transfer his audience's general approval of weapons searches as a condition for airplane travel to drug testing as a condition for federal employment. But he doesn't want his audience to linger too long on the analogy. (Is a urine specimen for employment really analogous to a weapons search before an airplane trip?)

Using Extended Analogies

Sometimes writers elaborate an analogy so that it takes on a major role in the argument. As an example of a claim based on an extended analogy, consider the following excerpt from a professor's argument opposing a proposal to require a writing proficiency exam for graduation. In the following portion of his argument, the professor compares development of writing skills to the development of physical fitness.

> A writing proficiency exam gives the wrong symbolic messages about writing. It suggests that writing is simply a skill, rather than an active way of thinking and learning.

---

*James J. Kilpatrick, "What's Illegal About Urinalysis?" 1986. ©Universal Press Syndicate. Reprinted with permission. All rights reserved.

It suggests that once a student demonstrates proficiency then he or she doesn't need to do any more writing.

Imagine two universities concerned with the physical fitness of their students. One university requires a junior-level physical fitness exam in which students must run a mile in less than 10 minutes, a fitness level it considers minimally competent. Students at this university see the physical fitness exam as a one-time hurdle. As many as 70 percent of them can pass the exam with no practice; another 10–20 percent need a few months' training; and a few hopeless couch potatoes must go through exhaustive re-mediation. After passing the exam, any student can settle back into a routine of TV and potato chips having been certified as "physically fit."

The second university, however, believing in true physical fitness for its students, is not interested in minimal competency. Consequently, it creates programs in which its students exercise 30 minutes every day for the entire four years of the undergraduate curriculum. There is little doubt which university will have the most physically fit students. At the second university, fitness becomes a way of life with everyone developing his or her full potential. Similarly, if we want to improve our students' writing abilities, we should require writing in every course throughout the curriculum.

If you choose to write an extended analogy such as this, you will focus on the points of comparison that serve your purposes. The writer's purpose in the preceding case is to support the achievement of mastery rather than minimalist standards as the goal of the university's writing program. Whatever other disanalogous elements are involved (for example, writing requires the use of intellect, which may or may not be strengthened by repetition), the comparison reveals vividly that a commitment to mastery involves more than a minimalist test. The analogy serves primarily to underscore this one crucial point. In reviewing the different groups of students as they "prepare" for the fitness exam, the author makes clear just how irrelevant such an exam is to the whole question of mastery. Typically, then, in developing your analogy, you are not developing all possible points of comparison so much as you are bringing out those similarities consistent with the point you are trying to make.

For Class Discussion

The following is a two-part exercise to help you clarify for yourself how analogies function in the context of arguments. Part 1 is to be done outside class; part 2 is to be done in class.

PART 1 Think of an analogy that expresses your point of view toward each of the following topics. Your analogy can urge your readers toward either a positive view of the topic or a negative view, depending on the rhetorical effect you seek. Write your analogy in the following one-sentence format:

X is like Y: A, B, C . . . (where X is the main topic being discussed; Y is the analogy; and A, B, and C are the points of comparison).

EXAMPLES:

Topic: Cramming for an exam

Negative analogy: Cramming for an exam is like pumping iron for ten hours straight to prepare for a weight-lifting contest: exhausting and counterproductive.

Positive analogy: Cramming for an exam is like carbohydrate loading before a big race: it gives you the mental food you need for the exam, such as a full supply of concepts and details all fresh in your mind.

1. Using spanking to discipline children
2. Using racial profiling for airport security
3. Steroid use to increase athletic performance
4. Paying college athletes
5. Eating at fast-food restaurants

An effective analogy should influence both your audience's feelings toward the issue and your audience's understanding of the issue. For example, the writer of the negative analogy in the "cramming for an exam" illustration obviously believes that pumping iron for ten hours before a weight-lifting match is stupid. This feeling of stupidity is then transferred to the original topic— cramming for an exam. But the analogy also clarifies understanding. The writer imagines the mind as a muscle (which gets exhausted after too much exercise and which is better developed through some exercise every day rather than a lot all at once) rather than as a large container (into which lots of stuff can be "crammed").

PART 2 Bring your analogies to class and compare them to those of your class-mates. Select the best analogies for each of the topics and be ready to say why you think they are good.

Arguments by Precedent

Precedent arguments are like analogy arguments in that they make comparisons between an X and a Y. In precedent arguments, however, the Y term is usually a past event where some sort of decision was reached, often a moral, legal, or polit-ical decision. An argument by precedent tries to show that a similar decision should or should not be reached for the present issue X because the situation of X is or is not like the situation of Y.

A good example of a precedent argument is the following excerpt from a speech by President Lyndon Johnson in the early years of the Vietnam War:

> Nor would surrender in Vietnam bring peace because we learned from Hitler at Munich that success only feeds the appetite of aggression. The battle would be

renewed in one country and then another country, bringing with it perhaps even larger and crueler conflict, as we have learned from the lessons of history.[*]

Here the audience knows what happened at Munich: France and Britain tried to appease Hitler by yielding to his demand for a large part of Czechoslovakia, but Hitler's armies continued their aggression anyway, using Czechoslovakia as a staging area to invade Poland. By arguing that surrender in Vietnam would lead to the same consequences, Johnson brings to his argument about Vietnam the whole weight of his audience's unhappy knowledge of World War II. Administration white papers developed Johnson's precedent argument by pointing toward the similarity of Hitler's promises with those of the Viet Cong: If you give us this, we will ask for no more. But Hitler didn't keep his promise. Why should the Viet Cong?

Johnson's Munich precedent persuaded many Americans during the early years of the war and helps explain U.S. involvement in Southeast Asia. Yet many scholars attacked Johnson's reasoning. Let's use Toulmin's schema to analyze the Munich argument.

ENTHYMEME: The United States should not withdraw its troops from Vietnam because conceding to the Viet Cong will have the same disastrous consequences as did conceding to Hitler in Munich.

CLAIM: The United States should not withdraw its troops from Vietnam.

STATED REASON: because conceding to the Viet Cong will have the same disastrous consequences as did conceding to Hitler in Munich

GROUNDS: evidence of the disastrous consequences of conceding to Hitler at Munich: Hitler's continued aggression; his using Czechoslovakia as a staging area to invade Poland

WARRANT: What happened in Europe will happen in Southeast Asia.

BACKING: evidence of similarities between 1939 Europe and 1965 Southeast Asia (for example, similarities in political philosophy, goals, and military strength of the enemy; similarities in the nature of the conflict between the disputants)

CONDITIONS OF REBUTTAL: acknowledged differences between 1939 Europe and 1965 Southeast Asia that might make the outcomes different

---

[*]From *Public Papers of the Presidents of the United States*, vol. 2, *Lyndon B. Johnson* (Washington: GPO, 1965), 794.

Using Toulmin's schema, we see that the persuasiveness of the comparison depends on the audience's acceptance of the warrant, which posits close similarity between 1939 Europe and 1965 Southeast Asia. But many critics of the Vietnam War attacked this warrant. Thus, during the Vietnam era, historian Howard Zinn attacked Johnson's argument by claiming three crucial differences between Europe in 1939 and Southeast Asia in 1965: First, the Czechs were being attacked from without by an external aggressor (Germany), whereas Vietnam was being attacked from within by rebels as part of a civil war. Second, Czechoslovakia was a prosperous, effective democracy, whereas the official Vietnam government was corrupt and unpopular. Third, Hitler wanted Czechoslovakia as a base for attacking Poland, whereas the Viet Cong and North Vietnamese aimed at reunification of their country as an end in itself.[*]

The Munich example shows again how arguments of resemblance depend on emphasizing the similarities between X and Y and playing down the dissimilarities. One could try to refute the counterargument made by Zinn by arguing first that the Saigon government was more stable than Zinn thinks and second that the Viet Cong and North Vietnamese were driven by goals larger than reunification of Vietnam—namely, communist domination of Asia. Such an argument would once again highlight the similarities between Vietnam and prewar Europe.

For Class Discussion

1. Consider the following claims of precedent and evaluate how effective you think each precedent might be in establishing the claim.

   a. Gays should be allowed to serve openly in the U.S. military because they are allowed to serve openly in the militaries of most other Western countries.

   b. Gun control will reduce violent crime in the United States because many countries that have strong gun control laws (such as Japan and England) have low rates of violent crime.

2. Advocates for "right to die" legislation legalizing active euthanasia under certain conditions often point to the Netherlands as a country where acceptance of euthanasia works effectively. Assume for the moment that your state has a ballot initiative legalizing euthanasia. Assume further that you are being hired as a lobbyist for (or against) the measure and have been assigned to do research on euthanasia in the Netherlands. Working in small groups, make a list of research questions you would want to ask.

---

[*]Based on the summary of Zinn's argument in J. Michael Sproule, *Argument: Language and Its Influence* (New York: McGraw, 1980), 149–50.

Your long-range rhetorical goal is to use your research to support (or attack) the ballot initiative by making a precedence argument focusing on the Netherlands.

Organizing a Resemblance Argument

The most typical way to develop a resemblance argument is as follows:

- Introduce the issue and state your claim.
- Develop your analogy or precedent.
- Draw the explicit parallels you want to highlight between your claim and the analogy or precedent.
- Anticipate and respond to objections (optional depending on space and context).

Of course, this structure can be varied in many ways, depending on your issue and rhetorical context. Sometimes writers open an argument with the analogy, which serves as an attention grabber.

Questioning and Critiquing a Resemblance Argument

Once you have written a draft of your resemblance argument, you can test its effectiveness by role-playing a skeptical audience. What follows are some typical questions audiences will raise about arguments of resemblance.

Will a skeptic say I am trying to prove too much with my analogy or precedent? The most common mistake people make with resemblance arguments is to ask them to prove more than they're capable of proving. Too often, an analogy is treated as if it were a syllogism or algebraic ratio wherein necessary truths are deduced (*a* is to *b* as *c* is to *d*) rather than as a useful, but basically playful, figure that suggests uncertain but significant insight. The best way to guard against this charge is to qualify your argument and to find other means of persuasion to supplement an analogy or precedent argument.

For a good example of an analogy that tries to do too much, consider President Ronald Reagan's attempt to prevent the United States from imposing economic sanctions on South Africa. Reagan wanted to argue that harming South Africa's economy would do as much damage to blacks as to whites. In making this argument, he compared South Africa to a zebra and concluded that one couldn't hurt the white portions of the zebra without also hurting the black.

Now, the zebra analogy might work quite well to point up the interrelatedness of whites and blacks in South Africa. But it has no force whatsoever in supporting Reagan's assertion that economic sanctions would hurt blacks as well as whites. To refute this analogy, one need only point out the disanalogies between the zebra stripes and racial groups. (There are, for example, no differences in income, education, and employment between black and white stripes on a zebra.)

Will a skeptic point out disanalogies in my resemblance argument?   Although it is easy to show that a country is not like a zebra, finding disanalogies is sometimes quite tricky. As an example, we have shown you how Howard Zinn identified disanalogies between Europe in 1939 and Southeast Asia in 1965 (see p. 221).

Readings

Our first reading is a letter to the editor by student Megan Matthews, written for the assignment on page 225. The letter responds to a news story appearing in the *Seattle Times* on September 26, 2002, about whales damaged by Navy sonar. Notice how Megan uses an analogy to help readers imagine how the Navy's low-frequency sonar for finding submarines, along with other human-made noise in the ocean, might disturb the lives of sea mammals. Megan later wrote the researched argument shown on pages 229–306 and used this analogy for her introduction.

Whales Need Silence
Megan Matthews (student)

Re: "Whales beach themselves following NATO exercise" (news story, September 26). Imagine that you are forced to live in an apartment located next to Interstate 5 with its constant roar of engines and tires against concrete, its blaring horns and piercing sirens. When you open your windows in the summer, you have to shout to be heard. What if your apartment had no windows? What if your only housing alternatives were next to other freeways?

Seems impossible? Not for whales, dolphins, and other marine mammals. Jacques Cousteau's "world of silence" has been turned into an underwater freeway by the rumbling of cargo ships, the explosions of undersea mineral explorations, and the cacophony of the blasting devices used by fisheries. Now the Navy is adding a new and more dangerous source of sound with its sonar systems for detecting enemy submarines. The recent beaching incident in the Canary Islands reflects the danger that Navy sonar systems pose to whales. Navy sonar systems have also been linked to other beachings, including the infamous deaths several years ago of sixteen beaked whales in the Bahamas. The Navy concluded that its midrange sonar tests caused the inner ear trauma that killed these animals.

3   To supplement or replace midrange sonar, the Navy has just been given approval to deploy even more powerful low-frequency active sonar (LFA). Low-frequency waves travel farther than high-frequency waves, which is why the bumping bass of a car stereo reverberates after the car passes you. In this case, 215 dB "pings" reflect off submarines—and whales—hundreds of miles away. LFA may be even more dangerous to whales than midrange sonar, and few tests have been conducted to determine the real risk.

4   Marine mammals depend on sound to avoid predators, to communicate across great distances between pods and prospective mates, and to establish mother-bonds. The extreme noise of navy sonar apparently kills whales outright, while background "freeway" noise throughout the oceans may be threatening their ability to survive as communities.

5   Congress should not fund further implementation of LFA, which springs from an outdated Cold War model of warfare; the risks to our *environmental* security are too great.

Our second reading is another letter to the editor, which appeared in the *New York Times* on September 10, 2002, at the height of a national debate on whether the United States should invade Iraq to eliminate Saddam Hussein. Whereas the *New York Times* generally took a skeptical stance toward the war plans of the Bush administration, this writer uses a precedent argument to support President Bush. The writer's initial citing of "Blair" refers to a news story from September 8, 2002, reporting British Prime Minister Tony Blair's support of Bush in the face of growing British opposition.

Iraq War Plans
Jean Arbeiter

1   To the Editor:

2   Re "Opposition Is Growing to Blair's Stand on Iraq" (news article, Sept. 8):

3   You report that a Londoner who had to spend nights in air-raid shelters as a child during World War II does not wish to be on the side of the aggressor in going to war.

4   Doesn't she realize that if anyone had listened to Winston Churchill during the 1930's, when he argued that Germany's militaristic intentions toward Britain and the rest of Europe had to be countered, rather than appeased, the need for air-raid shelters could have been avoided, along with the deaths of millions in Europe?

5   Countering an aggressor does not make one the aggressor, as Churchill well knew; it merely makes one safer.

WRITING ASSIGNMENT
FOR CHAPTER 13

Write a letter to the editor of your campus or local newspaper or a slightly longer guest editorial in which you try to influence public opinion on some issue through the use of a persuasive analogy or precedent. Megan Matthews' pro-whale argument against Navy sonar (see pp. 223–224) is a student piece written in response to this assignment.

14 Evaluation and Ethical Arguments

X Is (Is Not) a Good Y;

X Is Right (Wrong)

EXAMPLE CASE

In early fall 2002, the Federal Drug Administration seemed ready to lift the ban on selling milk from cloned cows to the general public. Milk from cloned cows raises two kinds of evaluation issues. The first is this: Is milk from cloned cows "good milk"? (Does it contain the same nutritional value as ordinary milk? Does it taste like ordinary milk? Is it safe?) The second evaluation issue is more knotty and can't be resolved through science: Is it ethical to clone cows? If we start cloning cows, will we slide down a slippery slope toward the cloning of humans? Where do we draw the line between ethical and nonethical uses of cloning?

An Overview of Evaluation Arguments

In our roles as citizens and professionals, we are continually expected to make difficult evaluations and to persuade others to accept them. In this chapter we explain strategies for conducting two different kinds of evaluation arguments. First, we examine categorical evaluations of the kind "Is X a good Y?"* (Is Ramon a good committee chair? Is Design Approach A or Design Approach B the better solution to this engineering problem?) In such an evaluation, the writer determines the extent to which a given X meets or fulfills the qualities or standards of category Y. As we explain, these qualities or standards are usually based on the purposes of category Y. Second, we examine ethical arguments of the kind "Is X right or wrong?" (Was it a right or wrong action to drop an atomic bomb on Hiroshima and Nagasaki? Is it morally okay on a job application not to mention a briefly held job from which you were fired?) In these arguments, the writer evaluates a given X from the perspective of some system of morality or ethics.

---

*In addition to the term *good*, a number of other evaluative terms involve the same kind of thinking—*effective, successful, workable, excellent, valuable,* and so forth.

Criteria-Match Structure of Categorical Evaluations

A categorical evaluation follows the same criteria-match structure that we examined in definitional arguments (see Chapter 11). A typical claim for such an argument has the following structure:

> X is (is not) a good Y because it meets (fails to meet) criteria A, B, and C.

The main conceptual difference between this kind of evaluation argument and a definitional argument involves the Y term. In a definitional argument, one argues whether a particular Y term is the correct class or category in which to place X. (Does this swampy area qualify as a *wetland*? For purposes of federal fuel-efficiency regulations, is an SUV a *truck* or a *car*?) In a categorical evaluation argument, we know the Y term—that is, what class or category to put X into. For example, we know that this 1998 Ford Escort is a *used car*. For a categorical evaluation, the question is whether this 1998 Ford Escort is a *good used car*. Or, to place the question within a rhetorical context, Is this Ford Escort a *good used car for me to buy for college?*

As an illustration of the criteria-match structure of a categorical evaluation, let's continue with the Ford Escort example. Suppose you get in a debate with Parent or Significant Other about the car you should buy for college. Let's say that Parent or Significant Other argues that the following criteria are particularly important: (1) value for the initial money, (2) dependability, (3) safety, and (4) low maintenance costs. (If you are into muscle cars, coolness, or driving excitement, you might shudder at these criteria!) Here is how an argument supporting the first criterion could be analyzed using the Toulmin system. Note that in evaluation arguments, as in definitional arguments, warrants are the criteria for the evaluation while the stated reasons and grounds assert that the specific case meets these criteria.

TOULMIN ANALYSIS FOR CRITERION 1: HIGH VALUE FOR THE INITIAL MONEY

ENTHYMEME: This 1998 Ford Escort is a good used car for you at college because it provides the most value for the initial money.

CLAIM: This 1998 Ford Escort is a good used car for you at college.

STATED REASON: because it provides the most value for the initial money

GROUNDS: Used Ford Escorts give high value at less cost because they are basically boring but dependable cars that don't have high demand in the used car market; this lack of demand means that you can get a 1998 Escort for $1,500 less than a comparable 1998 Honda Civic with the same mileage; this particular Escort has only 65,000 miles; a 1998 Honda Civic for the same price would have 120,000 miles or more. This 1998 Ford Escort thus gives you a low-mileage car at a reasonable price—high value for the initial money.

WARRANT: High value for the initial money is an important criterion for buying your college car.

BACKING: arguments showing why it is important to get high value for the money: money saved on the car can be used for other college expenses; low initial mileage means you can get years of dependable use without having to rebuild an engine or transmission; buying in this conservative and wise way meets our family's image of being careful, utilitarian shoppers.

CONDITIONS OF REBUTTAL: *Attacking stated reason and grounds:* Perhaps this 1998 Ford Escort isn't as good a value as it seems; my research suggests it has high projected maintenance costs after 60,000 miles; initial savings may be blown on high maintenance costs.

Attacking warrant and backing: Other criteria are more important to me: I value great handling and acceleration, the fun of driving, and the status of having a cool car. The Ford Escort doesn't meet these criteria.

As this Toulmin schema shows, Parent or Significant Other needs to argue that getting high value for the initial money is an important consideration (the criterion argument) and that this 1998 Ford Escort meets this criterion better than competing choices (the match argument). If you can't see yourself driving a Ford Escort, you've either got to argue for other criteria (attack the warrant) or accept the criterion but argue that the Ford Escort's projected maintenance costs undermine its initial value (attack the reason and grounds).

Conducting a Categorical Evaluation Argument

Now that you understand the basic criteria-match structure of a categorical evaluation, let's consider the thinking strategies used for determining criteria and for arguing that your given X meets or does not meet the criteria.

Determining Criteria for a Categorical Evaluation Argument

How do you develop criteria for a categorical evaluation? What distinguishes a successful manager from a poor one, a good studying place from a bad one, or a more effective treatment for obesity from a less effective treatment? In this section we turn to the practical problem of finding criteria you'll need for conducting your categorical evaluation argument.

Step 1: Determine the Category in which the Object Being Evaluated Belongs
In determining the quality or value of any given X, you must first figure out the category in which X belongs. For example, if you asked one of your professors to write a recommendation for a summer job, what class of things should the professor put you into? Is he or she supposed to evaluate you as a student? A leader?

A worker? A storyteller? A party animal? Or what? This is an important question because the criteria for excellence in one class (student) may be very different from criteria for excellence in another class (party animal).

To write a useful letter, your professor should consider you first as a member of the general class "summer job holder" and base her evaluation of you on criteria relevant to that class. To write a truly effective letter, however, your professor needs to consider your qualifications in the context of the smallest applicable class of candidates: not "summer job holder," but "law office intern" or "highway department flagperson" or "golf course groundsperson." Clearly, each of these subclasses has very different criteria for excellence that your professor needs to address.

We thus recommend placing X into the smallest relevant class because of the apples-and-oranges law: To avoid giving a mistaken rating to a perfectly good apple, you need to make sure you are judging an apple under the class "apple" and not under the next larger class "fruit" or a neighboring class "orange." And to be even more precise, you may wish to evaluate your apple in the class "eating apple" as opposed to "pie apple" because the latter class is supposed to be tarter and the former class juicier and sweeter.

Step 2: Determine the Purpose or Function of This Class Once you have located X in its appropriate class, you should next determine what the purpose or function of this class is. Let's suppose that the summer job you are applying for is tour guide at the city zoo. The function of a tour guide is to make people feel welcome, to give them interesting information about the zoo, to make their visit pleasant, and so forth. Consequently, you wouldn't want your professor's evaluation to praise your term paper on Napoleon Bonaparte or your successful synthesis of some compound in your chemistry lab. Rather, the professor should highlight your dependability, your neat appearance, your good speaking skills, and your ability to work with groups. In contrast, if you were applying for graduate school, then your term paper on Bonaparte or your chem lab wizardry would be relevant. In other words, the professor has to evaluate you according to the class "tour guide," not "graduate student," and the criteria for each class derive from the purpose or function of the class.

Let's take another example. Suppose that you are the chair of a committee charged with evaluating the job performance of Lillian Jones, director of the admissions office at a small, private college. Ms. Jones has been a controversial manager because several members of her staff have filed complaints about her management style. In making your evaluation, your first step is to place Ms. Jones into an appropriate class, in this case, the general class "manager," and then the more specific class "manager of an admissions office at a small, private college." You then need to identify the purpose or function of these classes. You might say that the function of the general class "manager" is to "oversee actual operations of an organization so that the organization meets its goals as harmoniously and efficiently as possible," whereas the function of the specific class "manager of an admissions office at a small, private college" is "the successful recruitment of the best students possible."

Step 3: Determine Criteria Based on the Purposes or Function of the Class to Which X Belongs   Once you've worked out the purposes of the class, you are ready to work out the criteria by which you judge all members of the class. Criteria for judgment will be based on those features of Y that help it achieve the purposes of its class. For example, once you determine the purpose and function of the position filled by Lillian Jones, you can develop a list of criteria for managerial success:

1. Criteria related to "efficient operation"
   - articulates priorities and goals for the organization
   - is aggressive in achieving goals
   - motivates fellow employees
   - is well organized, efficient, and punctual
   - is articulate and communicates well
2. Criteria related to "harmonious operation"
   - creates job satisfaction for subordinates
   - is well groomed, sets good example of professionalism
   - is honest, diplomatic in dealing with subordinates
   - is flexible in responding to problems and special concerns of staff members
3. Criteria related to meeting specific goals of a college admissions office
   - creates a comprehensive recruiting program
   - demonstrates that recruiting program works

Step 4: Give Relative Weightings to the Criteria   Even though you have established criteria, you must still decide which of the criteria are most important. In the case of Lillian Jones, is it more important that she bring in lots of students or that she create a harmonious, happy office? These sorts of questions are at the heart of many evaluative controversies. Thus, a justification for your weighting of criteria may well be an important part of your argument.

Determining Whether X Meets the Criteria

Once you've established your criteria, you've got to figure out how well X meets them. You proceed by gathering evidence and examples. In the Lillian Jones case, the success of the college's recruiting program can probably be measured empirically, so you gather statistics about applications to the college, SAT scores of applicants, number of acceptances, academic profiles of entering freshmen, and so forth. You might then compare those statistics to those compiled by Ms. Jones's predecessor or to those of her competitors at other, comparable institutions.

You can also look at what the recruiting program actually does—the number of recruiters, the number of high school visitations, quality of admissions brochures, and other publications. You can also look at Ms. Jones in action, searching for specific incidents or examples that illustrate her management style. For example, you can't measure a trait such as diplomacy empirically, but you can find specific instances where the presence or absence of this trait was demonstrated. You could turn to examples where Ms. Jones may or may not have prevented a potentially divisive situation from occurring or where she offered or failed to offer encouragement at psychologically the right moment to keep someone from getting demoralized. As with criteria-match arguments in definition, one must provide examples of how the X in question meets each of the criteria that have been set up.

Your final evaluation of Ms. Jones, then, might include an overview of her strengths and weaknesses along the various criteria you have established. You might say that Ms. Jones has done an excellent job with recruitment (an assertion you can support with data on student enrollments over the last five years) but was relatively poor at keeping the office staff happy (as evidenced by employee complaints, high turnover, and your own observations of her rather abrasive management style). Nevertheless, your final recommendation might be to retain Ms. Jones for another three-year contract because you believe that an excellent recruiting record is the most important criterion for her position. You might justify this heavy weighting of recruiting on the grounds that the institution's survival depends on its ability to attract adequate numbers of good students.

For Class Discussion

The following small-group exercise can be accomplished in one or two class hours. It gives you a good model of the process you can go through in order to write your own categorical evaluation. Working in small groups, suppose that you are going to evaluate a controversial member of one of the following classes:

   a. an athlete, a coach, a component of an athletic team (for example, the offensive line of a football team) or a whole team; a politician or office-holder; a teacher or administrator

   b. a proposed or current law, a government regulation, or a government policy

   c. a student service provided by your school, or any school policy or regulation; a school newspaper or radio station, an intramural program, or a student government policy or service

   d. a teaching method, your school's plagiarism policy, a homework assignment, a library orientation, or some other controversial academic policy or method

   e. a play, a film, a music video, or a Web site; an actor, a director, a dancer or other performer

f. an advertising campaign or a specific advertisement, a store, or a customer service department

g. an employer, a boss, a work policy, or a particular work environment

h. a day care center or school; a physician, dentist, or health care agency or policy

i. a restaurant, a college hangout, a vacation spot, or a study place

j. any controversial X of your choice

1. Choose a controversial member within one of these classes as the specific person, thing, or event you are going to evaluate (your school's Computer Services Help Desk, the Invite-a-Professor-to-Lunch program in your dormitory, a recent controversial film, Harvey's Hamburger Haven).

2. If not already apparent, stipulate a rhetorical context that gives importance to the issue, focuses the argument, and places the controversial X within the smallest relevant class. (Do you want to evaluate Harvey's Hamburger Haven in the broad category of *restaurants*, in the narrow category of *hamburger joints*, or in a different narrow category such as *late-night study places*? If you are evaluating a recent film, are you evaluating it as an *action film for guys*, as a possible *Academy Award nominee*, or as *political filmmaking statements against corporate greed?*)

3. Make a list of the purposes or functions of that class, and then list the criteria that a good member of that class would have to have in order to accomplish the purpose or function. (What is the purpose or function of a Computer Services Help Desk, an action film for guys, or a late-night study place? What criteria for excellence can you derive from these purposes or functions?)

4. If necessary, rank your criteria in order to show that X is superior (inferior) to a close competitor. (For a late-night study place, what is more important: good music to study by or cheap coffee? An Internet connection or wide tables where you can spread out your work?)

5. Evaluate your X by matching X to each of the criteria. (As a late-night study place, Harvey's Hamburger Haven has the best lighting, the most space to spread out, the least expensive coffee, and the best music to study by, but it doesn't offer Internet access and sometimes has too many rowdies. Therefore it ranks second to Carol's Coffee Closet.)

An Overview of Ethical Arguments

A second kind of evaluation argument focuses on moral or ethical issues, which can often merge or overlap with categorical evaluations. For example, many apparently straightforward categorical evaluations can turn out to have an ethical dimension. Consider again the criteria for buying a car. Most people would base their evaluations on cost, safety, comfort, stylishness, and so forth. But some people might feel morally obligated to buy the most fuel-efficient car (perhaps even an electric or hybrid car despite the extra cost), or not to buy a car from a manufacturer whose investment or labor policies they find morally repugnant. Depending on how large a role ethical considerations play in the evaluation, we might choose to call this an ethical argument based on moral considerations rather than a categorical evaluation based on the purposes of a class or category.

It is uncertainty about "purpose" that makes ethical evaluations particularly complex. In making a categorical evaluation, we assume that every class or category of being has a purpose, that the purpose should be defined as narrowly as possible, and that the criteria for judgment derive directly from that purpose. For example, the purpose of a computer repair person is to analyze the problem with my computer, to fix it, and to do so in a timely and cost-efficient manner. Once I formulate this purpose, it is easy for me to define criteria for a good computer repair person.

In ethics, however, the place of purpose is much fuzzier. Just what is the purpose of human beings? Before I can begin to determine what ethical duties I have to myself and to others, I'm going to have to address this question. What is my purpose in life? What kind of life do I want to lead? In ethical discussions we don't ask what a "manager" or a "judge" or a "point guard" is supposed to do in situations relevant to the respective classes. Who persons are or what their social function is makes no difference to our ethical assessment of their actions or traits of character. A morally bad person may be a good judge, and a morally good person may be a bad manager and a worse point guard.

As the discussion so far has suggested, disagreements about ethical issues often stem from different systems of values that make the issue irresolvable. It is precisely this problem—the lack of shared assumptions about value—that makes it so important to confront issues of ethics with rational deliberation. The arguments you produce may not persuade others to your view, but they should lay out more clearly the reasons and warrants for your own beliefs. By writing about ethical issues, you see more clearly what you believe and why you believe it. Although the arguments demanded by ethical issues require rigorous thought, they force us to articulate our most deeply held beliefs and our richest feelings.

Major Ethical Systems

When we are faced with an ethical issue, we must move from arguments of good or bad to arguments of right or wrong. The terms *right* and *wrong* are clearly different from the terms *good* and *bad* when the latter terms mean simply "effective" (meets purposes of class, as in "This is a good stereo system") or "ineffective" (fails to meet purposes of class, as in "This is a bad cookbook"). But *right* and *wrong* often also differ from what seems to be a moral use of the terms *good* and *bad*. We might say, for example, that warm sunshine is good because it brings pleasure and that cancer is bad because it brings pain and death, but that is not quite the same thing as saying that sunshine is "right" and cancer is "wrong." It is the problem of "right" and "wrong" that ethical arguments confront.

Thus it is not enough to say that terrorism is "bad"; obviously everyone, including most terrorists, would agree that terrorism is "bad" in that it causes suffering and anguish. If we want to condemn terrorism on ethical grounds, we have to say that it's also "wrong" as well as "bad." From a nonethical standpoint, you could say that certain persons are "good" terrorists in that they fully realize the purposes of the class "terrorist": they cause great anguish and damage with a minimum of resources, and they bring much attention to their cause. The ethical question here is not whether a person fulfills the purposes of the class "terrorist," but whether it is wrong for such a class to exist.

There are many schools of ethical thought—too many to cover in this brief overview—so we'll limit ourselves to two major systems: arguments from consequences and arguments from principles.

Consequences as the Base of Ethics

Perhaps the best-known example of evaluating acts according to their ethical consequences is utilitarianism, a down-to-earth philosophy that grew out of nineteenth-century British philosophers' concern to demystify ethics and make it work in the practical world. Jeremy Bentham, the originator of utilitarianism, developed the goal of the greatest good for the greatest number, or "greatest happiness," by which he meant the most pleasure for the least pain. John Stuart Mill, another British philosopher, built on Bentham's utilitarianism using predicted consequences to determine the morality of a proposed action.

Mill's consequentialist approach allows you readily to assess a wide range of acts. You can apply the principle of utility—which says that an action is morally right if it produces a greater net value (benefits minus costs) than any available alternative action—to virtually any situation and it will help you reach a decision. Obviously, however, it's not always easy to make the calculations called for by the principle, since, like any prediction, an estimate of consequences is conjectural. In particular, it's often very hard to assess the long-term consequences of any action. Too often, utilitarianism seduces us into a short-term analysis of a moral problem simply because long-term consequences are very difficult to predict.

Principles as the Base of Ethics

Any ethical system based on principles will ultimately rest on moral tenets that we are duty bound to uphold, no matter what the consequences. Sometimes the moral tenets come from religious faith—for example, the Ten Commandments. At other times, however, the principles are derived from philosophical reasoning, as in the case of German philosopher Immanuel Kant. Kant held that no one should ever use another person as a means to his or her own ends and that everyone should always act as if his or her acts were the basis of universal law. In other words, Kant held that we were duty bound to respect other people's sanctity and to act in the same way that we would want all other people to act. The great advantage of such a system is its clarity and precision. We are never overwhelmed by a multiplicity of contradictory and difficult-to-quantify consequences; we simply make sure we are not violating a principle of our ethical system and proceed accordingly.

Constructing an Ethical Argument

To show you how to construct an ethical argument, let's now apply these two strategies to an example. In general, you can construct an ethical evaluation by using the frame for either a principles-based argument or a consequences-based argument or a combination of both.

> *Principles-Based Frame*: X is right (wrong) because it follows (violates) principles A, B, and C.

> *Consequences-Based Frame*: X is right (wrong) because it will lead to consequences A, B, and C, which are good (bad).

To illustrate how these frames might help you develop an ethical argument, let's use them to develop arguments for or against capital punishment.

Constructing a Principles-Based Argument

A principles-based arguments looks at capital punishment through the lens of one or more guiding principles. Kant's principle that we are duty bound not to violate the sanctity of other human lives could lead to arguments opposing capital punishment. One might argue as follows:

> *Principles-based argument opposing capital punishment*: The death penalty is wrong because it violates the principle of the sanctity of human life.

You could support this principle either by summarizing Kant's argument that one should not violate the selfhood of another person or by pointing to certain religious systems such as Judeo-Christian ethics, where one is told "Vengeance is Mine, saith the Lord" or "Thou shalt not kill." To develop this argument further, you might examine two exceptions where principles-based ethicists may allow killing—self-defense and war—and show how capital punishment does not fall into either category.

Principles-based arguments can also be developed to support capital punishment. You may be surprised to learn that Kant himself—despite his arguments for the sanctity of life—actually supported capital punishment. To make such an argument, Kant evoked a different principle about the suitability of the punishment to the crime:

There is no sameness of kind between death and remaining alive even under the most miserable conditions, and consequently there is no equality between the crime and the retribution unless the criminal is judicially condemned and put to death.

Stated as an enthymeme, Kant's argument is as follows:

Principles-based argument supporting capital punishment: Capital punishment is right because it follows the principle that punishments should be proportionate to the crime.

In developing this argument, Kant's burden is to show why the principle of proportionate retribution outweighs the principle of the supreme worth of the individual. Our point is that a principles-based argument can be made both for or against capital punishment. The arguer's duty is to make clear what principle is being evoked and then to show why this principle is more important than opposing principles.

Constructing a Consequences-Based Argument

Unlike a principles-based argument, which appeals to certain guiding maxims or rules, a consequences-based argument looks at the consequences of a decision and measures the positive benefits against the negative costs. Here is the frame that an arguer might use to oppose capital punishment on the basis of negative consequences:

Consequences-based argument opposing capital punishment: Capital punishment is wrong because it leads to the following negative consequences:

- The possibility of executing an innocent person
- The possibility that a murderer who might repent and be redeemed is denied that chance
- The excessive legal and political costs of trials and appeals
- The unfair distribution of executions so that one's chances of being put to death are much greater if one is a minority or is poor

To develop this argument, the reader would need to provide facts, statistics, and other evidence to support each of the stated reasons.

A different arguer might use a consequences-based approach to support capital punishment:

Consequences-based argument supporting capital punishment: Capital punishment is right because it leads to the following positive consequences:

- It may deter violent crime and slow down the rate of murder.
- It saves the cost of lifelong imprisonment.

- It stops criminals who are menaces to society from ever committing more murders.

- It helps grieving families reach closure and sends a message to victims' families that society recognizes their pain.

It should be evident, then, that adopting an ethical system doesn't lead to automatic answers to one's ethical dilemmas. A system offers a way of proceeding—a way of conducting an argument—but it doesn't relieve you of personal responsibility for thinking through your values and taking a stand. When you face an ethical dilemma, we encourage you to consider both the relevant principles and the possible consequences the dilemma entails. In many arguments, you can use both principles-based and consequences-based reasoning so long as irreconcilable contradictions don't present themselves.

For Class Discussion

Working as individuals or in small groups:

1. Try to formulate a consequences-based argument in favor of biotech agriculture (see the arguments in Chapter 2, pp. 21–24 and 35–39).

2. Now try to formulate a consequences-based argument opposing biotech agriculture.

3. What might a principles-based ethicist say about biotech agriculture? About cloning?

4. When people argue about owning SUVs, the controversies can be either categorical, ethical, or both.

   a. How would you make a categorical evaluation argument that SUVs are good (bad) cars for families in urban environments?

   b. How would you make an ethical argument that it is morally right or wrong to buy an SUV?

Common Problems in Making Evaluation Arguments

When conducting evaluation arguments (whether categorical or ethical), writers can bump up against recurring problems that are unique to evaluation. In some cases these problems complicate the establishment of criteria; in other cases they complicate the match argument. Let's look briefly at some of these common problems.

- *The problem of standards—What's commonplace versus what's ideal:* To appreciate this problem, consider again Young Person's archetypal argument with Parent about her curfew (see Chapter 1, pp. 6–8). She originally argued that staying out until 2 A.M. is fair "because all the other kids' parents let their kids stay out late," to which Parent might respond: "Well, *ideally*, all the other parents should not let their kids stay out that late." Young Person based her criterion for fairness on what is *commonplace*; her standards arose from common practices of a social group. Parent, however, argued from what is *ideal*, basing her or his criterion on some external standard that transcends social groups. We experience this dilemma in various forms all the time. Is it fair to get a ticket for going 70 mph on a 65-mph freeway when most of the drivers go 70 mph or higher? (Does what is *commonplace*—going 70—override what is *ideal*—obeying the law?) Is it better for high schools to pass out free contraceptives to students because students are having sex anyway (what's *commonplace*), or is it better not to pass them out in order to support abstinence (what's *ideal*)?

- *The problem of mitigating circumstances:* This problem occurs when an arguer claims that unusual circumstances should alter our usual standards of judgment. Ordinarily, it is fair for a teacher to reduce a grade if you turn in a paper late. But what if you were up all night taking care of a crying baby? Does that count as a *mitigating circumstance* to waive the ordinary criterion? What about your annual performance evaluation during a year when you had chronic back pain or were going through a divorce? When you argue for mitigating circumstances, you will likely assume an especially heavy burden of proof. People assume the rightness of usual standards of judgment unless there are compelling arguments for abnormal circumstances.

- *The problem of choosing between two goods or two bads:* Often an evaluation issue catches us between a rock and a hard place. Should we cut pay or cut people? Put our parents into a nursing home or let them stay at home where they have become a danger to themselves? Take the road trip I had planned across the United States or take the new job offer? In such cases one has to weigh conflicting criteria, knowing that the choices are too much alike—either both bad or both good.

- *The problem of seductive empirical measures:* The need to make high-stakes evaluations has led many persons to seek quantifiable criteria that can be weighed mathematically. Thus we use grade point averages to select scholarship winners, student evaluation scores to decide merit pay for teachers, SAT scores and GPAs for college admissions, and combined scores of judges to rank figure skaters. In some cases, empirical measures can be quite acceptable, but they are often dangerous because they discount important nonquantifiable traits. The problem with empirical measures is that they seduce us into believing that complex judgments can be made mathematically, thus rescuing us from the messiness of alternative points of view and conflicting criteria. Empirical measures seem extremely persuasive next to written arguments that try to qualify and hedge and raise questions. We suggest, however, that in many cases a fair evaluation may require such hedging.

- *The problem of cost:* A final problem that can crop up in evaluations is cost. X may be the best of all possible Ys, but if X costs too much, we have to go for second or third best. We can avoid this problem somewhat by placing items into different classes on the basis of cost. For example, a Mercedes will exceed a Hyundai on almost any criterion, but if we can't afford more than a Hyundai, the comparison is pointless. It is better to compare a Mercedes to a Lexus and a Hyundai to an equivalent Ford. Whether costs are expressed in dollars, personal discomfort, moral repugnance, or some other terms, our final evaluation of X must take cost into account.

Organizing an Evaluation Argument

As you write a draft, you might find useful the following prototypical structures for evaluation arguments. Of course, you can always alter these plans if another structure better fits your material.

Plan 1 (Criteria and Match in Separate Sections)

- Introduce the issue by showing disagreements about how to evaluate a problematic X. (Is X a good Y?) (Is X right or wrong?)
- State your claim.
- Present your criteria for making the evaluation.
   State and develop Criterion 1.
   State and develop Criterion 2.
   Continue with the rest of your criteria.
- Summarize and respond to possible objections to your criteria.
- Restate your claim asserting that X is (is not) a good member of class Y or that X is right (wrong).
   Apply Criterion 1 to your case.
   Apply Criterion 2 to your case.
   Continue the match argument.
- Summarize and respond to possible objections to your match argument.
- Conclude your argument.

Plan 2 (Criteria and Match Interwoven)

- Introduce the issue by showing disagreements about how to evaluate a problematic X. (Is X a good Y?) (Is X right or wrong?)
- Present your claim.
   State Criterion 1 and argue that your X meets (does not meet) this criterion.
   State Criterion 2 and argue that your X meets (does not meet) this criterion.
   Continue with criteria-match sections for additional criteria.

- Summarize opposing views.
- Refute or concede to opposing views.
- Conclude your argument.

Critiquing a Categorical Evaluation

To strengthen your draft of a categorical evaluation, you can role-play a skeptic by asking the following questions.

Will a skeptic accept my criteria?   Many evaluative arguments are weak because the writers have simply assumed that readers will accept their criteria. Whenever your audience's acceptance of your criteria is in doubt, you will need to make your warrants clear and provide backing in their support.

Are my criteria based on the "smallest applicable class" for X?   For example, the 1999 film *The Blair Witch Project* will certainly be a failure if you evaluate it in the general class "movies," in which it would have to compete with *Citizen Kane* and other great classics. But if you evaluated it as a "horror film" or a "low-budget film," it would have a greater chance for success and hence of yielding an arguable evaluation.

Will a skeptic accept my general weighting of criteria?   Another vulnerable spot in an evaluation argument is the relative weight of the criteria. How much anyone weights a given criterion is usually a function of his or her own interests relative to the X in question. You should always ask whether some particular group affected by the quality of X might not have good reasons for weighting the criteria differently.

Will a skeptic question my standard of reference?   In questioning the criteria for judging X, we can also focus on the standard of reference used—what's common versus what's ideal. If you have argued that X is bad because it doesn't live up to what's ideal, you can expect some readers to defend X on the basis of what's common. Similarly, if you argue that X is good because it is better than its competitors, you can expect some readers to point out how short it falls from what is ideal.

Will a skeptic criticize my use of empirical measures?   The tendency to mistake empirical measures for criteria is a common one that any critic of an argument should be aware of. As we have discussed earlier, what's most measurable isn't always significant when it comes to assessing the essential traits needed to fulfill whatever function X is supposed to fulfill. A 95-mph fastball is certainly an impressive empirical measure of a pitcher's ability. But if the pitcher doesn't get batters out, that measure is a misleading gauge of performance.

Will a skeptic accept my criteria but reject my match argument?   The other major way of testing an evaluation argument is to anticipate how readers might object to your stated reasons and grounds. Will readers challenge you by finding sampling errors in your data or otherwise find that you used evidence selectively? For example, if you think your opponents will emphasize Lillian Jones's abrasive management style much more heavily than you did, you may be able to undercut their arguments by finding counterexamples that show Ms. Jones acting diplomatically. Be prepared to counter objections to your grounds.

Critiquing an Ethical Evaluation

Perhaps the first question you should ask in setting out to analyze your draft of an ethical argument is "To what extent is the argument based on consequences or on ethical principles?" If it's based exclusively on one of these two forms of ethical thought, then it's vulnerable to the sorts of criticism discussed here. A strictly principled argument that takes no account of the consequences of its position is vulnerable to a simple cost analysis. What are the costs in the case of adhering to this principle? There will undoubtedly be some, or else there would be no real argument. If the argument is based strictly on consequentialist grounds, we should ask if the position violates any rules or principles, particularly such commandments as the Golden Rule—"Do unto others as you would have others do unto you"—which most members of our audience adhere to. By failing to mention these alternative ways of thinking about ethical issues, we undercut not only our argument but our credibility as well.

Let's now consider a more developed examination of the two positions, starting with some of the more subtle weaknesses in a position based on principle. In practice people will sometimes take rigidly "principled" positions because they live in fear of "slippery slopes"—that is, they fear setting precedents that might lead to ever more dire consequences. Consider, for example, the slippery slope leading from birth control to euthanasia if you have an absolutist commitment to the sanctity of human life. Once we allow birth control in the form of condoms or pills, the principled absolutist would say, then we will be forced to accept birth control "abortions" in the first hours after conception (IUDs, "morning after" pills), then abortions in the first trimester, then in the second or even the third trimester. And once we have violated the sanctity of human life by allowing abortions, it is only a short step to euthanasia and finally to killing off all undesirables.

One way to refute a slippery-slope argument of this sort is to try to dig a foothold into the side of the hill to show that you don't necessarily have to slide all the way to the bottom. You would thus have to argue that allowing birth control does not mean allowing abortions (by arguing for differences between a fetus after conception and sperm and egg before conception), or that allowing abortions does not mean allowing euthanasia (by arguing for differences between a fetus and a person already living in the world).

Consequentialist arguments have different kinds of difficulties. As discussed before, the crucial difficulty facing anyone making a consequentialist argument is to calculate the consequences in a clear and reliable way. Have you considered all significant consequences? If you project your scenario of consequences further into the future (remember, consequentialist arguments are frequently stronger

over the short term than over the long term, where many unforeseen consequences can occur), can you identify possibilities that work against the argument?

As also noted, consequentialist arguments carry a heavy burden of empirical
proof. What evidence can you offer that the predicted consequences will in fact
come to pass? Do you offer any evidence that alternative consequences won't
occur? And just how do you prove that the consequences of any given action are a
net good or evil?

In addition to the problems unique to each of the two positions, ethical arguments are vulnerable to the more general sorts of criticism, including consistency, recency, and relevance of evidence. Obviously, however, consequentialist
arguments will be more vulnerable to weaknesses in evidence, whereas arguments based on principle are more open to questions about consistency of application.

Readings

Our first reading, by student writer Tiffany Anderson, developed out of discussions of hip-hop music. Tiffany was torn between a general dislike of rap combined with a growing admiration for certain female rappers. This evaluation
argument took shape once she formulated her issue question: What makes a good
female hip-hop artist?

A Woman's View of Hip-Hop
Tiffany Anderson (student)

1   Is there anything good about hip-hop? If you had asked me this question several
years ago, I would have said no. I probably disliked hip-hop as much as any typical
middle-aged white suburbanite. I found the aggressive, ego-driven, star-powered,
competitive male image of hip-hop devoid of value, especially the beat and the strong
language. I also disliked many of the themes explored in gangster rap, such as the
derogatory terms for blacks, the treatment of women as sex objects, and the equation
of power and money. When some boys at summer camp six years ago first introduced
me to hip-hop, we listened to artists like Bone Thugs-n-Harmony, Tupak Shakur, and
Biggie Smalls. These boys who liked rap were also sniffing markers and gave me my
first encounter with drugs. In my sheltered white world, I associated rap with drugs
and gangs, and I gravitated toward the comfort of alternative rock and punk instead.

2   But my view of rap began to change when I started listening to the female rappers introduced to me by my friends. During my sophomore year in high school I remember going home because of a bomb threat, and we danced to *The Miseducation of
Lauryn Hill* in my living room. I liked what Lauryn was saying. Women hip-hop artists
have something different to offer in a male-dominated industry, and it has been

women artists who have converted me into a hip-hop fan, not the men. What exactly do these women have to offer that is so compelling? What makes a good female hip-hop artist? While many female rappers merely follow in the footsteps of male rappers by rapping about money, sex, or violence, the truly great female artists provide female listeners with a sense of self-empowerment and identity, they offer a woman's perspective on many topics, and they often create a hopeful message that counters the negativity of male rap. Through their songs, good female rappers spread positive, unique messages that not only benefit African Americans, but females of every race.

Very few male artists are able to provide women with a sense of self-empowerment or identity through their music. But excellent female hip-hop artists like Lauryn Hill address women's sense of self, as Hill does in her song "Doo Wop (That Thing)." In the first verse she criticizes a woman who loses her self-respect by doing what men want her to do ("It's silly when girls sell their souls because it's in"). She encourages women who "ain't right within" to take pride in themselves, regain their self-respect, and be true to themselves. The encouragement Lauryn offers her female audience is uplifting in an industry where women are often reduced to sex objects as scantily clad dancers, back-up singers, and eye candy in music videos. Rapper Trina, in her song "Take Me," criticizes the idea that females have to be sex objects: "I wanna go to a world where I ain't gotta be a freak ho/just so I can be noticed by people." Perhaps through such urging, girls can take pride in themselves and rebel against stereotypes. Foxy Brown addresses stereotypes in an entirely different, but equally effective, way. She uses her explicitly sexual lyrics to objectify men in her songs, where her heroine is always the dominant one. Her songs help break female sexual inhibitions, reverse the typical roles of the sexes, and allow us to be proud of our sexuality. These songs can be a cathartic release in a world that is all too often dominated by men. Female artists should address the reality of derogatory stereotypes and work to foster a positive female image; if this were left to the male rappers of the industry, females would not be as positively represented in the hip-hop industry.

Another mark of a good female hip-hop artist is that she makes songs that give a woman's perspective on the world or her songs include topics not usually addressed in hip-hop songs at all. For example, my favorite song by Lauryn Hill, "To Zion," is about how her world changed after the birth of her son, Zion. When she sings, "Now the joy of my world is Zion," I am filled with pride that I am a woman and have the ability to give birth. How often do male artists, like Nelly or DMX, sing about the joys of parenthood? It is refreshing to hear songs about the miracles of life, as opposed to the death, drugs, and destruction that are often the topics in typical rap songs. On *Eve-olution*, Eve's most recent album, she criticizes our world where she "can't trust the air," an allusion to an oncoming ecological crisis. Hip-hop artists are rarely concerned with problems that affect the entire world, but focus more on their communities. Eve shows her scope as an artist in addressing ecological problems. Another topic not often explored in hip-hop songs is religion. In her song "Confessions," Lady of Rage asks for forgiveness and calls for appreciation for the Lord: "Forgive me God, for I have forsaken thee/I'm not gonna say that it's the devil that's makin me." Hip-hop is so often used to name all the evils in the world and lay blame, so hearing an artist take responsibility for her actions and explore a religious theme in her music is refreshing. When a female rap artist can offer her listeners something that they don't often hear, she is truly great.

5   Most importantly, the best female rappers often see some kind of hope in life. Some people might argue that the negativity so blatant in much hip-hop music actually conveys important social and political messages, addressing racial profiling, police brutality, gun control, violence, the glorification of money and sex, and problems with education and welfare reform. These people might say that this influential urban folk art exposes economic and social realities that America needs to confront. I agree that sometimes male artists will reveal a heartbreaking perspective on this empty world by communicating how urban youth struggle with self-hatred, poverty, lack of education, hopelessness, discrimination, and injustice. For example, in Outkast's song "Git Up, Git Out," the lyrics speak of never-ending cycles of drugs, negativity, and lack of education that hold African Americans back: "I don't recall, ever graduatin at all/Sometimes I feel I'm just a disappointment to y'all . . . Every job I get is cruel and demeanin/Sick of taking trash out and toilet bowl cleanin/But I'm also sick and tired of strugglin/I never ever thought I'd have resort to drug smugglin." While male hip-hop often offers a unique, chilling perspective on the problems of urban America, their music often only serves to strengthen the cycles of despair and self-hatred. Where is hope in songs that often spend verse after verse on the negative aspects of life and the forces that hold people back?

6   In contrast, female hip-hop artists do identify the problems, but sometimes suggest ways to overcome the difficulties of their lives. For example, Eve's song "Heaven Only Knows" talks about the trouble she faced until she overcame her devastating situation by finding peace through music: "Do positive and positive will happen/Stay positive and positive was rapping/It was like my brain was clouded with unnecessary shit/But I chose to see through the negative and make hits." "Heaven Only Knows" demonstrates the power of rap music to heal. Through her songs, Eve encourages her listeners in new paths and reinforces the importance of overcoming the negative aspects of being an African American. In the title track of *The Miseducation of Lauryn Hill*, Lauryn deftly addresses the problems and offers her own personal story of how she overcame life's setbacks: "I look at my environment/And wonder where the fire went/What happened to everything we used to be/I hear so many cry for help/Searching outside themselves/Now I know His strength is within me/And deep in my heart the answer it was in me/And I made up my mind to find my own destiny." Lauryn sings about how she rejected what was expected of her from outside sources, turned to God, and found everything she needed in herself. To impoverished people of urban America, finding inner strength and self-empowerment could be encouraging. Although Lauryn and Eve usually direct their songs to an African American audience, their words of wisdom apply to all races. Every woman alive can benefit from knowing that we can find our "own destiny" within ourselves, as Lauryn raps about.

7   Because the lyrics of rap are its heart and soul, what a rapper says conveys a powerful world view. The worldview of male rap for me is too violent, negative, and antiwoman, but female rap often conveys the same gritty sense of urban life without succumbing to hopelessness and without reducing women to sex objects. The best female rappers are able to arouse a sense of pride and self-worth through their thoughtful lyrics, offer a woman's perspective on the world, and include hopeful messages among the harsh realities of urban life. Female artists like Lauryn Hill,

Eve, or Trina have taught me that not all hip-hop is bad, and that sometimes, I can even learn a little something from a song. I found hip-hop a surprising source of feminist pride, diversity, and hope, and this discovery served as a reminder that even in a male- and African American-dominated industry, any white girl can find something to relate to and learn from.

Our second reading, "Eight Is Too Many: The Case Against Octuplets," is an ethical argument by Dr. Ezekiel Emanuel, the chair of the department of clinical bioethics at the National Institutes of Health. He discusses the case of the McCaughey septuplets, born on November 17, 1997, and the Chukwu octuplets, one of whom was born vaginally on December 8, 1999, with the other seven born by Caesarian section on December 20, 1999. In both cases, the couple had been treated with fertility drugs. This article appeared in the *New Republic* on January 25, 1999.

Eight Is Too Many: The Case Against Octuplets

Dr. Ezekiel J. Emanuel

Just like the McCaughey septuplets of Iowa, whose first birthday recently made   1
headlines in *People* magazine, the Chukwu octuplets of Texas have become a media spectacle. Daily bulletins detailing each child's respiratory status, ultrasound results, and other developments fill the papers—not just the tabloids, but respectable outlets like the *New York Times* and the *Washington Post,* as well. Inevitably, writers describe the eight live births in glowing terms—amazing, wonderful, even a miracle; they describe the mother as the brave survivor of adversity; they portray the hard-battling physicians as heroes and champions.

But what are we all celebrating? Modern reproductive technologies have   2
brought the miracle of children to many infertile couples, thereby producing enormous good. The McCaughey septuplets and Chukwu octuplets, however, represent too much of that good thing. They are the product of fertility technology misused—an error, not a wonder, and one that even the few public voices of skepticism seem not fully to appreciate.

First and most obvious, large multiple births lead to all sorts of medical problems,   3
for mothers and children alike. Nkem Chukwu had to stay in the hospital for months prior to delivery, on a bed that tilted her nearly upside down. It's too early to know how well her surviving children will fare (one died seven days after birth), but the odds do not favor them. Among children born prematurely and weighing just two pounds or less—the largest of the Chukwu infants weighed one pound, eleven ounces at birth—breathing difficulties, brain damage, and fluid imbalances are not rare.

The result is a comparatively high level of infant mortality and, in the survivors,   4
long-term complications. Studies of low-birth-weight children (not from multifetal

pregnancies but from premature births) have shown that approximately 20 percent have severe disabilities; among those weighing less than 750 grams (1.7 pounds) at birth, 50 percent have functional impairments. A recent study that followed these very small infants to school showed that up to 50 percent of them scored low on standardized intelligence tests, including 21 percent who were mentally retarded. In addition, nine percent had cerebral palsy, and 25 percent had severe vision problems. As a result, 45 percent ended up enrolling in special-education programs.

5   Equally important, but rarely articulated, are the emotional health risks children in multiple births face. Loving and raising children through the normal developmental milestones is enormously wonderful and rewarding. But it is also hard work. Raising children is not a sprint to a healthy birth but a marathon through variable terrain until the goal of independent adulthood. The real way to assess these miraculous pregnancies—indeed, any pregnancy—is whether they are ultimately good for children. Quite clearly, they are not.

6   Attending to the physical, emotional, intellectual, and social needs of children for 18 years is hard and demanding. For infants and toddlers there are the simple physical demands—feeding, changing diapers, bathing, chasing after them to prevent injuries. Then there are the emotional and intellectual demands—cuddling them, talking to them, responding meaningfully to their smiles and first words, reading books to them, playing with them and their toys, handling the tantrums, and so on. And, while the physical demands may lessen once children grow (although parents who often feel like chefs, maids, chauffeurs, and all-around gofers may disagree with that), the emotional and intellectual demands become more complex with time. Older children need help with homework, mediation of sibling rivalry, constructive discipline, support in the trials and tribulations of friendships, encouragement in their participation in sports and other activities, help in coping with losses and defeats, and guidance through the many pitfalls of adolescence.

7   It is challenging enough to balance the demands of one or two children of different ages and attend to their needs; it is simply not physically possible for two parents to do this successfully for seven children of the same age, even if one of the parents is a full-time caregiver. Regardless of the motivation, dedication, love, or stamina of these parents, the sheer limitations of time make it impossible for each of seven identically aged children to receive appropriate parental attention and affection.

8   Just ask yourself: Would you trade being born a healthy single or twin for being born one of the "miraculous" septuplets, even a healthy one? Most of us would probably say "no" because of parental attention we would have lost. And we would be right to think that way.

9   The McCaugheys' experience proves the point. They have been able to raise their septuplets for one year only because they can fall back on a veritable army of volunteers—scores of people with tightly coordinated schedules who assist in the food preparation, feeding, diapering, and care of the seven babies. Few families with quintuplets or more children can expect or rely on such community effort. (Indeed, a Washington, D.C., couple who recently bore quintuplets, had hardly any community help at all until some belated publicity highlighted the family's plight.) And, while the McCaugheys' community-wide effort appears to have worked for the first year of life, it's hardly a sure thing that the assistance will always be there.

The first is the year when, despite the demands on time, parents are most interchangeable and caregiving has the greatest, most unmitigated emotional rewards. The terrible twos and threes will try the patience and dedication of volunteers.

What's more, having multiple caregivers cannot fully substitute for parental time. While it's true that many children do just fine spending large amounts of time in paid day care, where multiple providers care for them, these children at least have the chance to go home and have one-on-one parental time spread among just a few siblings, of different ages. (Having multiple caregivers also becomes more problematic as the children grow, because of child-rearing styles that may differ from those of the parents, particularly on issues like discipline.) This is not possible in the McCaughey or Chukwu families, and it never will be. Spending just 20 minutes a day focusing on each individual child—hardly a lavish amount—will take nearly two and a half hours each day. When competing with sleep, meals, shopping, and all the other demands of basic existence for a family with septuplets, this focused time is likely to disappear. 10

Remember, too, that, while the McCaughey septuplets seem to have brought together a community to support their care, such children also impose significant costs on the community. It is now estimated that the hospital costs from birth to discharge (or death) for the Chukwu infants will exceed $2 million. And the health care costs don't stop after birth. Any complications—neurological, vision, or other problems—can drive the medical care costs sky-high. Plus, no one knows how much will be required for permanent problems that require ongoing special-education and other accommodations. Yes, there's health insurance. But health insurance exists to cover ill health and problems such as cancer, genetic defects, and accidents that are the result of random chance. The birth of octuplets, by contrast, is not a chance event; it is the result of deliberate actions (or inactions) by physicians, patients, and society. Remember, too, that financial resources are limited; money spent on octuplets is money not spent on other children with special health care and educational needs. 11

For these reasons, the standard of medical care is not to proceed with such large multiple births. But this raises legitimate ethical problems for many couples. The most common method for interrupting multiple pregnancies is "selective reduction"—that is, doctors abort some of the fetuses for the sake of the mother's health. Many people believe couples who agree to infertility treatments must not only be informed about—but should consent to—the potential need for selective reduction even before beginning the treatments. Yet this is clearly not an option for families like the McCaugheys and the Chukwus, who oppose abortion on religious grounds. 12

Fortunately, this issue doesn't have to be so morally knotty. In the usual treatment for problems with egg maturation and release (this is what both the McCaughey and Chukwu families were treated for), doctors prescribe drugs such as human menopausal gonadotropin (hMG) or Clomiphene (commonly known as Clomid) to stimulate egg development. Then they administer an additional drug, human chorionic gonadatropin (hCG), to induce ovulation. Using measurements of estrogen and ultrasound monitoring, physicians can assess the number of egg follicles developing in the ovaries. If they observe too many developing follicles, making the likelihood of multiple fertilizations high, physicians can withhold the drugs necessary to stimulate ovulation and advise against intercourse or withhold sperm injection until the next cycle, when they can go through the process again. To be sure, 13 that treatment process can be a little more frustrating for aspiring parents. And many couples are reluctant to skip a cycle because it wastes thousands of dollars on the drugs and treatments, usually out of their own pockets. But carrying septuplets to term has costs, too.

14   In the end, new laws or regulations won't fix this problem. The real solution is leadership by the medical profession and by the media. Reproductive specialists who care for infertile couples are not simply passive technicians following the orders of the parents. They are engaged professionals guiding important technology that can create great joy—but also great pain. Professionalism requires deliberating with the parents about the goals and purposes of the treatments; doctors should draw upon their experience to advise and strongly recommend the best course to the parents, which is to avoid large multiple pregnancies.

15   And the media must stop glorifying the septuplets and octuplets. We live in an era that measures success in terms of quantity, that thinks bigger is necessarily better, where the best is defined by size. The best movie is the one that makes the most money; the best law firm is the one with the highest billings; the best painting is auctioned for the highest price; and the best book is the best-selling book. But, in this case, bigger may not be better—indeed, it may actually be worse. The true miracle of birth is the mysterious process by which the fusing of an egg and a sperm can create in just nine months the complex organism that is an infant with the potential to become an independent, thinking, feeling, socially responsible adult. In this way, the millions of babies born each year are miraculous whether born of singleton, twin, triplet, or octuplet pregnancies. It is the wonder of each infant that we should celebrate.

WRITING ASSIGNMENT
FOR CHAPTER 14

Write an argument in which you try to change someone's mind about the value of X. The X you choose should be controversial or at least problematic. By "controversial" or "problematic," we mean that people are likely to disagree with your evaluation of X, that they are surprised at your evaluation, or that you are somehow opposing the common or expected view of X. By choosing a controversial or problematic X, you will be able to focus on a clear issue. Somewhere in your essay you should summarize alternative views and either refute them or concede to them (see Chapter 8).

Note that this assignment asks you to do something different from a typical movie review, restaurant review, or product review in a consumer magazine. Many reviews are simply informational or analytical; the writer's purpose is to describe the object or event being reviewed and explain its strengths and weaknesses. In contrast, your purpose here is persuasive. You must try to change someone's mind about the worth or value of X.

15 Proposal Arguments
We Should (Should Not) Do X

EXAMPLE CASE

Many cultural commentators are alarmed by a new social disease brought on by addictive spending. Dubbed "affluenza" and "credititis," this disease is spreading through aggressive promotion of credit cards. Economic analysts are particularly concerned at the way credit card companies are deluging teenagers with credit card offers. Some argue that encouraging credit card debt among the young is highly irresponsible corporate behavior. To raise public awareness of the problem, a group of legislators proposed that the following warning label be placed prominently on all credit cards: "*Warning:* Failure to research interest rates and credit cards may result in personal financial loss or possible bankruptcy."*

The Nature of Proposal Arguments

Proposal arguments are among the most common arguments that you will encounter or be called on to write. Their essence is that they call for action. In reading a proposal, the audience is enjoined to make a decision and then to act on it—to *do* something. Proposal arguments are sometimes called *should* or *ought* arguments because these helping verbs express the obligation to act: "We *should* do X" or "We *ought* to do X."

For instructional purposes, we will distinguish between two kinds of proposal arguments, even though they are closely related and involve the same basic arguing strategies. The first kind we will call *practical proposals,* which propose an action to solve some kind of local or immediate problem. A student's proposal to change the billing procedures for scholarship students would be an example of a practical proposal, as would an engineering firm's proposal for the design of a new bridge being planned by a city government. The second kind

---

*"Credit Cards: Wealth Hazard," *Seattle Times,* 4 Feb. 1999: B2.

we will call *policy proposals,* in which the writer offers a broad plan of action to solve major social, economic, or political problems affecting the common good. An argument that the United States should adopt a national health insurance plan or that the electoral college should be abolished would be examples of policy proposals.

The Structure of Proposal Arguments

Proposal arguments, whether practical proposals or policy proposals, generally have a three-part structure: (1) description of a problem, (2) proposed solution, and (3) justification for the proposed solution. Luckily, proposal arguments don't require different sorts of argumentative strategies from the ones you have already been using. In the justification section of your proposal argument, you develop *because* clauses of the kinds you have practiced all along throughout this text.

Special Concerns of Proposal Arguments

In their call for action, proposal arguments entail certain emphases and audience concerns that you don't generally face with other kinds of arguments. Let's look briefly at some of these special concerns.

The Need for Presence

Your audience might agree with your proposal on an intellectual level, but how can you move them to *act* on your proposal, especially if the personal cost of acting may be high? Urging action often requires you to engage your audience's emotions as well as their intellects. Thus proposal arguments often require more attention to *pathos* than do other kinds of arguments (see pp. 112–116).

In most cases, convincing people to act means that an argument must have presence as well as intellectual force. By *presence* we mean an argument's ability to grip the readers' hearts and imaginations as well as their intellects. You can give presence to an argument through the effective use of details, provocative statistics, dialogue, illustrative narratives, vivid analogies, or compelling examples that show the reader the seriousness of the problem you are addressing or the consequences of not acting on your proposal. When an argument has presence, the problem it addresses ceases to be an abstraction to your audience. Such arguments call the reader beyond assent toward action.

The Need to Overcome People's Natural Conservatism

Another difficulty faced by a proposal maker is the innate conservatism of all human beings, whatever their political persuasion. One philosopher refers to this conservatism as the *law of inertia,* the tendency of all things in the universe, including human beings, to remain at rest if possible. The popular adage "If it ain't broke, don't fix it" is one expression of this tendency. Hence, proposers of change face an extraordinary burden of proof. Specifically, they have to prove that something needs fixing, that it can be fixed, and that the cost of fixing it will be outweighed by the benefits of fixing it.

The difficulty of proving that something needs fixing is compounded by the fact that frequently the status quo appears to be working. So sometimes when writing a proposal, you can't argue that what we have is bad, but only that what we could have would be better. Often, then, a proposal argument will be based not on present evils but on the evils of lost potential. And getting an audience to accept lost potential may be difficult indeed, given the inherently abstract nature of potentiality.

The Difficulty of Predicting Future Consequences

Further, most proposal makers will be forced to predict consequences of a given act. As we've seen in our earlier discussions of causality, it is difficult enough to argue backward from event Y in order to establish that X caused Y. Think how much harder it is to establish that X will, in the future, cause certain things to occur. We all know enough of history to realize that few major decisions have led neatly to their anticipated results. This knowledge indeed accounts for much of our conservatism. All the things that can go wrong in a causal argument can go wrong in a proposal argument as well; the major difference is that in a proposal argument we typically have less evidence for our conjectures.

The Problem of Evaluating Consequences

A final difficulty faced by all proposal arguments concerns the difficulty of evaluating the consequences of the proposal. In government and industry, managers often turn to a tool known as *cost-benefit analysis* to calculate the potential consequences of a given proposal. As much as possible, a cost-benefit analysis tries to reduce all consequences to a single scale for purposes of comparison. Most often, the scale will be money. Although this scale may work well in some circumstances, it can lead to grotesquely inappropriate conclusions in other situations.

Just how does one balance the money saved by cutting Medicare benefits against the suffering of the people denied benefits? How does one translate the beauty of a wilderness area into a dollar amount? On this score, cost-benefit analyses often run into a problem discussed in the previous chapter: the seductiveness of empirical measures (see p. 238). Because something can't be readily measured doesn't mean it can be safely ignored. And finally, what will be a cost for one group will often be a benefit for others. For example, if Social Security benefits are cut, those on Social Security will suffer, but current workers who pay for it with taxes will take home a larger paycheck.

These, then, are some of the general difficulties facing someone who sets out to argue in favor of a proposal. Although not insurmountable, they are at least daunting.

Developing a Proposal Argument

Writers of proposal arguments must focus in turn on three main phases or stages of the argument: showing that a problem exists, explaining the proposed solution, and offering a justification.

Convincing Your Readers That a Problem Exists

There is one argumentative strategy generic to all proposal arguments: awakening in the reader a sense of a problem. Typically, the development of a problem occurs in one of two places in a proposal argument—either in the introduction prior to the presentation of the arguer's proposal claim or in the body of the paper as the first main reason justifying the proposal claim. In the second instance the writer's first *because* clause has the following structure: "We should do X *because* we are facing a serious problem that needs a solution."

At this stage of your argument, it's important to give your problem presence. You must get people to see how the problem affects people, perhaps through examples of suffering or other loss or through persuasive statistics and so forth. Your goal is to awaken your readers to the existence of a problem, a problem they may well not have recognized before.

Besides giving presence to the problem, a writer must also gain the readers' intellectual assent to the depth, range, and potential seriousness of the problem. Suppose, for illustration, that you wanted to propose a special tax to increase funding for higher education in your state. In trying to convince taxpayers in your state that a problem exists, what obstacles might you face? First of all, many taxpayers never went to college and feel that they get along just fine without it. They tend to worry more about the quality of roads, social services, elementary and secondary schools, police and fire protection, and so forth. They are not too convinced that they need to worry about professors' salaries or better-equipped research labs. Thus, it's not enough to talk about the importance of education in general or to cite figures showing how paltry your state's funding of higher education is.

To convince members of your audience of the need for your proposal, you'll have to describe the consequences of low funding levels in terms they can relate to. You'll have to show them that potential benefits to the state are lost because of inadequate funding. Perhaps you can show the cost in terms of inadequately skilled graduates, disgruntled teachers, high turnover, brain drain to other states, inadequate educational services to farmers and businesspeople, lost productivity, and so forth. Or perhaps you can show your audience examples of benefits realized from better college funding in other states. Such examples give life to the abstract notion of lost potential.

All of this is not to say that you can't or shouldn't argue that higher education is inherently good. But until your reader can see low funding levels as "problematic" rather than "simply the way things are," your proposal stands little chance of being enacted.

Showing the Specifics of Your Proposal

Having decided that there is a problem to be solved, you should lay out your thesis, which is a proposal for solving the problem. Your goal now is to stress the feasibility of your solution, including costs. The art of proposal making is the art of the possible. To be sure, not all proposals require elaborate descriptions of the implementation process. If you are proposing, for example, that a local PTA chapter should buy new tumbling mats for the junior high gym classes, the procedures for buying the mats will probably be irrelevant. But in many arguments the specifics of your proposal—the actual step-by-step methods of implementing it—may be instrumental in winning your audience's support.

You will also need to show how your proposal will solve the problem either partially or wholly. Sometimes you may first need to convince your reader that the problem is solvable, not something intractably rooted in "the way things are," such as earthquakes or jealousy. In other words, expect that some members of your audience will be skeptical about the ability of any proposal to solve the problem you are addressing. You may well need, therefore, to "listen" to this point of view in your refutation section and to argue that your problem is at least partially solvable.

To persuade your audience that your proposal can work, you can follow any one of several approaches. A typical approach is to lay out a causal argument showing how one consequence will lead to another until your solution is effected. Another approach is to turn to resemblance arguments, either analogy or precedent. You try to show how similar proposals have been successful elsewhere. Or, if similar things have failed in the past, you try to show how the present situation is different.

The Justification: Convincing Your Reader That Your Proposal Should Be Enacted

This phase of a proposal argument will need extensive development in some arguments and minimal development in others, again depending on your particular problem and the rhetorical context of your proposal. If your audience already acknowledges the seriousness of the problem you are addressing and has simply been waiting for the right solution to come along, then your argument will be successful so long as you can convince your audience that your solution will work and that it won't cost too much. Such arguments depend on the clarity of your proposal and the feasibility of its being implemented.

But what if the costs are high? What if your readers don't think the problem is serious? What if they don't appreciate the benefits of solving the problem or the bad consequences of not solving it? In such cases you have to develop persuasive reasons for enacting your proposal. You may also have to determine who has the power to act on your proposal and apply arguments directly to that person's or agency's immediate interests. You need to know to whom or to what your power source is beholden or responsive and what values your power source holds that can be appealed to. You're looking, in short, for the best pressure points.

Proposal Arguments as Advocacy Posters or Advertisements

A frequently encountered kind of proposal argument is the one-page newspaper or magazine advertisement often purchased by advocacy groups to promote a cause. Such arguments also appear as Web pages or as posters or fliers. These condensed advocacy arguments are marked by their bold, abbreviated, tightly planned format. The creators of these arguments know they must work fast to capture our attention, give presence to a problem, advocate a solution, and enlist our support. These advocacy advertisements frequently use photographs, images, or icons that appeal to a reader's emotions and imagination. In addition to images, they often use different type sizes and styles. Large-type text in these documents frequently takes the form of slogans or condensed thesis statements written in an arresting style. To outline and justify their solutions, creators of advocacy ads often put main supporting reasons in bulleted lists and sometimes enclose carefully selected facts and quotations in boxed sidebars. To add an authoritative *ethos,* the arguments often include fine-print footnotes and bibliographies. (For more detailed discussion of how advocacy posters and advertisements use images and visual arrangement of text for rhetorical effect, see Chapter 9 on visual argument.)

Another prominent feature of these condensed, highly visual arguments is their appeal to the audience through a direct call to a course of action: go to an advocacy Web site to find out more information on how to support a cause; cut out a postcardlike form to send to a decision maker; vote for or against the proposition or the candidate; write a letter to a political representative; or donate money to a cause.

An example of a student-produced advocacy advertisement is shown in Figure 15.1. Here, student Lisa Blattner joins a heated debate in her city on whether to close down all-ages dance clubs. Frustrated because the evening dance options for under-twenty-one youth were threatened in Seattle, Lisa directed her ad toward the general readership of regional newspapers with the special intention of reaching adult voters and parents. Lisa's ad uses three documentary-like, emotionally loaded, and disturbing photographs to give immediacy and presence

**What Is Left for Teenagers to Do When the Teen Ordinance
Bans Them from Dance Clubs?**

Take Ecstasy   Drink at Places with   Roam the Streets
at Raves   No Adult Supervision

Is There an Answer to These Problems?

**Yes! Through your support of the All Ages Dance Ordinance,
teens will have a safe place to go where:**

- **No hard drugs, like ecstasy and cocaine, are present**
- **Responsible adults are watching over everyone**
- **All of their friends can hang out in one place indoors, instead
  of outside with drug dealers, criminals, and prostitutes**

Give Your Child a Safe Place to Have Fun at Night

**Let the Seattle City Committee Know
That You Support the
All Ages Dance Ordinance**

FIGURE 15.1   *A student-produced advocacy advertisement*

to the problem. The verbal text in the ad states the proposal claim and provides
three reasons in support of the claim. Notice how the reasons also pick up the
ideas in the three photo images. The final lines of text memorably reiterate the
claim and call readers to action. The success of this ad derives from the collabora-
tion of layout, photos, and verbal text in conveying a clear, direct argument.

Now that you have been introduced to the main elements of a proposal argument, including condensed visual arguments, we explain in the next two sections two invention strategies you can use to generate persuasive reasons for a proposal argument and to anticipate your audience's doubts and reservations. We call these the "claim-type strategy" and the "stock-issues strategy."

Using the Claim-Type Strategy to Develop a Proposal Argument

In Chapter 10 we explained how claim-type theory can help you generate ideas for an argument. Specifically, we explained how values claims often depend for their supporting reasons on the reality claims of category, cause, or resemblance. This principle leads to a powerful idea-generating strategy that can be schematized as follows:

Overview of Claim-Type Strategy

We should do X (proposal claim)

- because X is a Y (categorical claim)
- because X will lead to good consequences (causal claim)
- because X is like Y (resemblance claim)

With each of these *because* clauses, the arguer's goal is to link X to one or more good things the audience already values. For a specific example, suppose that you wanted insurance companies to pay for long-term psychological counseling for anorexia. The claim-type strategy could help you develop arguments such as these:

Insurance companies should pay for long-term psychological counseling for anorexia (proposal claim)

- because paying for such counseling is a demonstration of commitment to women's health (categorical claim)
- because paying for such counseling might save insurance companies from much more extensive medical costs at a later date (causal claim)
- because anorexia is like alcoholism or drug dependency, which is already covered by insurance (resemblance claim)

Proposal arguments using reality claims as reasons are very common. Here is another example, this time from a famous art exhibit controversy in the early 1990s when conservatives protested government funding for an exhibition of homoerotic photographs by artist Robert Mapplethorpe.

Taxpayer funding for the Mapplethorpe exhibit should be withdrawn (proposal claim)

- because the photographs are pornographic (a categorical claim linking the photographs to pornography, which the intended audience opposes)
- because the exhibit promotes community acceptance of homosexuality (a causal claim linking the exhibit to acceptance of homosexuality, which the intended audience opposes)
- because the photographs are more like political statements than art (a resemblance claim linking the exhibit to politics rather than art, a situation that the intended audience would consider unsuitable for arts funding)

Whatever you might think of this argument, it shows how the supporting reasons for a proposal claim can be drawn from claims of category, cause, and resemblance. Each of these arguments attempts to appeal to the value system of the audience. Each tries to show how the proposed action is within the class of things that the audience already values, will lead to consequences that the audience desires, or is similar to something that the audience already values. The invention procedure can be summarized in the following way.

Argument from Category

To discover reasons using this strategy, conduct the following kind of search:

We should (should not) do X because X is _____.

Try to fill in the blank with an appropriate adjective or noun (*good, just, ethical, criminal, ugly, violent, peaceful, wrong, inflationary, healing,* etc; *an act of kindness, terrorism, murder, true art, political suicide,* etc.). The point is to try to fill in the blank with a noun or adjective that appeals in some way to your audience's values. Your goal is to show that X belongs to the chosen class or category.

Argument from Consequence

To discover reasons using this category, conduct the following kind of search:

We should (should not) do X because X leads to these good (bad) consequences: _____, _____, _____, _____.

Then think of consequences that your audience will agree are good or bad as your argument requires.

Argument from Resemblance

To discover supporting reasons using this strategy, conduct the following kind of search:

We should (should not) do X because doing X is like _____.

Then think of analogies or precedents that are similar to doing X but that currently have greater appeal to your audience. Your task is then to transfer to X your audience's favorable or unfavorable feelings toward the analogy/precedent.

These three kinds of searches—supporting a proposal claim from the perspectives of category, consequence, and resemblance—are powerful means of invention. In selecting among these reasons, choose those most likely to appeal to your audience's assumptions, beliefs, and values.

For Class Discussion

1. Working individually or in small groups, use the strategies of category, consequence, and resemblance to create *because* clauses that support each of the following claims. Try to have at least one *because* clause from each of the claim types, but generate as many reasons as possible. Don't worry about whether any individual reason exactly fits the claim type. The purpose is to stimulate thinking, not fill in the slots.

   EXAMPLE

   CLAIM: People should not own pit bulls.

   REASON FROM CATEGORY: because pit bulls are vicious

   REASON FROM CONSEQUENCE: because owning a pit bull leads to conflicts with neighbors

   REASON FROM RESEMBLANCE: because owning a pit bull is like having a shell-shocked roommate—mostly they're lovely companions but they can turn violent if startled

   a. Marijuana should be legalized.
   b. Division I college athletes should receive salaries.
   c. High schools should pass out free contraceptives.

    d. Violent video games should be made illegal.

    e. Parents should be heavily taxed for having more than two children.

2. Repeat the exercise, taking a different position on each issue.

Using the Stock-Issues Strategy to Develop a Proposal Argument

Another effective way to generate ideas for a proposal argument is to ask yourself a series of questions based on the stock-issues strategy. Suppose, for example, you wanted to develop the following argument: "To solve the problem of students who won't take risks with their writing, the faculty should adopt a pass/fail method of grading in all writing courses." The stock-issues strategy invites the writer to consider stock ways (that is, common, usual, frequently repeated ways) that such arguments can be conducted.

Stock issue 1:   *Is there really a problem here that needs to be solved?* Is it really true that a large number of student writers won't take risks in their writing? Is this problem more serious than other writing problems such as undeveloped ideas, lack of organization, and poor sentence structure? This stock issue invites the writer to convince her audience that a true problem exists. Conversely, an opponent to the proposal might argue that a true problem does not exist.

Stock issue 2:   *Will the proposed solution really solve this problem?* Is it true that a pass/fail grading system will cause students to take more risks with their writing? Will more interesting, surprising, and creative essays result from pass/fail grading? Or will students simply put less effort into their writing? This stock issue prompts a supporter to demonstrate that the proposal will solve the problem, and it prompts an opponent to show that the proposal won't work.

Stock issue 3:   *Can the problem be solved more simply without disturbing the status quo?* An opponent of the proposal might agree that a problem exists and that the proposed solution might solve it. However, the opponent might say, "Are there not less radical ways to solve this problem? If we want more creative and risk-taking student essays, can't we just change our grading criteria so that we reward risky papers and penalize conventional ones?" This stock issue prompts supporters to show that *only* the proposed solution will solve the problem and that no minor tinkering with the status quo will be adequate. Conversely, opponents will argue that the problem can be solved without acting on the proposal.

Stock issue 4:   *Is the proposed solution really practical? Does it stand a chance of actually being enacted?* Here an opponent to the proposal might agree that the proposal would work but that it involves pie-in-the-sky idealism. Nobody will vote to change the existing system so radically; therefore, it is a waste of our time to debate it. Following this prompt, supporters would have to argue that pass/fail grading is workable and that enough members of the faculty are disposed to it that the proposal is worth debating. Opponents might argue that the faculty is so traditional that pass/fail has utterly no chance of being accepted, despite its merits.

Stock issue 5:   *What will be the unforeseen positive and negative consequences of the proposal?* Suppose we do adopt a pass/fail system. What positive or negative consequences might occur that are different from what we at first predicted? Using this prompt, an opponent might argue that pass/fail grading will reduce the effort put forth by students and that the long-range effect will be writing of even lower quality than we have now. Supporters would try to find positive consequences—perhaps a new love of writing for its own sake rather than for the sake of a grade.

For Class Discussion

The following collaborative task takes approximately two class days to complete. The exercise takes you through the process of creating a proposal argument.

1. In small groups, identify and list several major problems facing students in your college or university.

2. Decide among yourselves which are the most important of these problems and rank them in order of importance.

3. Take your group's number one problem and explore answers to the following questions. Group recorders should be prepared to present your group's answers to the class as a whole:

   a. Why is the problem a problem?

   b. For whom is the problem a problem?

   c. How will these people suffer if the problem is not solved? (Give specific examples.)

   d. Who has the power to solve the problem?

   e. Why hasn't the problem been solved up to this point?

   f. How can the problem be solved? (Create a proposal.)

   g. What are the probable benefits of acting on your proposal?

   h. What costs are associated with your proposal?

   i. Who will bear those costs?

   j. Why should this proposal be enacted?

   k. Why is it better than alternative proposals?

4. As a group, draft an outline for a proposal argument in which you:
   a. Describe the problem and its significance.
   b. Propose your solution to the problem.
   c. Justify your proposal by showing how the benefits of adopting that proposal outweigh the costs.
5. Recorders for each group should write their group's outline on the board and be prepared to explain it to the class.

Organizing a Proposal Argument

When you write your draft, you may find it helpful to have at hand some plans for typical ways of organizing a proposal argument. What follows are two common methods of organization. Option 1 is the plan most typical for practical proposals. Either Option 1 or Option 2 is an effective plan for a policy proposal.

Option 1

- Presentation of a problem that needs solving:
  Description of problem (Give the problem presence.)
  Background, including previous attempts to solve the problem
  Argument that the problem is solvable (optional)
- Presentation of writer's proposal:
  Succinct statement of the proposed solution serves as thesis statement.
  Explain specifics of the proposed solution.
- Summary and rebuttal of opposing views (In practical proposals, this section is often a summary and rejection of alternative ways of solving the problem.)
- Justification persuading the reader that the proposal should be enacted:
  Present and develop Reason 1.
  Present and develop Reason 2.
  Continue with additional reasons.
- Conclusion that exhorts the audience to act:
  Give presence to the final sentences.

Option 2

- Presentation of an issue, including background
- Presentation of the writer's proposal
- Justification:

Reason 1: Show that the proposal addresses a serious problem.

Reason 2: Show that the proposal will solve the problem.

Reason 3: Give additional reasons for enacting the proposal.

- Summary and refutation of opposing views
- Conclusion that exhorts the audience to act

Questioning and Critiquing a Proposal Argument

As we've suggested, proposal arguments need to overcome people's innate conservatism, the difficulty of anticipating all the consequences of a proposal, and so forth. What questions, then, can we ask about proposal arguments to help us anticipate these problems?

Will a skeptic deny that my problem is really a problem? The first question to ask of your proposal is "What's so wrong with the status quo that change is necessary?" The second question is "Who loses if the status quo is changed?" Be certain not to overlook the second question. Most proposal makers can demonstrate that some sort of problem exists, but often the problem exists only for certain groups of people. Solving the problem will thus prove a benefit to some people but a cost to others. Members of your audience who examine the problem from the perspective of the potential losers, rather than the winners, will often raise doubts about your proposal.

For example, one state recently held an initiative on a proposed "bottle bill" that would fight litter by permitting the sale of soda and beer only in returnable bottles. Sales outlets would be required to charge a substantial deposit on the bottles in order to encourage people to return them. Proponents of the proposal emphasized citizens as "winners" sharing in the new cleanliness of a landscape no longer littered with cans. To refute this argument, opponents showed consumers as "losers" burdened with the high cost of deposits and the hassle of collecting and returning bottles to grocery stores.

Will a skeptic doubt the effectiveness of my solution? Assuming that you've satisfied yourself that a significant problem exists for a significant number of people, a number of questions remain to be asked about the quality of the proposed solution to solve the problem. First, "Does the problem exist for the reasons cited, or might there be alternative explanations?" Here we return to the familiar ground of causal arguments. A proposal supposedly strikes at the cause of a problem. But perhaps striking at that "cause" won't solve the problem. Perhaps you've mistaken a symptom for a cause, or confused two commonly associated but essentially unlinked phenomena for a cause-effect relationship. For example, will paying teachers higher salaries improve the quality of teaching or merely attract greedier rather than brighter people? Maybe more good teachers would be attracted and retained if they were given some other benefit (fewer students? smaller classes? more sabbaticals? more autonomy? more prestige?).

Another way to test your solution is to list all the uncertainties involved. This might be referred to as "the Devil you know is better than the Devil you don't know" strategy. Remind yourself of all the unanticipated consequences of past changes. Who, for example, would have thought back in the days when aerosol shaving cans were being developed that they might lead to diminished ozone layers, which might lead to more ultraviolet rays getting through the atmosphere from the sun, which would lead to higher incidences of skin cancer? The history of technology is full of such cautionary tales that can be invoked to remind you of the uncertain course that progress can sometimes take.

Will a skeptic think my proposal costs too much? The most commonly asked question of any proposal is simply "Do the benefits of enacting the proposal outweigh the costs?" As we saw above, you can't foresee all the consequences of any proposal. It's easy, before the fact, to exaggerate both the costs and the benefits of a proposal. So, in asking how much your proposal will cost, we urge you to make an honest estimate. Will your audience discover costs you hadn't anticipated—extra financial costs or unexpected psychological or environmental or aesthetic costs? As much as you can, anticipate these objections.

Will a skeptic suggest counterproposals? Related to all that's been said so far is the counterproposal. Can you imagine an appealing alternative to both the status quo and the proposal that you're making? The more clearly your proposal shows that a significant problem exists, the more important it is that you be able to identify possible counterproposals. Any potential critic of a proposal to remedy an acknowledged problem will either have to make such a counterproposal or have to argue that the problem is simply in the nature of things. So, given the likelihood that you'll be faced with a counterproposal, it only makes sense to anticipate it and to work out a refutation of it before you have it thrown at you. And who knows, you may end up liking the counterproposal better and changing your mind about what to propose!

Reading

The following reading, by student writer Mark Bonicillo, is a researched public policy proposal written for the Option 3 assignment on page 270. Bonicillo's argument is based on research he conducted into the problem of Americans without health insurance. You will note that he supplemented library and Internet research with information from a personal interview he conducted with a leading local authority on health insurance issues. Bonicillo's argument is formatted as a formal research paper using the documentation system of the Modern Language Association (MLA). A brief explanation of this system is given in Appendix Two, "A Concise Guide to Finding, Evaluating, and Documenting Sources."

Mark Bonicillo

Professor Scharf

Humanities Seminar 300

June 15, 2002

A Proposal for Universal Health Insurance in the United States

1   Ian, a twenty-three-year-old college graduate and the son of one of my professors, hasn't yet found a career-type job in the current slow economy. He currently works as a waiter at a downtown restaurant that offers minimum wage plus tips with no health insurance. A few weeks ago, Ian hurt his back in a recreational soccer game, and the pain is getting worse. Unfortunately, he has no doctor to go to. Like many recent college graduates, he is no longer covered by his student insurance policy, nor can he be covered on his parents' health insurance now that he has graduated from college. He can't afford to buy health insurance on his waiter's pay (the premiums would be $300 per month), and in any case his back injury wouldn't be covered because it is a "pre-existing condition." Now he is trying to pay for food and rent on his waiter's earnings, while also paying off his student loans. Meanwhile his back is killing him.

2   Ian's frightening situation is common in the United States. According to a study from the Employee Benefit Research Institute, 32.8% of Americans ages 21–24 and 22.5% of Americans ages 25–35 do not have health insurance (Fronstin 22). But it's not just young adults who don't have health insurance. The working poor and unemployed constitute the majority of the uninsured. Based on statistical research, recent estimates suggest that almost 39 million Americans do not have any form of health insurance (Kaiser Commission on Medicaid and the Uninsured).

3   These uninsured Americans lead sicker lives than insured Americans and create an unnecessary financial drain on the health care industry. If they are sick, they have to go to hospital emergency rooms, hassle with the subsequent unpaid bills, and hope that the hospital will eventually write them off as charity expense. (This is what Ian plans to do with his bad back.) According to a recent study by the Institute of Medicine, uninsured Americans are less likely than insured Americans to get regular checkups or receive preventative care. They have higher mortality rates and sickness rates. Moreover, treating these persons in emergency rooms is extremely expensive. It costs more to amputate the leg of a seriously ill diabetic

than it would to diagnose the disease, prescribe insulin, and provide regular care
(Institute of Medicine 1).

     Why do so many Americans lack health insurance? The answer lies in the   4
way that insurance is paid for in the United States. In most European countries and
in Canada, medicine is socialized so that the government pays for medical care and
citizens pay the government through higher taxes. In such a system, coverage is
universal. But in the United States, medical insurance is linked to employment.
Employers pay for health insurance, which they purchase from competing
insurance companies. Generally, the employer pays a significant percentage of the
insurance costs as a fringe benefit of employment. This system works fine as long
as (1) you are employed; (2) your employer is a large enough company to be
required to purchase health insurance (many small companies don't have to provide
insurance); and (3) you have a long-term, full-time position in the company (many
companies don't provide benefits for temporary or other low-wage workers). If you
don't have employer-provided insurance, you can purchase individual policies
(assuming that you aren't already ill with disqualifying pre-existing conditions), but
the premiums are very expensive and they are rated according to your health risk.
People with illnesses such as diabetes often can't buy private insurance at any
price.

     For those who are retired or are low-income earners—and therefore do not   5
have access to employer-provided insurance or cannot afford individual insurance—
the federal or state governments try to help. The federal government provides
Medicare for citizens over sixty-five and Medicaid for poor people who meet certain
federal poverty guidelines. Additionally, some states provide subsidized health care
plans for certain categories of people near the poverty line who are not covered by
Medicaid. However, as shown in Figure 1 (based on data from the Kaiser
Commission on Medicaid and the Uninsured), a significant number of Americans—
16% of the adult population under sixty-five years of age—have no insurance.

     Furthermore, two additional problems are connected to this employer-based   6
system. First, insured Americans can quickly lose their insurance if they lose their
jobs. When the economy is in recession, the number of uninsured increases
significantly. Diane Rowland, Executive Director of the Kaiser Commission on
Medicaid and the Uninsured, estimates that "for every 100 workers added to the
unemployment rolls, 85 people will join the ranks of the uninsured" (10). She cites a

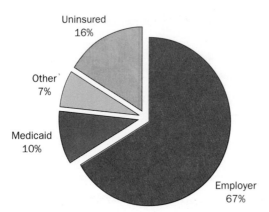

FIG. 1.   *Health Insurance Coverage in U.S., 2001, Adult Americans under 65.*

study that showed when unemployment rose from 4% in December 2000 to 5.8% in December 2001, the number of uninsured Americans increased by 2.2 million. As we can see, the current U.S. policy of distributing health insurance through employers leaves Americans in jeopardy of losing their health insurance at any time.

7   The second major problem with employer-provided insurance is that the attempts of the federal and state governments to create safety nets for the uninsured are underfunded and full of gaps. For example, Medicare certainly helps the elderly, but many persons fear that Medicare funding will collapse in the near future as baby boomers retire. Moreover, Medicare in some states is so poorly funded that many doctors will no longer take Medicare patients because the reimbursement payments are too low. According to a news report in the <u>Seattle Times</u>, some doctors in the state of Washington have even refused to accept new Medicare patients (Ostrom A1). In addition, the systems adopted by the states to provide insurance for persons at the poverty level are unevenly administered and burdened with red tape. In a personal interview I conducted with Randy Revelle, the director of health policy for the Washington State Hospital Association, I learned that in 1998 over fifteen thousand uninsured children in the state of Washington were eligible for state-subsidized insurance, but they and their parents did not know it because of inadequate advertising and red tape. Similar problems occur in other states. According to Rowland, even with the knowledge that one is eligible for government-sponsored health insurance, long and

burdensome application forms and language problems discourage many uninsured Americans from even applying for government health insurance (7). And so, many uninsured Americans who could have had public health insurance are still left uninsured.

Finally, we must ask why the American people haven't demanded a change   8
from this employer-based system. Why hasn't this problem already been solved?

I think there are three basic reasons. First, because the majority of Americans   9
have employer-provided insurance, they don't give this problem a high priority. Second, the general public is unwilling to support any real health care reform because they think it might lead to "socialized medicine," which raises the fearful specter of demoralized doctors, faceless patients, and long waiting lists for needed services. Finally, insurance companies, doctors, and drug companies benefit from the present system and lobby heavily to persuade politicians from adopting health care reform that might cut into their profits.

The solution to the problem of the uninsured is to dismantle the current   10
employer-provided system without leading to European- or Canadian-style socialized medicine that doesn't fit American values or business structures. Based on my research, the best approach is a compromise between liberals and conservatives evidenced in a series of interviews conducted by journalist Matthew Miller with two U.S. representatives—a liberal, Democrat Jim McDermott of Washington, who personally favors a European-style government-as-single-payer system, and a conservative, Republican Jim McCrery of Louisiana, who supports insurance companies and free markets for health care. The common ground between these two political opponents, evident in the interviews, leads to a possible solution. Based on my reading of these interviews, I offer the following three policy recommendations.

First, the federal government should break the linkage between health   11
insurance and employment. Instead, according to Rep. McCrery's suggestion, the government should mandate that all adult citizens purchase individual or family health insurance (Miller 84). This mandate would guarantee that all Americans would be insured. To help pay for this insurance, McCrery suggests that the insurance subsidies currently provided by employers as a fringe benefit could be passed on to employees as increased salary (Miller 86). Therefore employed persons would pay no additional costs under this system.

12   Second, McCrery and McDermott agree that the government should help unemployed or low-income people buy health insurance by providing tax subsidies on a sliding scale. The government would thus buy insurance for those at the poverty line and subsidize insurance on a sliding scale for those above it (Miller 86).

13   Third, McCrery and McDermott both agree that to make health insurance affordable for all, insurance companies must base their premiums on a community rating spread across all buyers instead of charging higher rates for persons with illnesses or identifiable risk factors. Because young, healthy Americans would be required to buy insurance, these persons would help fund the system by paying in more than they draw out and yet be fully covered if they need medical care (Miller 84).

14   These three policy recommendations would solve most of the problems with the current system and fit the American structure of business. An advantage of this proposal is that it does not eliminate insurance companies or interfere with a free-market approach to medicine. As Miller explains, insurance companies would still compete with each other for customers (85). The major change would be that health insurance companies would market to individuals rather than to employers in the same way that car and life insurance companies do. Also, drug companies would not be frightened by the prospect of the government setting prices for drugs.

15   A second advantage is that the majority of Americans would need no government subsidy because their increased insurance costs would be covered by a transfer into salary of the insurance benefit currently paid by the employer. At the same time employers would benefit by no longer having to undergo the hassles of negotiating for and providing insurance for their employees (Miller 85).

16   Third, this system provides a safety net for employed Americans who risk losing their jobs in times of recession. The government would immediately step in to help pay for insurance based on the sliding scale need of the unemployed person.

17   Finally, this system brings health care to low-wage workers who do not currently receive employer-subsidized insurance and to all currently ill or at-risk persons whose pre-existing conditions disqualify them for self-pay insurance. Because a community rating spreads the risk across all Americans, the many young and healthy people paying into the system (the ones who today are apt not to buy insurance because they aren't sick) help subsidize the health care needed by others (Miller 84).

Undoubtedly many problems with this proposal need to be worked out—   18
including the procedures for mandating every adult to buy insurance as well as the
political battle of determining how new taxes will be assessed to pay for the
substantial costs of subsidizing insurance for the poor and the unemployed. But
this proposal attacks the problem of the uninsured and the U.S. health care system
at its core. This nation has tried many different solutions, and they have all failed.
While genuine reform is painful and politically difficult, it is the only way to heal
our sickening health care system that leaves 39 million Americans without health
insurance. Under this system, Ian would have had government-subsidized health
insurance. He could have gone to a doctor when he first hurt his back instead of
waiting a month to go to a hospital emergency room and plead poverty.

[New Page]

Works Cited

Fronstin, Paul. <u>Sources of Health Insurance and Characteristics of the Uninsured: Analysis of the March 1997 Current Population Survey</u>. Employee Benefit Research Institute Issue Brief 192. Washington, D.C.: EBRI, Dec. 1997.

Institute of Medicine. <u>Care Without Coverage: Too Little, Too Late</u>. New York: Natl. Acad. P., 2002.

Kaiser Commission on Medicaid and the Uninsured. "The Uninsured and Their Access to Health Care." Feb. 2002. <u>Henry J. Kaiser Foundation</u>. 2 pp. 26 May 2002. <http://www.kff.org/content/ 2002/142003/142003.pdf>.

Miller, Matthew. "Health Care: A Bolt of Civic Hope." <u>Atlantic Monthly</u> Oct. 2000: 77–87.

Ostrom, Carol M. "Doctors Fleeing Medicare, Medicaid." <u>Seattle Times</u> 12 Mar. 2002: A1.

Revelle, Randy. Personal interview. 9 May 2002.

Rowland, Diane. "The New Challenge of the Uninsured: Coverage in the Current Economy." Kaiser Commission on Medicaid and the Uninsured 28 Feb. 2002. <u>Henry J. Kaiser Family Foundation</u>. 24 pp. 23 May 2002 <http://www.kff.org/content/2002/4042/4042.pdf>.

WRITING ASSIGNMENTS
FOR CHAPTER 15

Option 1: A Practical Proposal Addressing a Local Problem   Write a practical proposal offering a solution to a local problem. Your proposal should have three main sections: (1) description of the problem, (2) proposed solution, and (3) justification. You may include additional sections or subsections as needed. Longer proposals often include an *abstract* at the beginning of the proposal to provide a summary overview of the whole argument. (Sometimes called the *executive summary*, this abstract may be the only portion of the proposal read by high-level managers.) Sometimes proposals are accompanied by a *letter of transmittal*—a one-page business letter that introduces the proposal to its intended audience and provides some needed background about the writer.

Document design is important in practical proposals, which are aimed at busy people who have to make many decisions under time constraints. Because the writer of a practical proposal usually produces the finished document (practical proposals are seldom submitted to newspapers or magazines for publication), he or she must pay particular attention to the attractive design of the document. An effective design helps establish the writer's *ethos* as a quality-oriented professional and helps make the reading of the proposal as easy as possible. Document design includes effective use of headings and subheadings, attractive typeface and layout, flawless editing, and other features enhancing the visual appearance of the document.

Option 2: A Policy Proposal as a Guest Editorial   Write a two- or three-page policy proposal suitable for publication as a feature editorial in a college or city newspaper or in some publication associated with a particular group or activity such as a church newsletter or employee bulletin. The voice and style of your argument should be aimed at general readers of your chosen publication. Your editorial should have the following features:

1. The identification of a problem (Persuade your audience that this is a genuine problem that needs solving; give it presence.)
2. A proposal for action that will help alleviate the problem
3. A justification of your solution (the reasons why your audience should accept your proposal and act on it)

Option 3: A Researched Argument Proposing Public Policy   Write an eight- to twelve-page proposal argument as a formal research paper, using research data for development and support. In business and professional life, this kind of research proposal is often called a "white paper," which recommends a course of action internally within an organization or externally to a client or stakeholder.

An example of a researched policy proposal is student writer Mark Bonicillo's "A Proposal for Universal Health Insurance in the United States" on pages 264–269. **Option 4: *A One-Page Advocacy Advertisement*** Using the strategies of visual argument discussed in Chapter 9 and on pages 254–256 of this chapter, create a one-page advocacy advertisement urging action on a public issue. Your advertisement should be designed for publication in a newspaper or for distribution as a poster or flier. An example of a student-produced advocacy advertisement is shown in Figure 15.1.

Appendix One
Informal Fallacies

In this appendix we examine *informal fallacies*, which can fool us into thinking that an inconclusive argument is conclusive. Informal fallacies are quirky; they identify classes of less conclusive arguments that recur with some frequency, but they do not contain formal flaws that make their conclusions automatically illegitimate. An informal fallacy makes an argument more or less fallacious, and determining the degree of fallaciousness is a matter of judgment.

In arranging the fallacies, we have, for convenience, put them into three categories derived from classical rhetoric: *pathos, ethos,* and *logos.* Fallacies of *pathos* rest on a flawed relationship between what is argued and the audience for the argument. Fallacies of *ethos* rest on a flawed relationship between the argument and the character of those involved in the argument. Fallacies of *logos* rest on flaws in the relationship among statements of an argument.

Fallacies of *Pathos*

Argument to the People (Appealing to Stirring Symbols)

An argument to the people appeals to the fundamental beliefs, biases, and prejudices of the audience in order to sway opinion through a feeling of group solidarity. For example, when a politician says, "My fellow Americans, I stand here, draped in this flag from head to foot, to indicate my fundamental dedication to the values and principles of these sovereign United States," he's linking himself to the prime symbol of the group's nationalistic values, the flag.

Provincialism (Appealing to the Belief That the Known Is Always Better Than the Unknown)

Here is an example from the 1960s: "You can't sell small cars in the United States. Americans love their big cars. Those cramped little Japanese tin boxes will never win the hearts of American consumers." Although we may inevitably feel more comfortable with familiar things, ideas, and beliefs, we are not necessarily better off for sticking with them.

Appeal to Emotional Premises (Appealing to Comforting Reasons That Have No Basis in Logic)

This mode of short-circuiting reason may take one of three forms. In all three cases, we say that something is right, good, or necessary based on the comforting but irrational reason that it is common, traditional, or popular.

1. *Appeal to common practice.* (It's all right to do X because everyone else does it.) "Of course I borrowed money from the company slush fund. Everyone on this floor has done the same in the last eighteen months."
2. *Appeal to traditional wisdom.* (It's all right because we've always done it this way.) "We've got to require everyone to read *Hamlet* because we've always required everyone to read it."
3. *Appeal to popularity—the bandwagon appeal.* (It's all right because lots of people like it.) "You should buy a Ford Escort because it's the best-selling car in the world."

Red Herring (Shifting the Audience's Attention from a Crucial Issue to an Irrelevant One)

The *red herring* fallacy deliberately raises an unrelated or irrelevant point to throw an audience off the track. Politicians often employ this fallacy when they field questions from the public press. "You raise a good question about my support of continuing air strikes in country X. Let me tell you about my admiration for the bravery of our pilots."

Fallacies of *Ethos*

Appeals to False Authority and Bandwagon Appeals (Appealing to the Authority of a Popular Person or to the "Crowd" Rather Than to an Expert)

False authority fallacies offer as support for an argument the fact that a famous person or "many people" support it. Unless the supporters are themselves authorities in the field, their support is irrelevant. "Buy Freeble oil because Joe Quarterback always uses it in his fleet of cars." "How can abortion be wrong if millions of people support a woman's right to choose?"

Keep in mind, however, that occasionally the distinction between a false authority fallacy and an appeal to legitimate authority can blur. Suppose that Tiger Woods were to praise a particular company's golf club. Because he is an expert on golf, perhaps he speaks from authority about a truly superior golf club. But perhaps he is being paid to endorse a club that is no better than its competitors'. We could better determine the argument's conclusiveness if Woods presented an *ad rem* ("to the thing") argument showing us scientifically why the golf club in question is superior.

Appeal to the Person or *Ad Hominem* (Attacking the Character of the Arguer Rather Than the Argument Itself)

Literally, *ad hominem* means "to the person." When people can't find fault with an argument, they sometimes attack the arguer, substituting irrelevant assertions about that person's character for an analysis of the argument itself. It is better for an argument to be *ad rem* rather than *ad hominem*. Thus an *ad rem* critique of a politician would focus on her voting record, the consistency and cogency of her public statements, her responsiveness to constituents, and so forth. An *ad hominem* argument would shift attention to irrelevant features of her personality or personal life, perhaps a recent divorce or a long-ago reckless driving conviction.

But not all *ad hominem* arguments are *ad hominem* fallacies. It's not always fallacious to address your argument to the arguer. There are indeed times when the credibility of the person making an opposing argument is at issue. Lawyers, for example, in questioning expert witnesses who give damaging testimony, will often make an issue of their motives and credibility—and rightfully so.

Straw Man (Greatly Oversimplifying an Opponent's Argument to Make It Easier to Refute or Ridicule)

In committing a *straw man* fallacy, you basically make up the argument you *wish* your opponents had made and attribute it to them because it's so much easier to refute than the argument they actually made. Some political debates consist almost entirely of straw man exchanges, such as "You may think that taxing people out of their homes and onto park benches is the best way to balance the budget, but I don't," or "While my opponent would like to empty our prisons of serial killers and coddle kidnappers, I hold to the sacred principles of swift and sure justice."

Fallacies of *Logos*

Begging the Question (Supporting a Claim with a Reason That Is Really a Restatement of the Claim in Different Words)

We *beg the question* when we use as a reason the same assertion we make in our claim. "Abortion is murder because it involves the intentional killing of an unborn human being." Since murder is defined as the "intentional killing of a human being," the argument says, in effect, "Abortion is murder because it's murder."

False Dilemma/Either-Or (Oversimplifying a Complex Issue So That Only Two Choices Appear Possible)

A good extended analysis of this fallacy is found in sociologist Kai Erikson's analysis of President Harry Truman's decision to drop the A-bomb on Hiroshima. His analysis suggests that the Truman administration prematurely reduced numerous options to just two: either drop the bomb on a major city or suffer unacceptable losses in a land invasion of Japan. Erikson, however, shows there were other alternatives. Typically, we encounter *false dilemma* arguments when people try to justify a questionable action by creating a false sense of necessity, forcing us to choose between two options, one of which is clearly unacceptable.

But of course not all dilemmas are false. People who reject all binary oppositions are themselves guilty of a false dilemma. There are times when we might determine through a rational process of elimination that only two possible choices exist. Deciding whether a dilemma is truly a dilemma or only an evasion of complexity often requires a difficult judgment. Although we should initially suspect any attempt to convert a complex problem into an either/or choice, we may legitimately arrive at such a choice through thoughtful deliberation.

Confusing Correlation for Cause or *Post Hoc, Ergo Propter Hoc* (After This, Therefore Because of This—Assuming That Event X Causes Event Y Because Event X Preceded Event Y)

Here are two examples in which this fallacy may be at work:

> Cramming for a test really helps. Last week I crammed for a psychology test and I got an A on it.
>
> I am allergic to the sound of a lawn mower because every time I mow the lawn I start to sneeze.

We treat this fallacy at length in Chapter 12 in our discussion of correlation versus causation (pp. 200–203). The *post hoc, ergo propter hoc* fallacy occurs when a sequential relationship is mistaken for a causal relationship. The conjunction may be coincidental, or it may be attributable to some as-yet-unrecognized third factor. For example, your A on the psych test may be caused by something other than your cramming. Maybe the exam was easier, or perhaps you were luckier or more mentally alert. And perhaps a lawn mower makes you sneeze because it stirs up pollen rather than because it makes a loud noise.

Slippery Slope (Once We Move Slightly Toward an Unpleasant End, We Will Eventually Have to Go All the Way)

The *slippery-slope* fallacy appeals to the fear that once we take a first step in a direction we don't like, we will have to keep going.

> We don't dare send weapons to Country X. If we do so, next we will send in military advisers, then a special forces battalion, and then large numbers of troops. Finally, we will be in all-out war.
>
> Look, Blotnik, no one feels worse about your need for open-heart surgery than I do. But I still can't let you turn this paper in late. If I were to let you do it, then I'd have to let everyone turn in papers late.

The slippery-slope fear is that an apparently harmless first step in a dangerous direction dooms us to slide right out of sight.

The problem, of course, is that not every slippery-slope argument exhibits the slippery-slope fallacy. We all know that some slopes *are* slippery and that we sometimes have to draw the line, saying "to here, but no farther." And it is true also that making exceptions to rules is dangerous; the exceptions soon get established as regular procedures. The slippery slope becomes a fallacy, however, when we forget that some slopes don't have to be slippery unless we let them be slippery. Often we do better to imagine a staircase with stopping places all along the way. The assumption that we have no control over our descent once we take the first step makes us unnecessarily rigid.

Hasty Generalization (Making a Broad Generalization on the Basis of Too Little Evidence)

A *hasty generalization* occurs when we leap to a conclusion on insufficient evidence: "The food stamp program supports mostly freeloaders. Let me tell you about my worthless neighbor." But what constitutes "sufficient" evidence is a knotty problem. No generalization arrived at through empirical evidence would meet a logician's strict standard of certainty.

The Food and Drug Administration (FDA), for example, proceeds cautiously before certifying a drug as "safe." However, whenever doubts arise about the safety of an FDA-approved drug, critics accuse the FDA of having made a hasty generalization. At the same time, patients eager to get a new drug, or manufacturers eager to sell it, may lobby the FDA to quit dragging its feet and get the drug to market. Hence, the point at which a hasty generalization about drug safety passes over into the realm of a prudent generalization is nearly always uncertain and contested.

Mistaking the Part for the Whole or *Pars Pro Toto* (Assuming That What Is True for a Part Will Be True for the Whole)

We use the *pars pro toto* fallacy when we attack the whole of something by focusing on a part we don't like. Thus, critics who want to abolish the National Endowment for the Arts might focus on several controversial grants and use them as justification for wiping out all NEA programs.

False Analogy (Claiming That Because X Resembles Y in One Regard, X Will Resemble Y in All Regards)

Arguments by analogy are tricky because there are almost always significant differences between any two things being compared. If the two things differ greatly, the analogy can mislead rather than clarify. "You can't force a kid to become a musician any more than you can force a tulip to become a rose." For further discussion of reasoning by analogy, see Chapter 13.

Non Sequitur (Making a Claim That Doesn't Follow Logically from the Premises, or Supporting a Claim with Irrelevant Premises)

The *non sequitur* (literally, "it does not follow") fallacy is a miscellaneous category that includes any claim that doesn't follow logically from its premises or that is supported with irrelevant premises. Typically, *non sequitur* fallacies take the following forms:

> *An illogical leap:* "Our university has one of the best faculties in the United States because a Nobel Prize winner used to teach here." (How does the fact that a Nobel Prize winner used to teach at our university make its present faculty one of the best in the United States?)
>
> *Irrelevant premises:* "I should not receive a C in this course because I have received B's or A's in all my other courses (here is my transcript for evidence) and because I worked exceptionally hard in this course (here is my log of hours worked)." (Even though the arguer has solid evidence to support each premise, the premises themselves are irrelevant to the claim. Course grades should be based on actual performance, not on previous grades or on effort.)

Appendix Two

A Concise Guide to Finding, Evaluating, and Documenting Sources

When you research material for your arguments, you must be able to find materials from licensed databases and the World Wide Web as well as from a library's book collection. In addition, you must be able to evaluate your sources, use them effectively in your own arguments (avoiding plagiarism), and cite and document them accurately so that readers can retrace your steps. This appendix provides brief instruction for finding, evaluating, and using sources and for citing and documenting them using both the MLA (Modern Language Association) and APA (American Psychological Association) systems.

Finding Print Articles: Searching a Licensed Database

For many research projects, useful sources are print articles from your library's periodical collection, including newspapers, scholarly journals, and magazines. Some of these articles are available free on the World Wide Web, but most of them are not. Rather, they may be located physically in your library's periodical collection or located electronically in vast databases leased by your library.

What Is a Licensed Database?

Electronic databases of periodical sources, called "licensed databases" (our preferred term), "general databases," or "subscription services," are produced by for-profit companies that index articles in thousands of periodicals and construct engines that can search the database by author, title, subject, key word, date, genre, and other variables. In most cases the database contains an abstract of each article, and in many cases it contains the complete text of the article that you can download and print. Because access to these databases is restricted to fee-paying customers, they can't be searched through Web engines like Yahoo! or Google. Most university libraries allow students to access these databases from a remote computer by using a pass code. You can therefore use the Internet to connect your computer to licensed databases as well as to the World Wide Web (see Figure App. 2.1).

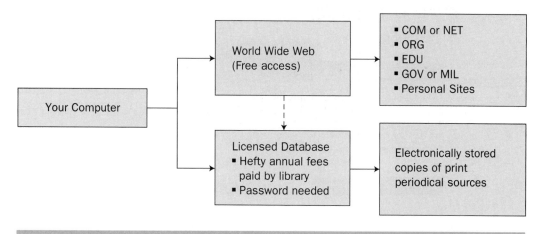

FIGURE APP. 2.1   *Licensed database versus free-access portions of Internet*

An example of a licensed database leased by many college libraries is *EBSCOhost*, which includes citations and abstracts from most disciplines as well as the full text of many articles from over three thousand journals; its *Academic Search Elite* function covers material published as long ago as the early 1980s. Other important databases include *UMI ProQuest Direct, InfoTrac,* and *LexisNexis Academic Universe.* Generally, one of these databases will be the "default method" chosen by your library for most article searches. Your reference librarian will be able to direct you to the most useful licensed database for your purpose.

Illustration of a Database Search

As an illustration of a database search, we'll draw on the experience of student writer Megan Matthews as she researched the effect on sea mammals, particularly whales, of the Navy's experimental submarine-detecting sonar systems. (Megan's completed research paper is reprinted on pages 299–306.) Using the database EBSCOhost, Megan entered the key words *Navy sonar* AND *whales*, which revealed the six articles shown in Figure App. 2.2. As this Results shows, EBSCOhost carries the full text for the first three records: "Baffling Boing Identified," "US Navy Sonar Blocked," and "Sonic Blast." The results list also notes that the Lemieux Library (the name of her college's library) subscribes to all the listed periodicals except for *Science Now* (Record 1) and *Ecologist* (Record 2). Thus Megan had access to all six articles, either from her college's periodical collection or from the online database. Because she wanted to decide whether the *New Scientist* article (Record 6) was worth tracking down, she clicked on its title "Noises Off," which revealed the screen shown in Figure App. 2.3. This screen provides an abstract of the article and indicates that it is four pages long and includes a graph and four color photographs or drawings.

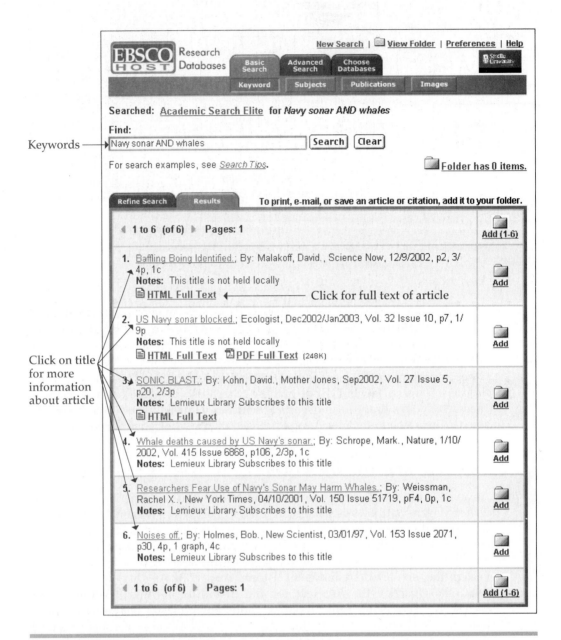

FIGURE APP. 2.2 *Results list from a search using EBSCOhost*

After you've identified articles you'd like to read, locate physically all those available in your library's periodical collection. (This way you won't lose important contextual cues for evaluating them.) For those unavailable in your library, print them from the database, if possible, or order them through interlibrary loan.

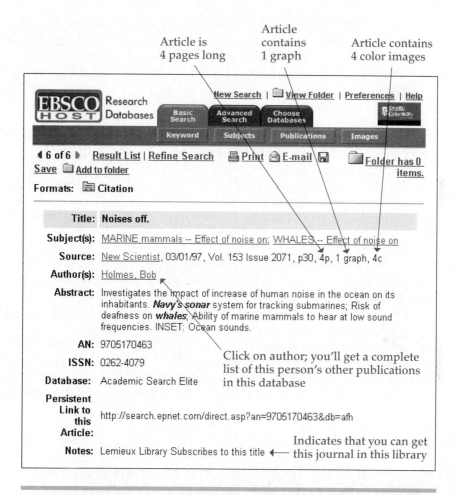

Article is
4 pages long

Article
contains
1 graph

Article contains
4 color images

Click on author; you'll get a complete
list of this person's other publications
in this database

Indicates that you can get
this journal in this library

FIGURE APP. 2.3   *Sample full display for an article on EBSCOhost*

Finding Cyberspace Sources: Searching the World Wide Web

To understand the logic of Web search engines, you need to keep in mind that the
Internet has restricted sections open only to those with special access rights as well
as a "free access" section. (See again Figure App. 2.1.) Web engines such as Yahoo!
or Google search only the free access portion of the Internet. When you type key
words into a Web search engine, it searches for matches in material posted on the
World Wide Web by all the users of the world's networked computers—government
agencies, corporations, advocacy groups, information services, individuals with
their own Web sites, and hosts of others.

The following example will quickly show you the difference between a
licensed database search and a Web search. When Megan entered the key words

Navy sonar AND *whales* into EBSCOhost, she received six "hits"—the titles of six articles on this subject appearing in print periodicals. In contrast, when she entered the same key words into the Web search engine Yahoo!, she received 5,180 hits; when she tried the search engine Google, she got even more—6,220. There are so many hits because Web search engines pick up not only the titles of print articles that someone may have posted on the Web, but all the references to Navy sonar and whales that may appear in advocacy Web sites, government publications, online news sources, chat rooms, course syllabi posted by professors, student papers posted to the Web, and so forth.

Although the hits you receive from a Web search frequently include useless, shoddy, trivial, or irrelevant material, the Web's resources for researchers are breathtaking. At your fingertips you have access to government documents and statistics, legislative and corporate white papers, court cases, persuasive appeals of advocacy groups, consumer information—the list seems endless.

The World Wide Web can be searched by a variety of engines that collect and categorize individual Web files and search them for key words. Most of these engines will find not only text files but also graphic, audio, and video files. Some engines look through the titles of files, whereas others scan the entire text of documents. Different engines search the Web in different ways, so it is important that you try a variety of search engines when you look for information. Although the Web is evolving rapidly, some of the best search engines are fairly stable. For starters, you might try Google (http://www.google.com), Yahoo! (http://www.yahoo.com), or Altavista (http://www.altavista.com). Again, if you are in doubt, your reference librarians can help you choose the most productive search engine for your needs.

Evaluating Sources

When you read sources for your research project—whether published in print or in cyberspace—you need to evaluate them as you proceed. Clues needed for evaluating a source often come indirectly. For example, when you look at an article in a magazine (rather than downloaded from a computer), the features of the magazine itself—its format, its table of contents, its editorial information, its advertisements, its use of photographs, the length and range and style of its articles—can help you infer valuable information about the article's author, intended audience, and political bias. In contrast, when you print materials from a licensed database or from the Web, these contextual clues are lost: A mindless rant from Joe's Web page can have the same appearance as a downloaded article from a serious journal.

When you evaluate a source, begin by asking yourself questions about an author's angle of vision, degree of advocacy, reliability, and credibility.

Angle of Vision

By "angle of vision," we mean the way that a piece of writing gets shaped by the underlying values, assumptions, and beliefs of the author so that the text reflects a certain perspective, worldview, or belief system. The angle of vision is revealed by internal factors such as the author's word choice (especially note connotations of words), selection and omission of details, overt statements, figurative language, and grammatical emphasis and by external factors such as the politics of the author, the genre of the source, the politics of the publisher, and so forth. When reading a source, see if you can detect underlying assumptions or beliefs that suggest a writer's values or political views.

You can also get useful clues about a writer's angle of vision by looking at external data. What are the writer's credentials? Is the writer affiliated with an advocacy group or known for a certain ideology? (If you know nothing about an author who seems important to your research, try keying the author's name into a Web search engine. You might discover useful information about the author's other publications or about the author's reputation in various circles.) Also pay attention to publishing data. Where was this source originally published? What is the reputation and editorial slant of the publication in which the source appears? For example, editorial slants of magazines can range from very liberal to very conservative. Likewise, publications affiliated with advocacy organizations (the Sierra Club, the National Rifle Association) will have a clear editorial bias.

Degree of Advocacy

By "degree of advocacy" we mean the extent to which an author unabashedly takes a persuasive stance on a contested position as opposed to adopting a more neutral, objective, or exploratory stance. When a writer has an ax to grind, you need to weigh carefully the writer's selection of evidence, interpretation of data, and fairness to opposing views. Although objectivity is itself an "angle of vision" and no one can be completely neutral, it is always useful to seek out authors who offer a balanced assessment of the evidence. Evidence from a more detached and neutral writer may be more trusted by your readers than the arguments of a committed advocate. For example, if you want to persuade corporate executives of the dangers of global warming, evidence from scholarly journals may be more persuasive than evidence from an environmentalist Web site or from a freelance writer in a leftist popular magazine like *Mother Jones*.

Reliability

"Reliability" refers to the accuracy of factual data in a source as determined by external validation. If you check a writer's "facts" against other sources, are they correct? Does the writer distort facts, take them out of context, or otherwise use them unreasonably? In some controversies, key data are highly disputed—for example, the number of homeless persons in the United States, the frequency of date rape, or the risk factors for many diseases. A reliable writer will acknowledge these controversies and not treat disputed data as fact. Furthermore, if you check the sources used by a reliable writer, they will reveal accurate and careful research—respected primary sources rather than hearsay or secondhand reports.

Credibility

"Credibility" is similar to "reliability" except that it is based on internal rather than external factors. It refers to the reader's trust in the writer's honesty, goodwill, and trustworthiness and is derived from the writer's tone, reasonableness, fairness in summarizing opposing views, and respect for different perspectives. Audiences differ in how much credibility they will grant to certain authors. Nevertheless a writer can achieve a reputation for credibility, even among bitter political opponents, by applying to issues a sense of moral courage, integrity, and consistency of principle.

Evaluating Web Sites

If some of your sources come from Web sites, you also need to become skilled in evaluating the Web site itself. The Web is a great vehicle for democracy, giving voice to the otherwise voiceless. Anyone with a cause and a rudimentary knowledge of Web page design can create a Web site. Before the invention of the Web, persons with a message would have to stand on street corners passing out fliers or invest in newsletters or advocacy advertisements. The Web, in contrast, is cheap. The result is a rhetorical medium that differs in significant ways from print.

Analyzing the Purpose of a Site and Your Own Research Purpose

When you do research on the Web, your first question should be, Who placed this piece on the Web and why? You can begin answering this question by analyzing the site's home page, where you will often find navigational buttons linking to "Mission," "About us," or other identifying information about the site's sponsors. You can also get hints about the site's purpose by asking, What kind of Web site is it? As we explained earlier, different kinds of Web sites have different purposes, often revealed by the domain identifier following the server name (.com, .net, .org, .gov, .mil). As you evaluate the Web site, also consider your own purpose for using it. For instance, are you trying to get an initial understanding of various points of view on an issue, or are you looking for reliable information? An advocacy site may be an excellent place for researching a point of view but a doubtful source of data and evidence for your own argument.

Sorting Sites by Domain Type

One powerful research strategy for evaluating Web sites is to use the "advanced search" feature of a search engine to sort sites by domain type. As an example, consider again Megan's research dilemma when she plugged *Navy sonar* AND *whales* into Google and received 6,220 "hits." How could she begin to navigate through such a huge number? Using Google's "advanced search" feature, Megan first sorted through her hits by selecting only .com sites (2,790 hits). These, she discovered, were primarily the sites of newspapers, news services, and tourist sites catering to "whale-watching"—a billion-dollar business she discovered from one source. These sites tended to repeat the same news stories and offer superficial coverage. She next looked at .org sites (1,400 hits). These were primarily the sites of environmental advocacy groups—organizations such as the National Resources Defense Council, the Sierra Club, the Humane Society, the League for Coastal Protection, the Cetacean Society International, the Ocean Futures Society, and so forth—all dedicated to protecting marine life. These advocacy sites were strongly pro-whale; in their arguments against Navy sonar they either discounted or ignored issues of national security. Next she looked at .edu sites (449 hits), which were primarily references to course descriptions and syllabi that included this controversy as a source of study. She didn't find these helpful. Finally, she sorted by .gov (348 hits) and .mil (138 hits). The .gov sites revealed documents on whales and sonar submitted to congressional hearings; they also included the sites of two key government agencies involved in the sonar dispute: the National Marine Fisheries Service and the National Oceanic and Atmospheric Administration. The .mil sites gave access to white papers and other documents provided by the Navy to justify its use of low-frequency sonar.

This overview of the territory helped Megan understand the angle of vision or bias of different sources. The .org sites focused on protecting marine life. In contrast, the .mil and the .gov sites helped her understand the national security issue. In the middle, trying to balance the competing demands of the environment, national security, and preservation of commerce were the sites of government agencies not directly connected to the military. All of these sites provided valuable information and most of them included links to scientific and research studies.

Making an Evaluation of a Web Site

Given this overview of the territory, Megan still had to decide which specific sites to use for her research. We offer the following criteria developed by scholars and librarians as points to consider when you are evaluating Web sites.

Criterion 1: Authority

- Is the author or sponsor of the Web site clearly identified?
- Does the site identify the occupation, position, education, experience, and credentials of the site's authors?
- Does the introductory material reveal the author's or sponsor's motivation for publishing this information on the Web?
- Does the site provide contact information for the author or sponsor such as an e-mail or organization address?

Criterion 2: Objectivity or Clear Disclosure of Advocacy

- Is the site's purpose (to inform, explain, or persuade) clear?
- Is the site explicit about declaring its author's or sponsor's point of view?
- Does the site indicate whether its author is affiliated with a specific organization, institution, or association?
- Does the site indicate whether it is directed toward a specific audience?

Criterion 3: Coverage

- Are the topics covered by the site clear?
- Does the site exhibit suitable depth and comprehensiveness for its purpose?
- Is sufficient evidence provided to support the ideas and opinions presented?

Criterion 4: Accuracy

- Are the sources of information stated? Can you tell whether this information is original or taken from someplace else?
- Does the information appear to be accurate? Can you verify this information by comparing this source with other sources in the field?

Criterion 5: Currency

- Are dates included in the Web site?
- Do the dates apply to the material itself or to its placement on the Web? Is the site regularly revised and updated?
- Is the information current or at least still relevant for the site's purpose?

To illustrate how these criteria can help you evaluate a site, consider how they could be applied to the article "Spread of Active Sonar Threatens Whales" found on the site of the National Resources Defense Council. The first screen of this article is shown in Figure App. 2.4. The site is clearly from an advocacy group as indicated by the boxed text on the right side urging readers to "ACT NOW!" and "SUPPORT OUR WORK!" The article is four pages long and gives a detailed overview of the history of Navy sonar and its negative impact on whales and other marine mammals. However, no author is identified. Is the article trustworthy or is it from an unreliable environmental group apt to suppress or distort evidence? Using the criteria for evaluating Web sites, Megan was able to identify the strengths and weaknesses of this site in light of her research purpose.

The site does very well against the criteria "authority" and "clear disclosure of advocacy." Megan located the home page of the site, clicked on "About us," and discovered that the National Resources Defense Council has been around for more than thirty years and established its first Web site in 1995. It is a large

NATURAL RESOURCES DEFENSE COUNCIL

Home   Join Us/Give Now   About Us   Act Now   Search

NRDC
THE EARTH'S BEST DEFENSE

- **Wildlife & Fish**
  Animals & Birds
  Fish
  - Whales & Marine Animals
    In Brief
    In Depth
    Related Links
    Habitat Preservation

○ Clean Air & Energy
○ Global Warming
○ Clean Water & Oceans
○ Wildlife & Fish
○ Parks, Forests & Wildlands
○ Toxic Chemicals & Health
○ Nuclear Weapons & Waste
○ Cities & Green Living
○ Environmental Legislation

Magazine
Reference/Links
Publications
Fun Features
Subscribe
Media Center
En Español
Site Map
Contact Us

Wildlife & Fish Whales & Marine Animals In Brief: News
✉ **Email This Article**

Spread of Active Sonar Threatens Whales

The U.S. Navy wants to flood the world's oceans and coastal waters with sonar technology that deafens -- and kills -- whales and other marine mammals.

Around the globe, nations are testing and beginning to deploy "active sonar" technology, which uses extremely loud sound to detect submarines. The problem? Active sonar can injure and even kill marine mammals. It has been conclusively linked to the deaths of seven whales in the Bahamas in March 2000, and is thought to have caused a 1996 mass stranding of beaked whales on the west coast of Greece.

ACT NOW!
Protect whales and other marine life from dangerous Navy sonar.

SUPPORT OUR WORK!
Make a donation to NRDC.

The U.S. Navy has led the push toward use of active sonar. In full knowledge of the disastrous effects that active sonar's intense noise may have on whale populations all over the world, the Navy has also conducted testing in complete secrecy and has consistently evaded and violated environmental law.

In July 2002, despite strong concerns from many leading scientists, the Bush administration issued a long-sought permit allowing the Navy to use the biggest gun in its active-sonar arsenal, the SURTASS LFA system, in as much as 75 percent of the world's oceans. (NRDC has filed a lawsuit to stop deployment of the system.) In addition, the Navy is attempting to expand its active-sonar program into U.S. coastal waters, and wants to do so without conducting the environmental analysis required by law.

The Bahamas Whale Deaths

In March 2000, four different species of whales and dolphins were stranded on beaches in the Bahamas after a U.S. Navy battle group used active sonar in the area. Despite efforts to save the whales, seven of them died. The Navy initially denied that active sonar was to blame, but its own investigation later found hemorrhaging around the dead whales' eyes and ears, indicating severe acoustic trauma. The government's study of the incident established with virtual certainty that the strandings in the Bahamas had been caused by mid-frequency active sonar used by Navy ships passing through the area. Since the

Of the 13 beaked whales that stranded in the Bahamas in March 2000 after exposure to active sonar, seven died, including this one.
Center for Whale Research

incident, the area's population of beaked whales has disappeared, leading researchers to conclude that they abandoned their habitat or died at sea. Scientists are concerned that, under the right circumstances, even the transient use of high-intensity active sonar can have a severe impact on populations of marine mammals.

FIGURE APP. 2.4   *First screen from article on Web site*

national organization with three regional offices, puts out numerous publications, and does extensive lobbying on environmental issues. The "About us" section states:

> NRDC uses law, science, and the support of more than 500,000 members nationwide to protect the planet's wildlife and wild places and to ensure a safe and healthy environment for all living things. . . . We work to foster the fundamental right of all people to have a voice in decisions that affect their environment. We seek to break down the pattern of disproportionate environmental burdens borne by people of color and others who face social or economic inequities. Ultimately, NRDC strives to help create a new way of life for humankind, one that can be sustained indefinitely without fouling or depleting the resources that support all life on Earth.

The site provides contact information, the addresses of regional and national offices, and lists of phone numbers and e-mail addresses.

In terms of coverage (Criteria 3), the site is unusually broad and deep. It covers hundreds of different environmental issues and has fun features for children as well as in-depth technical articles written for specialists. Megan also determined that the site was accurate (Criteria 4). Technical articles were well documented, and throughout the site, references to factual data had notes about sources. She discovered that information on this site corroborated well with references to the same data from other sites. Finally, the site was current (Criteria 5). The home page has a "tip of the day," updated daily, and items within the site have clear indications of dates. This is an active, ongoing site.

Megan concluded that the site was an excellent source for both arguments and data from a pro-environmental perspective. She could use the site to understand potential dangers of Navy sonar to whales and other marine life. However, the site was not helpful for understanding the Navy's reasons for needing low-frequency sonar or for understanding the role of this sonar in the war against terrorism.

Using Sources and Avoiding Plagiarism

Once you have evaluated a source and determined that it is worth using in your own argument, you need to learn how to use the source, how to avoid plagiarism, and how to cite and document it properly. We now turn to these concerns.

Using Sources for Your Own Purposes

To illustrate the purposeful use of sources, we will use the following short argument from the Web site of the American Council on Science and Health—a conservative organization of doctors and scientists devoted to providing scientific information on health issues and to exposing health fads and myths. Please read the argument carefully in preparation for the discussions that follow.

IS VEGETARIANISM HEALTHIER THAN NONVEGETARIANISM?

Many people become vegetarians because they believe, in error, that vegetarianism is uniquely conducive to good health. The findings of several large epidemiologic studies indeed suggest that the death and chronic-disease rates of vegetarians—primarily vegetarians who consume dairy products or both dairy products and eggs—are lower than those of meat eaters. . . .

The health of vegetarians may be better than that of nonvegetarians partly because of nondietary factors: Many vegetarians are health-conscious. They exercise regularly, maintain a desirable body weight, and abstain from smoking. Although most epidemiologists have attempted to take such factors into account in their analyses, it is possible that they did not adequately control their studies for nondietary effects.

People who are vegetarians by choice may differ from the general population in other ways relevant to health. For example, in Western countries most vegetarians are more affluent than nonvegetarians and thus have better living conditions and more access to medical care.

An authoritative review of vegetarianism and chronic diseases classified the evidence for various alleged health benefits of vegetarianism:

- The evidence is "strong" that vegetarians have (a) a lower risk of becoming alcoholic, constipated, or obese and (b) a lower risk of developing lung cancer.
- The evidence is "good" that vegetarians have a lower risk of developing adult-onset diabetes mellitus, coronary artery disease, hypertension, and gallstones.
- The evidence is "fair to poor" that vegetarianism decreases risk of breast cancer, colon cancer, diverticular disease, kidney-stone formation, osteoporosis, and tooth decay.

For some of the diseases mentioned above, the practice of vegetarianism itself probably is the main protective factor. For example, the low incidence of constipation among vegetarians is almost certainly due to their high intakes of fiber-rich foods. For other conditions, nondietary factors may be more important than diet. For example, the low incidence of lung cancer among vegetarians is attributable primarily to their extremely low rate of cigarette smoking. Diet is but one of many risk factors for most chronic diseases.

What we want to show you is that the way you use this article depends on your own research question and purpose. Sometimes you may decide to summarize a source completely—particularly if the source represents an opposing or alternative view that you intend to address. (See Chapter 2, pp. 24–27.) At other times you may choose to use only parts of a source. To illustrate how your rhetorical purpose governs your use of a source, we show you three different hypothetical examples:

- *Writer 1, arguing for an alternative treatment for alcoholism:* On some occasions, you will draw details from a source for use in a different context.

Another approach to fighting alcoholism is through naturopathy, holistic medicine, and vegetarianism. Vegetarians generally have better health than the rest of the population and particularly have, according to the American Council on Science and Health, "a lower risk of becoming alcoholic."[1] This lower risk has been borne out by other studies showing that the benefits of the holistic health movement are particularly strong for persons with addictive tendencies. . . . [goes on to other arguments and sources]

- *Writer 2, arguing for the value of vegetarianism:* Sometimes you can use part of a source for direct support of your own claim. In this case, a summary of relevant parts of the argument can be used as evidence.

  Not only will a vegetarian diet help stop cruelty to animals, but it is also good for your health. According to the American Council on Science and Health, vegetarians have longer life expectancy than nonvegetarians and suffer from fewer chronic diseases. The Council summarizes evidence from the scientific literature strongly showing that vegetarians have reduced risk of lung cancer, obesity, constipation, and alcoholism. They also cite good evidence that they have a reduced risk of adult-onset diabetes, high blood pressure, gallstones, or hardening of the arteries. Although the evidence isn't nearly as strong, vegetarianism may also lower the risk of certain cancers, kidney stones, loss of bone density, and tooth decay.

- *Writer 3, arguing for a skeptical view of vegetarianism:* Here Writer 3 uses portions of the article consciously excluded by Writer 2.

  The link between vegetarianism and death rates is a classic instance of correlation rather than causation. While it is true that vegetarians have a longer life expectancy than nonvegetarians and suffer from fewer chronic diseases, the American Council on Science and Health has shown that the causes can mostly be explained by factors other than diet. As the Council suggests, vegetarians are apt to be more health conscious than nonvegetarians and thus get more exercise, stay slender, and avoid smoking. The Council points out that vegetarians also tend to be wealthier than nonvegetarians and see their doctors more regularly. In short, they live longer because they take better care of themselves, not because they avoid meat.

Avoiding Plagiarism

Plagiarism, a form of academic cheating, is always a serious academic offense. You can plagiarize in one of two ways: (1) By borrowing another person's ideas without indicating the borrowing with attributive tags in the text and a proper citation or (2) by borrowing another person's language without putting the borrowed language in quotation marks or using a block indentation. The first kind of

---

[1]If the writer had found this quotation in a print source such as a book or magazine, the page number would be placed in parentheses immediately after the quotation (see p. 292 later in this chapter). Because the writer found this passage in a Web site, no page citation is possible. If this were an actual essay, rather than a hypothetical illustration, readers would find full information about the source in the bibliography at the end. In this case, the author would be listed as "American Council on Science and Health," indicated in the attributive tag preceding the quotation.

plagiarism is usually outright cheating; the writer usually knows he is stealing material and tries to disguise it.

The second kind of plagiarism, which often begins in a hazy never-never land between paraphrasing and copying, is much more common than the first, perhaps because inexperienced writers don't understand that you must indicate the borrowing of language through quotation marks just as you must acknowledge the borrowing of ideas through citation. It is not enough to change the order of phrases in a sentence or to replace a few words with synonyms. Thus, in our classes, we would fail a paper that included the following passage.

WRITER 4: PLAGIARISM

The link between vegetarianism and death rates is a classic instance of correlation rather than causation. While it is true that vegetarians have a longer life expectancy than nonvegetarians and suffer from fewer chronic diseases, the American Council on Science and Health has shown that the health of vegetarians may be better than that of nonvegetarians partly because of nondietary factors. Many vegetarians are very conscious of their health. They exercise regularly, keep a desirable body weight, and abstain from smoking. The Council points out that in Western countries most vegetarians are more affluent than nonvegetarians and thus have better living conditions and more access to medical care. In short, they live longer because they take better care of themselves, not because they avoid meat.

The best way to avoid plagiarism is to be especially careful at the note-taking stage. If you copy from your source, copy exactly, word for word, and put quotation marks around the copied material. If you paraphrase or summarize material, change the grammatical structure and wording so that you don't follow the writer's original language.

For Class Discussion

Do you think it was fair to flunk Writer 4's essay? He claimed he wasn't cheating because he used attributive tags to indicate his source throughout this passage, and he listed the American Council on Science and Health article accurately in his "Works Cited" list (bibliography) at the end of his paper. Before answering, compare Writer 4's passage with the original article on page 289; also compare the passage with Writer 3's passage on page 290. What justification could an instructor use for giving a high grade to Writer 3 and a failing grade to Writer 4?

Citing Sources in MLA Style

When academic writers cite sources, they use the conventions appropriate to their discipline. In this section we will explain briefly the MLA style used in the humanities. (We explain the APA system used in the social sciences later in this appendix.)

In the MLA system, you place the author's last name and the page number of the cited source in parentheses, usually at the end of the material you wish to cite. (If the author's name is mentioned in a preceding attributive tag, such as "according to Karnow" or "Karnow says," only the page number is placed in parentheses. In the following examples, note that the citation precedes the period. If you are citing a quotation, the parenthetical citation follows the quotation mark but precedes the final period.

> The Spanish tried to reduce the status of Filipina women who had been able to do business, get divorced, and sometimes become village chiefs (Karnow 41).
>
> According to Karnow, the Spanish tried to reduce the status of Filipina women who had been able to do business, get divorced, and sometimes become village chiefs (41).
>
> "And, to this day," Karnow continues, "women play a decisive role in Filipino families" (41).

A reader who wishes to look up the source will find the bibliographic information in the Works Cited section by looking for the entry under "Karnow." If more than one work by Karnow was used in the paper, the writer would also include an abbreviated title of the book or article following Karnow's name in the in-text citation.

> (Karnow, *In Our Image* 41)

When citing sources and page numbers, you should know about two special cases:

- *Special case 1: Citing from an indirect source* Occasionally you may wish to use a quotation that you have seen cited in one of your sources. You read Jones, who has a nice quotation from Smith, and you want to use Smith's quotation. To do so, quote Smith, but then cite Jones in your text preceded by the terms "qtd in." List only Jones in your "Works Cited."

  > According to the ex-mayor of Gotham City, Rupert Smith, "the rate of crime was at an all-time low" during his term of office (qtd. in Jones 25).

- *Special case 2: Citing page numbers for downloaded material* Although you always cite page numbers for material retrieved from its original print source (such as a magazine), material downloaded from the Web or a licensed database often provides no clues about original pagination (unless it is retrieved in *.pdf* format that duplicates the original appearance of the source). In such cases, MLA says to omit page references from the parenthetical citation under the assumption that researchers can locate the source on a computer and then use a search engine to find a specific quotation or passage.

Documenting Sources in a "Works Cited" List (MLA)

In the MLA system, you place a complete bibliography, titled "Works Cited," at the end of the paper. Entries in the Works Cited list are arranged alphabetically by author or by title if there is no author. Here are some general formatting guidelines for the Works Cited list:

- The list begins on a new sheet of paper with the words "Works Cited" centered one inch from the top of the page.

- Sources are listed alphabetically, the first line flush with the left margin and succeeding lines indented one-half inch or five spaces. (Use the "hanging indentation" feature on your word processor.)

- MLA formatting style uses abbreviations for months of the year (except for May, June, and July) and publishers' names (for example, "Random House" is shortened to "Random" and "University Press" is shortened to "UP"). For a complete list of abbreviations, consult the sixth edition of the *MLA Handbook for Writers of Research Papers.*

- Author entries include the name as it appears in the article byline or on the book's title page.

- MLA style recommends underlines rather than italics for book titles and names of journals and magazines (because underlines stand out better on the page). Do not underline any punctuation marks following an underlined title.

Here is a typical example of a work, in this case a book, cited in MLA form.

> Karnow, Stanley. In <u>Our Image: America's Empire in the Philippines</u>. New York: Random, 1989.

Special Case: Two or More Listings for One Author   When two or more works by one author are cited, the works are listed alphabetically by title. For the second and all additional entries, type three hyphens and a period in place of the author's name.

> Dombrowski, Daniel A. <u>Babies and Beasts: The Argument from Marginal Cases</u>. Urbana: U of Illinois P, 1997.
> ---.<u>The Philosophy of Vegetarianism</u>. Amherst: U of Massachusetts P, 1984.

MLA Quick Reference Guide for the Most Common Citations

Table App. 2.1 provides MLA models for the most common kinds of citations. This table will help you distinguish the forest from the trees when you try to cite sources. All the major categories of sources are displayed in this table. For further

TABLE APP. 2.1   *Quick Reference Guide for MLA Citations*

Kind of Source	Basic Citation Model
Print Sources When You Have Used the Original Print Version	
Book	Tannen, Deborah. <u>The Argument Culture: Moving From Debate to Dialogue</u>. New York: Random, 1998.
Article in anthology with an editor	Shamoon, Linda. "International E-mail Debate." <u>Electronic Communication Across the Curriculum</u>. Ed. Donna Reiss, Dickie Self, and Art Young. Urbana: NCTE, 1998. 151–61.
Article in scholarly journal	Pollay, Richard W., Jung S. Lee, and David Carter-Whitney. "Separate, but Not Equal: Racial Segmentation in Cigarette Advertising." <u>Journal of Advertising</u> 21.1 (1992): 45–57.
Article in magazine or newspaper	Beam, Alex. "The Mad Poets Society." <u>Atlantic Monthly</u> July–Aug. 2001: 96–103. Lemonick, Michael D. "Teens Before Their Time." <u>Time</u> 30 Oct. 2000: 66–74. Cauvin, Henri E. "Political Climate Complicates Food Shortage in Zimbabwe." <u>New York Times</u> 18 July 2001: A13.
Print Sources That You Have Downloaded from a Database or the Web	
Article downloaded from database	Barr, Bob. "Liberal Media Adored Gun-Control Marchers." <u>Insight on the News</u> 5 June 2000: 44. <u>Research Library Complete</u>. ProQuest. Lemieux Lib., Seattle U. 15 Aug. 2001 <http://proquest.umi.com>.
Article downloaded from Web	Goodman, Ellen. "The Big Hole in Health Debate." <u>Boston Globe</u> 24 June 2001: D7. <u>Boston Globe Online</u> 18 July 2001 <http://www. boston.com/dailyglobe 2/175/oped/ The_big_hole_in_health_debate+.shtml>.
Web Sources That Haven't Appeared in Print	
Home page (use for citing an entire Web site)	<u>Menstuff: The National Men's Resource</u>. 2003. National Men's Resource Center. 12 Mar. 2003 <http://www.menstuff.org/frameindex.html>.
Authored document within a Web site	Tobin, Sally. "Getting the Word Out on the Human Genome Project: A Course for Physicians." <u>Stanford University Center for Biomedical Ethics</u>. 2000. 18 July 2001 <http://scbe.stanford.edu/research/current_programs.html#genomics>.
Document with corporate or unnamed author within a Web site	"Ouch! Body Piercing." <u>Menstuff: The National Men's Resource</u>. 1 Feb. 2001. National Men's Resource Center. 17 July 2001 <http//www.menstuff.org/issues/byissue/ tattoo.html>.
Miscellaneous Sources	
Interview	Van der Peet, Rob. Personal interview. 24 June 2001.
Lecture, address, or speech	Jancoski, Loretta. "I Believe in God, and She's a Salmon." University Congregational United Church of Christ, Seattle. 30 Oct. 2001.

explanation of citations, along with instructions on citing variations and sources not listed in the Quick Reference Guide, see Joseph Gibaldi, *MLA Handbook for Writers of Research Papers,* 6th ed. New York: MLA, 2003.

Formatting an Academic Paper in MLA Style

An example research paper in MLA style is shown on pages 264–269. Here are the distinctive formatting features of MLA papers.

- Double-space throughout including block quotations and the Works Cited list.
- Use one-inch margins top and bottom, left and right. Indent one-half inch or five spaces from the left margin at the beginning of each paragraph.
- Number pages consecutively throughout the manuscript including the Works Cited list, which begins on a new page. Page numbers go in the upper right-hand corner, flush with the right margin, and one-half inch from the top of the page. The page number should be preceded by your last name. The text begins one inch from the top of the page.
- Do *not* create a separate title page. Type your name, professor's name, course number, and date in the upper left-hand corner of your paper (all double-spaced), beginning one inch from the top of the page; then double-space and type your title, centered, without underlines or any distinctive fonts (capitalize the first word and important words only); then double-space and begin your text.
- Start a new page for the Works Cited list. Type "Works Cited" centered, one inch from the top of the page in the same font as the rest of the paper; do not enclose it in quotation marks. Use hanging indentation of five spaces or one-half inch for each entry longer than one line. Format entries according to the instructions in Table App. 2.1.

Student Example of an MLA-Style Research Paper

For an illustration of a student research paper written in MLA style, see Mark Bonicillo's researched policy proposal on pages 264–269.

Citing Sources in APA Style

To cite sources in the APA system, you follow procedures very similar to those in the MLA system except that you also include the year of the source and you place a "p." or "pp." before the page number. The author's last name, date, and page numbers are separated by commas. When the author is mentioned in an attributive tag, place only the date and page number in parentheses, usually directly after the author's name.

> The Spanish tried to reduce the status of Filipina women who had been able to do business, get divorced, and sometimes become village chiefs (Karnow, 1989, p. 41).

According to Karnow (1989, p. 41), the Spanish tried to reduce the status of Filipina women who had been able to do business, get divorced, and sometimes become village chiefs.

If your readers wish to follow up on this source, they will look for "Karnow" in the References section at the end of the essay. If Karnow had more than one entry in the References section, they would look for the 1989 source. If Karnow had published more than one work in 1989, you would add a lower case "a" to the date of the first one and a lowercase "b" to the date of the second one. Your in-text parenthetical citation would then be either

(Karnow, 1989a)

or

(Karnow, 1989b)

APA style also makes provision for quoting or using data from an indirect source (see p. 292). In your parenthetical citation use "as cited in" rather than the MLA's "qtd in."

According to the ex-mayor of Gotham City, Rupert Smith, "the rate of crime was at an all-time low" during his term of office (as cited in Jones, 1995, p. 25).

Documenting Sources in a "References" List (APA)

Like the MLA system, the APA system includes a complete bibliography, called "References," at the end of the paper. Entries are listed alphabetically, with a similar kind of hanging indentation to that used in MLA style. If you list more than one item for an author, repeat the author's name each time and arrange the items in chronological order beginning with the earliest. If two works appeared in the same year, arrange them alphabetically, adding an "a" and a "b" after the year for purposes of in-text citation. Here is a hypothetical illustration:

Smith, R. (1995). *Body image in Western cultures, 1750–present.* London: Bonanza Press.

Smith, R. (1999a). *Body image in non-Western cultures.* London: Bonanza Press.

Smith, R. (1999b). Eating disorders reconsidered. *Journal of Appetite Studies, 45,* 295–300.

APA Quick Reference Guide for the Most Common Citations

Table App. 2.2 provides examples in APA style for the most common kinds of citations to be placed in a "References" list at the end of the paper. For a complete

TABLE APP. 2.2   *Quick Reference Guide for APA Citations*

Kind of Source	Basic Citation Model
	Print Sources When You Have Used the Original Print Version
Book	Tannen, D. (1998). *The argument culture: Moving from debate to dialogue.* New York: Random House.
Article in anthology with an editor	Shamoon, L. (1998). International e-mail debate. In D. Reiss, D. Self, & A. Young (Eds.), *Electronic communication across the curriculum* (pp. 151–161). Urbana, IL: National Council of Teachers of English.
Article in scholarly journal	Pollay, R. W., Lee, J.S., & Carter-Whitney, D. (1992). Separate, but not equal: Racial segmentation in cigarette advertising. *Journal of Advertising, 21*(1), 45–57.
Article in magazine or newspaper	Beam, A. (2001, July–August). The mad poets society. *Atlantic Monthly, 288,* 96–103. Lemonick, M. D. (2000, October 30). Teens before their time. *Time, 156,* 66–74. Cauvin, H. E. (2001, July 18). Political climate complicates food shortage in Zimbabwe. *The New York Times,* p. A13.
	Print Sources That You Have Downloaded from a Database or the Web
Article downloaded from database	Barr, B. (2000, June 5). Liberal media adored gun-control marchers. *Insight on the News,* 44. Retrieved August 15, 2001, from ProQuest database.
Article downloaded from Web	Goodman, E. (2001, June 24). The big hole in health debate. *Boston Globe Online,* D7. Retrieved July 18, 2001, from http://www.boston.com/dailyglobe2/175/oped/The_big_hole_in_health_debate+.shtml
	Web Sources That Haven't Appeared in Print
Authored document within a Web site	Tobin, S. (2000). *Getting the word out on the human genome project: A course for physicians.* Retrieved July 18, 2001, from Stanford University, Center for Biomedical Ethics Web site: http://scbe.stanford.edu/research/current_programslhtml#genomics
Document with corporate or unnamed author within a Web site	National Men's Resource Center. (2001, February 1). *Ouch! Body piercing.* Retrieved July 17, 2001, from http://www.menstuff.org/issues/byissue/tattoo.html
	Miscellaneous Sources
Interview, personal communication	R. Van der Peet (personal communication, June 24, 2001) stated that ... [In-text citation only; not included in References]
Lecture, address, or speech	According to Jancoski (speech to University Congregational United Church of Christ, Seattle, October 30, 2001), salmon ... [In-text citation only; not included in References; further details about speech can be included in text]

explanation of citations, consult the *Publication Manual of the American Psychological Association*, 5th ed. Washington, DC: APA, 2001.

Student Example of an APA-Style Research Paper

An example of a paper in APA style is Megan Matthews researched argument on Navy sonar and whales, pages 299–306.

Sounding the Alarm:
Navy Sonar and the Survival of Whales
Megan Matthews
English 260
November 1, 2002

Sounding the Alarm:

Navy Sonar and the Survival of Whales

1   Imagine that you are forced to live in an apartment next to a city freeway with a constant roar of engines and tires against concrete. Cars cruise by on the surface streets with bass systems so powerful that your windows shake and your ears hurt. You tolerate the din day after day, but you and your friends have to shout to be heard. What if you had no alternative place to live?

2   This scenario is, of course, preposterous. We can move to find the coveted sound of silence. For whales, dolphins, and sea turtles, however, noise is becoming an inescapable catastrophe that threatens far more than their aesthetic sensibilities. The incessant rumbling of cargo ships, the loud explosions of undersea mineral explorations, and the annoying cacophony of the blasting devices used by fisheries have turned Jacques Cousteau's world of silence into an underwater freeway. Now, however, a new and more dangerous source of sound has been approved for use in the oceans—the United States Navy's Low Frequency Active Sonar System (LFA sonar), which will track enemy submarines. The Navy claims that the technology is needed to ensure national security, since it detects submarines at greater distances than previous sonar systems. However, the potential damage to marine life and to the long-term health of the oceans themselves outweighs the Navy's questionable claims about national security. The U.S. Congress should cut funds for further deployment of LFA sonar.

3   Since the mid-1980s, the Navy has developed and tested LFA sonar systems. LFA is *active* because it does more than just listen for nearby submarines, like our older systems. With LFA, 18 acoustic transmitters the size of bathtubs act like giant woofer speakers suspended beneath the ship on cables. The speakers emit bursts of sound every 6 to 100 seconds. These bursts can be as powerful as 215 decibels, a sound level equivalent to standing 1 meter away from a departing commercial jet (National Marine Fisheries Service [MNFS], 2002a, p. 3). The Navy prefers low-frequency sonar because low-frequency waves travel farther than high-frequency waves, which is why the bumping bass of a car stereo reverberates after the car spins around a street corner. In this case, the sonar's sound waves reflect off objects from hundreds of miles away and alert the ship's crew to the presence of submarines. In its Environmental Impact Statement, the Navy explains that it needs LFA sonar because modern submarines are quieter than clunky Cold War versions.

Their ability to run quietly makes the new subs virtually undetectable until they are close by, leaving the Navy only minutes to respond to a potential submarine threat (Department of Navy [DON], 2001, p.ES-2) After studying possible solutions, the Navy believes LFA sonar is the only system capable of providing reliable and dependable long-range detection of quieter, harder-to-find submarines (DON, 2001, p. ES-2). Unfortunately, the far-traveling waves that bounce off enemy submarines also can pierce the inner ears of whales and dolphins.

     To its credit, the Navy has acted to protect marine mammals and other sea life. The Navy studied existing research reports on the levels of sounds that can cause hearing damage to marine mammals and concluded that protecting whales and dolphins from levels above 180 dB would prevent any harm to their hearing and behavior. Based on these studies, the National Oceanic and Atmospheric Administration's National Marine Fisheries Service determined that the Navy's employment of LFA sonar at levels below 180 dB would have no more than a negligible impact on marine mammal species and stocks (National Oceanic and Atmospheric Administration [NOAA], 2002). The Navy therefore plans to use a maximum volume of 180 dB when marine mammals are nearby. As an initial protective measure, the sonar will not be allowed to operate above 180 dB if it is within 12 nautical miles of coastlines and islands to ensure that coastal stocks of marine mammals and sea turtles will be relatively unaffected by LFA sonar (NMFS, 2002b). This measure protects critically endangered species, like northern right whales, who feed in coastal areas. The Navy also plans to avoid damaging whale hearing and behavior by trying to prevent animals from swimming near the ships. The Navy wants to detect animals that wander within 1 kilometer of the vessel, where they might be exposed to sounds of 180 dB or more. The protective monitoring systems will rely on humans and technology to protect sea animals. Sailors who have been trained to detect and identify marine mammals and sea turtles will stand on deck to look for whales and dolphins (Schregardus, 2002, p.48149). Underwater microphones will also listen for sounds that whales and dolphins make. Finally, the Navy has developed a second active sonar system called the High Frequency Marine Mammal Monitoring sonar. It will locate and monitor animals who enter the 180 dB area and will run before and during the LFA sonar transmissions. If whales, dolphins, or sea turtles are observed, the crew will turn off the LFA system until the animals move away.

5   These efforts to protect sea life are commendable, but current marine research shows that LFA sonar poses a much higher risk to marine mammals than the Navy acknowledges. The conclusions drawn by the Navy about potential hearing damage to marine mammals are open to serious doubt, and their measures to protect the sea environment are inadequate.

6   To begin, biologists generally agree that hearing is the primary sense of marine mammals. No one knows precisely what functions hearing performs, but it is likely that whales depend on sound to avoid predators, to communicate across great distances between pods and prospective mates, and to establish mother-calf bonds. According to a detailed study by the National Resources Defense Council (Jasny, 1999), significant noise interference could threaten individual mammals or entire populations if biologically important behaviors like these are disrupted. Furthermore, like the members of a rock band, whales and dolphins may experience hearing loss after repeated exposure to sounds at the same frequency. In 1996, two sperm whales residing in a heavily trafficked area of the Canary Islands made no apparent efforts to avoid a collision with a cargo ship and were killed. Autopsies revealed damage to their inner ears, which some environmental scientists believe could have been caused by repeated exposure to the sounds of cargo ships (Jasny, 1999). The Navy's tests of different kinds of sonar systems are also suspected to have caused 16 Cuvier's beaked whales to beach and die in the Bahamas. The Navy had been testing midrange active sonar in the area; autopsies of four whales revealed extensive bleeding in the inner ears and around the brain. The conclusions of the Navy and Fisheries Service interim and final reports named the sonar tests as the most likely cause of the beachings (DON and NMFS, 2001). Although the type of sonar was midrange, rather than low-frequency, the link still implies that whales can be harmed or even killed by sonar—and that the effects can be unanticipated. Beachings also occurred after naval sonar exercises in Greece and the Canary Islands. In Greece, sonar is the likely culprit; scientists cannot establish the cause of death, however, because the initial examination of the bodies was not thorough (Jasny, 1999). Finally, according to Jasny, the long-term effects of noise pollution may not be limited to hearing; noise pollution can increase stress levels, which lead to shorter life spans and lower birth rates—effects that humans may not notice for decades. One ping from a low-frequency system may only *harass* whales, to use

the term commonly encountered in Navy or Fisheries Service discussions of low frequency sonar, but if whales are exposed to LFA sound waves repeatedly, the effects may be long-lasting and even irreversible.

    The importance of hearing to marine mammals means that the effect of LFA   7 sonar on the sea environment needs to be extensively studied. Unfortunately, the studies used by the Navy to demonstrate that LFA sonar poses little threat to marine life are scant, scientifically flawed, and inconclusive. No one actually knows how loud or frequent sounds need to be to cause permanent or temporary hearing loss to whales and sea turtles. Most studies have focused on captive species like seals and some dolphins; the data is extrapolated to estimate the hearing capacities of other species. The Navy uses the findings of several scientific workshops that studied the range where serious hearing problems could occur. Based upon these conclusions, as well as the Navy's own examinations of marine mammal inner ear models and extrapolation from human results, the Navy believes that protecting marine mammals from levels above 180 dB will be sufficient (DON, 2001, p.14). Yet the Navy itself admits, in its own environmental impact statement, that data regarding underwater hearing capabilities of marine mammals are rare and limited to smaller species that can be studied in laboratories (DON, 2001, p.11). The Navy has tried to dispel fears that mammals are physically and behaviorally harmed by LFA sonar by releasing the results of three separate tests Navy scientists conducted on baleen whale populations in California and Hawaii; these studies concluded that most whales did not alter any observable aspect of their behavior for more than a few tenths of minutes (DON, 2001, p. 16). Nevertheless, three tests on baleen whales is hardly adequate to conclude that other species of whales, as well as other marine mammals, would react in the same way as the baleen whale. Moreover, none of these studies examined the long-term effects of repeated exposures, nor were whales exposed to sounds above 155 dB, even though the estimated LFA safety level is 180 dB. One has difficulty understanding how the Navy can set 180 dB as their safety threshold when their own tests did not monitor whales at this level. Moreover, some scientists claim that *less intense* sounds can be harmful. Dr. Marsh Green, the President of the Ocean Mammal Institute and an animal behavior specialist, claims that a significant body of research show[s] that whales avoid underwater sounds starting at 110 to 120 decibels (Knickerbocker, 2001). If the scientific community continues to debate this issue, it seems unlikely that the Navy could have indisputable evidence that the sonar will not harm whales.

8   Clearly the Navy's claim that LFA sonar will not hurt marine mammals and other sea life will not survive close scrutiny. Of even greater concern is the dangerous precedent that the U.S. Navy will set if it deploys LFA sonar on its surface ships. There is a strong possibility that other nations might develop LFA sonar systems in order to keep up with the United States. The nuclear weapons race of the past proves that military powers constantly compete with each other to be prepared for armed conflicts. This often results in a frantic struggle to develop the same technologies worldwide with no regard for environmental and social effects. Already, according to Jasny (1999), NATO countries are investigating their own use of similar LFA systems. If additional countries deploy the technology, whales and dolphins will face much greater risks of meeting sonar systems in open water. In addition, the world's governments have not discussed treaties that would require nations to turn off sonar systems in arctic waters, which the Navy currently plans to do. Whales, dolphins and sea turtles will have no permanent safe havens if other militaries choose to run their systems worldwide.

9   The Navy's justifies developing LFA sonar for the sake of national security; in light of the September 11, 2001, terrorist attacks, this claim almost guarantees unquestioned public support. Even so, in the age of terrorism, do enemy submarines present significant threats? A confusing array of Navy documents makes it nearly impossible for the general public to find out the facts about potential danger from submarines. The Navy argues that 224 diesel-electric submarines are operated by nonallied nations but never explains who these nations are or how much of a threat they actually pose (Schregardus, 2002, p. 48146). This long-standing anxiety about submarines feels like part of the old Cold War mentality when the nation to fear was the Soviet Union. Perhaps now we should be more concerned about cargo ships than submarines. A large percentage of freight containers are never inspected at our ports, and these seem to be easier targets for terrorists than our Navy ships. Finally, the most recent attack on a Navy ship, the USS *Cole,* came from another boat, not a submarine. The number of terrorists who have sophisticated submarine technology must be smaller than the number who can place a small bomb on a small boat, train, car, or cargo ship.

Sounding the Alarm   7

Moreover long-term national security also depends on healthy oceans. Millions of   10
people incorporate fish into their diet, and oceans provide materials for countless
human products. Any changes to the balance of marine life could degrade the entire
ecosystem. If the health of the oceans is damaged by LFA sonar, it will be only a
matter of time before humans feel the effects. Our national environmental security,
which never receives much attention in the media, should be as important to the
United States as our military readiness. The proposed widespread use of LFA sonar on
the Navy's surface ships opens up a range of questions about the long-term effects of
our underwater activities. When combined with other sources of human noise
pollution, LFA sonar poses dangerous threats to marine life. According to Dr. Sylvia
Earle, former Chief Scientist at the National Oceanic & Atmospheric Administration,
undersea noise pollution is like the death of a thousand cuts (as cited in Jasny, 1999,
executive summary, first sidebar). Each time we turn up the volume in the oceans, we
make it more difficult for marine animals to communicate with each other. We may
even diminish their hearing capacities, endangering their abilities to migrate safely
and to avoid countless ships that crisscross their routes. Until more is known about
the long-term effects of LFA sonar, the Navy should delay operation of LFA sonar
voluntarily. If it does not do so, the U.S. Congress should cut off further funding. The
debate over LFA sonar cannot be defined as a simple environment-versus-government
battle. It is a discussion about whether or not environmental security and ocean health
matter to humans. At its core, it is a debate about our futures.

[New Page]

Sounding the Alarm   8

References

Department of the Navy (2001). *Executive summary: Final overseas environmental im-
    pact statement and environmental impact statement for Surveillance Towed Array
    Sensor System Low Frequency Active (SURTASS LFA) Sonar.* Retrieved October 5,
    2002, from http://www.surtass-lfa-eis.com/ docs/ EXSUM%20FEIS%201–15.pdf
Department of the Navy and National Marine Fisheries Service (2001, December 20).
    Joint interim report: Bahamas marine mammal stranding event of 15-16 March 2000.
    Retrieved October 15, 2002, from http://www.nmfs.noaa.gov/prot_res/overview/
    Interim_Bahamas_Report.pdf

Jasny, Michael (1999, March). *Sounding the depths: Supertankers, sonar, and the rise of undersea noise.* Retrieved October 15, 2002, from the National Resources Defense Council Web site: http://www.nrdc.org/wildlife/marine/sound/sdinx.asp.

Knickerbocker, Brad. (2001, August 20). US Navy plans for loud sonar raises fears for whales. *Christian Science Monitor.* Retrieved October 20, 2002, from http://news.nationalgeographic.com/news/ 2001/08/0815_wirenavyboom.html.

National Marine Fisheries Service. (2002a). *Biological opinion on proposed employment of Surveillance Towed Array Sensor System Low Frequency Active Sonar.* Retrieved October 8, 2002, from http://www.nmfs.noaa.gov/prot_res/readingrm/ESAsec7/7pr_surtass-2020529.pdf

National Marine Fisheries Service. (2002b). *Final determination and rulemaking on the harassment of marine mammals incidental to Navy operations of Surveillance Towed Array Sensor System Low Frequency Active (SURTASS LFA) Sonar.* Retrieved October 5, 2002, from http:// www.nmfs.noaa.gov/prot_res/readingrm/ MMSURTASS/ LFAexecsummary.PDF

National Oceanic and Atmospheric Administration (2002, July 15). *Strong protection measures for marine mammals tied to operation of Low Frequency Sonar* (NOAA news release 2002–90). Retrieved October 15, 2002, from http:// www.publicaffairs.noaa.gov/releases2002/july02/noaa02090.html

Schregardus, D. R. (2002, July 16). *Record of decision for Surveillance Towed Array Sensor System Low Frequency Active (SURTASS LFA) Sonar,* Fed Reg 67 (141), pp. 48145-48154 (July 23, 2002). Retrieved October 12, 2002, from http:// www.surtass-lfa-eis.com/docs/ LFA%20EIS%20ROD.pdf

Credits

Page 12. Sara Jean Green, excerpt from "Mosh Pits: It's Not All Fun, Music" from the *Seattle Times* (June 4, 2002), pp. A1, A9. **Page 14.** Gordon F. Adams, "Petition to Waive the University Mathematics Requirement." Reprinted with the permission of the author. **Page 21.** Lisa Turner, "Playing with Our Food" from *Better Nutrition*, Vol. 62, No. 6 (June 2000), pp. 56–59. Copyright © 2000 Lisa Turner. Reprinted by permission of the author. **Page 35.** Council for Biotechnology Information, "Why Biotech Labeling Can Confuse Consumers." http://www.whybiotech.com/index.asp?id=1812. Accessed July 30, 2002. Courtesy of the Council for Biotechnology Information. **Page 106.** David Langley, "'Half-Criminals' or Urban Athletes? A Plea for Fair Treatment of Skateboarders." Reprinted with the permission of the author. **Page 124.** George C. Lodge and Jeffrey F. Rayport, "Knee-Deep and Rising: America's Recycling Crisis," *Harvard Business Review* (Sept.–Oct. 1991), p. 132. **Page 124.** John Tierney, "Recycling Is Garbage," *New York Times Magazine* (June 30, 1996), p. 28. **Page 128.** Ellen Goodman, "Minneapolis Pornography Ordinance" from the *Boston Globe* (1985). Copyright © 1985 The Washington Post Writers Group. Reprinted with permission. **Page 133.** Rebekah Taylor, "Letter to Jim." Reprinted with the permission of the author. **Page 190.** Jack K. C. Chiang, "Letter to the Editor." *The Seattle Times* (March 24, 2002), p. B7. Copyright © 2002 Jack K. C. Chiang. Reprinted by permission. **Page 191.** Kathy Sullivan, "Oncore, Obscenity, and the Liquor Control Board." Reprinted with the permission of the author. **Page 210.** Daeha Ko, "The Monster That Is High School." *University of Washington Daily* (May 9, 1999). Copyright © 1999 by the *University of Washington Daily*. Reprinted with permission of the publisher. **Page 223.** Megan Matthews, "Whales Need Silence." Reprinted with the permission of the author. **Page 224.** Jean Arbeiter, "Iraq War Plans" letter to the editor. *The New York Times* (September 10, 2002), p. A30. **Page 242.** Tiffany Anderson, "A Woman's View of Hip-Hop." Reprinted with the permission of the author. **Page 245.** Ezekiel J. Emanuel, "Eight Is Too Many: The Case Against Octuplets" from the *New Republic* (January 25, 1999). Copyright © 1999 by the New Republic, Inc. Reprinted with the permission of the *New Republic*. **Page 264.** Mark Bonicillo, "A Proposal for Universal Health Insurance in the United States." Reprinted with the permission of the author. **Page 289.** American Council on Science and Health, "Is Vegetarianism Healthier Than Nonvegetarianism?" *Priorities*, Vol. 9, No. 3, 1997, at www.acsh.org/publications/priorities/0903/vegetarianism.html, accessed October 31, 2002. Copyright © 1997 American Council on Science and Health. Used with permission. **Pages 299–306.** Megan Matthews, "Sounding the Alarm: Navy Sonar and the Survival of Whales." Reprinted with the permission of the author. **Images: Page 5.** Ron Haviv/CORBIS Saba **Page 117T.** AP/Wide World Photos **Page 117B.** Getty Images **Page 140.** Courtesy of the Seattle Field Division of the Drug Enforcement Administration and NW-HIDTA, and *The Seattle Times.* **Page 145 L & R.** AP/Wide World Photos **Page 146.** Reuters New Media Inc./CORBIS **Page 153.** Leah Johnson, "Drink and Then Drive?" poster. Reprinted with permission of Leah Johnson. **Page 163.** Library of Congress **Page 212.** Courtesy of United Way of King County **Page 255.** Lisa Blattner, "What Is Left for Teens to Do When the Teen Dance Ordinance Bans Them from Dance Clubs?" ad. Reprinted with permission of Lisa Blattner. **COLOR PLATES: COLOR PLATE A** Courtesy of Sustain USA **COLOR PLATE B** Courtesy of the Council for Biotechnology Information **COLOR PLATE E** Courtesy of Save the Children **COLOR PLATE F** Courtesy of Earthjustice **COLOR PLATE H** Courtesy of The Center for Consumer Freedom

Index